Blackmagic Design
Fusion 7 Studio
A Tutorial Approach

CADCIM Technologies
525 St. Andrews Drive
Schererville, IN 46375, USA
(www.cadcim.com)

Contributing Author
Sham Tickoo
Professor
Purdue University Calumet
Hammond, Indiana, USA

CADCIM Technologies

Blackmagic Design Fusion 7 Studio: A Tutorial Approach
Sham Tickoo

CADCIM Technologies
525 St Andrews Drive
Schererville, Indiana 46375, USA
www.cadcim.com

ISBN 978-1-942689-15-7

www.cadcim.com

DEDICATION

THANKS

Online Training Program Offered by CADCIM Technologies

CADCIM Technologies provides effective and affordable virtual online training on various software packages including Computer Aided Design and Manufacturing (CAD/CAM), computer programming languages, animation, architecture, and GIS. The training is delivered 'live' via Internet at any time, any place, and at any pace to individuals as well as the students of colleges, universities, and CAD/CAM training centers. The main features of this program are:

Training for Students and Companies in a Classroom Setting

Highly experienced instructors and qualified engineers at CADCIM Technologies conduct the classes under the guidance of Prof. Sham Tickoo of Purdue University Calumet, USA. This team has authored several textbooks that are rated "one of the best" in their categories and are used in various colleges, universities, and training centers in North America, Europe, and in other parts of the world.

Training for Individuals

CADCIM Technologies with its cost effective and time saving initiative strives to deliver the training in the comfort of your home or work place, thereby relieving you from the hassles of traveling to training centers.

Training Offered on Software Packages

CADCIM provides basic and advanced training on the following software packages:

***CAD/CAM/CAE**: CATIA, Pro/ENGINEER Wildfire, PTC Creo Parametric, Creo Direct, SOLIDWORKS, Autodesk Inventor, Solid Edge, NX, AutoCAD, AutoCAD LT, AutoCAD Plant 3D, Customizing AutoCAD, EdgeCAM, and ANSYS*

***Architecture and GIS**: Autodesk Revit Architecture, AutoCAD Civil 3D, Autodesk Revit Structure, AutoCAD Map 3D, Revit MEP, Navisworks, Primavera, and Bentley STAAD Pro*

***Animation and Styling**: Autodesk 3ds Max, Autodesk 3ds Max Design, Autodesk Maya, Autodesk Alias, The Foundry NukeX, MAXON CINEMA 4D, Adobe Flash, and Adobe Premiere*

***Computer Programming**: C++, VB.NET, Oracle, AJAX, and Java*

*For more information, please visit the following link: **http://www.cadcim.com***

Note
If you are a faculty member, you can register by clicking on the following link to access the teaching resources: ***http://www.cadcim.com/Registration.aspx***. The student resources are available at ***http://www.cadcim.com***. We also provide **Live Virtual Online Training** on various software packages. For more information, write us at ***sales@cadcim.com***.

Table of Contents

Dedication   iii

Preface   vii

Chapter 1
Exploring the Blackmagic Design Fusion 7 Studio Interface.................................1-1

Chapter 2
Creating Network of Tools...2-1

Chapter 3
Creator Tools...3-1

Chapter 4
Transform Tools...4-1

Chapter 5
Warp Tools..5-1

Chapter 6
Mask Tools..6-1

Chapter 7
Color Tools..7-1

Chapter 8
Matte Tools..8-1

Chapter 9
Tracking..9-1

Chapter 10
Effect Tools..10-1

Chapter 11
Deep Pixel and Position Tools 11-1

Chapter 12
Paint Tools...12-1

Chapter 13

3D Tools and Stereo 3D..13-1

Chapter 14

Particles...14-1

Project 1

Converting a Day Scene to a Night Scene...P1-1

Project 2

Compositing Render Passes...P2-1

Index   I-1

Preface

Blackmagic Design Fusion 7 Studio

Blackmagic Design Fusion 7 Studio is one of the world's leading node-based compositing software. It is a powerful VFX production application. It comprises of flexible, precise, and powerful compositing tools. This software uses various techniques such as color-correction, 2D tracking, keying, masking, depth-based compositing, 3D compositing, and stereo 3D for compositing. This software has been used in many movies such as Avatar, 300, Terminator Salvation, Final Destination II, and so on. Capability of using a wide range of techniques makes this software application an ideal platform for compositing and the first choice for compositors and visual effect artists.

Blackmagic Design Fusion 7 Studio: A Tutorial Approach textbook has been written to enable the users to learn the techniques and enhance creativity required to create a composition. The textbook caters to the needs of compositors and visual effects artists.

This textbook will help users learn how to create different effects such as of rain, snow, fireworks, smoke, and so on. Also, they will learn to composite 3D objects with 2D images, create moving water effect, track and stabilize a footage, create volume fog, and convert day scene to night scene. In totality, this book covers each and every concept of the software with the help of progressive examples and numerous illustrations.

The salient features of this textbook are as follows:

- **Tutorial Approach**

  The author has adopted the tutorial point-of-view and the learn-by-doing approach throughout the textbook. This approach helps the users through the process of compositing in the tutorials.

- **Tips and Notes**

  Additional information related to various topics is provided to the users in the form of tips and notes.

- **Learning Objectives**

  The first page of every chapter summarizes the topics that will be covered in that chapter. This will help the users to easily refer to a topic.

- **Self-Evaluation Test and Review Questions**

  Every chapter ends with Self-Evaluation Test so that the users can assess their knowledge of the chapter. The answers to Self-Evaluation Test are given at the end of the chapter. Also, the Review Questions are given at the end of each chapter and they can be used by the instructors as test questions.

- **Screen Captures**
  About 300 screen captures are given throughout the textbook to facilitate the understanding of various concepts.

Symbols Used in the Textbook

Note

 The author has provided additional information related to various topics in the form of notes.

Tip

 The author has provided a lot of information to the users about the topic being discussed in form of tips.

Formatting Conventions Used in the Textbook

Please refer to the following list for the formatting conventions used in this textbook.

• Names of tools, buttons, menu, panels, button, and tabs are written in boldface.	Example: The **Loader** tool, the **Color** tab, the **Tools** menu, the **BG** button, and so on.
• Names of dialog boxes, windows, drop-down lists, areas, and check boxes are written in boldface.	Example: The **Open File** dialog box, the **Bins** window, the **Apply Mode** drop-down list, the **Flow** area, the **Post-Multiply by Alpha** check box, and so on.
• Values entered in edit boxes are written in boldface.	Example: Enter the value **0.02** in the **Size** edit box.
• Names of the files saved are italicized.	Example: *c03tut1.comp*

Naming Conventions Used in the Textbook

Tool

If you choose an item from the toolbar or menubar, a tool tile is inserted in the **Flow** area.

For example:
Choose **Tools > Color > Color Corrector** from the menubar; the **ColorCorrector1** tool tile is inserted in the **Flow** area.

When a tool tile is inserted in the **Flow** area, its controls are displayed on the right side of the interface in a control window, refer to Figure 1.

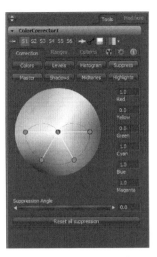

*Figure 1 The **ColorCorrect1** tool control window*

Dialog Box

In a dialog box, there are different options. Different terms are used to indicate various options in a dialog box. Refer to Figure 2 for terminologies used in a dialog box in Fusion.

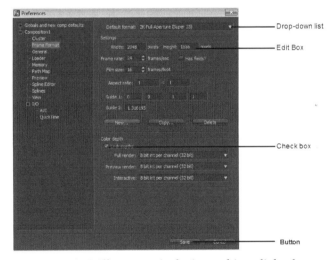

Figure 2 Different terminologies used in a dialog box

Button

The item in a dialog box that has a 3d shape is termed as **Button**, refer to Figure 2. For example, **OK** button, **Save** button, **Apply** button, and so on.

Drop-down List

A drop-down list is one in which a set of options are grouped together. You can identify a drop-down with a down arrow on it. These drop-downs are given a name based on the tools grouped in them. For example, **Apply Mode** drop-down list, refer to Figure 3.

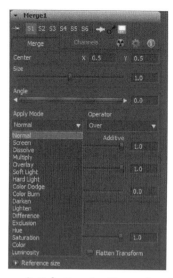

Figure 3 *Selecting the **Normal** option from the **Apply Mode** drop-down list*

Options

Options are the items that are available in shortcut menu, flyout, drop-down list, dialog box, and so on. For example, choose the **Force All Tile Pictures** option from the shortcut menu, refer to Figure 4.

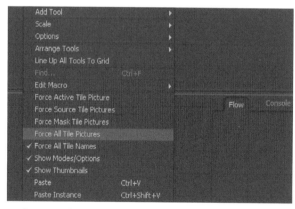

Figure 4 *Choosing the **Force All Tile Pictures** option from the shortcut menu*

Free Companion Website

It has been our constant endeavor to provide you the best textbooks and services at affordable price. In this endeavor, we have come out with a free companion website that will facilitate the process of teaching and learning of Blackmagic Design Fusion 7 Studio.

If you purchase this textbook, you will get access to the companion website.

The following resources are available for the faculty and students in this website:

Faculty Resources

- **Technical Support**
  The faculty can get online technical support by contacting *techsupport@cadcim.com*.

- **Instructor Guide**
  Solutions to all review questions and exercises in the textbook are provided in this guide to help faculty members test the skills of the students.

- **PowerPoint Presentations**
  The contents of the book are arranged in customizable powerpoint slides that can be used by the faculty for their lectures.

- **Compositions**
  The compositions and other media files used in tutorials are available for free download.

- **Rendered Images**
  If you do a tutorial, you can compare your rendered output with the one provided in the CADCIM website.

- **Additional Resources**
  You can access additional learning resources by visiting *http://eyeonfusionexperts.blogspot.com*.

- **Colored Images**
  You can download the PDF file containing color images of the screenshots used in this textbook from CADCIM website.

Student Resources

- **Technical Support**
  The faculty can get online technical support by contacting *techsupport@cadcim.com*.

- **Compositions**
  The compositions and other media files used in tutorials are available for free download.

- **Rendered Images**
  If you do a tutorial, you can compare your rendered output with the one provided in the CADCIM website.

- **Additional Resources**
  You can access additional learning resources by visiting *http://eyeonfusionexperts.blogspot.com*.

- **Colored Images**
  You can download the PDF file containing color images of the screenshots used in this textbook from CADCIM website.

If you face any problem in accessing these files, please contact the publisher at *sales@cadcim.com* or the author at *stickoo@purduecal.edu* or *tickoo525@gmail.com*.

Stay Connected

You can now stay connected with us through Facebook and Twitter to get the latest information about the textbooks, videos, and teaching/learning resources. To stay informed of such updates, follow us on Facebook (*www.facebook.com/cadcim*) and Twitter (*@cadcimtech*). You can also subscribe to our You Tube channel (*www.youtube/cadcimtech*) to get the information about our latest video tutorials.

Chapter *1*

Exploring the Black Magic Fusion 7 Studio Interface

Learning Objectives

After completing this chapter, you will be able to:
- *Start the Black Magic Fusion 7 Studio interface*
- *Work with the Fusion interface*
- *Understand the functions of various tools in Fusion*
- *Open, save, and close a composition*

INTRODUCTION TO Blackmagic Design Fusion 7 Studio

Welcome to the world of Fusion, a node-based compositing software, that helps in creating visual effects and digital compositing for an array of films and commercials. Formerly known as Digital Fusion, it is used to combine two or more images and video sequences. Fusion has a node-based interface in which intricate processes are developed by linking up different nodes, called tools. It provides you greater flexibility and helps improve the artistic creativity. This software was originally developed by New York Production & Design in 1987 for its in-house use. Fusion has found its application in a number of movies, such as Avatar, Terminator Salvation, Final Destination II, and so on.

In this chapter, you will learn how to start Fusion as well as to load and save an image in Fusion. Also, you will explore the interface of Fusion.

Starting Blackmagic Design Fusion 7 Studio

To start Blackmagic Design Fusion 7 Studio, choose **Start > All Programs > Blackmagic Design > Fusion > Fusion** from the **taskbar**, refer to Figure 1-1; the default Fusion interface will be displayed with its different components, as shown in Figure 1-2.

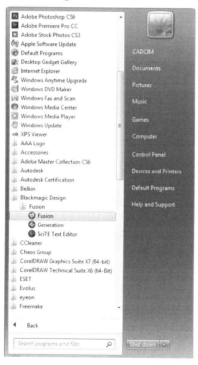

Figure 1-1   *Starting **Fusion** from the taskbar*

Fusion 7 Studio INTERFACE

The Fusion 7 Studio interface consists of menubar, Display Views, Work area, and Time Ruler, refer to Figure 1-2. These components of Fusion interface are discussed next.

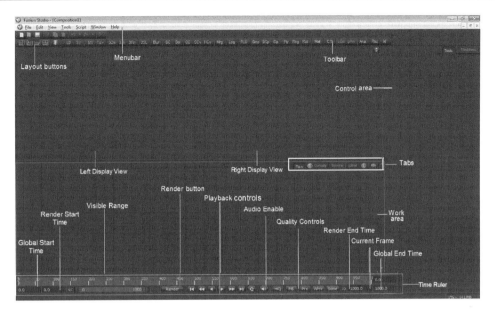

Figure 1-2 The Fusion 7 Studio interface

Menubar

The menubar is located on the top of the Fusion 7 Studio interface. It is used to access disk operations, editing functions, various tools, built-in scripts, and Fusion documentation.

Display View Area

The Display View area is used to view the output of the tools. By default, there are two views, namely left Display View and right Display View, refer to Figure 1-2. In this area, you can switch between the single view and separate views of a composite image by using the layout buttons in the toolbar.

Control Area

The Control area is located on the right of the Fusion interface and has two tabs: **Tools** and **Modifiers**. In the **Tools** tab, the attributes of a tool are specified. In the **Modifiers** tab, the modifiers will appear only if they are applied to the tool. The modifiers are used to create values for a control.

Work Area

The Work area is available below the Display Views, refer to Figure 1-2. It consists of six tabs. These tabs are discussed next.

Flow Tab

The **Flow** tab is used to create a network of tools. This network is formed by connecting nodes of the tools with the help of pipes. This tab is active by default.

Console Tab

The **Console** tab is used to display errors and status messages. This tab also displays output for scripts as well as render statistics.

Timeline Tab

The **Timeline** tab is used to adjust the timing of footage in a composition.

Spline Tab

The **Spline** tab is used to edit the animation curves, paths, and modifiers.

Comments Tab

The **Comments** tab is used to store comments and notes about a composition.

Chat Tab

The **Chat** tab is used to share comments with other users of the composition.

Time Ruler

The Time Ruler is available below the Work area. The Time Ruler consists of total number of frames in the current time segment. It consists of Timeline, buttons, and fields which are discussed next.

Global Start Time and Global End Time

These fields are used to define the length of a composition in frames.

Render Start Time and Render End Time

These fields are used to represent the frames of a composition's output for the final and preview renders.

Render Button

This button is used for rendering the composition.

Playback Controls

These buttons are used to control the playback of a composition.

Audio Enable

This is a toggle button is used to enable or disable the audio in the composition.

Quality Controls

The buttons in this category help you to control the quality of a composition. There are five buttons in this category, **HiQ**(high quality), **MB** (Motion Blur), **Prx** (Proxy), **APrx** (Auto proxy), and **Some**. Generally, Fusion shows a low resolution version of the composition in the Display Views to provide faster interactive performance. With default settings, Fusion skips anti-aliasing, motion blur, and other computationaly expensive processes. You can use the buttons in the **Quality** control category to re-enable these features. When the **MB** and **HiQ** buttons are chosen, Fusion will display the output exactly what is seen during a final render. The **Some** button is a toggle button that you can use to toggle between three modes: **Some**, **None**, and **All**. With default mode (**Some**), Fusion render the tools that are required to display image in the Display Views. The **None** mode is used to prevent interactive rendering of the tools. The **All** mode is used to force all tools to render.

Working with the Layout

There are various predefined layout styles available in Fusion. These styles can be accessed by choosing the layout buttons which are located below the toolbar, refer to Figure 1-3. In Fusion, you can also make modifications in different areas of the layout. The methods to make such modifications are discussed next.

Figure 1-3 *The layout buttons*

1. To change the size of Display Views, move the cursor over the divider line between them; a double-headed arrow will be displayed, as shown in Figure 1-4. You can drag the divider line to either side to resize the Display Views.

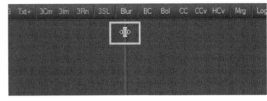

Figure 1-4 *Resizing the Display View*

2. To change the size of the Work area, move the cursor over the divider line between the Display Views and Work area; a double-headed arrow cursor will be displayed, as shown in Figure 1-5. Drag to resize the Work area.

Figure 1-5 *Resizing the Work area*

3. To change the size of the Control area, move the cursor over the divider line between the Display Views and Control area; a double-headed arrow will be displayed, as shown in Figure 1-6. Drag the divider line to resize the Control area.

USING THE TOOLBAR

The toolbar is located below the menubar. It is used to access commonly used tools in Fusion, refer to Figure 1-7. You can also access the tools in Fusion 7 Studio from the **Tools** menu in the menubar, as shown in Figure 1-8. The tools in the **Tools** menu are discussed next.

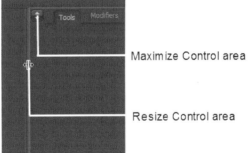

Figure 1-6 *Resizing the Control area*

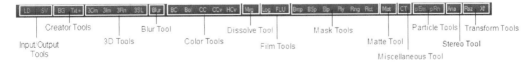

Figure 1-7 *The Fusion toolbar*

3D Tools

The 3D tools are used to apply light, assign shaders, apply textures, and so on to an object. These tools can be accessed by choosing **Tools > 3D** from the menubar, refer to Figure 1-9.

Light

The tools under the Light category are used to illuminate a scene. These tools can be accessed by choosing **Tools > 3D > Light** from the menubar, refer to Figure 1-10.

The tools in this category are discussed next.

Ambient Light

This tool is used to illuminate a 3D scene globally from all directions.

Directional Light

This tool is used to simulate a distant light source which casts parallel light rays in single direction.

Point Light

This tool is used to illuminate a scene by emitting the light in all directions.

Spot Light

This tool is used to simulate a conical shaped focussed beam of light. This is the only light in Fusion which casts shadows.

Figure 1-8 The Tools menu

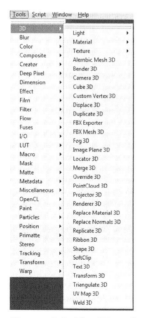

Figure 1-9 The 3D tools

Figure 1-10 The Light tools

Material

Materials are used to add realism to a scene. A material defines how a 3D object reflects or transmits light. You can apply materials to an object by using the Material tools. The Material tools can be accessed by choosing **Tools > 3D > Material** from the menubar, refer to Figure 1-11. The tools used for applying material are discussed next.

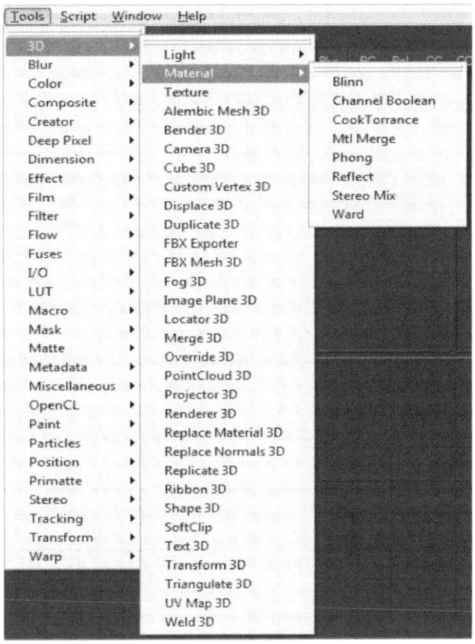

Blinn
This tool is used to apply basic illumination material on a 3D object.

Channel Boolean
This tool is used to modify the channels of a 3D object by using mathematical operations.

CookTorrance
The use of this tool is similar to that of the **Blinn** tool. However, the specular highlights are calculated using Fresnal/ Beckham equation when this tool is used. This tool is mainly used to shade shiny and highly reflective surfaces.

Mtl Merge
This tool is used to combine two different materials to form a complex shader.

Figure 1-11 *The Material tools*

Phong
This tool is used to simulate shiny plastic surfaces. It produces highlights similar to that produced by the **Blinn** tool.

Reflect
This tool is used to add environment map reflection and refraction to the material. It is usually connected with basic material to form a reflection or refraction pattern.

Stereo Mix
This tool is used to apply separate materials to the left and right eyes in a stereo pair.

Ward
This material is applied to a 3D object to give it a brushed metal look. The highlights can be adjusted in the U or V direction of the mapping coordinates.

Texture
Texture is a bitmap that can be wrapped on a 3D object to change the appearance of the existing texture. The tools in the Texture category can be accessed by choosing **Tools > 3D > Texture** from the menubar, as shown in Figure 1-12. The tools in this category are discussed next.

BumpMap
This tool is used to convert a bitmap to a bump material.

Catcher

This tool is used to intercept projections cast from the **Projector 3D** and **Camera 3D** tools. The projections are then converted to a texture map and applied by the **Catcher** material to the geometry it is connected to.

CubeMap

This tool is used to create texture maps using separate images for each face of the cube. It also provides coordinates for texture rotation.

Falloff

This tool is used to blend two materials based on the incidence angle between the object on which the material is applied and the camera.

Fast Noise Texture

This tool is used to generate a noise texture directly as a material on an object.

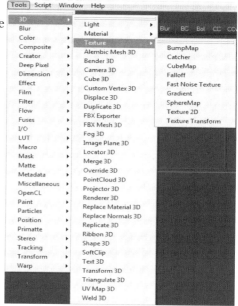

Figure 1-12 The Texture tools

Gradient

This tool is used to apply texture on an object with a variety of gradients types.

SphereMap

This tool is used to create a spherical texture map from an image.

Texture 2D

This tool is used to convert an image to a 3D material.

Texture Transform

This tool is used to translate, rotate, and scale image textures on the input material along the U, V, and W axes.

Alembic Mesh 3D

Alembic is a file format for meshes and animated scenes. You can easily import an Alembic mesh in Fusion using this option.

Bender 3D

This tool is used to bend, taper, or twist a 3D geometry. However, it only affects the geometry in a 3D scene.

Camera 3D

This tool is used to create a virtual camera through which a 3D scene can be viewed.

Cube 3D

This tool is used to create a simple cube. On using this tool, six additional image inputs for each face are displayed. You can apply texture on these faces individually.

Displace 3D
This tool is used to displace vertices along normals based on a reference image.

Duplicate 3D
This tool is used to duplicate a geometry in a 3D scene. You can create repeating transformation patterns using this tool.

FBX Exporter
This tool is used to export a Fusion 3D scene to the FBX interchange format. It also supports formats like *.3ds, .dae, .dxf,* and *.obj.*

FBX Mesh 3D
This tool is used to import complex polygonal geometry saved using the FBX format. It imports geometry in the *FBX, OBJ, 3DS, DAE,* and *DXF* file formats.

Note

In Fusion 7's 3D system you can import geometry from FBX and Alembic file formats, as well as OBJ, 3DS, and Collada formats. Now, you can easily import meshes with millions of polygons, complex shaders, Ambient Occlusion, Deep Volumetric Atmospherics, Particles Systems, and so on.

Fog 3D
This tool is used to generate depth-based fog in a 3D scene.

Image Plane 3D
This tool is used to used to create a 2D planar geometry in 3D space.

Locator 3D
This tool is used to transform, scale, or rotate a point in 3D space along 2D coordinates so that other tools can use it as a part of expressions.

Merge 3D
This tool is used to merge 3D elements into 3D environment.

Override 3D
This tool is used to override settings of a 3D object in a 3D scene.

PointCloud 3D
This tool is used to create a point cloud by importing a 3D scene and collects all the null points created by a 3D tracking software.

Projector 3D
This tool is used to project an image onto a 3D geometry.

Renderer 3D
This tool is used to render 3D environment into a 2D image by using one of the cameras present in the scene. It supports two render engines: Software and Open GL.

Replace Material 3D

This tool is used to change the material applied to all geometries in the input scene with its own material input.

Replace Normal 3D

The **Replace Normal 3D** tool is used to replace the normals on geometry. The geometry must have texture coordinates. All geometry in the scene is affected except the lights, camera, point clouds, and locators. Other non mesh tools are not affected by this tool.

Replicate 3D

The **Replace 3D** tool is used to replicate two or more geometries at the position of the target vertices. The geometries can be replicated at the vertices of a mesh. You can also replace particles with the geometry. You can apply various transformations for each copy of replicated geometry.

Ribbon 3D

Ribbon 3D is used to generate a segments or a line between two points. You can use this tool for creating motion graphics art work.

Shape 3D

This tool is used to create a basic primitive 3D shape including planes, spheres, and cylinders, which can be transformed, rotated, scaled, and rendered.

SoftClip

This tool is used to fade out the geometry or particles which are close to the camera.

Text 3D

This tool is a 3D version of the 2D **Text+** tool. Most of the controls found in this tool are similar to that of the **Text+** tool except that it supports all shading elements. The **Text+** tool will be discussed later in this chapter.

Transform 3D

This tool is used to translate, scale, and rotate 3D objects in a scene.

UV Map 3D

This tool is used to replace the UV texture coordinates on the geometry in a scene.

Weld 3D

This tool is used to weld adjustment vertices. It does not weld normals, texture coordinates, or any other vertex stream.

Blur Tools

Blur tools are used to blur or sharpen an image. These tools can be accessed by choosing **Tools > Blur** from the menubar, as shown in Figure 1-13. The Blur tools are discussed next.

Blur
This tool is used to blur the input image.

Defocus
This tool is used to defocus an image by simulating an out-of-focus camera lens effect.

Directional Blur
This tool is used to create directional and radial blurs. It is also useful in creating motion blur glow.

Glow
This tool is used to generate glow effect on an image by blurring an image and then brightening the image to produce glow.

Sharpen
This tool is used to enhance the detail of an image.

Soft Glow
This tool is used to simulate natural and soft glow effects in an image.

Unsharp Mask
This tool is used to sharpen only the edges within an image.

VariBlur
This tool is used to add per pixel blur to an image. It uses a second image to control the magnitude of the blur.

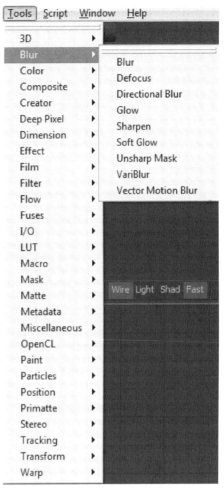

Figure 1-13 The Blur tools

Vector Motion Blur
This tool is used to create directional blur on an input image based on the vector channel.

Color Tools
Color tools are used to adjust the appearance of the images in a composition, make tonal adjustment, set gain, make gamma correction, and so on. These tools can be accessed by choosing **Tools > Color** from the menubar, as shown in Figure 1-14. The tools in this category are discussed next.

Auto Gain
This tool is used to adjust the color range of an image automatically to set the darkest and brightest pixels to the user-specified values.

Brightness / Contrast

This tool is used to control the gain, brightness, contrast, gamma, and saturation of an input image.

Channel Booleans

This tool is used to perform mathematical and logical operations on channels of an image.

Color Corrector

This tool is used to adjust the appearance of an image. It helps to correct the color with the help of histograms, levels, curves, and color compression functions.

Color Curves

This tool is used to perform LUT (Look Up Tables) color manipulations. It is an animatable spline-based tool.

Color Gain

This tool is used to adjust the gain, gamma, saturation, and hue of an image. It renders faster as compared to the **Color Corrector** tool.

Color Matrix

This tool is used to modify values independently in different color channels.

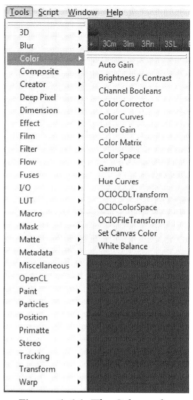

Figure 1-14 *The Color tools*

Color Space

This tool is used to convert a color space from one format to another. The default color space in Fusion is RGB (Red, Green, Blue).

Gamut

This tool is used to convert a color from one gamut to another.

Hue Curves

This tool is used to adjust the color of an image by using spline curves. This tool is different from other color correction tools because this tool allows you to manipulate the splines to restrict the tools effect to a range of colors.

OCIO CDLTransform

Fusion supports the OCIO (Open Color IO) workflow specified by Sony Imageworks. The color pipeline is made up from a set of color transformations defined by the OCIO-specific cofiguration files. The extention of these is *.ocio*.

OCIO ColorSpace

This tool allows for color space conversions based on an OCIO Configuration file. The RGB color space defines a color as the percentages of red, green, and blue hues mixed together.

OCIO File Transform

This tool is used to control the LUT files.

Set Canvas Color

This tool is used to set the color of the workspace A workspace is the area beyond the defined pixels within an image (the DOD).

White Balance

This tool is used to correct the color casts in an image which are usually caused by incorrect setup of a camera or lighting conditions.

Composite Tools

Composite tools are used to combine two images to form a single image. The composite tools can be accessed by choosing **Tools > Composite** from the menubar, refer to Figure 1-15. The Composite tools are discussed next.

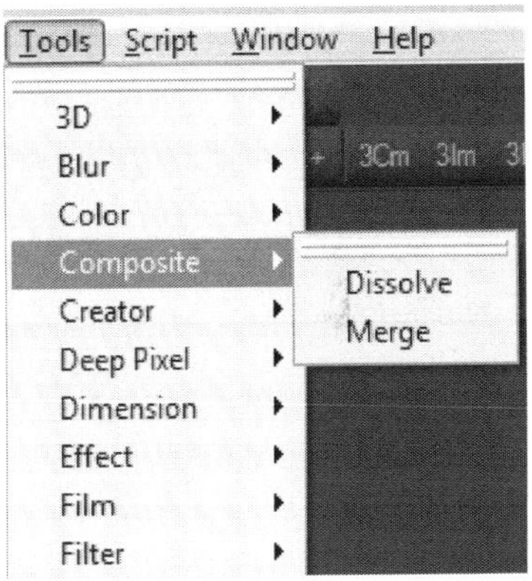

Dissolve

This tool is used to dissolve/mix two images together, thereby providing a gradual transition between the two images. It generates a smooth transition between foreground and background images.

Merge

This tool is used to combine two images: background and foreground. This operation is based on the alpha channel associated with the foreground.

Figure 1-15 The Composite tools

Creator Tools

Creator tools are used to produce solid backgrounds, noise, fractal pattern, and 2D text. These tools can be accessed by choosing **Tools > Creator** from the menubar, as shown in Figure 1-16. The Creator tools are discussed next.

Background

This tool is used to produce color backgrounds and also complex loopable gradients.

DaySky

This tool is used to create a procedural sky pattern based on a specific time and location on earth.

FastNoise

This tool is used to create a wide variety of noise effects using gradients such as procedural skies.

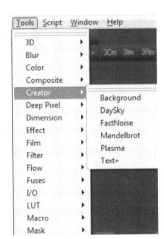

Figure 1-16 The Creator tools

Mandelbrot

This tool is used to generate an image based on the Mandlebrot fractal theory set.

Plasma

This tool is used to create circular shapes, thereby generating a plasma-like effect.

Text+

This tool is used to create 2D characters capable of 3D transformations. It also provides multiple styles and shading options to be applied on the text.

Deep Pixel Tools

Deep Pixel tools are used to generate various effects based on the Z-depth of the image. These tools can be accessed by choosing **Tools > Deep Pixel** from the menubar, refer to Figure 1-17. The different Deep Pixel tools are discussed next.

Depth Blur

This tool is used to generate the focal length or depth of field effects.

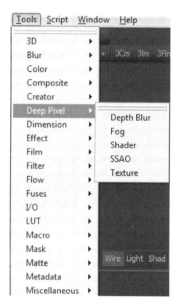

Figure 1-17 The Deep Pixel tools

Fog

This tool is used to simulate fog effect on a 3D rendered image. It uses Z buffer channel to generate the 3D fog effect.

Shader

This tool is used to control lighting, reflection mapping, and 3D shading of elements in the rendered image. It uses X, Y, and Z normal maps in the image to control the light.

SSAO

SSAO stand for Screenspace ambient occlusion. It generates global lighting effects in a 3D scenes.

Texture

This tool is used to control the texture mapping of an element in a rendered image. It can also be used to replace current texture of an image. It relies on the U and V map channels in the rendered image.

Effect Tools

Effect tools are used to generate various effects. These tools can be accessed by choosing **Tools > Effect** from the menubar, as shown in Figure 1-18. The various Effect tools are discussed next.

Highlight

This tool is used to create star-shaped highlights in the bright areas of an image.

Hot Spot

This tool is used to create lens flare, spotlight, and burn/dodge effect on an image.

Pseudo Color

This tool is used to create color variations, based on the waveforms generated by the tool controls.

Shadow

This tool is used to generate shadows based on the alpha channel information of an image.

Trails

This tool is used to generate trails effect. It first creates a frame buffer, then it takes the image data from the previous frames, and then merges that data over the current frame.

TV

This tool is used to replicate the flaws seen in analog television broadcasts and screens.

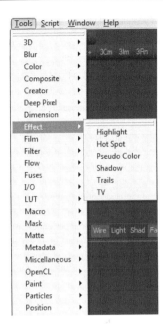

Figure 1-18 *The Effect tools*

Film Tools

Film tools are used to work with films. These tools can be accessed by choosing **Tools > Film** from the menubar, as shown in Figure 1-19. The various Film tools are discussed next.

Cineon Log

This tool is used to convert an image data from logarithmic to linear.

File LUT

This tool is used to apply Look Up Table (LUT) to the image.

Film Grain

This tool is used to apply grain to an image so that the grain resembles the grain profiles of the modern film stocks.

Grain

This tool is used to apply simulated grain to a video or 3D rendered image sequence.

Light Trim

This tool is used to emulate film scanner light trims. Generally, it is used with linear logarithmic images.

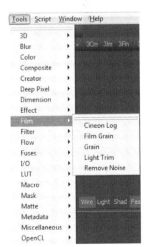

Figure 1-19 *The Film tools*

Remove Noise

This tool is used to remove noise from an image sequence.

Filter Tools

Filter tools are used to filter the RGB and alpha channels from an image. These tools can be accessed by choosing **Tools > Filter** from the menubar, as shown in Figure 1-20. The various Filter tools are discussed next.

Rank Filter

This tool is used to sort the pixel by value and then replace the color of all pixels by the color of the pixel with the specified rank.

Flow Tools

Flow tools are used to manage tool tiles in the **Flow** area. These tools can be accessed by choosing **Tools > Flow** from the menubar, refer to Figure 1-21. The various Flow tools are discussed next.

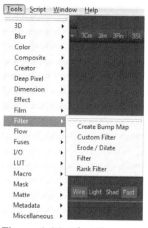

Figure 1-20 The Filter tools

Sticky Note

This tool is used to write notes and comments for the specific area of a composition.

Underlay

This tool is used to visually organize the tool tiles in the **Flow** area.

Fuse Tools

The Fuse tools are created by using scripting language (eyeonScript). Fuses are like normal tools and they contain scripting commands. These tools can be accessed by choosing **Tools > Fuses** from the menubar.

I/O Tools

I/O tools are used to load or import and save an image sequence. I/O represents Input and Output. These tools can be accessed by choosing **Tools > I/O** from the menubar, refer to Figure 1-22. The various I/O tools are discussed next.

Loader

This tool is used to select and load the footage from hard-drive or network storage.

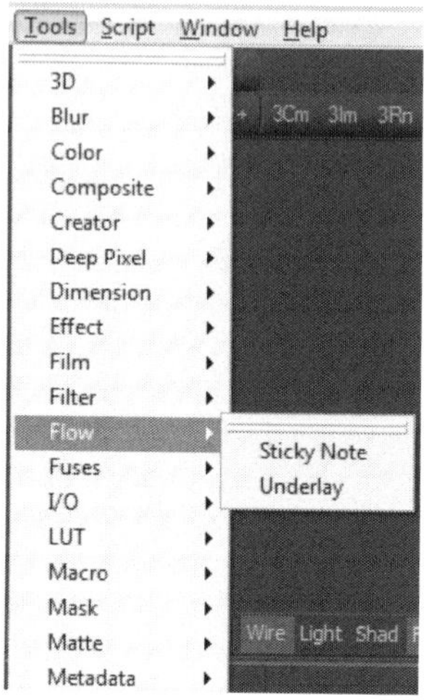

Figure 1-21 The Flow tools

Saver

This tool is used to write the render of a composition to disk.

Macro Tools

These tools are used to collapse the complex tool effects into single customized tool.

Mask Tools

Mask tools are used to mask out an area of an image. Each mask has its own set of controls unique to that mask type. These tools can be accessed by choosing **Tools > Mask** from the menubar, as shown in Figure 1-23. The various Mask tools are discussed next.

Bitmap
This tool allows an image from the flow to act as a mask.

BSpline
This tool is used to create smooth mask by using the B-spline handles.

Ellipse
This tool is used to create a mask by using circular shapes.

Mask Paint
This tool is used to directly paint on the mask images using mouse pointer as a brush.

Polygon
This tool is used to mask irregular-shaped objects.

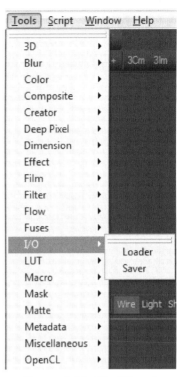

Figure 1-22 The I/O tools

Ranges
This tool is used to generate masks based on the tonal range.

Rectangle
This tool is used to create a rectangular or square shape mask.

Triangle
This tool is used to create a mask that has no centre, size, or angle control.

Wand
This tool is used to mask out an image based on the magic wand style selection.

Matte Tools

Matte tools are used to generate alpha channels by removing selected colors from the footage. These tools can be accessed by choosing **Tools > Matte** from the menubar, as shown in Figure 1-24. The Matte tools are discussed next.

Figure 1-23 The Mask tools

Alpha Divide
This tool is used to divide an input image with it's alpha channel.

Alpha Multiply
This tool is used to multiply an input image with it's alpha channel.

Chroma Keyer
This tool is used to generate an alpha channel by removing selected colors from the image.

Difference Keyer
This tool is used to create matte based on the differences between the two images.

Luma Keyer
This tool is used to generate an alpha channel by using the luminance of an image.

Matte Control
This tool is used to manipulate an existing alpha channel.

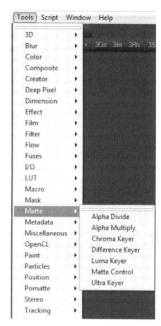

Figure 1-24 *The Matte tools*

Ultra Keyer
This tool is used to pull a key from the images using the bluescreen and greenscreen backgrounds.

Metadata Tools
Metadata tools are used for storing data within the data. These tools can be accessed by choosing **Tools > Metadata** from the menubar, refer to Figure 1-25. The Metadata tools are discussed next.

Copy Metadata
This tool is used to copy and filter the metadata.

Set Metadata
This tool is used to set the metadata.

Set Time Code
This tool is used to insert dynamic time code values into the meta-data table based on the FPS settings.

Miscellaneous Tools
These tools can be accessed by choosing **Tools >Miscellaneous** from the menubar, as shown in Figure 1-26. The Miscellaneous tools are discussed next.

Figure 1-25 *The Metadata tools*

Auto Domain

This tool is used to set the Domain of Definition (DoD) of an image automatically.

Change Depth

This tool is used to change bits per channel depth of an image.

Custom Tool

This tool is used to create custom expressions and filters to modify an image.

Fields

This tool offers several functions related to interlaced video frames.

RunCommand

This tool is used to execute external commands or batch files at certain points while rendering.

Set Domain

This tool is used to set the active area of an image without changing its physical dimension.

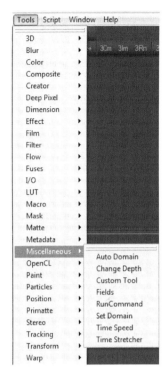

Figure 1-26 *The Miscellaneous tools*

Time Speed

This tool is used to speed up, slow down, reverse, or delay the image sequences.

Time Stretcher

This tool is used to animate the speed of the clip.

OpenCL Tools

These tools are OpenCL (Open Computing Language) clones of source native compiled tools. Open CL language allows you to take the full advantage of modern day graphic cards.

These tools can be accessed by choosing **Tools > OpenCL** from the menubar.

Paint Tool

This tool is used to paint directly on the image by using brush strokes. It is used for cloning, wire removal, and masking. This tool can be accessed by choosing **Tools > Paint** from the menubar.

Particles Tools

Particles are computer generated points in 3D space and help in creating a wide variety of effects. These tools can be accessed

Figure 1-27 *The Particles tools*

by choosing **Tools > Particles** from the menubar, as shown in Figure 1-27. The Particles tools are discussed next.

pAvoid
This tool is used to create an area within an image so that the affected particles do not enter or cross.

pBounce
This tool is used to create an area wherein the particles will bounce away when they come in contact with it.

pChangeStyle
This tool is used to change the appearance and style of particles when they come in contact with a defined region.

pCustom
This tool is used to create custom expressions. These expressions affect the properties of the particles.

pDirectionalForce
This tool is used to apply a unidirectional force. As a result, on invoking this tool, particles move along the defined direction.

pEmitter
This tool is used to emit particles. It is the first tool in a particle tools network.

pFlock
This tool is used to simulate the behavior of organic systems such as a flock of birds. Each particle attempts to stay close to the other particle.

pFriction
This tool is used to apply friction to particles on a specified region.

pGradientForce
This tool is used to increase the speed of particles by a force generated by gradients. Particles accelerate from white to black area of the gradient.

pImageEmitter
This tool is used to emit particles from an input image. The color of the particles depends on the input image.

pKill
This tool is used to kill the particle, if it crosses or intersects the tool's region.

pMerge
This tool is used to combine particles from two different emitters.

pPointForce

This tool is used to attract or repel particles within its sphere of influence by applying a force to them.

pRender

This tool is used to convert a particle system to 2D image.

pSpawn

This tool is used to spawn particles from existing particles, thereby making each affected particle produce more particles on its own.

pTangentForce

This tool is used to apply a tangential force on particles.

pTurbulence

This tool is used to generate frequency-based turbulence to particles.

pVortex

This tool is used to apply a circular force to each particle in the particle system.

Position Tools

The Position tools are used to work with masks and volumetrics for images having XYZ position channels. These tools can be accessed by choosing **Tools > Position** from the menubar, as shown in Figure 1-28. The Position tools are discussed next.

Volume Fog

This tool is used to create volumetric fog on images containing XYZ Position channels.

Volume Mask

This tool is used to create volumetric masks from images containing XYZ Position channels.

Z to WorldPos

This tool is used to either generate a world position pass from a Z-channel and a 3D camera or a Z-channel from a world position pass and a 3D camera.

Figure 1-28 The Position tools

Primatte Tool

The **Primatte** tool is an advanced green/blue screen keyer. It provides advanced techniques for extremely fine manipulations of the color regions. This tool can be accessed by choosing **Tools > Primatte** from the menubar.

Stereo Tools

Stereo tools are used for creating and processing stereoscopicimages. These tools can be accessed by choosing **Tools > Stereo** from the menubar, refer to Figure 1-29. The Stereo tools are discussed next.

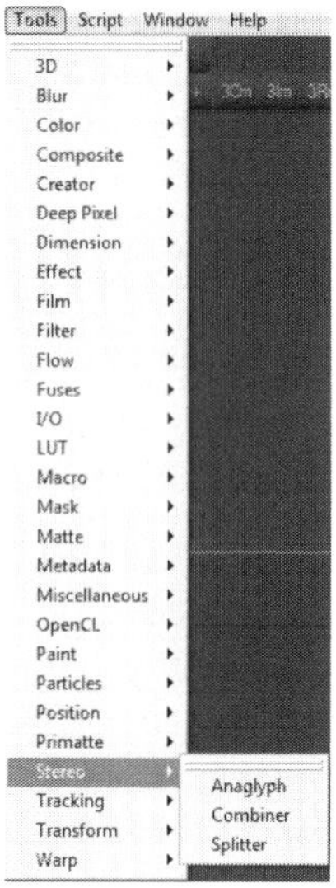

Anaglyph

This tool is used to create stereoscopic images by combining the left and the right eye images.

Combiner

This tool is used to stack two stereoscopic images side by side or on top of each other.

Splitter

This tool takes input of the **Combiner** tool and provides two output images one each for the left and right eyes.

Figure 1-29   The Stereo tools

Tracking Tool

This tool is used to detect and follow pixel patterns across frames in an image sequence. Additionally, you can use this tool for stabilizing and reverse stabilizing an image sequence.

Transform Tools

These tools are used to transform a 2D image by moving, scaling, or rotating it. These tools can be accessed by choosing **Tools > Transform** from the menubar, refer to Figure 1-30. The Transform tools are discussed next.

Camera Shake

This tool is used to generate a variety of camera shape style motions from organic to mechanical.

Crop

This tool is used to crop a portion of an image or offset the image into a larger image area.

DVE

This tool is used to transform an image and also to add perspective to an image.

Figure 1-30 The Transform tools

Letterbox

This tool is used to change the frame size and aspect ratio of an input image to the frame size and aspect ratio of another image.

Resize

This tool is used to increase or decrease the resolution of an image.

Scale
This tool is similar to the **Resize** tool but it uses relative dimensions to specify the changes.

Transform
This tool is used for 2D transformations of an image.

Warp Tools
Warp tools are used to distort the input image. These tools can be accessed by choosing **Tools > Warp** from the menubar, as shown in Figure 1-31. The various Warp tools are discussed next.

Figure 1-31 *The Warp tools*

Coordinate Space
This tool is used to modify the coordinate space of an input image from rectangular to polar and polar to rectangular.

Corner Positioner
This tool is used to modify the position of four corners of an image interactively.

Dent
This tool is used to distort an image by creating a circular deformation.

Displace
This tool is used to displace/refract an image based on the displacement map.

Drip
This tool is used to create ripple effects of different shapes in an image such as circular, square, and so on.

Grid Warp
This tool is used to deform an image by using a 2D deformation grid which has flexible vertices.

Lens Distort
This tool is used to add or remove the lens distortion in an image.

Perspective Positioner
This tool is used to modify the position of an image by adjusting corner points to remove the perspective from an image.

Vector Distortion
This tool is used to distort the input image along the X and Y axes individually based on vector channel data.

Vortex

This tool is used to create a swirling whirlpool effect on the specified region of an image.

OPENING A COMPOSITION

To open a composition in Fusion, choose **File > Open** from the menubar; the **Open** dialog box will be displayed, as shown in Figure 1-32. In this dialog box, navigate to the desired folder and select the composition. Next, choose the **Open** button; the composition will be displayed.

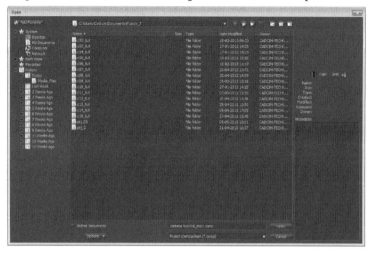

Figure 1-32 The **Open** dialog box

 Note
The extension of Fusion file is .comp

SAVING A COMPOSITION

To save a composition, choose **File > Save** from the menubar. Alternatively, press CTRL+S; the **Save File** dialog box will be displayed, as shown in Figure 1-33. Now, enter the desired name of the composition and then choose the **Save** button.

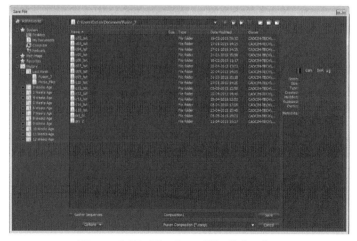

Figure 1-33 The **Save File** dialog box

CLOSING A COMPOSITION

To close a composition, choose **File > Close** from the menubar; a message box will be displayed, as shown in Figure 1-34. Choose the **Yes** button to save the changes made, the **No** button to discard the changes, or the **Cancel** button to close the message box.

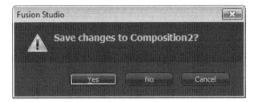

Figure 1-34 *A message box prompting to save the changes made*

Using the Undo and Redo Commands in Fusion

In Fusion, you can use the **Undo** and **Redo** commands to undo and redo the steps performed earlier. To undo a step, choose **Edit > Undo** from the menubar or press CTRL + Z. To redo a step, choose **Edit > Redo** from the menubar or press CTRL+Y. You can also delete tools by first selecting them and then pressing DEL.

General HotKeys

In Fusion, you can invoke some of the commands by using hotkeys. The main hotkeys and their functions are given next.

Hotkey	Function
CTRL+ N	Creates a new composition
CTRL + O	Opens an existing composition
CTRL + S	Saves the composition
CTRL + Z	Used to undo the last action performed
CTRL+ Y	Used to redo the last action performed
CTRL + X or SHIFT+DEL	Cuts the selected item in the clipboard
CTRL + C	Copies the selected tools in the clipboard
CTRL + G	Creates a group of selected tools
CTRL + V	Pastes the selected tools from the clipboard
[	Moves forward one frame on the timeline
]	Moves backward one frame on the timeline
ALT + [	Advances to the next keyframe
ALT +]	Moves back to the previous keyframe

Function Keys

The function keys are used to perform various functions. The main function keys and their functions are given next.

Key	Function
F1	Displays the help for the selected tool
F2	Renames the selected tools
F4	Maximizes and restores the selected area
F5	Activates the **Flow** area in the Work area
F6	Activates the **Console** area in the Work area
F7	Activates the **Timeline** area in the Work area
F8	Activates the **Spline** area in the Work area
F11	Activates the **Modifiers** area in the Control area
F12	Displays the **Render Settings** dialog box

Display Views Keys

These keys are used to view the composition in different channels. These keys and their functions are given next.

Key	Function
R	Displays the red channel in the selected Display View
G	Displays the green channel in the selected Display View
B	Displays the blue channel in the selected Display View
A	Displays the alpha channel in the selected Display View
Z	Displays the Z channel in the selected Display View
C	Displays full color image in the selected Display View
V	Displays the selected sub views in the Display View
SHIFT + V	Swaps the content of the Display View and sub view
CTRL + L	Locks the Display View
CTRL + Q	Toggles quad view in the selected Display View
CTRL + K	Toggles the **Show Controls** button
CTRL + G	Toggles the display of guides
SHIFT + H	Toggles the display of handles on spline keypoints
, (comma)	Switches the view to use the A image buffer
. (period)	Switches the view to use the B image buffer
/	Switches the view so that it shows both the A and B buffers and enables splitwipe

Flow Area Keys

These keys are used to perform various functions in the **Flow** area. These keys and their functions are given next.

Key	Function
CTRL + F	Displays the **Find tools** dialog box
CTRL + L	Toggles the lock mode of the selected tool
V	Toggles the display of the navigator

Spline Area Keys

These keys are used to perform various functions in the **Spline** area. These keys and their functions are given next.

Key	Function
S	Smoothens the curve of the selected points on a spline or polyline
V	Reverses the selected keyframes on a spline
CTRL + drag	Copies the selected points on a spline

Time Ruler Keys

These keys are used to perform functions in the Time Ruler area. These keys and their functions are given next.

Key	Function
CTRL + SHIFT+ double-click	Sets the render range to the slider range
CTRL + Drag	Sets the render range to frames enclosed by dragging mouse

Self-Evaluation Test

Answer the following questions and then compare them to those given at the end of this chapter:

1. Which of the following components is located at the bottom of the Fusion interface?

   (a) Control area   (b) Timeline
   (c) Toolbar   (d) Display View

2. The _____ is located on the right of the Fusion interface.

3. The Work area consists of _____ tabs.

4. The _____ tool is used to combine two images.

5. The _____ View displays the output of the tools in a composition.

6. The _____ tool uses luminance of an image to create the alpha channel.

7. The _____ tool is used to increase or decrease the resolution of an image.

8.   The _____ tool is used to load a footage.

9.   The _____ tool is used to color-correct the image.

10. The **Dissolve** and **Merge** tools are Composite tools. (T/F).

Review Questions

Answer the following questions:

1.   Which of the following Material tools is used to modify 3D material by using mathematical operations?

     (a) **Mtl Merge**   (b) **Ward**
     (c) **Phong**   (d) **Channel Boolean**

2.   Which of the following Mask tools is used to mask an irregular shape?

     (a) **Range**   (b) **Polygon**
     (c) **Triangle**   (d) **Ellipse**

3.   Which of the following combinations of shortcut keys is used to open a new composition?

     (a) CTRL+O   (b) CTRL+S
     (c) CTRL+N   (d) CTRL+Z

4.   The Work area is located below the _____ views.

5.   The **Mask** tool comprises of _____ tools.

6.   The extension of a Fusion file is _____ .

7.   The _____ tool is used to stabilize or destabilize an image sequence.

8.   The _____ light emits light in all directions.

9.   The I/O tools help you load and save an image. (T/F)

10. The **Soft Glow** tool is used to give natural and soft glow effect to an image. (T/F)

Answers to Self-Evaluation Test
1. b, **2.** Control area, **3.** six, **4. Merge**, **5.** Display, **6. Luma Keyer**, **7. Resize**, **8. Loader**, **9. Color Corrector**, **10.** T

Chapter 2

Creating Network
of Tools

Learning Objectives

After completing this chapter, you will be able to:
- *Set the frame format for the composition*
- *Merge multiple images*
- *Load a footage*
- *Color-correct the footage*
- *Connect and disconnect connections between tools*
- *Save and render a composition*

INTRODUCTION

Fusion is an advanced node-based compositing application for visual effects artists. Compositing is an art of combining multiple images to create a single image. You can create complex effects simply by connecting various nodes together. In this chapter, you will learn to create, save, and render a composition. You will also learn how to load and merge images.

A Fusion composition consists of a network of nodes called tools. These tools are connected through pipes to form a composition. You can connect or disconnect pipes easily by using various methods which are discussed later in this chapter.

In this chapter, you will also learn about **Bins**, where you can store references, compositions, and large quantity of data across the network. You can also access tools from this folder.

TUTORIALS

Before you start the tutorials of this chapter, you need to download the *c02_fusion_7_tut.zip* file from *http://www.cadcim.com*. The path of the file is as follows:

> *Textbooks > Animation and Visual Effects > Fusion > Blackmagic Design Fusion 7 Studio: A Tutorial Approach*

Next, you need to extract the contents of the zip file. To do so, navigate to the *Documents* folder and then create a new folder with the name *Fusion_7*. Next, extract the contents of the downloaded zip file to the *Fusion_7* folder.

Tutorial 1

In this tutorial, you will composite three images to create a single image. The final output of the composition is shown in Figure 2-1.   **(Expected time: 25 min)**

Figure 2-1 The final output of the composition

The following steps are required to complete this tutorial:

a. Set the frame format.
b. Download and import images.
c. View the output of the tools in Display Views.
d. Resize images.
e. Color-correct the image.
f. Merge images.
g. Prepare the composition for rendering.
h. Save and render the composition.

Setting the Frame Format

In this section, you will set the frame format for the composition.

1. Choose **File > New** from the menubar; a new composition is displayed in the Fusion interface, as shown in Figure 2-2.

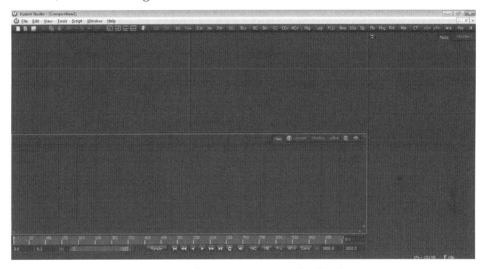

Figure 2-2 The new composition displayed

2. Choose **File > Preferences** from the menubar; the **Preferences** dialog box is displayed, as shown in Figure 2-3.

3. In this dialog box, select **Frame Format** from the **Composition#** preferences tree; various frame format settings are displayed in the right of the **Preferences** dialog box. Next, select the **NTSC (Square Pixel)** option from the **Default format** drop-down list and then choose the **Save** button to save the changes made.

Note

*If you generally work in a particular frame format, you can set it in the **Global and new comp defaults** preferences tree of the **Preferences** dialog box. As a result, the next time when you create a new composition, Fusion will inherit the preference settings for the new composition from the global preferences.*

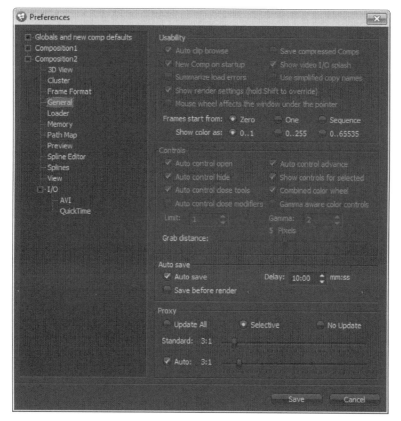

*Figure 2-3 The **Preferences** dialog box*

The **Frame Format** option allows you to set the various aspects(width, height, frame rate, aspect ratio) of the frame format settings for the composition. The footage may be NTSC, PAL, HD, or even Multimedia.

4. In the Time Ruler area, enter **0** in the **Global End Time** edit box.

    The Time Ruler area control the playback as well as sets the composition options like current frame, quality, proxy level and motion blur.

Downloading and Importing the Images

In this section, you will download the images and import them to the composition.

1. Open the link *http://www.freeimages.com/photo/1252649*; an image is displayed.

2. Download the image to */Documents/Fusion_7/c02_tut/c02_tut_01/Media_Files* and save it with the name *sunset.jpg*.

Note
*Footage Courtesy: **Colin Broug** (http://www.freeimages.com/profile/ColinBroug).*

3. Choose the **LD** button from the toolbar; the **Open File** dialog box is displayed, refer to Figure 2-4. Next, choose **Documents > Fusion_7 > c02_tut > c02_tut_01 > Media_Files > sunset. jpg** from the dialog box and then choose the **Open** button; the **Loader1** tool tile is inserted in the **Flow** area, refer to Figure 2-5.

The **Loader** tool is used to select and load the footage from hard-drive or network storage.

*Figure 2-4 The **Open File** dialog box*

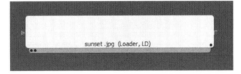

*Figure 2-5 The **Loader 1** tool tile inserted in the **Flow** area*

 Note
*You can add the tools in the **Flow** area using one of the following methods:*

*1. Using the **Tool** menu from the menubar.*

*2. Right click in the **Flow** area; a shortcut menu is displayed. Choose **Add Tool** from the shortcut menu to add the tools.*

*3. Press CTRL+SPACEBAR to add the tools in the **Flow** area.*

4. You can access the tools from toolbar.

Viewing the Output of the Tools in the Display Views

In this section, you will view the output of the tools in the Display Views.

1. Make sure the **Loader1** tool tile is selected in the **Flow** area and then press 1; the output of the **Loader1** tool is displayed in the left Display View. Choose the **Fit** button from the left Display View toolbar to fit the image into the left Display View.

 Note
You can create additional Display Views to view the output of the tools. To do so, choose **Window > New Image View** *from the menubar; the* **View1** *window is displayed, as shown in Figure 2-6. Now, to display the footage in the new Display View, press 3 or drag and drop the* **Loader1** *tool tile in the* **View1** *window.*

 Tip: *1. You can also drag and drop the loader tools into the Display Views to view the output of the tools. Alternatively, you can click on the black dots available at the bottom left corner of the tool tile to display the footage in the left, right, and additional views that you have created, refer to Figure 2-5.*

2. If you choose the third dot in the tool tile, Fusion will display the output in full screen mode. Press Esc to exit this mode.

2. Click on the empty space in the **Flow** area to deselect the **Loader1** tool tile. Import *tree.png* from the location specified in step 3; the **Loader2** tool tile is inserted in the **Flow** area, as shown in Figure 2-7.

3. Press 2; the output of the **Loader2** tool is displayed in the right Display View. Next, choose the **Fit** button from the right Display View toolbar to fit the image in the right Display View.

Figure 2-6 The **View 1** *window*

4. In the control window of the **Loader2** tool, choose the **Import** tab and then select the **Post-Multiply by Alpha** check box, refer to Figure 2-8; the transparency is displayed in the Display View.

   When you select the **Post-Multiply by Alpha** check box, the color values of the pixels are multiplied by their alpha values, thereby producing clear transparency.

Resizing the Images

In this section, you will resize the images.

1. Select the **Loader1** tool tile from the **Flow** area and then choose the **Rsz** button from the toolbar; the **Resize1** tool tile is inserted in the **Flow** area and a connection between **Loader1** and **Resize1** tools is established.

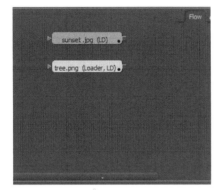

Figure 2-7 *The* **Loader2** *tool tile inserted in the* **Flow** *area*

Figure 2-8 *Choosing the* **Import** *tab from the* **Loader2** *tool control window*

The **Resize1** tool is used to increase or decrease the resolution of an image.

Note

To break the connection between two tools, click on the connecting arrow head and drop it into an empty space of the **Flow** *area.*

2. Select the **Loader2** tool tile from the **Flow** area and then choose the **Rsz** button from the toolbar; the **Resize2** tool tile is inserted in the **Flow** area and a connection between the **Loader2** and **Resize2** tools is established.

3. Set the values of the **Width** and **Height** parameters in the **Resize1** and **Resize2** tool control windows to **640** and **480**, respectively.

Color-Correcting the Image

In this section, you will color-correct the tree image.

1. Select the **Resize2** tool tile from the **Flow** area and then choose **Tools > Color > Color Corrector** from the menubar; the **ColorCorrector1** tool is inserted in the **Flow** area and a connection between the **ColorCorrector1** and **Resize2** tools is established.

   The **Color Corrector** tool is used to set the color of an image. It helps to manipulate the colors with the help of histograms, levels, curves, and color compression functions.

2. Make sure the **ColorCorrector1** tool tile is selected in the **Flow** area and then press 2; the output of the **ColorCorrector1** tool is displayed in the right Display View.

3. In the control window of the **ColorCorrector1** tool, set the values of the parameters as follows:

   Master - RGB - Gain: **0.18**   Master - RGB - Brightness: **-0.64**

4. Choose the **Suppress** button in the **ColorCorrector1** tool control window; the Suppress color wheel is displayed. In this color wheel, move the circles corresponding to yellow and green colors to the center of the color wheel, refer to Figure 2-9.

   The **Suppress** button is used to suppress the individual colors on an image.

Merging the Images

In this section, you will merge the images.

1. Drag the red output node of the **ColorCorrector1** tool tile to the red output node of the **Resize1** tool tile; the **Merge1** tool tile is inserted in the **Flow** area and a connection between the **Resize1**, **ColorCorrector1**, and **Merge1** tools is established.

   The **Merge1** tool is used to combine background and foreground images.

 Note
   *If you click on the red output node of a tool and then drag the cursor to the red output node of another tool, the **Merge** tool will appear automatically and pipes will be drawn between the tools.*

2. Press 2; the output of the **Merge1** tool is displayed in the right Display View.

3. In the **Merge1** tool control window, enter **1.49** in the **Size** edit box.

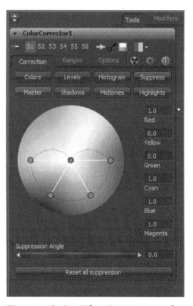

Figure 2-9 The Suppress color wheel in the control window

4. Click on the empty space in the **Flow** area to deselect the selected tool tile, if any. Choose the **LD** button from the toolbar; the **Open File** dialog box is displayed, refer to Figure 2-4. In this dialog box, choose **Documents > Fusion_7 > c02_tut > c02_tut_01 > Media_Files > man standing.png**; the **Loader3** tool tile is inserted in the **Flow** area.

5. Press 1; the output of the **Loader3** tool is displayed in the left Display View.

6. In the control window of the **Loader3** tool, choose the **Import** tab and then select the **Post-Multiply by Alpha** check box.

7. Make sure the **Loader3** tool tile is selected in the **Flow** area. Next, choose the **Rsz** button from the toolbar; the **Resize3** tool tile is inserted in the **Flow** area and a connection between the **Loader3** and **Resize3** tools is established.

8. Click on the empty space in the **Flow** area to deselect the selected tool tile, if any. Choose the **Mrg** button from the toolbar; the **Merge2** tool tile is inserted in the **Flow** area. Drag the red output node of the **Merge1** tool to the orange node of the **Merge2** tool to connect these tools. Similarly, connect the red output node of the **Resize3** tool to the green node of the **Merge2** tool. Next, press 2; the output of the **Merge2** tool is displayed in the right Display View.

9. In the control window of the **Merge2** tool, set the values of the parameters as follows:

   Center
   X: **0.54**   Y: **0.26**

   Size: **0.21**

10. Make sure the **Merge2** tool tile is selected in the **Flow** area and then choose the **CC**  button from the toolbar; the **ColorCorrector2** tool tile is inserted in the **Flow** area and a connection between the **Merge2** and **ColorCorrector2** tools is established. Next, press 2; the output of the **ColorCorrector2** tool is displayed in the right Display View.

11. In the **ColorCorrector2** tool control window, set the values of the parameters as follows:

   Tint: **0.11**   Strength: **0.28**   Master - RGB - Gain: **0.92**

   The **Tint** option is used to make the original color lighter and the **Strength** option controls the tint applied to the selected range of colors.

   After entering the values, the output of the **ColorCorrector2** tool is displayed in the right Display View, as shown in Figure 2-10.

*Figure 2-10 The output of the **ColorCorrector2** tool*

12. Click on the empty space of the **Flow** area to deselect the selected tool tile, if any. Choose **Tools > Blur > Blur** from the toolbar; the **Blur1** tool tile is inserted in the **Flow** area.

   The **Blur** tool is used to blur the input images.

13. Drag the red output node of the **ColorCorrector2** tool tile to the orange input node of the **Blur1** tool tile; a pipe is drawn between the **ColorCorrector2** and **Blur1** tools to represent the connection between them.

14. Press 1; the output of the **Blur1** tool is displayed in the left Display View.

15. In the control window of the **Blur1** tool, enter **1.05** in the **Blur Size** edit box.

    The **Blur Size** option controls the amount of blur applied to the image.

Preparing the Composition for Rendering
Next, you will prepare the composition for rendering.

1. Make sure the **Blur1** tool tile is selected in the **Flow** area. Choose the **SV** button from the toolbar; the **Save File** dialog box is displayed, as shown in Figure 2-11.

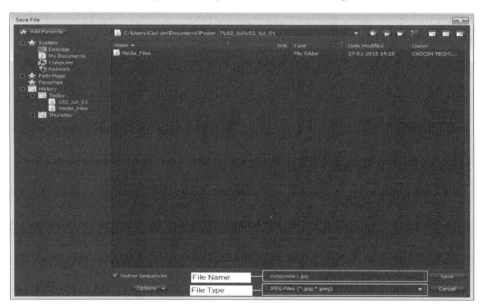

*Figure 2-11 The **Save File** dialog box*

2. Choose **Documents > Fusion_7 > c02_tut > c02_tut_01** from the dialog box. Select **JPEG Files (*.jpg; *.jpeg)** from the File Type drop-down list. Next, enter **composite.jpg** in the File Name edit box. Next, choose the **Save** button.

3. Choose the **Format** tab in the **Saver1** tool control window and move the **Quality** slider to **100**.

Saving and Rendering the Composition
In this section, you will save and render the composition. You can also view the final render of the composition by downloading the file *c02_fusion_7_rndr.zip* from *http://www.cadcim.com*. The path of the file is given at the beginning of the chapter.

1. Choose **File > Save** from the menubar; the **Save File** dialog box will be displayed. In this dialog box, choose **Documents > Fusion_7 > c02_tut > c02_tut_01** and then enter **c02tut1** in the File Name edit box. Next, choose the **Save** button to close the dialog box and save the composition.

2. Choose the **Render** button from the Time Ruler available below the **Flow** area, refer to Figure 2-12; the **Render Settings** dialog box is displayed, as shown in Figure 2-13. Next, choose the **Start Render** button; the rendering process starts. On completion of rendering, the **c02tut1.comp** message box is displayed, as shown in Figure 2-14. Next, choose the **OK** button to close the message box.

Render Start Time   Render button   Render End Time

Figure 2-12 *The Time Ruler showing the* ***Render*** *button*

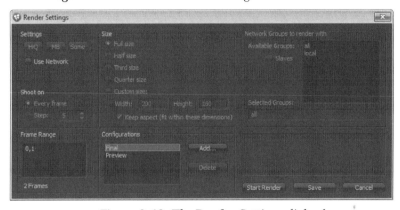

Figure 2-13 *The* ***Render Settings*** *dialog box*

Figure 2-14 *The* ***c02tut1.comp*** *message box informing about the completion of the rendering process*

3. Navigate to */Documents/Fusion_7/c02_tut/c02_tut_01* and double-click on the *composite0000.jpg* file to view the final rendered output.

Tutorial 2

In this tutorial, you will create a composition and then render it. The final output of the composition is shown in Figure 2-15.   (**Expected time: 20 min**)

The following steps are required to complete this tutorial:

a.   Create a new composition.
b.   Load the footage.
c.   Color-correct the footage.
d.   Resize the footage.
e.   Prepare the composition for rendering.
f.   Save and Render the composition.

Figure 2-15 *The final output of the composition*

Creating a New Composition

In this section, you will create a new composition.

1.   Choose **File > New** from the menubar; a new composition is displayed in the Fusion screen, refer to Figure 2-2.

     Before you start working on the composition, you need to set the frame format, frame rate, and other parameters of the composition.

2.   Choose **File > Preferences** from the menubar; the **Preferences** dialog box is displayed, refer to Figure 2-3.

3. In this dialog box, select **Frame Format** from the **Composition#** preferences tree; various frame format settings are displayed in the right of the **Preferences** dialog box. Next, select the **Pal / SECAM (D1)** option from the **Default format** drop-down list and then choose the **Save** button to save the changes made.

Loading the Footage

Image or image sequences are loaded into Fusion by using the **Loader** tool. In this section, you will load the footage in the **Flow** area.

1. Choose the **LD** button from the toolbar; the **Loader1** tool tile is inserted in the **Flow** area and the **Open File** dialog box is displayed.

2. In this dialog box, choose **Documents > Fusion_7 > c02_tut > c02_tut_02 > Media_Files > beach clip.mov**. Next, choose the **Open** button.

3. Make sure the **Loader1** tool tile is selected in the **Flow** area and then press 1; the output of the **Loader1** tool is displayed in the left Display View. Similarly, press 2 to display the **Loader1** tool in the right Display View, refer to Figure 2-16.

*Figure 2-16 The output of the **Loader 1** tool displayed in left and Right Display Views*

Color-Correcting the Footage

In this section, you will color-correct the footage by using the **Color Corrector** tool.

1. Click on the empty space in the **Flow** area to deselect the selected tool tile, if any. Choose the **Fit** button from the left **Display View** toolbar to fit the image into the left Display View.

2. Choose **Tools > Color > Color Corrector** from the menubar; the **ColorCorrector1** tool tile is inserted in the **Flow** area and its properties are displayed in the control window on the right of the interface, refer to Figure 2-17.

3. Drag the red output node of the **Loader1** tool tile to the orange input node of the **ColorCorrector1** tool tile; a pipe is drawn between the **Loader1** and **ColorCorrector1** tools to make a connection between them.

4. Select the **ColorCorrector1** tool tile from the **Flow** area and press 2; the output of the **ColorCorrector1** tool is displayed in the right Display View. Next, choose the **Fit** button from the right **Display View** toolbar to fit the image into the right Display View.

5. In the control window of the **ColorCorrector1** tool, set the values of the parameters as follows:

Tint: **0.33**   Strength: **0.072**

Master - RGB - Contrast: **1.05**

Master - RGB - Gain: **1.15**

Notice the change in the colors of the footage in the right Display View.

Resizing the Footage

In this section, you will resize the footage by using the **Resize** tool.

1. Make sure the **ColorCorrector1** tool tile is selected in the **Flow** area and then choose the **Bins** button from the toolbar; the **Bins** window is displayed. Expand **Library on localhost** in the left pane of the **Bins** window by clicking on the plus sign placed before it.

Figure 2-17 The ColorCorrector1 tool control window

2. Expand the **Tools** node and then select the **Transform** node from the left pane in the **Bins** window; the tools under the **Transform** category are displayed in the right pane. Double-click on the **Resize** tool in the **Bins** window; the **Resize1** tool is connected to the **ColorCorrector1** tool and its properties are displayed in the control window. Next, close the **Bins** window.

 Note
*You can also drag and drop tools from the **Bins** window to the **Flow** area and then make connections between the tools based on your requirement.*

3. Press 2; the output of the **Resize1** tool is displayed in the right Display View.

4. In the control window of the **Resize1** tool, set the values of the parameters as follows:

Width: **625**   Height: **391**

After entering the values in the **Resize1** tool control window, the output of the tool is displayed, refer to Figure 2-18.

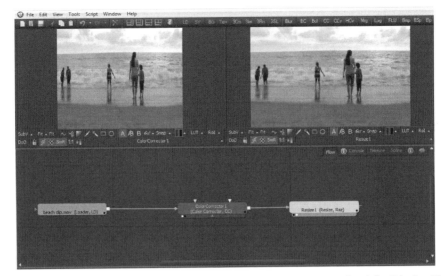

*Figure 2-18 The **Resize1** tool in the **Flow** area and its output in the right Display View*

Preparing the Composition for Rendering

In this section, you will prepare the composition for rendering.

1. Make sure the **Resize1** tool tile is selected in the **Flow** area and then right-click on it; a shortcut menu is displayed. Choose **Insert Tool > I/O > Saver** from the shortcut menu; the **Saver1** tool tile is inserted in the **Flow** area and the **Save File** dialog box is displayed.

2. Choose **Documents > Fusion_7 > c02_tut > c02_tut_02** from the dialog box. Select **Quick Time Movies (*.mov; *.qt; *.gp; *.mp4)** from the File Type drop-down list. Next, enter **beach clip** in the File Name edit box. Next, choose the **Save** button.

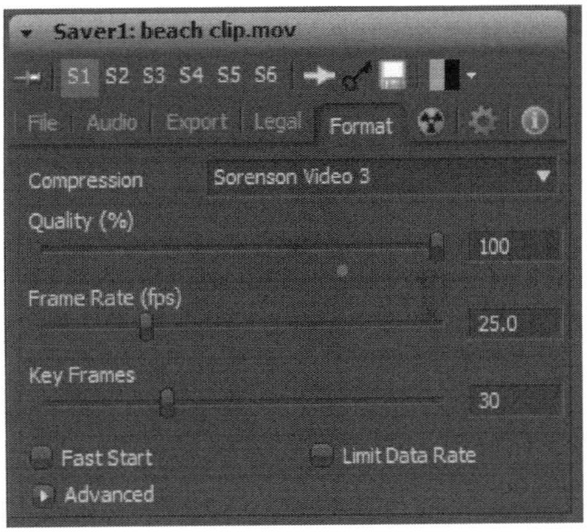

*Figure 2-19 The **Saver1** tool control window*

3. Choose the **Format** tab in the **Saver: beach clip. mov** tool control window and select **Sorenson Video 3** or **H.264** from the **Compression** drop-down list. Next, move the **Quality** slider to **100**, refer to Figure 2-19.

Saving and Rendering the Composition

In this section, you will save and render the composition. You can also view the final render of the composition by downloading the file *c02_fusion_7_rndr.zip* from *http://www.cadcim.com*. The path of the file is given at the beginning of the chapter.

1. Choose **File > Save** from the menubar; the **Save File** dialog box is displayed. In this dialog box, choose **Documents > Fusion_7 > c02_tut > c02_tut_02** and then enter **c02tut2** in the File Name edit box. Next, choose the **Save** button to close the dialog box and save the composition.

2. Choose **File > Start Render** from the menubar; the **Render Settings** dialog box is displayed, as shown in Figure 2-20.

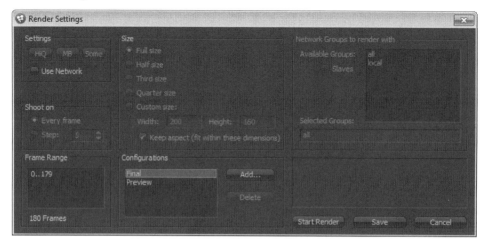

*Figure 2-20 The **Render Settings** dialog box*

3. Choose the **Start Render** button; the rendering process is started. On completion of rendering, a message box is displayed with the information about the frame range rendered and the time taken to render the frame range, as shown in Figure 2-21. Next, choose the **OK** button to close the message box.

*Figure 2-21 The **c02tut2.comp** message box informing about the completion of the rendering process*

4. Navigate to */Documents/Fusion_7/c02_tut/c02_tut_02* and double-click on the *beach clip.mov* file to view the final rendered output, refer to Figure 2-15.

 Tip: *You can also open the **Render Settings** dialog box by pressing F12 or by choosing the green **Render** button available in the Time Ruler.*

Self-Evaluation Test

Answer the following questions and then compare them to those given at the end of this chapter:

1. Which of the following combination of shortcut keys is used to access the tools?

    (a) CTRL+H   (b) CTRL+SPACE
    (c) CTRL+G   (d) CTRL+Z

2. The _____ and _____ numeric keys are used to view the output of the tools in the primary Display Views.

3. The _____ button in the toolbar is used to load an image or video sequence.

4. The _____ button in the toolbar is used to add the **Color Corrector** tool to the **Flow** area.

5. The _____ is an art of combining multiple images to create a new image.

6. The _____ window is used to store references, composition, and various other data across the network.

7. The **Merge** tool is used to combine background and foreground images together. (T/F)

Review Questions

Answer the following questions:

1. Which of the following colors is used to represent the output node of a tool?

    (a) Green   (b) Orange
    (c) Red   (d) None of these

2. The Suppress parameters in the **Color Corrector** tool control window are used to _____ the color of an image.

3. The **Merge** tool is represented as _____ button on the toolbar.

4. A Fusion composition consists of a network of nodes called tools. These tools are connected through _____.

5. The _____ button in the Time Ruler is used to start the rendering process.

6. The _____ shortcut key is used to lock the Display View.

7. On pressing the F12 key, the **Render Settings** dialog box is displayed. (T/F)

8. You can save the composition by using the CTRL + Z keys. (T/F)

Answers to Self-Evaluation Test
1. b, **2.** 1, 2, **3. LD**, **4. CC**, **5.** compositing, **6. Bins**, **7.** T

Chapter 3

Creator Tools

Learning Objectives

After completing this chapter, you will be able to:

- *Create a composition using Creator tools*
- *Create a basic animation*
- *Create and animate text*
- *Create the sky and clouds effects*
- *Create the plasma effect*

INTRODUCTION

Creator tools are used to create backgrounds, noise patterns, and various other types of effects. In this chapter, you will learn to create some basic effects. Also, you will learn to animate objects in Fusion.

TUTORIALS

The compositions created in this chapter can be downloaded from *http://www.cadcim.com*. These compositions are contained in the *c03_fusion_7_tut.zip* file. The path of the file is as follows:

> *Textbooks > Animation and Visual Effects > Fusion > Blackmagic Design Fusion 7 Studio: A Tutorial Approach*

Tutorial 1

In this tutorial, you will create a rolling ball animation by using the **Background** tool. The ball animation pose at frame 12 is shown in Figure 3-1.   **(Expected time: 30 min)**

Figure 3-1 *The ball animation pose at frame 12*

The following steps are required to complete this tutorial:

a. Set the frame format.
b. Create a new background.
c. Create a wooden plank.
d. Create the shadow of the wooden plank.
e. Create the base of the wooden plank.
f. Create a ball.
g. Animate the ball, wooden plank, and the wooden plank shadow.

Setting the Frame Format

In this section, you will specify the frame format settings.

1. Choose **File > New** from the menubar; a new composition is displayed in the Fusion screen.

2. Choose **File > Preferences** from the menubar; the **Preferences** dialog box is displayed.

3. In this dialog box, select **Frame Format** from the **Composition#** preferences tree; various frame format settings are displayed on the right in the **Preferences** dialog box.

4. Choose the **New** button from the right pane in the **Settings** area of the **Preferences** dialog box; the **Enter a name for the new image format** dialog box is displayed. Next, enter **2048x1556** in the edit box and then choose the **OK** button.

5. In the **Settings** area, enter **2048** and **1556** in the **Width** and **Height** edit boxes, respectively.

6. Enter **24** in the **Frame rate** edit box. Next, choose the **Save** button to save the changes made.

Creating a New Background

In this section, you will create a background for the composition.

1. Choose the **BG** button from the toolbar; the **Background1** tool tile is inserted in the **Flow** area.

    The **Background** tool is used to generate solid color and gradient images.

2. Press 1; the output of the **Background1** tool is displayed in the left Display View. Next, choose the **Fit** button from the left **Display View** toolbar to fit the image in the left Display View.

3. In the **Background1** tool control window, choose the **Pick** button; the **Color** dialog box is displayed. In this dialog box, select the white color swatch from the **Basic Colors** area and then choose the **OK** button; the white color output is displayed in left Display View.

    By default, the **Solid Color** button is chosen in the **Color** tab of the **Background1** tool control window. To use two or more colors, you can choose the **Horizontal**, **Vertical**, **Four Corner**, or **Gradient** button. If you choose the **Gradient** button, a green line appears in the Display View. You can change the appearance of the gradient in the Display View by dragging either end of the green line. You can also define the custom gradient by adding keys to the gradient ramp.

Creating a Wooden Plank

In this section, you will create a wooden plank by using the **Background** tool.

1. Click on the empty space in the **Flow** area to deselect the selected tool tile, if any. Choose the **BG** button from the toolbar; the **Background2** tool tile is inserted in the **Flow** area. Next, press F2; the **Rename Tool** dialog box is displayed. Enter **WoodenPlank1** in the edit box and then choose the **OK** button.

2. In the control window of the **WoodenPlank1** tool, choose the **Vertical** button; the **Top** and **Bottom** areas are displayed in the **Color** tab. Parameters in these areas are used to specify two colors for the vertical gradient. Enter the following values in the **Top** area:

    R: **0.5**   G: **0.25**

3. Select the **WoodenPlank1** tool tile in the **Flow** area. Press 1; the output of the **WoodenPlank1** tool is displayed in the left Display View.

4. Make sure the **WoodenPlank1** tool tile is selected in the **Flow** area and then choose
    the **Add a Rectangle Mask** button from the left **Display View** toolbar; the **Rectangle1**
    tool tile is inserted in the **Flow** area and gets automatically connected to the purple
    effect mask node of the **WoodenPlank1** tool.

    Note

    *An effect mask is an animatable shape that can be used to restrict an effect to a specific area of an
    image. You can attach any number of masks to a tool. Effect masks are connected to the purple
    effect mask node of a tool.*

5. Make sure the **Rectangle1** tool tile is selected in the **Flow** area. Next, specify the parameters
    in the control window of the **Rectangle1** tool as follows:

    Center
    Y: **0.26**

    Width: **0.72**   Height: **0.016**

6. Drag the red output node of the **WoodenPlank1** tool to the red output node of the
    Background1 tool; the **Merge1** tool tile is inserted in the **Flow** area and a connection between
    the **Background1**, **WoodenPlank1**, and **Merge1** tools is established, refer to Figure 3-2.

7. Press 2; the output of the **Merge1** tool is displayed in the right Display View, refer to
    Figure 3-2. Next, choose the **Fit** button from the right **Display View** toolbar to fit the image
    in the Display View.

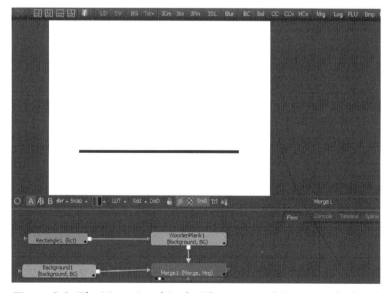

Figure 3-2 *The **Merge1** tool in the **Flow** area and its output displayed
in the right Display View*

8. In the **Merge1** tool control window, enter the value of the **Center** parameter as follows:

Center
Y: **0.49**

After entering the value, the output of the **Merge1** tool is displayed in the right Display View.

Next, you will create the left corner of the wooden plank.

9. Select the **Rectangle1** tool tile from the **Flow** area and then choose the **Add a Rectangle** **Mask** button from the left **Display View** toolbar; the **Rectangle2** tool tile is created in the **Flow** area.

10. In the **Rectangle2** tool control window, select **Add** from the **Paint Mode** drop-down list and then set the parameters as follows:

Center
X: **0.23**   Y: **0.27**

Width: **0.03**   Height: **0.03**

Next, you will create the right corner of the wooden plank.

11. Make sure the **Rectangle2** tool tile is selected from the **Flow** area and then choosethe **Add a Rectangle Mask** button from the left **Display View** toolbar; the **Rectangle3** tool tile is inserted in the **Flow** area and a connection between the **Rectangle2** and **Rectangle3** tools is established.

12. In the **Rectangle3** tool control window, select **Add** from the **Paint Mode** drop-down list and then specify the parameters as follows:

Center
X: **0.75**   Y: **0.27**

Width: **0.03**   Height: **0.03**

After setting the parameters, the output of the **Merge1** tool is displayed in the right Display View, as shown in Figure 3-3.

Creating the Shadow of the Wooden Plank
In this section, you will create the shadow of the wooden plank.

1. Select the **WoodenPlank1** tool tile from the **Flow** area. Next, press and hold CTRL and then select the **Rectangle1** tool tile.

2. Choose **Edit > Copy** from the menubar. Next, click on the empty space in the **Flow** area to deselect the selected tool tile, if any. To paste copied tools, choose **Edit > Paste** from the menubar; two new tool tiles with the name **Rectangle1_1** and **WoodenPlank1_1** are inserted in the **Flow** area.

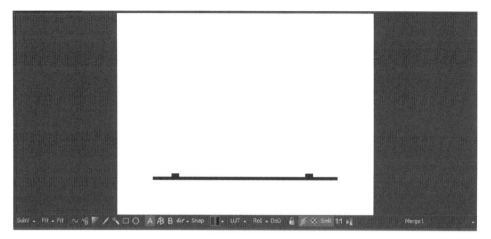

*Figure 3-3 The output of the **Merge1** tool*

3. Press F2 to rename the **WoodenPlank1_1** tool as **WoodenPlankShadow1** and **Rectangle1_1** tool as **Rectangle4**.

4. Drag the red output node of the **Rectangle4** tool tile to the purple node of the **WoodenPlankShadow1** tool tile; a connection between the **Rectangle4** and **WoodenPlankShadow1** tools is established.

5. Drag the red output node of the **WoodenPlankShadow1** tool tile to the red output node of the **Merge1** tool tile; the **Merge2** tool tile is inserted in the **Flow** area and a connection is established between the **Merge2**, **WoodenPlankShadow1**, and **Merge1** tools.

6. Press 2; the output of the **Merge2** tool is displayed in the right Display View.

7. In the **Merge2** tool control window, enter the value of the **Center** parameter as follow:

    Center
    Y: **0.456**

8. Select the **Rectangle4** tool tile from the **Flow** area and enter **0.02** in the **Soft Edge** edit box of the **Rectangle4** tool control window.

    After entering the values, the output of the **Merge2** tool is displayed in the right Display view, as shown in Figure 3-4.

Creating Base of the Wooden Plank

In this section, you will create base of the wooden plank.

1. Select the **WoodenPlank1** tool tile from the **Flow** area and press CTRL+C. Next, click on the empty space in the **Flow** area and then press CTRL+V. Rename the pasted tool as **Base1**. Choose the **Add a Rectangle Mask** button from the left **Display View** toolbar; the **Rectangle5** tool tile is inserted in the **Flow** area and a connection between the **Base1** and **Rectangle5** tools is established.

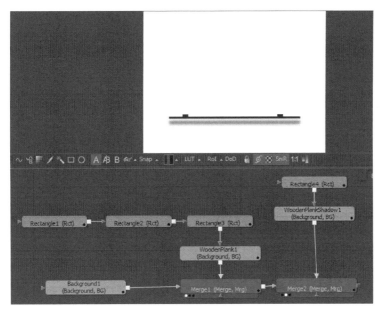

*Figure 3-4 The **Merge2** tool in the **Flow** area and its output displayed in the right Display View*

2. Drag the red output node of the **Base1** tool tile to the red output node of the **Merge2** tool tile; the **Merge3** tool tile is inserted in the **Flow** area and a connection between the **Base1**, **Merge2**, and **Merge3** tools is established.

3. Press 2; the output of the **Merge3** tool is displayed in the right Display View.

4. Select the **Rectangle5** tool tile from the **Flow** area. In the control window, set the parameters as follows:

    Center
    X: **0.23**   Y: **0.3**

    Width: **0.016**   Height: **0.02**

5. Select the **Merge3** tool tile from the **Flow** area. In the control window, set the parameters as follows:

    Center
    X: **0.77**   Y: **0.447**

6. Select the **Base1** tool tile from the **Flow** area and press CTRL+C. Next, click on the empty space in the **Flow** area and then press CTRL+V. Next, press F2 to rename the pasted tool tile as **Base2**.

7. Select the **Rectangle1** tool tile from the **Flow** area and press CTRL+C. Next, click on the empty space of the **Flow** area and then press CTRL+V. Rename the pasted tool as **Rectangle6**.

8. Drag the red output node of the **Base2** tool tile to the red output node of the **Merge3** tool tile; the **Merge4** tool tile is inserted in the **Flow** area and a connection between the **Merge3**, **Base2**, and **Merge4** tools is established.

9. Press 2; the output of the **Merge4** tool is displayed in the right Display View.

10. Drag the red output node of **Rectangle6** tool tile to the purple node of the **Base2** tool tile; a connection between the **Rectangle6** and **Base2** tools is established.

11. Select the **Rectangle6** tool tile from the **Flow** area. In the control window, set the parameters as follows:

    Center
    Y: **0.198**

    Width: **0.033**   Height: **0.067**

    Corner Radius: **0.56**

12. Select the **Merge4** tool tile from the **Flow** area. In the control window, set the parameters as follows:

    Center
    Y: **0.508**

    After entering the values, the output of the **Merge4** tool is displayed in the right Display View, as shown in Figure 3-5.

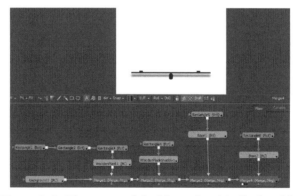

Figure 3-5 *The output of the **Merge4** tool is displayed in the right Display View*

Creating a Ball

In this section, you will create a ball.

1. Click on the empty space in the **Flow** area to deselect the selected tool tile, if any. Next, choose the **BG** button from the toolbar; the **Background2** tool tile is inserted in the **Flow** area. Next, rename the **Background2** tool as **Ball**.

2. Press 1; the output of the **Ball** tool is displayed in the left Display View.

3. In the **Ball** tool control window, choose the **Gradient** button; controls corresponding to the **Gradient** button are displayed. Next, choose the **Radial** button and then specify the parameters as follows:

   Start
   X: **0.69**   Y: **0.69**

   End
   X: **0.33**   Y: **0.31**

4. Click on the first key of the Gradient ramp to select it and set the values as follows:

   R: **0.4**   Position: **0.51**

5. Click on the last key of the Gradient ramp to select it and set the values as follows:
   R: **0**   G: **0**   B: **0**

6. Drag the red output node of the **Ball** tool tile to the red output node of the **Merge4** tool tile; the **Merge5** tool tile is inserted in the **Flow** area and a connection between the **Ball**, **Merge4**, and **Merge5** tools is established.

7. Press 2; the output of the **Merge5** tool is displayed in the right Display View.

8. Select the **Ball** tool tile from the **Flow** area and then choose the **Add an Ellipse Mask** tool from the left **Display View** toolbar; the **Ellipse1** tool is connected to the **Ball** tool.

9. In the **Ellipse1** tool control window, enter **0.01** in the **Soft Edge** edit box.

10. Select the **Merge5** tool tile from the **Flow** area and then set the parameters of the **Merge5** tool in the control window as follows:

    Center
    X: **0.88**   Y: **0.68**

    Size: **0.15**
    After entering the values, the output of the **Merge5** and **Ball** tools is shown in the Display Views, as shown in Figure 3-6.

Figure 3-6 *The output of the* **Merge5** *and* **Ball** *tools*

Animating the Ball, the Wooden Plank, and the Wooden Plank Shadow

In this section, you will animate the ball by using the **Transform** tool.

1. Select the **Ball** tool tile from the **Flow** area and then choose **Tools > Transform > Transform** from the menubar or choose the **Xf** button from the toolbar; the **Transform1** tool tile is inserted in the **Flow** area and a connection between the **Transform1**, **Ball,** and **Merge5** tools is established.

2. In the Time Ruler area, enter **50** in the **Render End Time** edit box.

   Note
   In Fusion, you can animate the controls. When you animate a control in Fusion, it gets connected to an animation curve. The animation curves are made of splines. By default, bezier spline type is used during animation. You can change the default spline type from the **Preferences** *dialog box.*

   Next, you will animate the **Center** control of the **Transform1** tool.

3. In the control window of the **Transform1** tool, set the parameters as follows:

   Center
   X: **2.57**   Y: **0.86**

4. Right-click on the **Center** control; a shortcut menu is displayed. Choose the **Animate** option from the shortcut menu; a keyframe is added at frame 0.

   Note
   Keyframes are automatically updated when the values of a control are changed. If a keyframe exists on that particular frame, it will be updated otherwise a new keyframe will be created. To set a keyframe without changing the value of the control, right-click on the control; a shortcut menu is displayed. Next, choose the **Set Key** *from the shortcut menu.*

Tip: *To move the CTI forward or backward frame by frame, press the [key or the] key. To play the animation, press SPACEBAR, and to stop the animation, press SPACEBAR again.*

5. Now, create keyframes by using the values given next.

Frame	Center X	Center Y
10	-0.35	-1.82
20	-1.9	-0.6
30	-3.87	-2
40	-5.72	-0.716
50	-7.16	-2.822

When you add keyframes to an animation curve, a green spline with control points is displayed in the Display View. You can modify the animation curve interactively by moving the control points or by adjusting the spline handles, refer to Figure 3-7.

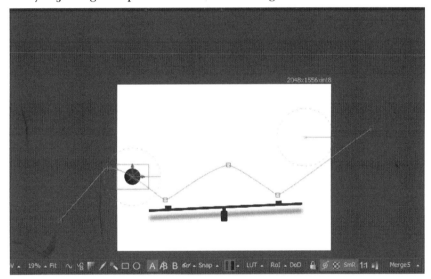

*Figure 3-7 The **Transform1** tool animation spline displayed in the right Display View*

6. Scrub the timeline to view the animation.

7. Select the top 2 keyframes and then press SHIFT+S to smooth the spline.

8. Select the **WoodenPlank1** tool tile from the **Flow** area and then choose the **Xf** button from the toolbar; the **Transform2** tool tile is inserted in the **Flow** area and a connection between the **WoodenPlank1** and **Merge1** tools is established.

9. Enter **0** in the **Current Time** edit box; the current time indicator (CTI) moves at the beginning of the timeline.

10. Right-click on the **Angle** control; a shortcut menu is displayed. Choose the **Animate** option from the shortcut menu; a keyframe is added at frame 0.

11. Animate the **Angle** control of the **Transform2** tool by using the values given next.

Frame	Angle
0	2.033
10	0
12	-2.28
20	-2.71
30	3.23
40	1.9

12. Scrub the timeline to view the animation.

Animating the Shadow of the Wooden Plank
In this section, you will animate the shadow of the wooden plank.

1. Click on the empty space in the **Flow** area to deselect the selected tool tile, if any. Next, copy the **Transform2** tool and rename it as **Transform3** in the **Flow** area.

2. Make sure the **Transform3** tool tile is selected in the Flow area. Press and hold SHIFT and then drag the **Transform3** tool tile over the pipe between the **Merge2** and **WoodenPlankShadow1** tools; the pipe is highlighted. The **Transform3** tool tile is inserted between the **Merge2** and **WoodenPlankShadow1** tool tiles. Next, press SPACEBAR to play the animation.

    Figure 3-8 displays the network of tools of the final composition.

    Now, save the composition with the name *c03tut1* at the location *Documents > Fusion_7 > c03_tut > c03_tut_01*. Next, you need to render the composition. For rendering, refer to Tutorial 2 of Chapter 2. The output of the composition at frame 12 is shown in Figure 3-1. You can also view the final render of the composition by downloading the *c03_fusion_7_rndr.zip* file from *http://www.cadcim.com*. The path of the file is mentioned at the beginning of the chapter.

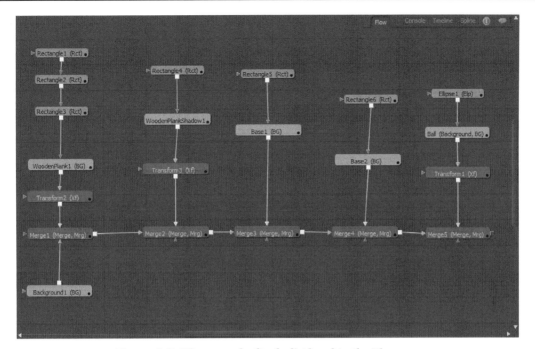

Figure 3-8 *The network of tools displayed in the **Flow** area*

Tutorial 2

In this tutorial, you will create and animate text by using the **Text+** tool. The final output of the composition at frame 80 is shown in Figure 3-9.   **(Expected time: 25 min)**

Figure 3-9 *The final output of the composition at frame 80*

The following steps are required to complete the tutorial:

a.   Set the frame format.
b.   Create the text.
c.   Create the shadow of the text.
d.   Add more text.
e.   Create borders around the text.
f.   Prepare the text to render.

Setting the Frame Format

In this section, you will specify the frame format settings.

1. Choose **File > New** from the menubar; a new composition is displayed in the Fusion screen.

2. Choose **File > Preferences** from the menubar; the **Preferences** dialog box is displayed.

3. In this dialog box, select **Frame Format** from the **Composition#** preferences tree; various frame format settings are displayed on the right in the **Preferences** dialog box.

4. Select the **HDTV 1080** option from the **Default Format** drop-down list and then choose the **Save** button to save the changes made.

Creating the Text

In this section, you will create the text by using the **Text+** tool.

1. Choose the **Txt+** button from the toolbar; the **Text1** tool tile is inserted in the **Flow** area.

   The **Text1** tool is used to add the text for motion graphics.

2. In the **Text1** tool control window, set the parameters as follows:

   Styled Text: **Blackmagic Design Fusion**   Font: **Impact**

3. Select the **Underline** check box to underline the text.

   Next, you will scramble the text.

4. Press 1; the output of the **Text1** tool is displayed in the left Display View. Next, choose the **Fit** button on the left **Display View** toolbar to fit the image in the Display View.

5. In the **Text1** tool control window, right-click in the **Styled Text** area; a shortcut menu is displayed. Next, choose the **TextScramble** option from the menu; the **TextScramble** modifier is applied to the **Text1** tool.

6. Choose the **Modifiers** tab in the control window, as shown in Figure 3-10. Next, click on the triangle located on the left of the modifier's title bar to expand the **TextScramble on Text1: Styled Text**. Set the value of the **Randomness** control to **1.61**.

7. Enter **bBlLaAcCkKmMaAgGiIcCdDeEsSiIgGnNfFuUsSiIoOnN** in the **Substitute Chars** text box.

Figure 3-10 *Choosing the Modifiers tab in control window*

8. In the Time Ruler area, enter **80** in the **Render End Time** edit box, refer to Figure 3-11.

9. Right-click on the **Randomness** control; a shortcut menu is displayed. Choose the **Animate** option from the shortcut menu; a keyframe is added at frame 0.

Figure 3-11 *The Timeline view*

10. Animate the **Randomness** control by using the values given in the table below:

Frame	Randomness
0	1.61
30	1.61
50	0

 Note
*After entering 1.61 in the Randomness control at frame 30, you can set the key frame by right-clicking on the **Randomness** control and choosing the **Set Key** option from the shortcut menu.*

11. Scrub the timeline to view the animation.

12. Enter **0** in the **Current Time** edit box; the current time indicator (CTI) moves at the beginning of the timeline.

13. Choose the **Tools** tab in the control window and then choose the **Layout** tab. Right-click on the **Center** control; a shortcut menu is displayed. Choose the **Animate** option from the shortcut menu; a keyframe is added at frame 0.

14. Animate the **Center** control by using the values given in the table below:

Frame	Center X	Center Y
0	1.5	1
20	0.5	0.76
30	0.5	0.86

15. Scrub the timeline to view the animation.

16. Enter **0** in the **Current Time** edit box; the current time indicator (CTI) moves at the beginning of the timeline.

17. Choose the **Text** tab and then right-click on the **Size** control; a shortcut menu is displayed. Next, choose the **Animate** option from the shortcut menu; a keyframe is added at frame 0.

18. Animate the **Size** control by using the values given in the table below:

Frame	Size
0	0.037
10	0.09
20	0.11
30	0.13

19. Scrub the timeline to view the animation.

    Next, you will create the background for the text and change the color of the text.

20. Choose the **Layout** tab and then choose the **Pick** button; the **Color** dialog box is displayed, as shown in Figure 3-12. Choose the white color swatch from the dialog box and then choose the **OK** button.

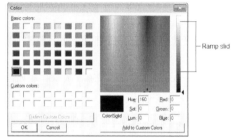

21. To change the color of the text, choose the **Shading** tab. In this tab, the **1** button is chosen by default. Choose the **Pick** button in the **Color** area; the **Color** dialog box is displayed. Move the ramp slider to black color and then choose the **OK** button.

Figure 3-12 The Color dialog box

Creating the Shadow of the Text
In this section, you will create the shadow of the text.

1. Make sure the **Text1** tool tile is selected in the **Flow** area. In the **Text1** tool control window, make sure the **Shading** tab is chosen. Next, choose the **3** button from the **Shading** tab and then select the **Enabled** check box.

2. Enter **0.63** in the **Opacity** edit box.

Adding More Text
In this section, you will add more text to the composition.

1. Click on the empty space of the **Flow** area to deselect the selected tool tile, if any. Choose **Tools > Creator > Text+** from the menubar; the **Text2** tool tile is inserted in the **Flow** area.

2. Press 2; the output of the **Text2** tool is displayed in the right Display View. Next, choose the **Fit** button from the right **Display View** toolbar to fit the image in the Display View.

3. In the **Text2** tool control window, set the parameters as follows:

Styled Text: **.Compositing**   Font: **Impact**

4. Choose the **Shading** tab in the **Text2** tool control window and then set the text color to black, as discussed earlier.

5. Choose the **3** button from the **Shading** tab and then select the **Enabled** check box; the black shadow is added to the text. Next, enter **0.63** in the **Opacity** edit box.

6. Choose the **Text** tab in the **Text2** tool control window and animate the **Size** control by using the values given in the table below:

Frame	Size
0	0
23	0
30	0.08

7. Choose the **Layout** tab in the **Text2** tool control window and animate the **Center** controls by using the following values given in the table below:

Frame	Center X	Center Y
0	0.5	0.47
30	0.5	0.34

8. Click on the empty space in the **Flow** area to deselect the selected tool tile, if any. Choose the **Mrg** button from the toolbar; the **Merge1** tool tile is inserted in the **Flow** area.

9. Drag the red output node of the **Text1** tool tile to the orange node of the **Merge1** tool tile. Next, drag the red output node of the **Text2** tool tile to the green node of the **Merge1** tool tile; a connection between the **Text1**, **Text2**, and **Merge1** tools is established.

10. Press 2; the output of the **Merge1** tool is displayed in the right Display View.

11. Click in the empty space of the **Flow** area and then choose the **Txt+** from the toolbar; the **Text3** tool tile is inserted in the **Flow** area.

12. Drag the red output node of the **Text3** tool tile to the red output node of the **Merge1** tool tile; the **Merge2** tool tile is inserted in the **Flow** area and a connection between the **Merge1**, **Merge2**, and **Text3** tools is established.

13. In the **Text3** tool control window, set the parameters as follows:

Styled Text: **.Keying**   Font: **Impact**

14. Choose the **Shading** tab and then change the color of the text to black, as discussed earlier. Next, choose the **3** button and then select the **Enabled** check box to enable black shadows. Next, enter **0.63** in the **Opacity** edit box.

15. Choose the **Text** tab and animate the **Size** control by using the values given in the table below:

Frame	Size
0	0
30	0
50	0.08

16. Choose the **Layout** tab in the **Text3** tool control window and then enter **0.22** in the **Y** edit box of the **Center** area.

17. Click on the empty space in the **Flow** area to deselect the selected tool tile, if any. Choose the **Txt+** button from the toolbar; the **Text4** tool tile is inserted in the **Flow** area.

18. Drag the red output node of the **Text4** tool tile to the red output node of the **Merge2** tool tile; the **Merge3** tool is inserted in the **Flow** area and a connection between the **Merge2**, **Merge3**, and **Text4** tools is established.

19. Press 2; the output of the **Merge3** tool is displayed in the right Display View.

20. Select the **Text4** tool tile in the **Flow** area. In the control window of the **Text4** tool, set the parameters as follows:

    Styled Text: **.Motion Tracking**   Font: **Impact**

21. Choose the **Shading** tab and then change the color of text to black. Next, choose the **3** button and then select the **Enabled** check box to enable black shadows.

22. Choose the **Text** tab in the control window and animate the **Size** control by using the values given in the table below:

Frame	Size
50	0
70	0.08

23. Select the **Merge3** tool tile from the **Flow** area and enter **0.11** in the **Y** edit box of the **Center** control in the control window.

24. Scrub the timeline to view the animation.

Creating Borders Around the Text
In this section, you will create borders around the text.

1. Click on the empty space in the **Flow** area to deselect the selected tool tile, if any.

2. Choose the **BG** button from the toolbar; the **Background1** tool tile is inserted in the **Flow** area.

3. Press 1; the output of the **Background1** tool is displayed in the left Display View.

4. Choose the **Add a Rectangle Mask** button from the left **Display View** toolbar; the **Rectangle1** tool gets automatically connected to the effect mask node of the **Background1** tool.

5. Enter **0.015** in the **Width** edit box of the **Rectangle1** tool control window.

6. Drag the red output node of the **Background1** tool tile to the red output node of the **Merge3** tool tile; the **Merge4** tool tile is inserted in the **Flow** area.

7. Press 2; the output of the **Merge4** tool is displayed in the right Display View.

8. Enter **0.006** in the **X** edit box of the **Center** control in the **Merge4** tool control window.

9. Select the **Background1** and **Rectangle1** tool tiles from the **Flow** area.

10. Choose **Edit > Copy** from the menubar. Next, click on the empty space in the **Flow** area to deselect the selected tool tile, if any. Now, choose **Edit > Paste** from the menubar; the **Background1_1** and **Rectangle1_1** tool tiles are inserted in the **Flow** area.

11. Drag the red output node of the **Background1_1** tool tile to the red output node of the **Merge4** tool tile; the **Merge5** tool tile is inserted in the **Flow** area.

12. Press 2; the output of the **Merge5** tool is displayed in the right Display View.

13. Enter **0.996** in the **X** edit box of the **Center** control in the **Merge5** tool control window.

After entering the values, the output of the **Merge5** tool is displayed at frame 70 in the right Display View, as shown in Figure 3-13. Figure 3-14 displays the network of tools used for creating the final composition.

Now, save the composition with the name *c03tut2* at the location *Documents > Fusion_7 > c03_tut > c03_tut_02*. Next, you need to render the composition. For rendering, refer to Tutorial 2 of Chapter 2. You can also view the final render of the composition by downloading the *c03_fusion_7_rndr.zip* file from *http://www.cadcim.com*. The path of the file is mentioned at the beginning of the chapter.

*Figure 3-13 The output of the **Merge5** tool at frame 70*

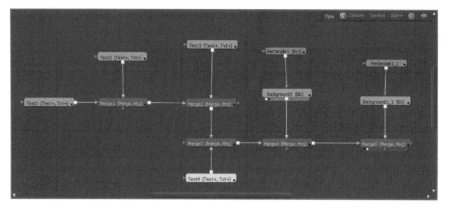

Figure 3-14 *All tools used in the composition displayed in the **Flow** area*

Tutorial 3

In this tutorial, you will create clouds by using the **Fast Noise** tool and then merge clouds with the image of sea bridge. The final output of the composition is shown in Figure 3-15.

(Expected time: 20 min)

The following steps are required to complete this tutorial:

a.   Set the frame format.
b.   Download and import the image.
c.   Create the clouds.
d.   Merge the images of clouds and sea bridge.
e.   Add perspective to the image.
f.   Create the shadows of the clouds.

Figure 3-15 *The final output of the composition*

Setting the Frame Format

In this section, you will specify the frame format settings.

1. Choose **File > New** from the menubar; a new composition is displayed in the Fusion screen.

2. Choose **File > Preferences** from the menubar; the **Preferences** dialog box is displayed.

3. In this dialog box, select **Frame Format** from the **Composition#** preferences tree; various frame format settings are displayed on the right in the **Preferences** dialog box. Make sure **2K Full Aperture (Super 35)** is selected in the **Default format** drop-down list and then choose the **Save** button to save the changes made.

4. In the Time Ruler area, enter **48** in the **Render End Time** edit box.

Downloading and Importing the Image

In this section, you will download the image and import it to the composition.

1. Open the following link: *http://www.freeimages.com/photo/1327985*; an image is displayed.

2. Download the image at the location */Documents/Fusion_7/c03_tut/c03_tut_03/Media_Files* and save it with the name *1327985.jpg*.

3. Open the *1327985.jpg* image in the Photoshop application and erase sky from it. Now, save the file in *TGA* format with the name *seabridge.tga* at the location specified in step 2.

> **Note**
> *Footage Courtesy: **Peter Mazurek** (http://www.freeimages.com/profile/mazwebs)*

4. Choose the **LD** button from the toolbar; the **Open File** dialog box is displayed. In the dialog box, choose **Documents > Fusion_7 > c03_tut > c03_tut_03 > Media_Files > seabridge.tga** and then choose the **Open** button; the **Loader1** tool tile is inserted in the **Flow** area. In the **Loader1** tool control window, choose the **Import** tab and then select the **Post-Multiply by Alpha** check box.

5. Press 1; the output of the **Loader1** tool is displayed in the left Display View. Next, choose the **Fit** button from the left **Display View** toolbar to fit the image in the left Display View.

Creating the Clouds

In this section, you will create the clouds.

1. Click on the empty space of the **Flow** area and then choose **Tools > Creator > FastNoise** from the menubar; the **FastNoise1** tool tile is inserted in the **Flow** area.

   The **FastNoise** tool is used to add noise. This tool is useful for creating wide range of effects such as cloud, smoke, and other organic textures.

2. Press 2; the output of the **FastNoise1** tool is displayed in right Display View. Next, choose the **Show Checker Underlay** button from the **Display View** toolbar to enable

transparency in the right Display View. Next, choose the **Fit** button from the right **Display View** toolbar to fit the image in the right Display View.

3. In the **FastNoise1** tool control window, choose the **Color** tab. Next, choose the **Pick** button from the **Color1** area; the **Color** dialog box is displayed. In this dialog box, specify the following values and then choose the **OK** button to close the dialog box, refer to Figure 3-16.

Red: **175**   Green: **185**   Blue: **250**

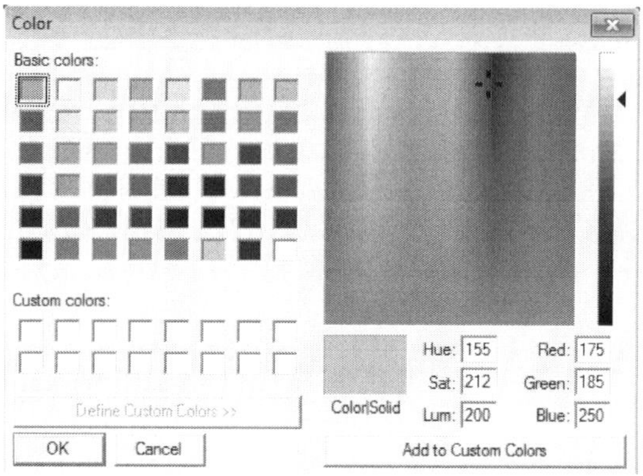

Figure 3-16 *Selecting color from the **Color** dialog box*

4. In the **FastNoise1** tool control window, choose the **Noise** tab and set the parameters as given next, refer to Figure 3-17.

Detail: **3.71**   Scale: **5.54**

Seethe: **0.07**   Seethe Rate: **0.10**

The **Detail** parameter is used to enhance the level of detailing in the noise pattern. The larger the value of this parameter, better will be the result but the render time will increase. The **Scale** parameter is used to define the scale of the noise pattern. The **Seethe** parameter is used to produce drifting effects such as drifting fog. The **Seethe Rate** parameter determines the rate at which the noise changes in each frame.

*Figure 3-17 The **FastNoise1** tool control window*

Merging the Images of Clouds and Sea bridge

In this section, you will merge the images.

1. Click on the empty space in the **Flow** area to deselect the selected tool tile, if any. Next, choose the **Mrg** button from the toolbar; the **Merge1** tool tile is inserted in the **Flow** area. Press 2; the output of the **Merge1** tool is displayed in the right Display View.

2. In the **Flow** area, drag the red output node of the **FastNoise1** tool tile to the orange node of the **Merge1** tool tile. Next, drag the red output node of the **Loader1** tool tile to the green node of the **Merge1** tool tile. Press 2; the output of the **Merge1** tool is displayed in the right Display View.

Adding Perspective to the Image

In this section, you will add perspective to the image.

1. Select the **FastNoise1** tool tile from the **Flow** area. Next, choose **Tools > Transform > DVE** from the menubar; the **DVE1** tool tile is inserted in the **Flow** area and a connection between the **DVE1** and **FastNoise1** tools is established.

2. In the **DVE1** tool control window, choose the **YZX** button from the **Rotation Order** area and then set the parameters as given next, refer to Figure 3-18.

   Center
   Y: **0.012**

   Z Move: **0.57**　　　　　　　　　　Z Pivot: **0.25**

   X Rotation: **66.6**　　　　　　　　　Perspective: **0.94**

Figure 3-18 *The DVE1 tool control window*

Creating the Shadows of the Clouds

In this section, you will create animated shadows of the clouds on the ground.

1. Select the **FastNoise1** tool tile in the **Flow** area and then press CTRL+C. Next, click on the empty space in the **Flow** area to deselect the **FastNoise1** tool tile and then press CTRL+V; the **FastNoise1_1** tool tile is inserted in the **Flow** area.

2. Drag the red output node of the **FastNoise1_1** tool tile to the red output node of the **Merge1** tool tile; the **Merge2** tool tile is inserted in the **Flow** area and a connection between the **FastNoise1_1**, **Merge1**, and **Merge2** tools is established.

3. Press 2; the output of the **Merge2** tool is displayed in the right Display View.

4. Select the **FastNoise1_1** tool tile in the **Flow** area and then choose **Tools > Transform > DVE** from the menubar; the **DVE2** tool tile is inserted between the **FastNoise1_1** and **Merge2** tools in the **Flow** area, as shown in Figure 3-19.

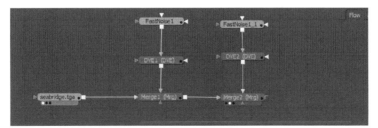

Figure 3-19 *The DVE2 tool inserted between the **FastNoise1_1** and **Merge2** tools*

5. In the **DVE2** tool control window, enter the values of the parameters as follows:

Center
Y: **0.4**

Z Move: **0.32**   Z Pivot: **0.21**   X Rotation: **-52**

6. Select the **Merge2** tool tile from the **Flow** area and select **Soft Light** from the **Apply Mode** drop-down list in the control window.

7. Press SPACEBAR to play the animation.

    Now, save the composition with the name *c03tut3* at the location *Documents > Fusion_7 > c03_tut > c03_tut_03*. Next, you need to render the composition. For rendering, refer to Tutorial 2 of Chapter 2. The output of the composition is shown in Figure 3-15. You can also view the final render of the composition by downloading the *c03_fusion_7_rndr.zip* file from *http://www.cadcim.com*. The path of the file is mentioned at the beginning of the chapter.

Tutorial 4

In this tutorial, you will create the plasma effect. The final output of the composition at frame 160 is shown in Figure 3-20.   **(Expected time: 20 min)**

The following steps are required to complete this tutorial:

a. Set the frame format.
b. Create the plasma effect.

Figure 3-20 *The final output of the composition at frame 160*

Setting the Frame Format
In this section, you will specify the frame format settings.

1. Choose **File > New** from the menubar; a new composition is displayed in the Fusion screen.

2. Choose **File > Preferences** from the menubar; the **Preferences** dialog box is displayed.

3. In this dialog box, select **Frame Format** from the **Composition#** preferences tree; various frame format settings are displayed on the right in the **Preferences** dialog box. Make sure **2K Full Aperture (Super 35)** is selected in the **Default format** drop-down list and then choose the **Save** button to save the changes made.

4. In the Time Ruler area, enter **300** in the **Render End Time** edit box.

Creating the Plasma Effect

In this section, you will create plasma effect using the **Plasma** tool.

1. Choose **Tools > Creator > Plasma** from the menubar; the **Plasma1** tool tile is inserted in the **Flow** area.

    The **Plasma** tool is used to create circular patterns to generate image similar to plasma.

2. Press 1; the output of the **Plasma1** tool is displayed in the left Display view. Next, choose the **Fit** button from the left **Display View** toolbar to fit the image in the left Display View.

3. Choose the **Show Checker Underlay** button in the left **Display View** toolbar to viewthe output without transparency in the left Display View.

4. Select the **Plasma1** tool tile from the **Flow** area, if it is not already selected. Now, animate the **Scale** control in the **Circles** tab to create the keyframes by using the values given in the table below:

Frame	Scale
0	10
50	10
100	8.3
150	6.4
200	4.5
250	2.6
300	0.8

5. Animate the **Scale** control in the **Circle1** and **Circle3** areas in the **Circles** tab by using the values given next.

Frame	Circle 1- Scale	Circle 3 - Scale
0	0.26	4.85
50	0.26	4.85
100	0.34	4.82
150	0.45	4.85

Frame	Circle 1- Scale	Circle 3 - Scale
200	0.56	4.85
250	0.67	4.85
300	0.72	4.85

6. In the **Circle4** area, make sure that the **Type 2** button is chosen and then enter **0.27** in the **Scale** edit box.

7. Press SPACEBAR to play the animation.

The final output of the **Plasma1** tool at frame 280 is shown in Figure 3-21.

Figure 3-21   *The final output of the **Plasma1** tool at frame 280*

Now, save the composition with the name *c03tut4* at the location *Documents > Fusion_7 > c03_tut > c03_tut_04*. Next, you need to render the composition. For rendering, refer to Tutorial 2 of Chapter 2. The output of the composition at frame 280 is shown in Figure 3-21. You can also view the final render of the composition by downloading the *c03_fusion_7_rndr.zip* file from *http://www.cadcim.com*. The path of the file is mentioned at the beginning of the chapter.

Tutorial 5

In this tutorial, you will create a daylight time-lapse simulation by using the real-world data. The final output of the composition at frame 20 is shown in Figure 3-22.

(Expected time: 20 min)

The following steps are required to complete this tutorial:

a. Set the frame format.
b. Download and import the image.
c. Create the daylight time-lapse simulation.
d. Create the reflection of sky.

Figure 3-22 The final output of the composition at frame 20

Setting the Frame Format
In this section, you will specify the frame format settings.

1. Choose **File > New** from the menubar; a new composition is displayed in the Fusion screen.

2. Choose **File > Preferences** from the menubar; the **Preferences** dialog box is displayed.

3. In this dialog box, select **Frame Format** from the **Composition#** preferences tree; various frame format settings are displayed on the right in the **Preferences** dialog box. Make sure **2K Full Aperture (Super 35)** is selected in the **Default format** drop-down list and then choose the **Save** button to save the changes made.

Downloading and Importing the Image
In this section, you will download image and import it to the composition.

1. Copy the *seabridge.tga* file that you have created in Tutorial 3 at the location */Documents/ Fusion_7/c03_tut/c03_tut_05/Media_Files*.

2. Choose the **LD** button from the toolbar; the **Open File** dialog box is displayed. In the dialog box, choose **Documents > Fusion_7 > c03_tut > c03_tut_05 > Media_Files > seabridge.tga** and then choose the **Open** button; the **Loader1** tool tile is inserted in the **Flow** area. In the **Loader1** tool control window, choose the **Import** tab and then select the **Post-Multiply by Alpha** check box.

3. Press 1; the output of the **Loader1** tool is displayed in the left Display View. Next, choose the **Fit** button from the left **Display View** toolbar to fit the image in the left Display View.

4. To hide the transparency of the image, choose the **Show Checker Underlay** button from the left **Display View** toolbar.

The output of the **Loader1** tool is displayed in the left Display View, as shown in Figure 3-23.

Figure 3-23 *The output of the **Loader1** tool*

Creating the Daylight Time-lapse Simulation
In this section, you will create a daylight simulation based on the real-word data.

1. Make sure the **Loader1** tool tile is selected in the **Flow** area and then choose **Tools > Transform > Resize** from the menubar; the **Resize1** tool tile is inserted in the **Flow** area and a connection is established between the **Loader1** and **Resize1** tools.

2. Make sure the **Resize1** tool tile is selected in the **Flow** area and then choose **Tools > Creator > DaySky** from the menubar; the **DaySky1** and **Merge1** tool tiles are inserted in the **Flow** area and a connection is established between the **Resize1**, **Merge1**, and **DaySky1** tools, as shown in Figure 3-24.

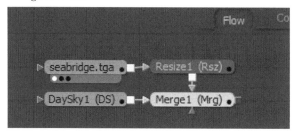

Figure 3-24 *The **DaySky1** tool tile inserted in the **Flow** area*

The **DaySky** tool is used to generate the effect of day light produced at specific time and location of earth.

3. Make sure the **Merge1** tool tile is selected in the **Flow** area and then press 2; the output of the **Merge1** tool is displayed in the right Display View. Next, choose the **Fit** button from the right **Display View** toolbar to fit the image in the right Display View.

4. Select the **DaySky1** tool tile in the **Flow** area and press 1; the output of the **DaySky1** tool is displayed in the right Display View.

5. In the control window of the **DaySky1** tool, choose the **Image** tab and then enter **1556** in the **Height** edit box.

6. Select the **Merge1** tool tile in the **Flow** area and then press CTRL+W to swap the background and foreground inputs of the **Merge1** tool. After entering the values, the output of the **DaySky1** and **Merge1** tools is displayed, as shown in Figure 3-25.

*Figure 3-25 The output of the **DaySky1** and **Merge1** tools*

7. Make sure the **DaySky1** tool tile is selected in the **Flow** area and then choose **Tools > Transform > Transform** from the menubar; the **Transform1** tool tile is inserted in the **Flow** area and a connection is established between the **DaySky1**, **Transform1**, and **Merge1** tools.

8. In the **Transform1** tool control window, enter **1.03** in the **Y** edit box of the **Center** control; the horizon line meets with the sea.

9. Select the **DaySky1** tool tile from the **Flow** area. Next, choose the **Controls** tab and then select **5** from the **Day** drop-down list. Similarly, select **August** from the **Month** drop-down list in the **Date and Time** area.

   The **Day** and **Month** drop-down lists are used to specify the day and month for the DaySky simulation

10. In the **Location** area, enter **25.47** and **80.7** in the **Latitude** and **Longitude** edit boxes, respectively.

   The latitude and longitude used here are of Miami beach.

11. Choose the **Advanced** tab and enter **1.1** in the **Brightness** edit box of the **Horizon** area.

   Next, you will animate the **Time** control.

12. In the Time Ruler area, enter **96** in the **Render End Time** edit box.

13. Choose the **Controls** tab and then animate the **Time** control in the **Date and Time** area to create the keyframe by using the values given in the table below:

Frame	Time
0	5
96	17

14. Press SPACEBAR to play the animation.

Creating the Reflection of the Sky
In this section, you will create reflection of the sky.

1. Click on the empty space in the **Flow** area and then choose **Tools > Transform > DVE** from the menubar; the **DVE1** tool tile is inserted in the **Flow** area.

2. Drag the red output node of the **Transform1** tool tile to the orange node of the **DVE1** tool tile; a connection between the **Transform1** and **DVE1** tools is established.

3. Drag the red output node of the **DVE1** tool tile to the red output node of the **Merge1** tool tile; the **Merge2** tool tile is inserted in the **Flow** area and a connection between the **Merge1**, **Merge2**, and **DVE1** tools is established.

4. Press 2; the output of the **Merge2** tool is displayed in the right Display View.

5. Select the **DVE1** tool tile from the **Flow** area. In the **DVE1** tool control window, specify the parameters as follows:

   Center
   Y: **0.57**

   Z Move: **1.05**   X Rotation: **144.76**   Perspective: **0.5**

6. Select the **Merge2** tool tile from the **Flow** area and select **Hue** from the **Apply Mode** drop-down list and then enter **0.67** in the **Blend** edit box. Figure 3-26 displays the final output of the composition at frame 20.

   Now, save the composition with the name *c03tut5* at the location *Documents > Fusion_7 > c03_tut > c03_tut_05*. Next, you need to render the composition. For rendering, refer to Tutorial 2 of Chapter 2. The output of the composition at frame 20 is shown in Figure 3-22. You can also view the final render of the composition by downloading the *c03_fusion_7_rndr.zip* file from *http://www.cadcim.com*. The path of the file is mentioned at the beginning of the chapter.

Figure 3-26 *The final output of the composition*

Self-Evaluation Test

Answer the following questions and then compare them to those given at the end of this chapter:

1. Which of the following combination of shortcut keys is used to copy the tools?

    (a) CTRL+Z   (b) CTRL+C
    (c) CTRL+Y   (d) CTRL+X

2. Which of the following keys is used to play the animation?

    (a) ENTER   (b) SHIFT
    (c) CTRL   (d) SPACEBAR

3. The _____ tools category is used to create new backgrounds, noise, and many other effects in the composition.

4. _____ is the process of giving motion to an object.

5. The _____ tool is used to rotate, scale, and move the objects in a scene.

6. You can choose the **Xf** button from the toolbar to transform elements in the composition. (T/F)

Review Questions

Answer the following questions:

1. To create a shadow of the text, you have to choose the _____ button from the **Shading** tab and then select the _____ check box.

2. The _____ tool is used to create circular shapes, thereby generating a plasma like effect.

3. The _____ tool is used to create a procedural sky pattern based on a specific time and location on earth.

4. To play an animation forward or backward frame by frame, press the _____ or _____ key.

5. Perspective can be added to an input image by using the _____ tool.

Answers to Self-Evaluation Test
1. b, **2**. d, **3**. **Creator**, **4**. Animation, **5. Transform**, **6**. T

Chapter 4

Transform Tools

Learning Objectives

After completing this chapter, you will be able to:

- *Resize, scale, and crop the images*
- *Add perspective to an image*
- *Create a camera shake effect*

INTRODUCTION

In Fusion, you can transform an image or image sequence by using the Transform tools. Transforming an image implies changing its appearance. You can change the appearance of an image by moving, rotating, and scaling it. In this chapter, you will learn about Transform tools. In addition, you will learn about cropping an image and adding perspective to it.

TUTORIALS

The compositions created in this chapter can be downloaded from *http://www.cadcim.com*. These compositions are contained in the *c04_fusion_7_tut.zip* file. The path of the file is as follows:

> *Textbooks > Animation and Visual Effects > Fusion > Blackmagic Design Fusion 7 Studio: A Tutorial Approach*

Tutorial 1

In this tutorial, you will crop, transform, and add perspective to an image. The final output of the composition at frame 80 is shown in Figure 4-1.   **(Expected time: 30 min)**

Figure 4-1 *The final output of the composition at frame 80*

The following steps are required to complete this tutorial:

a. Set the frame format.
b. Download and import images.
c. Crop and animate the image of clouds.
d. Add perspective to clouds.
e. Color-correct the composition.

Setting the Frame Format

In this section, you will specify the frame format settings.

1. Choose **File > New** from the menubar; a new composition is displayed in the Fusion screen.

2. Choose **File > Preferences** from the menubar; the **Preferences** dialog box is displayed.

3. In this dialog box, select **Frame Format** from the **Composition#** preferences tree; various frame format settings are displayed on the right in the **Preferences** dialog box. Next, select the **HDTV 720** option from the **Default format** drop-down list and then choose the **Save** button to save the changes made.

4. In the Time Ruler area, enter **300** in the **Render End Time** edit box.

Downloading and Importing the Images

In this section, you will download the images and import them to the composition.

1. Download one image each from the following two links and then save them with the names *river.jpg* and *clouds.jpg*, respectively at */Documents/Fusion_7/c04_tut/c04_tut_01/Media_Files*.

   http://www.freeimages.com/photo/1232159 and *http://www.freeimages.com/photo/1161955*

2. Open *river.jpg* in the Photoshop application and then erase the sky portion from it. Save the file with the name **river.tga** at the location specified above. Make sure that you save the transparency information in the *river.tga* file.

   Note
   Footage Courtesy: **Rafa Moskovita** *(http://www.freeimages.com/profile/fael_m)* and **Johan Colon** *(http://www.freeimages.com/profile/johancolon).*

3. Choose the **LD** button from the toolbar; the **Open File** dialog box is displayed. In this dialog box, choose **Documents > Fusion_7 > c04_tut > c04_tut_01 > Media_Files > clouds.jpg** and then choose the **Open** button; the **Loader1** tool tile is inserted in the **Flow** area.

4. Press 1; the output of the **Loader1** tool is displayed in the left Display View.

5. Choose the **Fit** button from the left **Display View** toolbar to fit the image in the left Display View. The output of the **Loader1** tool is displayed in the left Display View, refer to Figure 4-2.

6. Click on the empty space in the **Flow** area to deselect the selected tool, if any.

7. Import *river.tga* in the **Flow** area as done in step 3; the **Loader2** tool tile is inserted in the **Flow** area. Press 2; the output of the **Loader2** tool is displayed in the right Display View. Choose the **Fit** button from the right **Display View** toolbar to fit the image in the right Display View.

8. In the control window of the **Loader2** tool, choose the **Import** tab and then select the **Post-Multiply by Alpha** check box; the output of the **Loader2** tool is displayed in the right Display View, refer to Figure 4-2.

Figure 4-2 *The output of the* **Loader1** *and* **Loader2** *tools*

Cropping and Animating the Image of Clouds

In this section, you will crop the image of clouds and then animate them.

1. Click on the empty space in the **Flow** area. Choose **Tools > Transform > Crop** from the menubar; the **Crop1** tool tile is inserted in the **Flow** area.

2. In the **Flow** area, drag the red output node of the **Loader1** tool tile to the orange node of the **Crop1** tool tile; a connection between the **Loader1** and **Crop1** tools is established. Next, press 1; the output of the **Crop1** tool is displayed in the left Display View.

   The **Crop** tool is used to crop a portion of an image or offset the image into a larger image area.

3. In the **Crop1** tool control window, animate the **X Offset** control to create the keyframes by using the values given next, as discussed in Chapter 3.

Frame	X Offset
0	0
300	1020

   The **X Offset** and **Y Offset** parameters are measured in pixels and represent the top left corner of the cropping window.

4. Press SPACEBAR to start the playback of the composition. The clouds starts moving from right to left in the left Display View. Press SPACEBAR again to stop the playback.

   Next, you will add the **Transform** tool to flip the image of the clouds and then you will add another **Crop** tool tile and animate the **X Offset** control of it. Next, you will blend outputs of the two **Crop** tools to give depth to the clouds.

5. Click on the empty space in the **Flow** area to deselect the selected tool tile, if any. Choose the **Xf** button from the toolbar; the **Transform1** tool tile is inserted in the **Flow** area.

   The **Transform** tool is used to transform a 2D image by moving, scaling, and rotating the image.

6. Drag the white output node of the **Loader1** tool tile to the orange node of the **Transform1** tool tile; a connection between the **Loader1** and **Transform1** tool tiles is established, as shown in Figure 4-3.

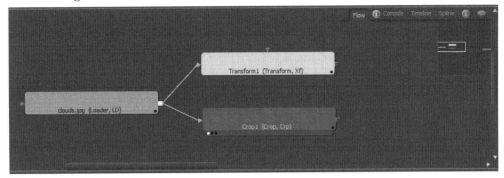

*Figure 4-3 The **Transform1** tool connected to the **Loader1** tool*

7. In the **Transform1** tool control window, select the **Flip Horizontally** check box. This check box is used to flip the image along the X axis.

8. Click on the empty space in the **Flow** area to deselect the selected tool tile, if any. Choose **Tools > Transform > Crop** from the menubar; the **Crop2** tool tile is inserted in the **Flow** area.

9. Drag the red output node of the **Transform1** tool tile to the orange node of the **Crop2** tool tile; a connection between the **Crop2** and **Transform1** tools is established.

10. In the **Crop2** tool control window, animate the **X Offset** control to create the keyframes by using the values given next.

Frame	X Offset
0	0
300	500

11. Drag the red output node of the **Crop1** tool tile in the **Flow** area to the red output node of the **Crop2** tool tile; the **Merge1** tool tile is inserted in the **Flow** area and a connection between the **Crop1**, **Crop2**, and **Merge1** tools is established, as shown in Figure 4-4.

12. Press 2; the output of the **Merge1** tool is displayed in the right Display View.

13. In the **Merge1** tool control window, select **Lighten** from the **Apply Mode** drop-down list to blend the two layers of clouds. Next, press SPACEBAR; the playback of the composition starts. You will notice that the clouds are blended together and have depth as well.

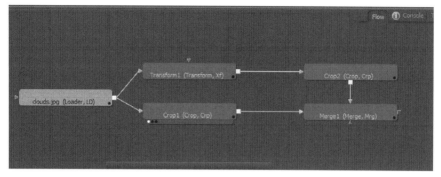

*Figure 4-4 The **Merge1** tool and its connections in the **Flow** area*

14. Select the **Loader2** tool tile in the **Flow** area and then choose the **Rsz** button from the toolbar; the **Resize1** tool tile is inserted in the **Flow** area and a connection between the **Loader2** and **Resize1** tools is established.

15. Drag the red output node of the **Resize1** tool tile to the red output node of the **Merge1** tool tile; the **Merge2** tool tile is inserted in the **Flow** area and a connection between the **Resize1**, **Merge1**, and **Merge2** tools is established, as shown in Figure 4-5.

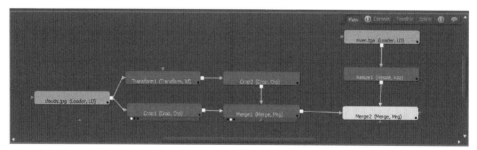

*Figure 4-5 The **Merge2** tool and its connections in the **Flow** area*

16. Press 2; the output of the **Merge2** tool is displayed in the right Display View, as shown in Figure 4-6.

*Figure 4-6 The output of the **Merge2** tool*

Adding Perspective to the Clouds

In this section, you will add perspective to the clouds.

1. Select the **Merge1** tool tile in the **Flow** area and then choose **Tools > Transform > DVE** from the menubar; the **DVE1** tool tile is inserted between the **Merge1** and **Merge2** tools.

   The **DVE** tool is used to transform an image and also to add perspective to an image.

2. In the **DVE1** tool control window, enter the values of the parameters as follows:

   X Rotation: **0.36**   Perspective: **0.72**

   Next, you will create reflection of the clouds in the lake.

3. Click on the empty space in the **Flow** area and then choose **Tools > Transform > DVE** from the menubar; the **DVE2** tool is inserted in the **Flow** area.

4. Drag the white output node of the **Merge1** tool tile in the **Flow** area to the orange input node of the **DVE2** tool tile; a connection is established between the **Merge1** and **DVE2** tools.

5. Drag the red output node of the **DVE2** tool tile to the red output node of the **Merge2** tool tile; the **Merge3** tool tile is inserted in the **Flow** area and a connection between the **DVE2**, **Merge2**, and **Merge3** tools is established. Select the **Merge3** tool tile in the **Flow** area and then press 2; the output of the **Merge3** tool is displayed in the right Display View.

6. Select the **DVE2** tool tile from the **Flow** area and then in the **DVE2** tool control window, enter the values of the parameters as follows:

   Center
   X: **-0.46**

   Z Move: **0.314**   X Rotation: **120**

7. Choose the **Add a Polyline Mask** button from the right **Display View** toolbar; the **Polygon1** tool tile is inserted in the **Flow** area and a connection between the **Merge3** and **Polygon1** tools is established. Next, draw a polyline shape, as shown in Figure 4-7.

8. In the **Merge3** tool control window, choose **Multiply** from the **Apply Mode** drop-down list and then enter **0.5** in the **Blend** edit box; the reflection of clouds gets blended with the lake, as shown in Figure 4-8.

Figure 4-7 *The polygon shape drawn*

Figure 4-8 *The reflection of cloud blended with lake*

Color-Correcting the Composition

In this section, you will color-correct the composition.

1. Make sure the **Merge3** tool tile is selected in the **Flow** area and then choose the **CC** button from the toolbar; the **ColorCorrector1** tool tile gets connected to the **Merge3** tool.

2. Press 1; the output of the **ColorCorrector1** tool is displayed in the left Display View.

3. In the **ColorCorrector1** tool control window, enter the values of the parameters as follows:

    Tint: **1.67**   Strength: **0.04**

    The **Tint** parameter indicates the angle of the tint color on the color wheel. The **Strength** parameter is used to control the amount of tint applied.

4. Press SPACEBAR to start the playback of the composition.

    The final output at frame 80 after specifying all parameters is shown in Figure 4-1.

Now, save the composition with the name *c04tut1* at the location *Documents > Fusion_7 > c04_tut > c04_tut_01*. Next, you need to render the composition. For rendering, refer to Tutorial 2 of Chapter 2. The output of the composition at frame 80 is shown in Figure 4-1. You can also view the final render of the composition by downloading the *c04_fusion_7_rndr.zip* file from *http://www.cadcim.com*. The path of the file is mentioned at the beginning of the chapter.

Tutorial 2

In this tutorial, you will create a composition and then change the resolution using the **Scale** tool. The final output of the composition is shown in Figure 4-9.   **(Expected time: 30 min)**

Figure 4-9 The final output of the composition

The following steps are required to complete the tutorial:

a. Set the frame format.
b. Download and import the images.
c. Color-correct the glass image.
d. Merge the images.

Setting the Frame Format

In this section, you will specify the frame format settings.

1. Choose **File > New** from the menubar; a new composition is displayed in the Fusion screen.

2. Choose **File > Preferences** from the menubar; the **Preferences** dialog box is displayed.

3. In this dialog box, select **Frame Format** from the **Composition#** preferences tree; various frame format settings are displayed on the right in the **Preferences** dialog box. Next, select the **HDTV 720** option from the **Default format** drop-down list and then choose the **Save** button to save the changes made.

4. In the Time Ruler area, enter **0** in the **Global End Time** edit box.

Downloading and Importing the Images

In this section, you will download the images and import them to the composition.

1. Open the link *http://www.freeimages.com//photo/1275249*; an image is displayed.

2. Download the image at */Documents/Fusion_7/c04_tut/c04_tut_02/Media_Files* with the name *table.jpg*.

Note
Footage Courtesy: **shho** *(http://www.freeimages.com/profile/shho)*

3. Choose the **LD** button from the toolbar; the **Open File** dialog box is displayed. In this dialog box, choose **Documents > Fusion_7 > c04_tut > c04_tut_02 > Media_Files > table.jpg** and then choose the **Open** button; the **Loader1** tool tile is inserted in the **Flow** area.

4. Press 1; the output of the **Loader1** tool is displayed in the left Display View. Choose the **Fit** button from the left **Display View** toolbar to fit the image in the left Display View, refer to Figure 4-10.

5. Click on the empty space in the **Flow** area to deselect the selected tool tile, if any. Import *glass.png* in the **Flow** area, as done in step 3; the **Loader2** tool tile is inserted in the **Flow** area. Press 2; the output of the **Loader2** tool is displayed in the right Display View.

6. Make sure the **Loader2** tool tile is selected in the **Flow** area. In the control window of the **Loader2** tool, choose the **Import** tab and then select the **Post-Multiply by Alpha** check box. Next, choose the **Fit** button from the right **Display View** toolbar to fit the image in the right Display View, refer to Figure 4-10.

*Figure 4-10 The output of the **Loader1** and **Loader2** tools*

Color-Correcting the Glass Image

In this section, you will color-correct the image of the glass.

1. Make sure the **Loader2** tool tile is selected in the **Flow** area and choose the **CC**button from the **Flow** area; the **ColorCorrector1** tool tile is inserted in the **Flow** area and a connection between the **Loader2** and **ColorCorrector1** tools is established.

2. Press 2; the output of the **ColorCorrector1** tool is displayed in the right Display View.

3. In the control window of the **ColorCorrector1** tool, enter **0.9** in the **Master-RGB-Gain** edit box.

Merging the Images

In this section, you will merge the images.

1. Select the **Loader1** tool tile in the **Flow** area and then choose the **Rsz** button from the toolbar; the **Resize1** tool tile is inserted in the **Flow** area and a connection is established between the **Loader1** and **Resize1** tools.

2. Drag the red output node of the **ColorCorrector1** tool tile to the red output node of the **Resize1** tool tile; the **Merge1** tool tile is inserted in the **Flow** area and a connection is established between the **ColorCorrector1**, **Resize1**, and **Merge1** tools.

3. Press 2; the output of the **Merge1** tool is displayed in the right Display View.

4. In the **Merge1** tool control window, set the values of the parameters as follows:

Center
X: **0.34**   Y: **0.49**

Size: **0.82**

The output of the **Merge1** tool after specifying all parameters is shown in Figure 4-11.

Figure 4-11 *The output of the **Merge1** tool*

Next, you will make the upper part of the glass image transparent.

5. Choose the **Add a Polyline Mask** button from the right **Display View** toolbar; the
    Polygon1 tool tile is inserted in the **Flow** area and a connection between the **Merge1**
    and **Polygon1** tools is established in the **Flow** area.

6. In the control window of the **Polygon** tool, select the **Invert** check box. Next, draw a polyline
    shape in the right Display View, as shown in Figure 4-12.

Figure 4-12 The polyline shape drawn in the right Display View

7. In the **Polygon1** tool control window, enter **0.11** in the **Soft Edge** edit box.

8. Select the **Merge1** tool tile from the **Flow** area and then choose the **CC** button from
    the toolbar; the **ColorCorrector2** tool tile is inserted in the **Flow** area and a connection
    between the **Merge1** and **ColorCorrector2** tools is established.

9. Press 2; the output of the **ColorCorrector2** tool is displayed in the right Display View.

10. In the **ColorCorrector2** tool control window, enter the values of the parameters as follows:

    Tint: **1.15**   Strength: **0.5**   Master-RGB-Gain: **0.85**

    The output of the **ColorCorrector2** tool after specifying all parameters is shown in
    Figure 4-13.

11. Make sure the **ColorCorrector2** tool tile is selected in the **Flow** area and then choose **Tools >
    Transform > Scale** from the menubar; the **Scale1** tool tile is inserted in the **Flow** area and
    a connection is established between the **ColorCorrector2** and **Scale1** tools.

    The **Scale** tool is used to change the dimension of the image.

12. Press 1; the output of the **Scale1** tool is displayed in the left Display View.

*Figure 4-13 The output of the **ColorCorrector2** tool*

13. Enter **0.5** in the **Size** edit box of the **Scale1** tool control window; the image is reduced to fifty percent of its original size.

Figure 4-14 displays all tools used in the composition.

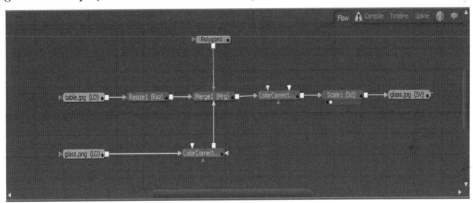

*Figure 4-14 All tools used in the composition displayed in the **Flow** area*

Now, save the composition with the name *c04tut2* at the location *Documents > Fusion_7 > c04_tut > c04_tut_02*. Next, you need to render the composition. For rendering, refer to Tutorial 1 of Chapter 2. The final output of the composition is shown in Figure 4-9. You can also view the final render of the composition by downloading the *c04_fusion_7_rndr.zip* from *http://www.cadcim.com*. The path of the file is mentioned at the beginning of the chapter.

Tutorial 3

In this tutorial, you will create the cell phone vibration effect by using the **CameraShake** tool. The final output of the composition at frame 225 is shown in Figure 4-15.

(Expected time: 35 min)

The following steps are required to complete this tutorial:

a. Set the frame format.
b. Download and import the images.

c.   Merge images.
d.   Add perspective to the cellphone image.
e.   Create the cellphone vibration effect.
f.   Create shadow of cellphone.
g.   Add glow to the cellphone screen.

Figure 4-15 The final output of the composition at frame 225

Setting the Frame Format

In this section, you will specify the frame format settings.

1.   Choose **File > New** from the menubar; a new composition is displayed in the Fusion screen.

2.   Choose **File > Preferences** from the menubar; the **Preferences** dialog box is displayed.

3.   In this dialog box, select **Frame Format** from the **Composition#** preferences tree; various frame format settings are displayed in the right in the **Preferences** dialog box. Next, select the **HDTV 720** option from the **Default format** drop-down list and then choose the **Save** button to save the changes made.

4.   In the Time Ruler area, enter **350** in the **Render End Time** edit box.

Downloading and Importing the Images

In this section, you will download the images and import them to the composition.

1.   Open the link *http://www.freeimages.com/photo/1243927*; an image is displayed.

2.   Download the image at */Documents/Fusion_7/c04_tut/c04_tut_03/Media_Files* and save it with the name *coffee.jpg*.

   Note
   Footage Courtesy: **Catalin Pop** *(http://www.freeimages.com/profile/catalin82)*

3. Choose the **LD** button from the toolbar; the **Open File** dialog box is displayed. In this dialog box, choose **Documents > Fusion_7 > c04_tut > c04_tut_03 > Media_Files > coffee.jpg** and then choose the **Open** button; the **Loader1** tool tile is inserted in the **Flow** area.

4. Press 1; the output of the **Loader1** tool is displayed in the left Display View. Choose the **Fit** button from the left **Display View** toolbar to fit the image into the left Display View, refer to Figure 4-16. Next, click on the empty space of the **Flow** area to deselect the selected tools, if any.

5. Import *mobile.png* in the **Flow** area as done in step 3; the **Loader2** tool tile is inserted in the **Flow** area. Press 2; the output of the **Loader2** tool is displayed in the right Display View.

6. Select the **Loader2** tool tile from the **Flow** area. In the control window of the **Loader2** tool, choose the **Import** tab and then select the **Post-Multiply by Alpha** check box. Next, choose the **Fit** button from the right **Display View** toolbar to fit the image into the right Display View, refer to Figure 4-16.

*Figure 4-16 The output of the **Loader1** and **Loader2** tools*

7. Make sure the **Loader1** tool tile is selected in the **Flow** area. Choose the **Rsz** button from the toolbar; the **Resize1** tool tile is inserted in the **Flow** area and a connection between the **Loader1** and **Resize1** tools is established.

The **Resize** tool is used to increase or decrease the resolution of an image.

8. Select the **Loader2** tool tile from the **Flow** area and choose the **Rsz** button from the toolbar; the **Resize2** tool tile is inserted in the **Flow** area and a connection between the **Loader2** and **Resize2** tools is established.

Merging the Images
In this section, you will merge the images.

1. Drag the red output node of the **Resize2** tool tile to the red output node of the **Resize1** tool; the **Merge1** tool tile is inserted in the **Flow** area and a connection between the **Resize1**, **Resize2**, and **Merge1** tools is established, as shown in Figure 4-17.

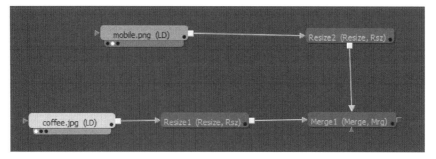

*Figure 4-17 The **Resize1** and **Resize2** tools connected with the **Merge1** tool*

2. Press 2; the output of the **Merge1** tool is displayed in the right Display View.

3. In the **Merge1** tool control window, enter the values of the parameters as follows:

Center
X: **0.94**   Y: **0.03**

Size: **0.35**   Angle: **-6.0**

After entering the values, the output of the **Merge1** tool is displayed in the right Display View, as shown in Figure 4-18.

*Figure 4-18 The output of the **Merge1** tool*

Adding Perspective to the Cellphone Image

In this section, you will add perspective to the cellphone image.

1. Select the **Resize2** tool tile from the **Flow** area and then choose **Tools > Transform > DVE** from the menubar; the **DVE1** tool tile is inserted in the **Flow** area and a connection between the **Resize2** and **DVE1** tools is established.

2. In the **DVE1** tool control window, set the values of the parameters as follows:

Center
X: **0.46**   Y: **0.63**

Z Move: **1.26**   Z Pivot: **0.078**

Rotation Order: **XYZ**

X Rotation: **-32**   Y Rotation: **-24.78**   Z Rotation: **3.8**

The **Center** parameter is used to position the center of the image in the Display View. The **Z Move** parameter allows to zoom the image in or out along the **Z** axis. The **Z Pivot** parameter is used to position the axis of rotation and scaling.

Creating the Cellphone Vibration Effect

In this section, you will create cellphone vibration effect by using the **Camera Shake** tool. This tool is used to simulate the real life camera shake effect.

1.   Select the **DVE1** tool tile from the **Flow** area and choose **Tools > Transform > Camera Shake** from the menubar; the **CameraShake1** tool tile is inserted in the **Flow** area and a connection between the **DVE1** and **CameraShake1** tools is established.

     The **CameraShake** tool is used to generate a variety of camera shape style motions from organic to mechanical.

2.   In the **CameraShake1** tool control window, animate the **Overall Strength** control to create the keyframes by using the values given in the following table:

Frame	Overall Strength
0, 44	0
45	0.04
50, 94	0
95	0.04
100, 144	0
145	0.04
150, 194	0
195	0.04
200, 244	0
245	0.027
250, 294	0
295	0.03
300, 344	0
345	0.04

The **Overall Strength** parameter is used to adjust the overall effect of all the parameters of the **Camera Shake** tool. The value of this parameter ranges from 0 to 1.

Creating the Shadow of the Cellphone

In this section, you will create the shadow of the cellphone.

1. Click on the empty space in the **Flow** area to deselect the selected tool tiles, if any. Next, choose the **CC** button from the toolbar; the **ColorCorrector1** tool tile is inserted in the **Flow** area. Drag the white output node of the **CameraShake1** tool tile to the orange node of the **ColorCorrector1** tool tile; a connection between the **ColorCorrector1** and **CameraShake1** tools is established, as shown in Figure 4-19.

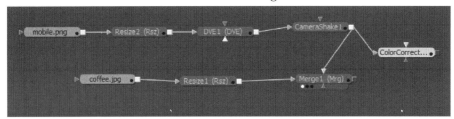

*Figure 4-19 The **CameraShake1** tool connected with the **ColorCorrector1** tool*

2. Press 2; the output of the **ColorCorrector1** tool is displayed in the right Display View.

3. Enter **0** in the **Master-RGB-Gain** edit box of the **ColorCorrector1** tool control window.

4. Drag the red output node of the **ColorCorrector1** tool tile to the red output node of the **Merge1** tool tile; the **Merge2** tool tile is inserted in the **Flow** area and a connection between the **ColorCorrector1** and **Merge1** tools is established.

5. Press 2; the output of the **Merge2** tool is displayed in the right Display View.

6. In the **Merge2** tool control window, set the values of the parameters as follows:

   Center
   X: **0.935**   Y: **0.012**

   Size: **0.35**   Angle: **-6**

   After entering the values, the output of the **Merge2** tool is displayed in the right Display View, as shown in Figure 4-20.

7. Make sure the **Merge2** tool tile is selected in the **Flow** area. Next, choose the **Add a Polyline Mask** button from the right **Display View** toolbar; the **Polygon1** tool tile is inserted in the **Flow** area and a connection between the **Polygon1** and **Merge2** tools is established.

8. Draw a polyline shape, as shown in Figure 4-21.

Figure 4-20 *The output of the **Merge2** tool*

Figure 4-21 *The polyline shape drawn in the Display View*

9. In the **Polygon1** tool control window, select the **Invert** check box and then enter **0.001** in the **Soft Edge** edit box to soften the edges of the mask.

Adding Glow to the Cellphone Screen

In this section, you will animate the controls of **Color Corrector** tool to create the glow effect on the screen of the cellphone.

1. Select the **Merge2** tool tile from the **Flow** area. Next, choose the **CC** button from the toolbar; the **ColorCorrector2** tool tile is inserted in the **Flow** area and a connection between the **Merge2** and **ColorCorrector2** tools is established in the **Flow** area, as shown in Figure 4-22.

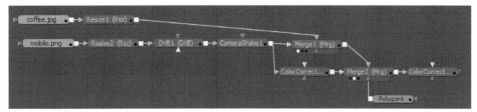

Figure 4-22 *The **ColorCorrector2** tool connected with the **Merge2** tool*

2. Press 2; the output of the **ColorCorrector2** tool is displayed in the right Display View.

3. In the **ColorCorrector2** tool control window, set the values of the parameters as follows:

Tint: **0.62**   Strength: **0.91**

4. Make sure the **ColorCorrector2** tool tile is selected in the **Flow** area and choose the **Add a Polyline Mask** button from the **Display View** toolbar; the **Polygon2** tool tile is inserted in the **Flow** area and a connection between the **Polygon2** and **ColorCorrector2** tools is established.

5. Draw a polyline shape, as shown in Figure 4-23.

Figure 4-23 *The polyline shape drawn in the right Display View*

6. Select the **ColorCorrector2** tool tile in the **Flow** area and then animate the **Master-RGB-Gain** control to create keyframes by using the values given in the following table:

Frame	Master-RGB-Gain	Frame	Master-RGB-Gain
0, 45	3.5	196, 199	0
46, 49	0	200, 245	3.5
50, 95	3.5	246, 249	0
96, 99	0	250, 295	3.5
100, 145	3.5	296, 299	0
146, 149	0	300, 345	3.5
150, 195	3.5	350	0

7. Press SPACEBAR to start the playback of the composition.

You will notice vibrations in the cellphone and also its screen will glow. The rendered output of the **ColorCorrector2** tool at frame 225 is shown in Figure 4-24.

Figure 4-24 The rendered output of the composition at frame 225

Figure 4-25 displays all tools used in the composition.

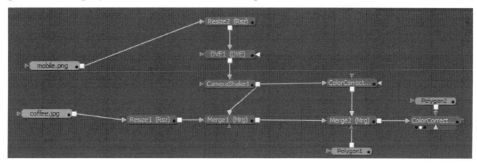

*Figure 4-25 All tools used in the composition displayed in the **Flow** area*

Now, save the composition with the name *c04tut3* at the location *Documents > Fusion_7 > c04_ tut > c04_tut_03*. Next, you need to render the composition. For rendering, refer to Tutorial 2 of Chapter 2. The final output of the composition is shown in Figure 4-15. You can also view the final render of the composition by downloading the *c04_fusion_7_rndr.zip* file from *http://www.cadcim.com*. The path of the file is mentioned at the beginning of the chapter.

Self-Evaluation Test

Answer the following questions and then compare them to those given at the end of this chapter:

1. Which of the following tools is used to transform an image or an image sequence?

    (a) **Transform**   (b) **Creator**
    (c) **Warp**   (d) None of these

2. The **Transform** tool is used to_____, _____, and _____the images.

3. The _____ tool is used to crop a portion of an image.

4. The _____ tool is used to add perspective to an image.

Review Questions

Answer the following questions:

1. Which of the following buttons in the toolbar is used to insert the **Color Corrector** tool in the **Flow** area?

    (a) **CC**   (b)   **BC**
    (c) **Bol**   (d)   **BG**

2. Which of the following buttons in the toolbar is used to insert the **Resize** tool in the **Flow** area?

    (a)   **Rng**   (b)   **Log**
    (c)   **Rsz**   (d)   **3Rn**

3. Which of the following buttons in the toolbar is used to insert the **Transform** tool in the **Flow** area?

    (a)   **Xf**   (b) **CT**
    (c)   **3SL**   (d) **Mat**

4. The _____ tool is used to increase or decrease the resolution of an image.

Answers to Self-Evaluation Test
1. a, **2.** move, rotate, scale, **3. Crop**, **4. DVE**

Chapter 5

Warp Tools

Learning Objectives

After completing this chapter, you will be able to:

- *Use different types of Warp tools*
- *Create the smoke effect*
- *Create the swirling motion effect*
- *Create the fisheye lens effect*
- *Create the moving water effect*
- *Create the lens distortion effect*

INTRODUCTION

The Warp tools are used to distort an image. These tools can be used to interactively position the four corners of an image, create a circular deformation on an image, create a swirling whirlpool effect in specified regions of the image, and create fisheye lens effect. In this chapter, you will create various effects using the Warp tools.

TUTORIALS

The compositions created in this chapter can be downloaded from *http://www.cadcim.com*. These compositions are contained in the *c05_fusion_7_tut.zip* file. The path of the file is as follows:

> *Textbooks > Animation and Visual Effects > Fusion > The Blackmagic Design Fusion 7 Studio: A Tutorial Approach*

Tutorial 1

In this tutorial, you will create the smoke effect by using the **Vector Distortion** and **FastNoise** tools. The final output of the composition is shown in Figure 5-1. **(Expected time: 25 min)**

Figure 5-1 *The final output of the composition*

The following steps are required to complete this tutorial:

a. Set the frame format.
b. Download and import the images.
c. Merge the images.
d. Distort the image.
e. Color-correct the composition.

Setting the Frame Format

In this section, you will specify the frame format settings.

1. Choose **File > New** from the menubar; a new composition is displayed in the Fusion screen.

2. Choose **File > Preferences** from the menubar; the **Preferences** dialog box is displayed.

3. In this dialog box, select **Frame Format** from the **Composition#** preferences tree; various frame format settings are displayed on the right in the **Preferences** dialog box. Next, select the **HDTV 720** option from the **Default format** drop-down list and then choose the **Save** button to save the changes made.

4. In the Time Ruler area, enter **300** in the **Global End Time** edit box.

Downloading and Importing the Images

In this section, you will download the images and import them to the composition.

1. Open the following link: *http://www.freeimages.com/photo/787925*; an image is displayed.

2. Download the image at the location */Documents/Fusion_7/c05_tut/c05_tut_01/Media_Files* and save it with the name *street.jpg*.

 Note
*Footage Courtesy: **Michael & Christa Richert** (http://www.freeimages.com/profile/Ayla87)*

3. Choose the **LD** button from the toolbar; the **Open File** dialog box is displayed. In this dialog box, choose **Documents > Fusion_7 > c05_tut > c05_tut_01 > Media_Files > street.jpg** and then choose the **Open** button; the **Loader1** tool tile is inserted in the **Flow** area.

4. Press 1; the output of the **Loader1** tool is displayed in the left Display View.

5. Choose the **Fit** button from the left **Display View** toolbar to fit the image into the Display View, refer to Figure 5-2.

6. Click on the empty space in the **Flow** area to deselect the selected tool tile, if any.

7. Load *car.png* in the **Flow** area as done in step 3; the **Loader2** tool tile is inserted in the **Flow** area. Press 2; the output of the **Loader2** tool is displayed in the right Display View. Choose the **Fit** button from the right **Display View** toolbar to fit the image into theDisplay View

8. In the **Loader2** tool control window, choose the **Import** tab and then select the **Post-Multiply by Alpha** check box. Figure 5-2 shows the output of the right display view.

*Figure 5-2 The output of the **Loader1** and **Loader2** tools*

Merging the Images

In this section, you will merge the images.

1. Select the **Loader1** tool tile from the **Flow** area and choose the **Rsz** button from the toolbar; the **Resize1** tool tile is inserted in the **Flow** area and a connection between the **Loader1** and **Resize1** tools is established.

2. Select the **Loader2** tool tile from the **Flow** area and choose the **Rsz** button from the toolbar; the **Resize2** tool tile is inserted in the **Flow** area and a connection between the **Loader2** and **Resize2** tools is established.

3. Drag the red output node of the **Resize2** tool tile to the red output node of the **Resize1** tool tile; the **Merge1** tool tile is inserted in the **Flow** area, refer to Figure 5-3.

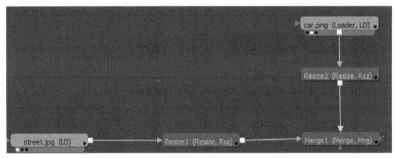

Figure 5-3 The **Resize1** and **Resize2** tools connected to the **Merge1** tool

4. Press 2; the output of the **Merge1** tool is displayed in the right Display View, as shown in Figure 5-4.

5. In the **Merge1** tool control window, set the values of the parameters as follows:

Center
Y: **0.16**

Size: **0.92**

Figure 5-4 The output of the **Merge1** tool

Distorting the Image

In this section, you will distort the image by using the **Vector Distortion** tool.

1. Select the **Resize1** tool tile from the **Flow** area. Next, choose **Tools > Warp > Vector Distortion** from the menubar; the **VectorDistortion1** tool tile is inserted in the **Flow** area and a connection between the **Resize1**, **Merge1**, and **VectorDistortion1** tools is established.

   The **Vector Distortion** tool is used to distort the image separately along the X and Y axes.

2. Press 2; the output of the **VectorDistortion1** tool is displayed in the right Display View.

3. Enter **5** in the **Scale** edit box of the **VectorDistortion1** tool control window.

   The **Scale** parameter is used to multiply to the values of the distortion reference image.

   Next, you will use the **FastNoise** tool to create a mask to restrict the effect of the **Vector Distortion1** tool.

4. Click on the empty space in the **Flow** area to deselect the selected tool tile, if any. Choose **Tools > Creator > FastNoise** tool from the toolbar; the **FastNoise1** tool is inserted in the **Flow** area.

5. Press 1; the output of the **FastNoise1** tool is displayed in the left Display View.

6. Choose the **Image** tab from the **FastNoise1** tool control window and set the values of the parameters as follows:

   Width: **1800**   Height: **912**

   The **Width** and **Height** parameters are used to set the width and height of the output generated by the **FastNoise** tool.

7. Choose the **Noise** tab from the **FastNoise1** tool control window and set the values of the parameters as follows:

   Center
   X: **0.47**   Y: **0.37**

   Detail: **5.5**   Contrast: **0.62**   Scale: **10.89**

   Seethe: **0.2**   Seethe Rate: **0.5**

8. Drag the red output node of the **FastNoise1** tool tile to the green node of the **VectorDistortion1** tool tile; the **FastNoise1** tool is connected to the **VectorDistortion1** tool, as shown in Figure 5-5.

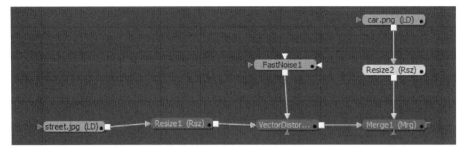

*Figure 5-5 The **FastNoise1** tool connected to the **VectorDistortion1** tool*

Next, you will position the effect generated by the **VectorDistortion1** and **FastNoise1** tools.

9. Make sure the **FastNoise1** tool tile is selected in the **Flow** area. Choose **Tools > Transform > DVE** from the menubar; the **DVE1** tool tile is inserted in the **Flow** area and a connection between the **FastNoise1**, **VectorDistortion1**, and **DVE1** tools is established.

10. In the **DVE1** tool control window, set the values of the parameters as follows:

Center
X: **0.57**   Y: **0.57**

Z Move: **1.93**   Z Pivot: **0.07**

X Rotation: **24.17**   Perspective: **0.18**

11. Select the **FastNoise1** tool tile from the **Flow** area. Next, choose the **Add an Ellipse Mask** button from the right **Display View** toolbar; the **Ellipse1** tool tile is inserted in the **Flow** area and a connection between the **FastNoise1** and **Ellipse1** tools is established.

12. In the **Ellipse1** tool control window, set the values of the parameters as follows:

Soft Edge: **0.065**   Border Width: **-0.038**

Center
X: **0.578**   Y: **0.68**
Width: **0.39**   Height: **0.3**

13. Select the **Merge1** tool tile in the **Flow** area and press 2; the output of the **Merge1** tool is displayed in the right Display View, as shown in Figure 5-6.

Color-Correcting the Composition

In this section, you will apply the color correction to the composition.

1. Select the **Resize2** tool tile from the **Flow** area and choose the **CC** button from the toolbar; the **ColorCorrector1** tool tile is inserted in the **Flow** area and a connection between the **Resize2** and **ColorCorrector1** tools is established .

2. Press 2; the output of the **ColorCorrector1** tool is displayed in the right Display View.

*Figure 5-6 The output of the **Merge1** tool*

3. Enter **0.59** in the **Master-RGB-Gain** edit box of the **ColorCorrector1** tool control window.

4. Select the **Merge1** tool tile from the **Flow** area and choose the **CC** button from the toolbar; the **ColorCorrector2** tool tile is inserted in the **Flow** area and a connection between the **Merge1** and **ColorCorrector2** tools is established.

5. Press 2; the output of the **ColorCorrector2** tool is displayed in the right Display View.

6. In the **ColorCorrector2** tool control window, set the parameters as follows:

    Tint: **-0.87**   Strength: **0.12**

    Now, save the composition with the name *c05tut1* at the location *Documents > Fusion_7 > c05_tut > c05_tut_01*. Next, you need to render the composition. For rendering, refer to Tutorial 2 of Chapter 2. The output of the composition is shown in Figure 5-1. You can also view the final render of the composition by downloading the *c05_fusion_7_rndr.zip* from *http://www.cadcim.com*. The path of the file is mentioned at the beginning of the chapter.

Tutorial 2

In this tutorial, you will interactively place the corners of an image using the **Corner Positioner** tool in the composition. The final output of the composition is shown in Figure 5-7.

(Expected time: 20 min)

The following steps are required to complete this tutorial:

a. Set the frame format.
b. Download and import the images.
c. Color-correct the beach chair image.
d. Merge the images.
e. Position the corners of the beach chair image.

Figure 5-7 *The final output of the composition*

Setting the Frame Format

In this section, you will specify the frame format settings.

1.   Choose **File > New** from the menubar; a new composition is displayed in the Fusion screen.

2.   Choose **File > Preferences** from the menubar; the **Preferences** dialog box is displayed.

3.   In this dialog box, select **Frame Format** from the **Composition#** preferences tree; various frame format settings are displayed on the right in the **Preferences** dialog box. Next, select the **NTSC (Square Pixel)** option from the **Default format** drop-down list and then choose the **Save** button to save the changes made.

4.   In the Time Ruler area, enter **0** in the **Global End Time** edit box.

Downloading and Importing the Images

In this section, you will download the images and import them to the composition.

1.   Open the following link: *http://www.freeimages.com/photo/230160*; an image is displayed.

2.   Download the image at the location */Documents/Fusion_7/c05_tut/c05_tut_02/ Media_Files* and save it with the name *chairs.jpg*.

3.   Open *chairs.jpg* in the Photoshop application and create transparency in it, as shown in Figure 5-8. Next, save it with the name *chairs.tga* at the location specified above.

 Note
*Footage Courtesy : **Andy Steele** (http://www.freeimages.com/profile/andysteele)*

4.   Choose the **LD** button from the toolbar; the **Open File** dialog box is displayed. In this dialog box, choose **Documents > Fusion_7 > c05_tut > c05_tut_02 > Media_Files > beach.jpg** and then choose the **Open** button; the **Loader1** tool tile is inserted in the **Flow** area.

5. Press 1; the output of the **Loader1** tool is displayed in the left Display View.

6. Choose the **Fit** button from the left **Display View** toolbar to fit the image into the left Display View, refer to Figure 5-8.

7. Click on the empty space in the **Flow** area and then load the *chairs.tga* file in the **Flow** area; the **Loader2** tool tile is inserted in the **Flow** area.

8. Choose the **Fit** button from the right **Display View** toolbar to fit the image into the right Display View.

9. In the **Loader2** tool control window, choose the **Import** tab and then select the **Post-Multiply by Alpha** check box. Next, press 2; the output of the **Loader2** tool is displayed in the right Display View, refer to Figure 5-8.

*Figure 5-8 The output of the **Loader1** and **Loader2** tools*

Color-Correcting the Beach Chair
In this section, you will apply the color-correction to the beach chair.

1. Make sure the **Loader2** tool tile is selected in the **Flow** area and choose the **CC** button from the toolbar; the **ColorCorrector1** tool tile is inserted in the **Flow** area and a connection between the **Loader2** and **ColorCorrector1** tools is established.

2. Press 1; the output of the **ColorCorrector1** tool is displayed in the left Display View.

3. In the **ColorCorrector1** tool control window, set the values of the parameters as follows:

Tint: **-0.25**   Master-RGB-Gain: **0.77**

Merging the Images
In this section, you will merge the images.

1. Select the **Loader1** tool tile from the **Flow** area. Choose **Tools > Transform > Resize** from the menubar; the **Resize1** tool tile is inserted in the **Flow** area and a connection between the **Loader1** and **Resize1** tools is established.

2. Select the **Loader2** tool tile from the **Flow** area. Choose **Tools > Transform > Resize** from the menubar; the **Resize2** tool tile is inserted in the **Flow** area and a connection between the **Loader2**, **Resize2**, and **ColorCorrector1** tools is established.

3. Drag the red output node of the **ColorCorrector1** tool tile to the red output node of the **Resize1** tool tile; the **Merge1** tool tile is inserted in the **Flow** area and a connection between the **ColorCorrector1**, **Resize1**, and **Merge1** tools is established.

4. Press 2; the output of the **Merge1** tool is displayed in the right Display View.

5. In the **Merge1** tool control window, set the values of the parameters as follows:

Center
X: **0.4**   Y: **0.49**

Size: **0.78**

After entering the values, the output of the **Merge1** tool is displayed in the right Display View, as shown in Figure 5-9.

Figure 5-9 *The output of the **Merge1** tool*

Positioning the Corners of the Beach Chair

In this section, you will position the corners of the beach chair by using the **Corner Positioner** tool.

1. Select the **ColorCorrector1** tool tile from the **Flow** area. Choose **Tools > Warp > Corner Positioner** from the menubar; the **CornerPositioner1** tool tile is inserted in the **Flow** area and a connection between the **ColorCorrector1**, **Merge1,** and **CornerPositioner1** tools is established.

2. In the **CornerPositioner1** tool control window, set the values of the parameters as follows:

Top Left   **Top Right**
X: **0.05**   Y: **0.83**   X: **0.84**   Y: **0.76**

Bottom left   **Bottom Right**
X: **0.06**   Y: **-0.04**   X: **0.98**   Y: **0.07**

Next, you will apply an overall color-correction to the composition.

3. Select the **Merge1** tool tile from the **Flow** area and choose the **CC** button from the toolbar; the **ColorCorrector2** tool tile is inserted in the **Flow** area and a connection between the **Merge1** and **ColorCorrector2** tools is established.

4. Press 2, the output of the **ColorCorrector2** tool is displayed in the right Display View.

5. In the **ColorCorrector2** tool control window, set the parameters as follows:

Tint: **0.15**   Strength: **0.15**

Now, save the composition with the name *c05tut2* at the location *Documents > Fusion_7 > c05_tut > c05_tut_02*. Next, you need to render the composition. For rendering, refer to Tutorial 1 of Chapter 2. The output of the composition is shown in Figure 5-7. You can also view the final render of the composition by downloading the *c05_fusion_7_rndr.zip* from *http://www.cadcim.com*. The path of the file is mentioned at the beginning of the chapter.

Tutorial 3

In this tutorial, you will create a swirling whirlpool effect by using the **Vortex** tool. The final output of the composition at frame 18 is shown in Figure 5-10.   **(Expected time: 20 min)**

Figure 5-10 *The final output of the composition at frame 18*

The following steps are required to complete this tutorial:

a. Set the frame format.
b. Create the background.
c. Download and import the images.
d. Create the swirl effect on the background image.
e. Merge the images.

f. Create the swirl effect on the notes image.

g. Color-correct the composition.

Setting the Frame Format

In this section, you will specify the frame format settings.

1. Choose **File > New** from the menubar; a new composition is displayed in the Fusion screen.

2. Choose **File > Preferences** from the menubar; the **Preferences** dialog box is displayed.

3. In this dialog box, select **Frame Format** from the **Composition#** preferences tree; various frame format settings are displayed on the right in the **Preferences** dialog box. Next, select the **NTSC (Square Pixel)** option from the **Default format** drop-down list and then choose the **Save** button to save the changes made.

4. In the Time Ruler area, enter **50** in both the **Render End Time** and **Global End Time** edit boxes.

Creating the Background

In this section, you will create the background image by using the **Background** tool.

1. Choose the **BG** button from the toolbar; the **Background1** tool is inserted in the**Flow** area.

2. Press 1; the output of the **Background1** tool is displayed in the left Display View.

3. In the **Background1** tool control window, choose the **Pick** button; the **Color** dialog box is displayed. Select the white color swatch in this dialog box. Next, choose the **OK** button to close the dialog box.

4. Choose the **Fit** button from the left **Display View** toolbar to fit the image into theDisplay View.

Downloading and Importing the Images

In this section, you will download the images and import them to the composition.

1. Open the following link: *http://www.freeimages.com/photo/1282214*; an image is displayed.

2. Download the image at */Documents/Fusion_7/c05_tut/c05_tut_03/Media_Files* and save it with the name *colors.jpg*.

3. Open the *colors.jpg* in the Photoshop application and erase the white background from it and then save the file in the TGA format with the name *colors.tga*.

  Note
*Footage Courtesy: **Robert Proksa** (http://www.freeimages.com/profile/fangol)*

4. Click on the empty space in the **Flow** area and then choose the **LD** button from the toolbar; the **Open File** dialog box is displayed. In this dialog box, choose **Documents > Fusion_7 >**

c05_tut > c05_tut_03 > Media_Files > colors.tga and then choose the **Open** button; the **Loader1** tool tile is inserted in the **Flow** area.

5. Press 1; the output of the **Loader1** tool is displayed in the left Display View. Next, choose the **Fit** button from the left **Display View** toolbar to fit the image into the left Display View.

6. Select the **Loader1** tool tile from the **Flow** area. In the control window of the **Loader1** tool, choose the **Import** tab and then select the **Post-Multiply by Alpha** check box.

7. Click on the empty space in the **Flow** area and then load *notes.png* in the **Flow** area; the **Loader2** tool tile is inserted in the **Flow** area.

8. Press 2; the output of the **Loader2** tool is displayed in the right Display View.

9. Make sure the **Loader2** tool tile is selected in the **Flow** area and then the control window of the **Loader2** tool, choose the **Import** tab and then select the **Post-Multiply by Alpha** check box.

Creating the Swirl Effect on the Background Image

In this section, you will create the swirl effect by using the **Vortex** tool.

1. Select the **Loader1** tool tile from the **Flow** area. Next, choose **Tools > Transform > Resize** from the menubar; the **Resize1** tool tile is inserted in the **Flow** area and a connection between the **Loader1** and **Resize1** tools is established.

2. Select the **Loader2** tool tile from the **Flow** area. Next, choose **Tools > Transform > Resize** from the menubar; the **Resize2** tool tile is inserted in the **Flow** area and a connection between the **Loader2** and **Resize2** tools is established.

3. Select the **Resize1** tool tile from the **Flow** area. Next, choose **Tools > Warp > Vortex** from the toolbar; the **Vortex1** tool tile is inserted in the **Flow** area and a connection between the **Resize1** and **Vortex1** tools is established.

   The **Vortex** tool is used to create a swirling whirlpool effect on the specified region of an image.

4. Press 1; the output of the **Vortex1** tool is displayed in the left Display View.

5. In the **Vortex1** tool control window, animate the **Size** and **Angle** parameters to create the keyframes by using the values given next.

Frames	Size	Angle
0	10	648.5
10	7.75	696
20	4.85	735.5
30	1.29	765
40	0.19	-

6. Enter **9.7** in the **Power** edit box.

    The **Power** parameter is used to make the vortex smaller.

7. Press SPACEBAR to start the playback of the composition.

Merging the Images

In this section, you will merge the images.

1. Drag the red output node of the **Vortex1** tool tile to the red output node of the **Background1** tool tile in the **Flow** area; the **Merge1** tool tile is inserted in the **Flow** area and a connection between the **Background1**, **Vortex1**, and **Merge1** tools is established.

2. Press 2; the output of the **Merge1** tool is displayed in the right Display View.

    After entering the values, the output of the **Merge1** tool is displayed in the right Display View, as shown in Figure 5-11.

Figure 5-11 *The output of the **Merge1** tool*

3. Drag the red output node of the **Resize2** tool tile to the red output node of the **Merge1** tool tile; the **Merge2** tool tile is inserted in the **Flow** area and a connection between the **Merge1** and **Resize2** tools is established.

4. Press 2; the output of the **Merge2** tool is displayed in the right Display View.

Creating the Swirl Effect on the Notes Image

In this section, you will create the swirl effect on the notes image.

1. Select the **Resize2** tool tile from the **Flow** area and then choose **Tools > Warp > Vortex** from the toolbar; the **Vortex2** tool tile is inserted in the **Flow** area and a connection between the **Resize2**, **Merge2**, and **Vortex2** tools is established.

2. Select the **Merge2** tool tile from the **Flow** area. In the **Merge2** tool control window, animate the **Size** control to create the keyframes by using the values given next.

Frame	Size
0	65
35	1.5
36	1.08
40	1
50	0.22

3. Select the **Vortex2** tool tile from the **Flow** area. Next, animate the **Size** and **Angle** controls to create the swirling effect by using the following values:

Frame	Size	Angle
0	10	648.5
10	7.76	697
15	6.63	720.95
20	4.85	735.5
30	1.29	765
40	0.19	765

4. Enter **9.7** in the **Power** edit box of the **Vortex2** tool control window.

After entering the values, the output of the **Merge2** tool at frame 42 is displayed in the right Display View, as shown in Figure 5-12.

*Figure 5-12 The output of the **Merge2** tool at frame 42*

Color-Correcting the Composition

In this section, you will blur and color-correct the composition by using the **Blur** and **Color Corrector** tools.

1. Select the **Loader1** tool tile from the **Flow** area. Next, choose the **Blur** button from the toolbar; the **Blur1** tool tile is inserted in the **Flow** area and a connection between the **Loader1** and **Blur1** tools is established.

   The **Blur** tool is used to blur the input image.

2. Enter **20** in the **Blur Size** edit box of the **Blur1** tool control window.

3. Select the **Loader2** tool tile from the **Flow** area and choose the **Blur** button from the toolbar; the **Blur2** tool tile is inserted in the **Flow** area and a connection between the **Loader2**, **Resize2**, and **Blur2** tools is established.

4. Enter **8.4** in the **Blur Size** edit box in the **Blur2** tool control window.

5. Select the **Loader2** tool tile from the **Flow** area. Next, choose the **CC** button from the toolbar; the **ColorCorrector1** tool tile is inserted in the **Flow** area and a connection between **Loader2**, **Blur2**, and **ColorCorrector1** tools is established.

6. In the **ColorCorrector1** tool tile control window, set the values of the parameters as follows:

   Tint: **0.65**   Strength: **0.93**

7. In the control window of the **ColorCorrector1** tool, animate the **Master-RGB-Gain** control to create the keyframes by using the values given next.

Frame	Master-RGB-Gain
0	0
10	0.25
20	0.46
30	0.62
40	0.64
50	0.29

   Now, save the composition with the name *c05tut3* at the location *Documents > Fusion_7 > c05_tut > c05_tut_03*. Next, you need to render the composition. For rendering, refer to Tutorial 2 of Chapter 2. The output of the composition at frame 18 is shown in Figure 5-10. You can also view the final render of the composition by downloading the *c05_fusion_7_rndr.zip* from *http://www.cadcim.com*. The path of the file is mentioned at the beginning of the chapter.

Tutorial 4

In this tutorial, you will create a fisheye lens effect by using the **Dent** tool. The final output of the composition is shown in Figure 5-13. **(Expected time: 20 min)**

Figure 5-13 The final output of the composition

The following steps are required to complete this tutorial:

a. Set the frame format.
b. Download and import the images.
c. Create the fisheye lens effect.

Setting the Frame Format

In this section, you will specify the frame format settings.

1. Choose **File > New** from the menubar; a new composition is displayed in the Fusion screen.

2. Choose **File > Preferences** from the menubar; the **Preferences** dialog box is displayed.

3. In this dialog box, select **Frame Format** from the **Composition#** preferences tree; various frame format settings are displayed on the right in the **Preferences** dialog box. Next, select the **NTSC (Square Pixel)** option from the **Default format** drop-down list and then choose the **Save** button to save the changes made.

4. In the Time Ruler area, enter **0** in the **Global End Time** edit box.

Downloading and Importing the Image

In this section, you will download the image and import it to the composition.

1. Open the following link: *http://www.freeimages.com/photo/1012596*; an image is displayed.

2. Download the image at the location */Documents/Fusion_7/c05_tut/c05_tut_04/ Media_Files* and save it with the name *building.jpg*.

Note
*Footage Courtesy: **Joven David** (http://www.freeimages.com/profile/jovenshado)*

3. Choose the **LD** button from the toolbar; the **Open File** dialog box is displayed. In this dialog box, choose **Documents > Fusion_7 > c05_tut > c05_tut_04 > Media_Files > building.jpg** and then choose the **Open** button; the **Loader1** tool tile is inserted in the **Flow** area.

4. Press 1; the output of the **Loader1** tool is displayed in the left Display View. Next, choose the **Fit** button from the left **Display View** toolbar to fit the image into the Display View, refer to Figure 5-14.

*Figure 5-14 The output of the **Loader1** tool*

5. Select the **Loader1** tool tile from the **Flow** area. Next, choose **Tools > Transform > Resize** from the menubar; the **Resize1** tool tile is inserted in the **Flow** area and a connection between the **Loader1** and **Resize1** tools is established.

Creating the Fisheye Lens Effect

In this section, you will create the fisheye lens effect by using the **Dent** tool.

1. Click on the empty space in the **Flow** area to deselect the selected tool tile, if any. Choose the **BG** button from the toolbar; the **Background1** tool tile is inserted in the **Flow** area.

2. Select the **Loader1** tool tile from the **Flow** area and then choose the **Add an Ellipse Mask** button from the toolbar; the **Ellipse1** tool tile is inserted in the **Flow** area and a connection between the **Loader1** and **Ellipse1** tools is established.

3. In the **Ellipse1** tool control window, set the values of the parameters as follows:

Soft Edge: **0.014**
Center
X: **0.47**   Y: **0.53**

Width: **0.79**   Height: **0.67**

After entering the values, the output of the **Loader1** tool is displayed in the left Display View, as shown in Figure 5-15.

Figure 5-15 *The output of the **Loader1** tool*

4. Drag the red output node of the **Resize1** tool tile and then drag the cursor to the red output node of the **Background1** tool tile; the **Merge1** tool tile is inserted in the **Flow** area and a connection between the **Resize1, Merge1,** and **Background1** tools is established.

5. Press 2; the output of the **Merge1** tool is displayed in the right Display View. Next, choose the **Fit** button from the right **Display View** toolbar to fit the image into the right Display View.

6. In the **Merge1** tool control window, set the values of the parameters as follows:

Center
X: **0.51**   Y: **0.54**

Size: **0.87**

After entering the values, the output of the **Merge1** tool is displayed in the right Display View, as shown in Figure 5-16.

Figure 5-16 *The output of the **Merge1** tool*

7. Make sure the **Merge1** tool tile is selected in the **Flow** area and then choose **Tools > Warp > Dent** from the menubar; the **Dent1** tool tile is inserted in the **Flow** area and a connection between the **Merge1** and **Dent1** tools is established.

8. Press 2; the output of the **Dent1** tool is displayed in the right Display View.

9. In the **Dent1** tool control window, choose the **Dent 2** button and then set the parameters as follows:

    Size: **0.80**   Strength: **0.3**

    Center
    Y: **0.37**

    After entering the values, the output of the **Dent1** tool is displayed, as shown in Figure 5-17.

Figure 5-17 *The output of the **Dent1** tool*

10. Click in the empty space in the **Flow** area to deselect the selected tool tile, if any. Choose the **Mrg** button from the toolbar; the **Merge2** tool tile is inserted in the **Flow** area.

11. Drag the red output node of the **Dent1** tool tile and then drag the cursor to the orange input node of the **Merge2** tool tile; a connection between the **Dent1** and **Merge2** tools is established.

12. Press 2; the output of the **Merge2** tool is displayed in the right Display View.

13. Drag the white output node of the **Resize1** tool tile and then drag the cursor to the green input node of the **Merge2** tool tile; a connection between the **Resize1** and **Merge2** tools is established.

Next, you will create the reflection of the city image.

14. Click on the empty space in the **Flow** area to deselect the selected tool tile, if any. Choose the **Xf** button from the toolbar; the **Transform1** tool tile is inserted in the **Flow** area.

15. Press and hold SHIFT. Next, drag and drop the **Transform1** tool tile on the pipe connecting the **Resize1** and **Merge2** tools; the **Transform1** tool tile is inserted between the **Resize1** and **Merge2** tools.

16. In the **Transform1** tool control window, select the **Flip Vertically** check box. Also, set the values of the parameters as follows:

Center
X: **0.53**   Y: **-0.32**

Size: **0.91**

17. In the **Merge2** tool control window, enter **0.4** in the **Blend** edit box.

After entering the values, the output of the **Merge2** tool is displayed in the right Display View, as shown in Figure 5-18.

Figure 5-18 *The output of the **Merge2** tool*

18. Make sure the **Merge2** tool tile is selected in the **Flow** area. Next, choose **Tools > Blur > SoftGlow** from the menubar; the **SoftGlow1** tool tile is inserted and a connection between the **Merge2** tool and **SoftGlow1** tools is established, refer to Figure 5-19.

The **SoftGlow** tool is used to simulate natural and soft glow effects in an image.

19. Press 2; the output of the **SoftGlow1** tool is displayed in the right Display View.

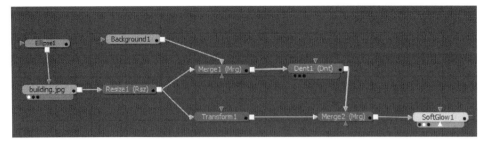

Figure 5-19 *The network of tools in the* **Flow** *area*

20. In the **SoftGlow1** tool control window, set the values of the parameters as follows:

Threshold: **0.052**   Gain: **0.5**

The **Threshold** parameter is used to control the effect of the glow and the **Gain** parameter is used to control the brightness of the glow.

Now, save the composition with the name *c05tut4* at the location *Documents > Fusion_7 > c05_tut > c05_tut_04*. Next, you need to render the composition. For rendering, refer to Tutorial 1 of Chapter 2. The output of the composition is shown in Figure 5-13. You can also view the final render of the composition by downloading the *c05_fusion_7_rndr.zip* from *http://www.cadcim.com*. The path of the file is mentioned at the beginning of the chapter.

Tutorial 5

In this tutorial, you will create the effect of moving water by using the **Displace** and **FastNoise** tools. The final output of the composition is shown in Figure 5-20.   **(Expected time: 25 min)**

The following steps are required to complete this tutorial:

a. Set the frame format.
b. Download and import the image.
c. Create a noise pattern.
d. Create a moving water effect.

Figure 5-20 *The final output of the composition*

Setting the Frame Format

In this section, you will specify the frame format settings.

1. Choose **File > New** from the menubar; a new composition is displayed in the Fusion screen.

2. Choose **File > Preferences** from the menubar; the **Preferences** dialog box is displayed.

3. In this dialog box, select **Frame Format** from the **Composition#** preferences tree; various frame format settings are displayed on the right in the **Preferences** dialog box. Next, select the **NTSC (Square Pixel)** option from the **Default format** drop-down list and then choose the **Save** button to save the changes made.

4. In the Time Ruler area, enter **100** in both the **Render End Time** and **Global End Time** edit boxes.

Downloading and Importing the Image

In this section, you will download the image and import it to the composition.

1. Open the following link: *http://www.freeimages.com/photo/1308135*; an image is displayed.

2. Download the image at the location */Documents/Fusion_7/c05_tut/c05_tut_05/ Media_Files* and save it with the name *bridge.jpg*.

Note
*Footage Courtesy: **Zedart** (http://www.freeimages.com/profile/zedart)*

3. Choose the **LD** button from the toolbar; the **Open File** dialog box is displayed. In this dialog box, choose **Documents > Fusion_7 > c05_tut > c05_tut_05 > Media_Files > bridge.jpg** and then choose the **Open** button; the **Loader1** tool tile is inserted in the **Flow** area.

4. Press 1; the output of the **Loader1** tool is displayed in the left Display View. Next, choose the **Fit** button from the left **Display View** toolbar to fit the image into the left Display View, refer to Figure 5-21.

Creating the Noise Pattern

In this section, you will create a noise pattern by using the **FastNoise** tool that will be used to displace the water in the scene.

1. Select the **Loader1** tool tile from the **Flow** area. Next, choose **Tools > Transform > Resize** from the menubar; the **Resize1** tool tile is inserted in the **Flow** area.

2. Click on the empty space on the **Flow** area to deselect the selected tool tile, if any. Choose **Tools > Creator > FastNoise** from the menubar; the **FastNoise1** tool tile is inserted in the **Flow** area.

Figure 5-21 *The output of the* ***Loader1*** *tool*

3. Press 2; the output of the **FastNoise1** tool is displayed in the right Display View. Next, choose the **Fit** button from the right **Display View** toolbar to fit the image into the right Display View.

4. In the control window of the **FastNoise1** tool, animate **Center X** and **Center Y** controls to create keyframes by using the values given next.

Frame	Center X	Center Y
20	0.58	0.5
40	0.6	0.5
60	0.69	0.5
80	0.78	0.5
100	0.87	0.5

5. In the **FastNoise1** tool control window, set the values of the parameters as follows:

Noise tab
Scale: **20**   Seethe Rate: **0.2**

Image tab
Width: **720**   Height: **540**

6. Choose the **Show Checker Overlay** button from the right **Display View** toolbar to disable the transparency in the Display View. The output of the **FastNoise1** tool is shown in Figure 5-22.

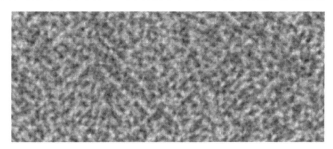

*Figure 5-22 The output of the **FastNoise1** tool*

Creating the Moving Water Effect

In this section, you will create the effect of moving water by using the **Displace** tool.

1. Select the **Resize1** tool tile from the **Flow** area. Next, choose **Tools > Warp > Displace** from the menubar; the **Displace1** tool tile is inserted in the **Flow** area and a connection between the **Resize1** and **Displace1** tools is established.

    The **Displace** tool is used to displace/refract an image based on the displacement map.

2. Press 1; the output of the **Displace1** tool is displayed in the left Display View.

3. Drag the red output node of the **FastNoise1** tool tile to the green node of the **Displace1** tool tile in the **Flow** area.

4. Select the **Displace1** tool tile from the **Flow** area. Then, choose the **Add a Polyline Mask** button from the left **Display View** toolbar; the **Polygon1** tool tile is inserted in the **Flow** area and a connection between the **Displace1** and **Polygon1** tools is established, as shown in Figure 5-23.

5. Draw the polyline shape in the left Display View, as shown in Figure 5-24.

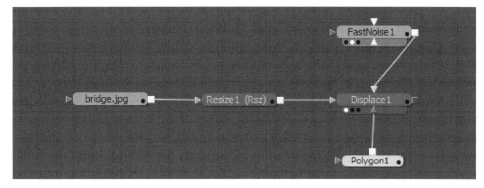

*Figure 5-23 The **Polygon1** tool connected to the **Displace1** tool*

Figure 5-24 *The polyline shape created in the Display View*

6. Select **Displace1** tool tile in the **Flow** area and enter **0.025** in the **Refraction Strength** edit box of the **Displace1** tool control window.

Higher the value of the **Refraction Strength** parameter, greater will be the displacement effect.

The final output of the composition is shown in Figure 5-25.

Figure 5-25 *The final output of the composition*

Now, save the composition with the name *c05tut5* at the location *Documents > Fusion_7 > c05_tut > c05_tut_05*. Next, you need to render the composition. For rendering, refer to Tutorial 2 of Chapter 2. The output of the composition is shown in Figure 5-25. You can also view the final render of the composition by downloading the *c05_fusion_7_rndr.zip* from *http://www.cadcim.com*. The path of the file is mentioned at the beginning of the chapter.

Tutorial 6

In this tutorial, you will create lens distortion effect in an image by using the **Lens Distort** tool. The final output of the composition is shown in Figure 5-26.   **(Expected time: 25 min)**

The following steps are required to complete this tutorial:

a. Set the frame format.
b. Download and import the image.
c. Create a distort effect.

Figure 5-26 The final output of the composition

Setting the Frame Format
In this section, you will specify the frame format settings.

1. Choose **File > New** from the menubar; a new composition is displayed in the Fusion screen.

2. Choose **File > Preferences** from the menubar; the **Preferences** dialog box is displayed.

3. In this dialog box, select **Frame Format** from the **Composition#** preferences tree; various frame format settings are displayed on the right of the **Preferences** dialog box. Next, select the **HDTV 720** option from the **Default format** drop-down list and then choose the **Save** button to save the changes made.

4. In the Time Ruler area, enter **0** in the **Global End Time** edit box.

Downloading and Importing the Image
In this section, you will download the image and import it to the composition.

1. Open the following link: *http://www.freeimages.com/photo/880191*; an image is displayed.

2. Download the image at the location */Documents/Fusion_7/c05_tut/c05_tut_06/Media_Files* and save it with the name *scene.jpg*.

 Note
*Footage Courtesy: **Ayla87** (http://www.freeimages.com/gallery/Ayla87)*

3. Choose the **LD** button from the toolbar; the **Open File** dialog box is displayed. In this dialog box, choose **Documents > Fusion_7 > c05_tut > c05_tut_06 > Media_Files > scene.jpg** and then choose the **Open** button; the **Loader1** tool tile is inserted in the **Flow** area.

4. Press 1; the output of the **Loader1** tool is displayed in the left Display View. Next, choose the **Fit** button from the left **Display View** toolbar to fit the image into the left Display View, refer to Figure 5-27.

Figure 5-27 *The output of the **Loader1** tool*

Creating a Distort Effect

In this section, you will create a distort effect by using the **Lens Distort** tool.

1. Select the **Loader1** tool tile in the **Flow** area and choose **Tools > Warp > Lens Distort** from the menubar; the **LensDistort1** tool tile is inserted in the **Flow** area and a connection between the **Loader1** and **LensDistort** tools is established.

   The **LensDistort** tool is used to remove or add lens distortion to an image.

2. Press 2; the output of the **LensDistort1** tool is displayed in the right Display View. Next, choose the **Fit** button from the right **Display View** toolbar to fit the image into the right Display View.

3. In the **LensDistort1** tool control window, choose the **Distort** button from the **Mode** area to distort the image.

   The **Distort** option is used to add original lens distortion to the input image.

4. Expand the **Camera Settings** area in the **LensDistort1** tool control window and set the values of the parameters as follows:

   Aperture Width (in): **1.87**   Aperture Height (in): **1.46**

   The **Aperture Width (in)** option is used to specify the width of lens. Similarly, the **Aperture Height (in)** option is used to specify the height of lens.

5. Expand the **Lens Distortion Model** area in the **LensDistort1** tool control window and set the values of the parameters as follows:

   Model: **3DE 4 Radial - Fisheye, Degree 8**

   Distortion Degree 2: **-0.38**   Quartic Distortion Degree 4: **0.088**

The options in the **Model** drop-down list are used to select appropriate 3D equalizer lens distortion model. The **Distortion** degree option is used to increase or decrease the distortion effect of an input image. The **Quartic Distortion Degree** option is used to distort the corners of an image.

6. Expand the **Sampling Options** area in the **LensDistort1** tool control window and choose the **4x4** button from the **Supersampling [HiQ]** area.

The buttons in the **Sampling Option** area are used to set the number of samples used to determine each destination pixel.

7. Choose the **Common Controls** tab from the **LensDistort1** tool control window and enter **0.8** in the **Blend** edit box.

Now, save the composition with the name *c05tut6* at the location *Documents > Fusion_7 > c05_tut > c05_tut_06*. Next, you need to render the composition. For rendering, refer to Tutorial 1 of Chapter 2. The output of the composition is shown in Figure 5-28. You can also view the final render of the composition by downloading the *c05_fusion_7_rndr.zip* from *http://www.cadcim.com*. The path of the file is mentioned at the beginning of the chapter.

Figure 5-28 The final output of the composition

Tutorial 7

In this tutorial, you will create the 3d effect on 2D image of a T-shirt by using the **Displace** tool. The final output of the composition is shown in Figure 5-29.   **(Expected time: 30 min)**

The following steps are required to complete this tutorial:

a. Set the frame format.
b. Import the image.
c. Merge the images.
d. Resize the images.
e. Color-correct the image.

Figure 5-29 *The final output of the composition*

Setting the Frame Format

In this section, you will specify the frame format settings.

1. Choose **File > New** from the menubar; a new composition is displayed in the Fusion screen.

2. Choose **File > Preferences** from the menubar; the **Preferences** dialog box is displayed.

3. In this dialog box, select **Frame Format** from the **Composition#** preferences tree; various frame format settings are displayed on the right in the **Preferences** dialog box. Next, select the **NTSC (Square Pixel)** option from the **Default format** drop-down list and then choose the **Save** button to save the changes made.

4. In the Time Ruler area, enter **0** in the **Global End Time** edit boxes.

Importing the Image

In this section, you will download the image and import it to the composition.

1. Choose the **LD** button from the toolbar; the **Open File** dialog box is displayed. In this dialog box, choose **Documents > Fusion_7 > c05_tut > c05_tut_07 > Media_Files > t_shirt** and then choose the **Open** button; the **Loader1** tool tile is inserted in the **Flow** area.

2. Press 1; the output of the **Loader1** tool is displayed in the left Display View. Next, choose the **Fit** button from the left **Display View** toolbar to fit the image into the left Display View, refer to Figure 5-30.

3. Click on the empty space in the **Flow** area and then choose the **LD** button from the toolbar; the **Open File** dialog box is displayed. In this dialog box, choose **Documents > Fusion_7 > c05_tut > c05_tut_07 > Media_Files > dog** and then choose the **Open** button; the **Loader2** tool tile is inserted in the **Flow** area.

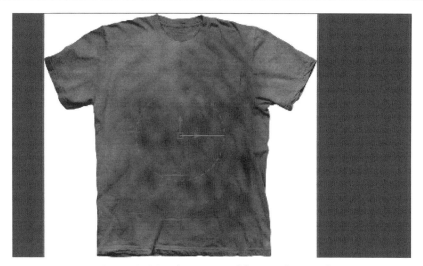

Figure 5-30 *The output of the **Loader1** tool*

4. Press 2; the output of the **Loader2** tool is displayed in the right Display View. Next, choose the **Fit** button from the left **Display View** toolbar to fit the image into the left Display View, refer to Figure 5-31.

Figure 5-31 *The output of the **FastNoise1** tool*

Merging the images

In this section, you will merge the images.

1. Click on the empty space in the **Flow** area and then choose the **Mrg** button from the toolbar; the **Merge1** tool tile is inserted in the **Flow** area.

2. Drag the red output node of the **Loader1** tool tile to the orange background node of the **Merge1** tool tile. Next, drag the red output node of the **Loader2** tool to the green foreground node of the **Merge1** tool. Press 2; the output of the **Merge1** tool is displayed in the right Display View, as shown in Figure 5-32.

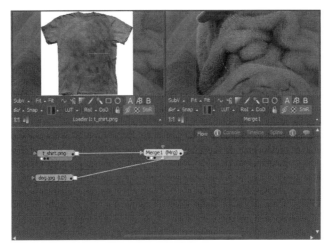

Figure 5-32 The output of the Merge1 tool

3. In the **Merge1** tool control window, enter **0.281**, **0.814**, and **0.3666** in the **Size**, **Alpha Gain**, and **Burn In** edit boxes. Enter **0.39** and **0.45** in the **X** and **Y** edit boxes in the **Center** area.

4. Select the **Loader2** tool tile in the **Flow** area and choose the **Add a Polyline Mask** button from the left Display view toolbar; the **Polygon1** tool tile is inserted in the **Flow** area and a connection between **Loader2** and **Polygon1** tool is established, as shown in Figure 5-33.

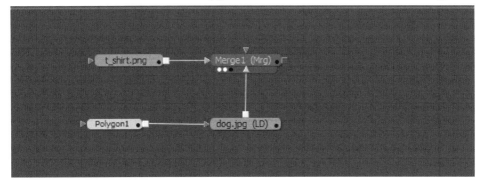

*Figure 5-33 The **Polygon1** tool connected to the **Loader1** tool*

5. Select the **Invert** check box in the **Polygon1** tool control window. Next, draw the polyline shape in the right Display View. Now, clear the **Invert** check box in the **Polygon1** tool control window; the image is displayed in the shape area, as shown in Figure 5-34

6. In the **Polygon1** tool control window, enter the **0.019** in the **Soft Edge** edit box.

Resizing the images

In this section, you will resize the images.

1. Select the **Loader2** tool tile in the **Flow** area, choose the **Rsz** button from the toolbar; a **Resize1** tool tile is inserted in the **Flow** area and a connection between the **Resize1** and **Merge1** tools is established.

Figure 5-34 *The output of the **Polygon1** tool*

2. Press 2; the output of the **Resize1** tool is displayed in the right Display View.

3. Make sure the **Resize1** tool tile is selected in the **Flow** area. Next, set the values for the following parameters.

    Width: **2263**   Height: **1815**

    After entering the values, the output of the **Resize1** tool is displayed, as shown in Figure 5-35.

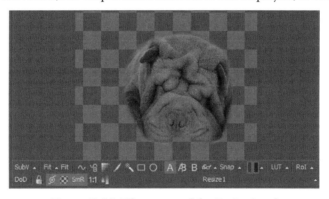

Figure 5-35 *The output of the **Resize1** tool*

4. Select the **Merge1** tool tile in the **Flow** area. Choose **Tools > Warp > Displace** from the menu bar; the **Displace1** tool tile is inserted in the **Flow** area.

5. Press 2; the output of the **Displace1** tool is displayed in the right Display View.

6. Make sure the **Displace1** tool tile is selected in the **Flow** area and then set the following parameters in the **Displace1** tool control window.

    Offset: **0.0619**   Refraction Strength: **0.4**   Loight Power: **1.657**
    Spread: **1.557**

    After entering the values, the output of the **Displace1** tool is displayed, as shown in Figure 5-36.

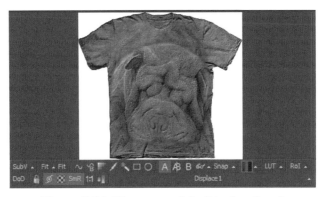

*Figure 5-36 The output of the **Displace1** tool*

Color-Correcting the image

In this section, you will apply the color-correction tool.

1. Make sure the **Displace1** tool tile is selected in the **Flow** area and then choose the **CC** button
    from the toolbar; the **ColorCorrector1** tool tile is inserted in the **Flow** area and a connection
    between the **Displace1** and **ColorCorrector1** tools is established.

2. Press 1; the output of the **ColorCorrector1** tool is displayed in the left Display View.

3. In the **ColorCorrector1** tool control window, set the values of the parameters as follows:

    Hue: **-0.657**   Saturation: **0.9809**

    Tint: **-0.25**   Highlights-Hue:**-0.657**   Master-RGB-Gain: **0.77**

The final output of the composition is shown in Figure 5-37.

Figure 5-37 The final output of the composition

Now, save the composition with the name *c05tut7* at the location *Documents > Fusion_7 >
c05_tut > c05_tut_07*. Next, you need to render the composition. For rendering, refer to
Tutorial 1 of Chapter 2. The output of the composition is shown in Figure 5-37. You can also
view the final render of the composition by downloading the *c05_fusion_7_rndr.zip* file from
http://www.cadcim.com. The path of the file is mentioned at the beginning of the chapter.

Self-Evaluation Test

Answer the following questions and then compare them to those given at the end of this chapter:

1. Which of the following tools is used to create a swirling effect?

    (a) **Vector Distortion**   (b) **Vortex**
    (c) **Displace**   (d) **Dent**

2. Which of the following tools does not belong to the **Warp** category?

    (a) **Corner Positioner**   (b) **DVE**
    (c) **Vortex**   (d) None of these

3. The _____ tool is used to interactively position the corners of an image.

4. The _____ tools are used to distort an image.

5. The **Corner Positioner** tool is used to distort an image along the x and y axes based on the alpha channel.(T/F)

Review Questions

Answer the following questions:

1. The _____ tool is used to distort an image into a circular pattern.

2. The _____ tool is used to blur an image.

3. The _____ button in the **Display View** toolbar is used to insert the **Rectangle** tool in the **Flow** area.

4. The **Add an Ellipse Mask** button is available only in the **Display View** toolbar. (T/F)

Answers to Self-Evaluation Test
1. b, **2.** b, **3. Corner Positioner**, **4. Warp**, **5.** F

Chapter 6

Mask Tools

Learning Objectives

After completing this chapter, you will be able to:

• *Create a composition using the Mask tools*
• *Convert a day scene into a night scene*
• *Create a mask using brush strokes*

INTRODUCTION

The Mask tools are used to restrict the effect of any tool on specific areas of an image. These tools are used to create animatable shapes, both primitive and complex polygon shapes. You can also use another image in the composition to create a mask.

When you apply a mask to an image, the output of the tool is calculated over the entire image and then mask is used to filter the final result. However, on some tools such as **DVE**, **Glow**, and **Highlight** the mask is applied before the result. This type of masking is known as pre-masking.

In this chapter, you will use different Mask tools to create different types of effects using them.

TUTORIALS

The compositions created in this chapter can be downloaded from *http://www.cadcim.com*. These compositions are contained in the *c06_fusion_7_tut.zip* file. The path of the file is as follows:

> *Textbooks > Animation and Visual Effects > Fusion > Blackmagic Design Fusion 7 Studio: A Tutorial Approach*

Next, you need to extract the contents of the downloaded zip file to *\Documents\Fusion_7*.

Tutorial 1

In this tutorial, you will convert a day scene into a night scene by using the Mask tools. The final output of the composition is shown in Figure 6-1.   **(Expected time: 45 min)**

Figure 6-1 *The final output of the composition*

The following steps are required to complete this tutorial:

a. Set the frame format.
b. Download and import the image.
c. Color-correct the image.
d. Create the street light.

e.   Group the tools.
f.   Add more lights.
g.   Create hotspot on the ground.
h.   Add canopy lights.

Setting the Frame Format

In this section, you will specify the frame format settings.

1.   Choose **File > New** from the menubar; a new composition is opened in the Fusion screen.

2.   Choose **File > Preferences** from the menubar; the **Preferences** dialog box is displayed.

3.   In this dialog box, select **Frame Format** from the **Composition#** preferences tree; various frame format settings are displayed on the right in the **Preferences** dialog box. Next, select the **NTSC (Square Pixel)** option from the **Default format** drop-down list and then choose the **Save** button to save the changes made.

4.   In the Time Ruler area, enter **0** in the **Global End Time** edit box.

Downloading and Importing the Image

In this section, you will download and import the image of a day scene that will be converted to a night scene.

1.   Open the following link: *http://www.freeimages.com/photo/1342702;* an image is displayed.

2.   Download the image at the location */Documents/Fusion_7/c06_tut/c06_tut_01/Media_Files* and save it with the name *day.jpg*.

   Note
*Footage Courtesy: **Alexander King** (http://www.freeimages.com/profile/ajkTreno)*

3.   Choose the **LD** button from the toolbar; the **Open File** dialog box is displayed. In this dialog box, choose **Documents > Fusion_7 > c06_tut > c06_tut_01 > Media_Files > day.jpg** and then choose the **Open** button; the **Loader1** tool tile is inserted in the **Flow** area.

4.   Press 1; the output of the **Loader1** tool is displayed in the left Display View. Choose the **Fit** button from the left **Display View** toolbar to fit the image into the left Display View, as shown in Figure 6-2.

5.   Select the **Loader1** tool tile from the **Flow** area and then choose the **Rsz** buttonfrom the toolbar; the **Resize1** tool tile is inserted in the **Flow** area and a connection between the **Resize1** and **Loader1** tools is established.

Figure 6-2 *The output of the* **Loader1** *tool*

Color-Correcting the Image

In this section, you will darken the image by using the **Color Corrector** tool.

1. Select the **Resize1** tool tile from the **Flow** area. Choose the **CC** button from the toolbar; the **ColorCorrector1** tool tile is inserted in the **Flow** area and a connection between the **ColorCorrector1** and **Resize1** tools is established.

2. Press 2; the output of the **ColorCorrector1** tool is displayed in the right Display View. Next, choose the **Fit** button from the right **Display View** toolbar to fit the image into the Display View.

3. In the **ColorCorrector1** tool control window, set the parameters as follows:

    Master-RGB-Contrast: **0.95**   Master-RGB-Gain: **0.38**

    After entering the values, the output of the **ColorCorrector1** tool is displayed, as shown in Figure 6-3.

Creating the Street Light

In this section, you will create the street light.

1. Click on the empty space in the **Flow** area to deselect the selected tool tile, if any. Choose the **BG** button from the toolbar; the **Background1** tool tile is inserted in the **Flow** area.

2. Make sure the **Background1** tool tile is selected in the **Flow** area. By default, the **Color** tab is chosen in the **Background1** tool control window. Choose the **Pick** button from the control window; the **Color** dialog box is displayed. Select the white color swatch in this dialog box and then choose the **OK** button to close the dialog box.

Figure 6-3 *The output of the **ColorCorrector1** tool*

3. Press 1; the output of the **Background1** tool is displayed in the left Display View.

4. Make sure the **Background1** tool tile is selected in the **Flow** area. Next, choose the **Add an Ellipse Mask** button from the toolbar; the **Ellipse1** tool tile is inserted in the **Flow** area and a connection between the **Background1** and **Ellipse1** tools is established.

5. In the **Ellipse1** tool control window, enter the values of the parameters as follows:

Soft Edge: **0.05**   Width: **0.22**   Height: **0.22**

After entering the values, the output of the **Background1** tool is displayed, as shown in Figure 6-4.

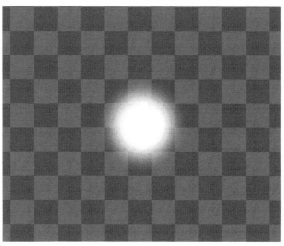

Figure 6-4 *The output of the **Background1** tool*

6. Drag the red output node of the **Background1** tool tile to the red output node of the

ColorCorrector1 tool tile in the **Flow** area; the **Merge1** tool tile is inserted in the **Flow** area and a connection between the **Merge1**, **Background1**, and **ColorCorrector1** tools is established.

7. Press 2; the output of the **Merge1** tool is displayed in the right Display View.

8. In the **Merge1** tool control window, enter the values of the parameters as follows:

   Center
   X: **0.847**   Y: **0.8512**

   Size: **0.29**

   After entering the values, the output of the **Merge1** tool is displayed, as shown in Figure 6-5.

Figure 6-5   *The output of the **Merge1** tool*

9. Select the **Background1** tool tile from the **Flow** area. Next, choose **Tools > Blur > Blur** from the menubar; the **Blur1** tool tile is inserted in the **Flow** area and a connection between the **Background1** and **Blur1** tools is established.

10. In the **Blur1** tool control window, enter **13.6** in the **Blur Size** edit box.

    Next, you will add soft glow to the light.

11. Make sure the **Blur1** tool tile is selected in the **Flow** area and then choose **Tools > Blur > Soft Glow** from the menubar; the **SoftGlow1** tool tile is inserted in the **Flow** area.

12. In the **SoftGlow1** tool control window, enter the values of the parameters as follows:

    Threshold: **0.52**   Gain: **2.3**   Blend: **0.88**

Grouping the Tools
In this section, you will group the tools to manage the tools network better.

1. Drag a marquee selection around the **Ellipse1**, **Background1**, **Blur1**, and **SoftGlow1** tools to select them.

2. Press CTRL+G; the **Group1** tile is created in the **Flow** area in place of the selected tools.

3. Press F2; the **Rename Tool** dialog box is displayed. Rename the group as **Light1** and choose the **OK** button; refer to Figure 6-6.

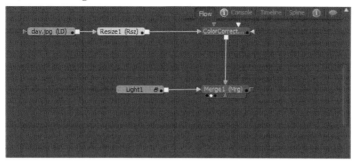

Figure 6-6   *The **Light1** group in the **Flow** area*

Adding More Lights

In this section, you will add more lights in the background using the **Background** tool.

1. Click on the empty space in the **Flow** area to deselect the selected tool tile, if any. Next, choose the **BG** button from the toolbar; the **Background2** tool tile is inserted in the **Flow** area.

2. Select the **Background2** tool tile from the **Flow** area. In the **Background2** tool control window, choose the **Pick** button; the **Color** dialog box is displayed. Select the white color swatch in this dialog box and then choose the **OK** button.

3. Press 1; the output of the **Background2** tool is displayed in the left Display View.

4. Drag the red output node of the **Background2** tool tile to the red output node of the **Merge1** tool tile; the **Merge2** tool tile is inserted in the **Flow** area and a connection between the **Background2**, **Merge1**, and **Merge2** tools is established. Press 2; the output of the **Merge2** tool is displayed in the right Display View.

5. Select the **Background2** tool tile from the **Flow** area. Choose the **Add an Ellipse** **Mask** button from the toolbar; the **Ellipse2** tool tile is inserted in the **Flow** area and a connection between the **Background2** and **Ellipse2** tools is established.

6. In the **Ellipse2** tool control window, enter the values of the parameters as follows:

    Soft Edge: **0.005**   Width: **0.15**   Height: **0.15**

7. In the **Merge2** tool control window, set the parameters as follows:

    Center
    X: **0.76**   Y: **0.57**

    Size: **0.05**

8. Select the **Background2** tool tile in the **Flow** area. Choose **Tools > Blur > Blur** from the menubar; the **Blur2** tool tile is inserted in the **Flow** area and a connection between the **Background2** and **Blur2** tools is established.

9. In the **Blur2** tool control window, enter **61.8** in the **Blur Size** edit box.

10. Choose **Tools > Blur > Soft Glow** from the menubar; the **SoftGlow2** tool is inserted in the **Flow** area and a connection between the **Blur2** and **SoftGlow2** tools is established.

11. In the **SoftGlow2** tool control window, enter the values of the parameters as follows:

Threshold: **0.71**   Gain: **2.64**   Glow Size: **89.0**

After entering the value, the output of the **Merge2** tool is displayed in the right Display View, as shown in Figure 6-7.

Figure 6-7   *The output of the **Merge2** tool*

12. Select the **Ellipse2**, **Background2**, **Blur2**, and **SoftGlow2** tool tiles from the **Flow** area and group them. Rename the group as **Light2**, as discussed earlier.

13. Click on the empty space in the **Flow** area to deselect any selected tool. Next, choose the **BG** button from the toolbar; the **Background3** tool tile is inserted in the **Flow** area.

14. Make sure the **Background3** tool tile is selected in the **Flow** area. In the control window, choose the **Pick** button; the **Color** dialog box is displayed. Select the white color swatch in this dialog box and then choose the **OK** button to close the dialog box.

15. Press 1; the output of the **Background3** tool is displayed in the left Display View.

16. Choose the **Add an Ellipse Mask** button from the toolbar; the **Ellipse3** tool tile is inserted in the **Flow** area and a connection between the **Background3** and **Ellipse3** tools is established.

17. Drag the red output node of the **Background3** tool tile to the red output node of the **Merge2** tool tile; the **Merge3** tool tile is inserted in the **Flow** area and a connection between the **Background3**, **Merge2**, and **Merge3** tools is established.

18. Press 2; the output of the **Merge3** tool is displayed in the right Display View.

19. In the **Ellipse3** tool control window, enter the values of the parameters as follows:

    Soft Edge: **0.007**   Width: **0.15**   Height: **0.15**

20. Select the **Background3** tool tile from the **Flow** area. Choose **Tools > Blur > Blur** from the menubar; the **Blur3** tool tile is inserted in the **Flow** area and a connection between the **Background3** and **Blur3** tools is established.

21. In the **Blur3** tool control window, enter **61.8** in the **Blur Size** edit box.

22. Choose **Tools > Blur > Soft Glow** from the menubar; the **SoftGlow3** tool is inserted in the **Flow** area and a connection between the **Blur3** and **SoftGlow3** tools is established.

23. In the **SoftGlow3** tool control window, enter the values of the parameters as follows:

    Threshold: **0.2**   Gain: **0.55**

24. In the **Merge3** tool control window, enter the values of the parameters as follows:

    Center:
    X: **0.71**   Y: **0.56**

    Size: **0.031**

    Press 2; the output of the **Merge3** tool is displayed in the right Display View.

25. Select the **Ellipse3**, **Background3**, **Blur3**, and **SoftGlow3** tool tiles from the **Flow** area and create a group with the name **Light3**.

26. Click on the empty space in the **Flow** area to deselect the selected tool tile, if any. Choose the **BG** button from the toolbar; the **Background4** tool tile is inserted in the **Flow** area.

27. In the **Background4** tool control window, choose the **Pick** button; the **Color** dialog box is displayed. Select the white color swatch in this dialog box and then choose the **OK** button to close the dialog box.

28. Press 1; the output of the **Background4** tool is displayed in the left Display View.

29. Choose the **Add an Ellipse Mask** button from the left **Display View** toolbar; the **Ellipse4** tool tile is inserted in the **Flow** area and a connection between the **Background4** and **Ellipse4** tools is established.

30. In the **Ellipse4** tool control window, enter the values of the parameters as follows:

    Soft Edge: **0.005**   Width: **0.15**   Height: **0.16**

31. Drag the red output node of the **Background4** tool tile to the red output node of the **Merge3** tool tile; the **Merge4** tool tile is inserted in the **Flow** area and a connection between the **Background4**, **Merge3**, and **Merge4** tools is established.

32. Press 2; the output of the **Merge4** tool is displayed in the right Display View.

33. In the **Merge4** tool control window, enter the values of the parameters as follows:

    Center
    X: **0.67**   Y: **0.55**

    Size: **0.021**

34. Select the **Background4** tool tile from the **Flow** area. Choose **Tools > Blur > Blur** from the menubar; the **Blur4** tool tile is inserted in the **Flow** area and a connection between the **Background4**, **Blur4**, and **Merge4** tools is established.

35. In the **Blur4** tool control window, enter **98** in the **Blur Size** edit box.

36. Select the **Blur4** tool tile from the **Flow** area and then choose **Tools > Blur > Soft Glow** from the menubar; the **SoftGlow4** tool tile is inserted in the **Flow** area and a connection between the **Blur4** and **SoftGlow4** tools is established.

37. In the **SoftGlow4** tool control window, enter the values of the parameters as follows:

    Threshold: **0.71**   Gain: **2.86**   Glow Size: **36.65**

    After entering the values, the output of the **Merge4** tool is displayed, as shown in Figure 6-8.

Figure 6-8 *The output of the **Merge4** tool*

38. Select the **Ellipse4**, **Background4**, **Blur4**, and **SoftGlow4** tool tiles from the **Flow** area and create a group with the name **Light4**.

Creating Hotspot on the Ground

In this section, you will create a hotspot on the ground.

1. Click on the empty space in the **Flow** area to deselect the selected tool tile, if any. Next, choose the **BG** button from the toolbar; the **Background5** tool tile is inserted in the **Flow** area.

2. Select the **Background5** tool tile from the **Flow** area. Choose the **Pick** button from the control window; the **Color** dialog box is displayed. Select the white color swatch in this dialog box and then choose the **OK** button to close the dialog box.

3. Press 1; the output of the **Background5** tool is displayed in the left Display View.

4. Drag the red output of the **Background5** tool tile to the red output node of the **Merge4** tool tile; the **Merge5** tool tile is inserted in the **Flow** area and a connection between the **Merge5** and **Background5** tools is established. Next, press 2; the output of the **Merge5** tool is displayed in the right Display View.

5. Select the **Background5** tool tile from the **Flow** area. Next, choose the **Add an Ellipse Mask** button from the toolbar; the **Ellipse5** tool tile is inserted in the **Flow** area and a connection between the **Background5** and **Ellipse5** tools is established.

6. In the **Ellipse5** tool control window, enter the values of the parameters as follows:

   Soft Edge: **0.16**   Width: **0.23**   Height: **0.32**

   Center
   X: **0.4**   Y: **0.5**

7. In the **Merge5** tool control window, enter the values of the parameters as follows:

   Center
   X: **0.81**   Y: **0.4**

8. Select the **Background5** tool tile from the **Flow** area. Next, choose **Tools > Transform > DVE** from the menubar; the **DVE1** tool tile is inserted in the **Flow** area and a connection between the **DVE1** and **Background5** tools is established.

9. In the **DVE1** tool control window, enter the values of the parameters as follows:

   Center
   X: **0.63**   Y: **0.35**

   Z Move: **1.31**   X Rotation: **-80**

10. Select the **DVE1** tool tile from the **Flow** area. Next, choose **Tools > Blur > Blur** from the menubar; the **Blur5** tool tile is inserted in the **Flow** area and a connection between the **DVE1** and **Blur5** tools is established.

11. In the **Blur5** tool control window, enter the values of the parameters as follows:

    Blur Size: **100**   Blend: **0.63**

12. Select the **Merge5** tool tile in the **Flow** area and then choose **Add a Polyline Mask**
    button from the **Display View** toolbar; the **Polygon1** tool tile is inserted in the **Flow**
    area and a connection is established between the **Merge5** and **Polygon1** tools.

13. Draw a polyline shape in the right Display View, as shown in Figure 6-9.

Figure 6-9 The polyline shape drawn in the right Display View

14. In the **Polygon1** tool control window, select the **Invert** check box and then enter **0.004** in
    the **Soft Edge** edit box.

    After entering the values, the output of the **Merge5** tool is displayed, as shown in Figure 6-10.

*Figure 6-10 The output of the **Merge5** tool*

15. Select the **Ellipse5**, **Background5**, **Blur5**, **DVE1**, and **Polygon1** tools from the **Flow** area
    and create a group with the name **Light5**.

Adding a Canopy Light

In this section, you will add a canopy light in the scene.

1. Click on the empty space in the **Flow** area to deselect the selected tool tile, if any. Next, choose the **BG** button from the toolbar; the **Background6** tool tile is inserted in the **Flow** area.

2. Select the **Background6** tool tile from the **Flow** area. Next, choose the **Pick** button from the control window; the **Color** dialog box is displayed. Select the white color swatch in this dialog box and then choose the **OK** button to close the dialog box.

3. Press 1; the output of the **Background6** tool is displayed in the left Display View.

4. Drag the red output of the **Background6** tool tile to the red output node of the **Merge5** tool tile; the **Merge6** tool tile is inserted in the **Flow** area and a connection between the **Background6**, **Merge5**, and **Merge6** tools is established.

5. Press 2; the output of the **Merge6** tool is displayed in the right Display View.

6. Select the **Background6** tool tile in the **Flow** area and then choose the **Add an Ellipse Mask** button from the toolbar; the **Ellipse6** tool tile is inserted in the **Flow** area and a connection between the **Background6** and **Ellipse6** tools is established.

7. In the **Ellipse6** tool control window, enter **0.16** in the **Soft Edge** edit box.

8. Select the **Background6** tool tile from the **Flow** area. Next, choose **Tools > Transform > DVE** from the menubar; the **DVE2** tool tile is inserted in the **Flow** area and a connection between the **DVE2** and **Background6** tools is established.

9. In the **DVE2** tool control window, enter the values of the parameters as follows:

    Center
    X: **0.56**   Y: **0.73**

    Z Move: **4.66**   Z Pivot: **0.16**   X Rotation: **-93.33**

10. In the **Merge6** tool control window, enter the values of the parameters as follows:

    Center
    X: **0.68**   Y: **0.54**

    Size: **0.45**

11. Select the **DVE2** tool tile from the **Flow** area. Next, choose **Tools > Blur > Blur** from the menubar; the **Blur6** tool tile is inserted in the **Flow** area and a connection between the **DVE2** and **Blur6** tools is established in the **Flow** area.

12. In the **Blur6** tool control window, enter **16** in the **Blur Size** edit box.

After entering the values, the output of the **Merge6** tool is displayed, as shown in Figure 6-11.

Figure 6-11 *The output of the* **Merge6** *tool*

13. Select the **Ellipse6**, **Background6**, **Blur6**, and **DVE2** tool tiles from the **Flow** area and create a group with the name **Light6**.

14. Click on the empty space of the **Flow** area to deselect the selected tool tile, if any. Choose the **BG** button from the toolbar; the **Background7** tool tile is inserted in the **Flow** area.

15. Select the **Background7** tool tile from the **Flow** area. Next, choose the **Pick** button from the control window; the **Color** dialog box is displayed. Select the white color swatch in this dialog box and then choose the **OK** button.

16. Press 1; the output of the **Background7** tool is displayed in the left Display View.

17. Drag the red output node of the **Background7** tool tile to the red output node of the **Merge6** tool tile; the **Merge7** tool tile is inserted in the **Flow** area and a connection between the **Background7**, **Merge6**, and **Merge7** tools is established.

18. Press 2; the output of the **Merge7** tool is displayed in the right Display View.

19. Make sure the **Background7** tool tile is selected in the **Flow** area. Choose the **Add a Polyline Mask** button from the toolbar; the **Polygon2** tool tile is inserted in the **Flow** area and it is connected to the purple node of the **Background7** tool.

20. In the **Polygon2** tool control window, enter the values of the parameters as follows:

    Soft Edge: **0.2**   Border Width: **-0.2**   Level: **0.5**

21. Draw a polyline shape in the right Display View, as shown in Figure 6-12.

Figure 6-12 *The polyline shape drawn in the right Display View*

Now, you can create more lights and stars in the scene, based on your requirement, refer to Figure 6-1.

Now, save the composition with the name *c06tut1* at the location *Documents > Fusion_7 > c06_tut > c06_tut_01*. Next, you need to render the composition. For rendering, refer to Tutorial 1 of Chapter 2. The output of the composition is shown in Figure 6-1. You can also view the final render of the composition by downloading the *c06_fusion_7_rndr.zip* file from *http://www.cadcim.com*. The path of the file is mentioned at the beginning of the chapter.

Tutorial 2

In this tutorial, you will change the sky in an image by using the **Wand** tool. The final output of the composition is shown in Figure 6-13.   **(Expected time: 20 min)**

Figure 6-13 *The final output of the composition*

The following steps are required to complete this tutorial:

a. Set the frame format.
b. Download and import the images.
c. Color-correct the image.
d. Create a sky mask.
e. Merge the images.

Setting the Frame Format

In this section, you will specify the frame format settings.

1. Choose **File > New** from the menubar; a new composition is opened in the Fusion screen.

2. Choose **File > Preferences** from the menubar; the **Preferences** dialog box is displayed.

3. In this dialog box, select **Frame Format** from the **Composition#** preferences tree; various frame format settings are displayed on the right in the **Preferences** dialog box. Next, select the **HDTV 720** option from the **Default format** drop-down list and then choose the **Save** button to save the changes made.

4. In the Time Ruler area, enter **0** in the **Global End Time** edit box.

Downloading and Importing the Images

In this section, you will download the images and import them to the composition.

1. Open the following link: *http://www.rgbstock.com/photo/n8cpkhq*; a page is displayed.

2. Download the image to */Documents/Fusion_7 /c06_tut/c06_tut_02/Media_Files* and save with the name *park.jpg*.

3. Open the following link: *http://freeimages.com/photo/1346769*; a page is displayed.

4. Download the image at the location */Documents/Fusion_7 /c06_tut/c06_tut_02/ Media_Files* and save it with the name *sky.jpg*.

  Note
Footage Courtesy: **Ayla** *(http://www.rgbstock.com/user/Ayla87),* **Roger Kirby** *(http://www.freeim-ages.com/profile/theswedish)*

5. Choose the **LD** button from the toolbar; the **Open File** dialog box is displayed. In this dialog box, choose **Documents > Fusion_7 > c06_tut > c06_tut_02 > Media_Files > park.jpg** and then choose the **Open** button; the **Loader1** tool tile is inserted in the **Flow** area.

6. Press 1; the output of the **Loader1** tool is displayed in the left Display View. Choose the **Fit** button from the left **Display View** toolbar to fit the image into the Display View, refer to Figure 6-14.

7. Click on the empty space in the **Flow** area and then load *sky.jpg* in the **Flow** area; the **Loader2** tool tile is inserted in the **Flow** area.

8. Press 2; the output of the **Loader2** tool is displayed in the left Display View. Choose the **Fit** button from the right **Display View** toolbar to fit the image into the Display View, refer to Figure 6-14.

*Figure 6-14 The output of the **Loader1** and **Loader2** tools*

9. Select the **Loader1** tool tile from the **Flow** area and then choose the **Rsz** buttonfrom the toolbar; the **Resize1** tool tile is inserted in the **Flow** area and a connection between the **Resize1** and **Loader1** tools is established.

Color-Correcting the Image
In this section, you will color-correct the image.

1. Click on the empty space in the **Flow** area to deselect the selected tool tile, if any. Choose the **CC** button from the toolbar; the **ColorCorrector1** tool tile is inserted in the **Flow** area.

2. Drag the red output of the **Resize1** tool tile to the orange input of the **ColorCorrector1** tool tile; the **ColorCorrector1** tool tile is connected to the **Resize1** tool tile.

3. Press 1; the output of the **ColorCorrector1** tool is displayed in the left Display View.

4. In the **ColorCorrector1** tool control window, enter the values of the parameters as follows:

Tint: **-0.05**   Strength: **0.16**

After entering the values, the output of the **ColorCorrector1** tool is displayed, as shown in Figure 6-15.

Creating a Mask
In this section, you will create a sky mask by using the **Wand** tool.

1. Click on the empty space in the **Flow** area to deselect the selected tools tile, if any. Choose **Tools > Mask > Wand** from the menubar; the **Wand1** tool tile is inserted in the **Flow** area.

2. Drag the white output of the **Resize1** tool tile to the orange input of the **Wand1** tool tile; a connection **Resize1** and **Wand1** tools is established.

Figure 6-15 *The output of the* ***ColorCorrector1*** *tool*

3. Make sure the **Wand1** tool tile is selected in the **Flow** area and then press 2; the output of the **Wand1** tool is displayed in the right Display View.

4. In the **Wand1** tool control window, choose the **YUV** button in the **Color Space** area and the **Y** button in the **Channel** area. Next, enter the values of the parameters as follows:

Soft Edge: **0.001**   Range: **0.303**

Selection Point
X: **0.62**   Y: **0.84**

Range Soft Edge: **0.502**

The **Soft Edge** parameter softens the edge of the mask.

The **Range** parameter limits the range of colors of input image that will be included in mask.

The **Selection Point** parameter is used to determine from where the input image derives the color sample.
The **Range Soft Edge** parameter is used to soften the edge of the selected color area.

5. In the **Wand1** tool control window, select the **Invert** check box.

After entering the values, the output of the **Wand1** tool is displayed, as shown in Figure 6-16.

Merging the Images
In this section, you will merge the images.

1. Select the **Loader2** tool tile in the **Flow** area and then choose **Tools > Transform > Crop** from the menubar; the **Crop1** tool tile is inserted in the **Flow** area and a connection is established between the **Loader2** and **Crop1** tools.

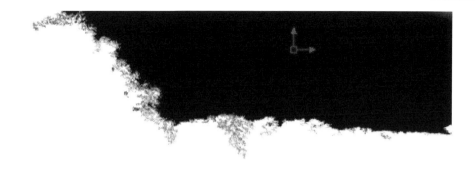

*Figure 6-16 The output of the **Wand1** tool*

2. Drag the red output of the **ColorCorrector1** tool tile to the red output node of the **Crop1** tool tile; the **Merge1** tool tile is inserted in the **Flow** area and a connection between the **Crop1**, **ColorCorrector1**, and **Merge1** tools is established.

3. Drag the red output node of the **Wand1** tool tile to the purple node of the **Merge1** tool; a connection between the **Merge1** and **Wand1** tools is established.

4. Press 2; the output of the **Merge1** tool is displayed in the right Display View.

5. Select the **Crop1** tool tile from the **Flow** area and choose **Tools > Transform > DVE** from the menubar; the **DVE1** tool tile is inserted in the **Flow** area and a connection between the **DVE1** and **Crop1** tools is established.

6. In the **Crop1** tool control window, enter **-300** in the **Y Offset** edit box.

7. In the **DVE1** tool control window, enter the values of the parameters as follows:

    X Rotation: **26**   Perspective: **0.6**

8. Select the **Merge1** tool tile from the **Flow** area and choose the **CC** button from the toolbar; the **ColorCorrector2** tool tile is inserted in the **Flow** area and a connection between the **Merge1** and **ColorCorrector2** tools is established. Press 2; the output of the **ColorCorrector2** tool is displayed in the right Display View.

9. In the **ColorCorrector2** tool control window, enter the values of the parameters as follows:

    Tint: **0.06**   Strength: **0.33**   Master-RGB-Gain: **1.3**

    After entering the values, the output of the **ColorCorrector2** tool is displayed, as shown in Figure 6-17. Figure 6-18 displays the network of tools used in the composition.

Figure 6-17 *The output of the* ***ColorCorrector2*** *tool*

Now, save the composition with the name *c06tut2* at the location *Documents > Fusion_7 > c06_tut > c06_tut_02*. Next, you need to render the composition. For rendering, refer to Tutorial 1 of Chapter 2. The output of the composition is shown in Figure 6-13. You can also view the final render of the composition by downloading the *c06_fusion_7_rndr.zip* file from *http://www.cadcim.com*. The path of the file is mentioned at the beginning of the chapter.

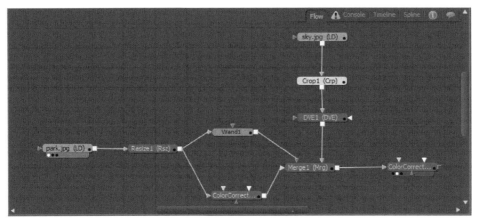

Figure 6-18 *The network of tools used in the composition*

Tutorial 3

In this tutorial, you will create a composition using the **Bitmap** tool. The final output of the composition is shown in Figure 6-19.	**(Expected time: 15 min)**

The following steps are required to complete this tutorial:

a.	Set the frame format.
b.	Download and import the images.

c.   Resize the images.
d.   Create a sky mask.
e.   Merge the images.

Figure 6-19 *The final output of the composition*

Setting the Frame Format

In this section, you will specify the frame format settings.

1.   Choose **File > New** from the menubar; a new composition is opened in the Fusion screen.

2.   Choose **File > Preferences** from the menubar; the **Preferences** dialog box is displayed.

3.   In this dialog box, select **Frame Format** from the **Composition#** preferences tree; various frame format settings are displayed on the right in the **Preferences** dialog box. Next, select the **NTSC (Square Pixel)** option from the **Default format** drop-down list and then choose the **Save** button to save the changes made.

4.   In the Time Ruler area, enter **0** in the **Global End Time** edit box.

Downloading and Importing the Images

In this section, you will download the images and import them to the composition.

1.   Open the following link: *http://www.rgbstock.com/photo/mXDlDly*; an image is displayed.

2.   Download the image at */Documents/Fusion_7/c06_tut/c06_tut_03/Media_Files* and save it with the name *fields.jpg*.

Note
Footage Courtesy: **Ayla** *(http://www.rgbstock.com/user/Ayla87)*

3.   Choose the **LD** button from the toolbar; the **Open File** dialog box is displayed. In this dialog box, choose **Documents > Fusion_7 > c06_tut > c06_tut_03 > Media_Files > sky.jpg** and then choose the **Open** button; the **Loader1** tool tile is inserted in the **Flow** area.

4. Press 1; the output of the **Loader1** tool is displayed in the left Display View. Choose the **Fit** button from the left **Display View** toolbar to fit the image into the left Display View, refer to Figure 6-20.

5. Click on the empty space in the **Flow** area and then load *fields.jpg* in the **Flow** area; the **Loader2** tool tile is inserted in the **Flow** area. Next, press 2 to view the output of the **Loader2** tool in the right Display View. Now, choose the **Fit** button from the right **Display View** toolbar to fit the image into the right Display View, refer to Figure 6-20.

Figure 6-20 *The output of the **Loader1** and **Loader2** tools*

Resizing the Images
In this section, you will resize the images.

1. Select the **Loader1** tool tile from the **Flow** area and then choose the **Rsz** button from the toolbar; the **Resize1** tool tile is inserted in the **Flow** area and a connection between the **Resize1** and **Loader1** tools is established.

2. Select the **Loader2** tool tile from the **Flow** area and then choose the **Rsz** buttonfrom the toolbar; the **Resize2** tool tile is inserted in the **Flow** area and a connection between the **Resize2** and **Loader2** tools is established.

Creating a Sky Mask
In this section, you will create a mask for the sky by using the **Bitmap** tool.

1. Click on the empty space in the **Flow** area to deselect the selected tool tile, if any. Next , choose the **Add a Bitmap Mask** button from the **Display View** toolbar; the **Bitmap1** tool tile is inserted in the **Flow** area.

2. Drag the red output node of the **Resize2** tool tile to the orange node of the **Bitmap1** tool tile; a connection between the **Resize2** and **Bitmap1** tools is established.

3. Press 2; the output of the **Bitmap1** tool is displayed in the right Display View.

   The **Bitmap** tool is used to create a mask based on the color, luminance, and auxiliary channels of the image.

4. In the control window of the **Bitmap1** tool, select **Blue** from the **Channels** drop-down list. Also, enter the values of the parameters as follows:

Low: **0.722**   High: **0.772**

On increasing the value of the **Low** parameter, the pixels will be converted to black. On decreasing the values of the **High** parameter, the pixels will be converted to white.

5.   Enter **0.007** in the **Soft Edge** edit box.

     After entering the values, the output of the **Bitmap1** tool is displayed, as shown in Figure 6-21.

Merging the Images

In this section, you will merge the images.

1.   Click on the empty space of the **Flow** area to deselect the selected tool tile, if any.
     Next, choose the **Mrg** button from the toolbar; the **Merge1** tool tile is inserted in the
     Flow area.

2.   Drag the red output node of the **Resize1** tool tile to the green node of the **Merge1** tool tile;
     a connection between the **Resize1** and **Merge1** tools is established.

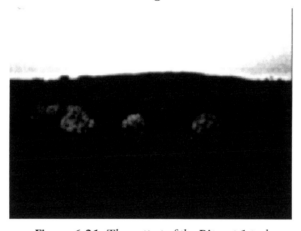

Figure 6-21 *The output of the **Bitmap1** tool*

3.   Drag the red output node of the **Resize2** tool tile to the orange node of the **Merge1** tool
     tile; a connection between the **Resize2** and **Merge1** tools is established. Press 2; the output
     of the **Merge1** tool is displayed in the right Display View.

4.   Drag the red output node of the **Bitmap1** tool tile to the purple node of the **Merge1** tool
     tile; a connection between the **Bitmap1** and **Merge1** tools is established.

5.   Make sure the **Merge1** tool tile is selected in the **Flow** area. Next, choose the **CC**
     button from the toolbar; the **ColorCorrector1** tool tile is inserted in the **Flow** area
     and a connection between the **ColorCorrector1** and **Merge1** tools is established.

6.   Press 1; the output of the **ColorCorrector1** tool is displayed in the left Display View.

7. In the **ColorCorrector1** tool control window, enter the values of the parameters as follows:

   Hue: **-0.078**   Tint: **1.11**   Strength: **0.24**

8. Choose the **Midtones** button and then enter **1.17** in the **MidTones-Saturation** edit box.

   Figure 6-22 displays the network of tools used in the composition.

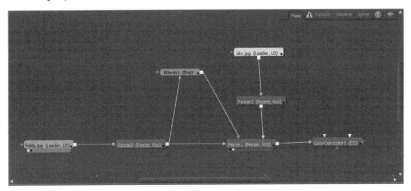

Figure 6-22 The network of tools in the composition

Now, save the composition with the name *c06tut3* at the location *Documents > Fusion_7 > c06_tut > c06_tut_03*. Next, you need to render the composition. For rendering, refer to Tutorial 1 of Chapter 2. The output of the composition is shown in Figure 6-19. You can also view the final render of the composition by downloading the *c06_fusion_7_rndr.zip* file from *http://www.cadcim.com*. The path of the file is mentioned at the beginning of the chapter.

Tutorial 4

In this tutorial, you will add an object to the composition by using the **Mask Paint** tool. The final output of the composition is shown in Figure 6-23.   **(Expected time: 25 min)**

Figure 6-23 The final output of the composition

The following steps are required to complete this tutorial:

a.   Set the frame format.
b.   Download and import the images.
c.   Create a mask.
d.   Merge the images.
e.   Create shadow of the dustbin.

Setting the Frame Format

In this section, you will specify the frame format settings.

1.   Choose **File > New** from the menubar; a new composition is opened in the Fusion screen.

2.   Choose **File > Preferences** from the menubar; the **Preferences** dialog box is displayed.

3.   In this dialog box, select **Frame Format** from the **Composition#** preferences tree; various frame format settings are displayed on the right in the **Preferences** dialog box. Next, select the **NTSC (Square Pixel)** option from the **Default format** drop-down list and then choose the **Save** button to save the changes made.

4.   In the Time Ruler area, enter **0** in the **Global End Time** edit box.

Downloading and Importing the Images

In this section, you will download and import the images.

1.   Open the following link: *http://www.rgbstock.com/photo/mYjldBo*; an image is displayed.

2.   Download the image at the location *Documents/Fusion_7/c06_tut/c06_tut_04/Media_Files* and save it with the name *scene.jpg*.

3.   Open the following link: *http://www.freeimages.com/photo/932570*; an image is displayed.

4.   Download the image at the location *Documents/Fusion_7/c06_tut/c06_tut_04/Media_Files* with the name *bin.jpg*.

Note
Footage Courtesy: **Ayla** *(http://www.rgbstock.com/user/Ayla87),* **Michal Zacharzewski** *(http://http://www.freeimages.com/profile/mzacha)*

5.   Choose the **LD** button from the toolbar; the **Open File** dialog box is displayed. In this dialog box, choose **Documents > Fusion_7 > c06_tut > c06_tut_04 > Media_Files > bin.jpg** and then choose the **Open** button; the **Loader1** tool tile is inserted in the **Flow** area.

6.   Press 1; the output of the **Loader1** tool is displayed in the left Display View.

7.   Click on the empty space in the **Flow** area and then load *scene.jpg* in the **Flow** area; the **Loader2** tool tile is inserted in the **Flow** area. Next, press 2 to view the output of the **Loader2** tool in the right Display View, refer to Figure 6-24.

8. Choose the **Fit** button from the **Display View** toolbar to fit the image into the [Fit] Display View, refer to Figure 6-24.

Figure 6-24 *The output of the **Loader1** and **Loader2** tools*

Creating a Mask

In this section, you will create a mask by using the **Mask Paint** tool.

1. Click on the empty space in the **Flow** area to deselect the selected tool tiles, if any. Choose **Tools > Mask > Mask Paint** from the menubar; the **MaskPaint1** tool tile is inserted in the **Flow** area.

2. Drag the red output node of the **MaskPaint1** tool tile to the purple effect mask node of the **Loader1** tool tile; a connection between the **Loader1** and **MaskPaint1** tools is established.

3. In the **MaskPaint1** tool control window, enter **0.32** in the **Size** edit box in the **Brush Controls** area. Next, choose the **Mask** tab and select the **Invert** check box.

4. Make sure the **MaskPaint1** tool tile is selected. Next, to generate transparency draw paint strokes on the white part of the image in the left Display View, refer to Figure 6-25.

5. Select the **Loader1** tool tile from the **Flow** area and then choose the **CC** button from the toolbar; the **ColorCorrector1** tool tile is inserted in the **Flow** area and a connection between the **Loader1** and **ColorCorrector1** tools is established.

6. Press 1; the output of the **ColorCorrector1** tool is displayed in the left Display View.

7. In the **ColorCorrector1** tool control window, enter the values of the parameters as follows:

Tint: **-0.98**   Strength: **0.76**

Figure 6-25 *The output of the **Loader1** tool*

Master - RGB - Gain: **0.88**

Merging the Images

In this section, you will merge the images.

1. Drag the red output of the **ColorCorrector1** tool tile to the red output node of the **Loader2** tool tile; the **Merge1** tool tile is inserted in the **Flow** area and a connection between the **Loader2**, **ColorCorrector1**, and **Merge1** tools is established.

   Press 1; the output of the **Crop1** tool is displayed in the left Display View.

2. Select the **Loader2** tool tile in the **Flow** area and then choose **Tools > Transform > Crop** from the menubar; the **Crop1** tool tile is inserted between the **Loader2** and **Merge1** tools. Press 1; the output of the **Crop1** tool is displayed in the left Display View.

3. In the **Crop1** tool control window, enter **700** in the **X Offset** edit box.

4. Select the **Merge1** tool tile from the **Flow** area. In the control window of the **Merge1** tool, set the parameters as follows:

   Center
   X: **0.52**   Y: **0.3**

   Size: **0.19**

5. Select the **ColorCorrector1** tool tile from the **Flow** area and choose **Tools > Transform > DVE** from the toolbar; the **DVE1** tool tile is inserted in the **Flow** area and a connection between the **ColorCorrector1** and **DVE1** tools is established.

6. In the **DVE1** tool control window, enter the values of the following parameter:

   Center
   X: **-0.5**

   Y Rotation: **19.05**

   After entering the values, the output of the **Merge1** tool is displayed, as shown in Figure 6-26.

Figure 6-26 *The output of the **Merge1** tool*

Creating the Shadow of the Dustbin

In this section, you will create a shadow of the dustbin.

1. Click on the empty space of the **Flow** area to deselect the selected tools, if any. Choose the **Mrg** button from the toolbar; the **Merge2** tool tile is inserted in the **Flow** area.

2. Drag the white output node of the **Loader1** tool tile to the green input node of the **Merge2** tool tile; a connection between the **Loader1** and **Merge2** tools is established.

3. Drag the red output node of the **Merge1** tool tile to the orange input node of the **Merge2** tool tile; a connection between the **Merge1** and **Merge2** tools is established.

4. Press 2; the output of the **Merge2** tool is displayed in the right Display View.

5. In the **Merge2** tool control window, enter the values of the parameters as follows:

    Center
    X: **0.52**   Y: **0.31**

    Size: **0.19**

6. Hover the cursor over the pipe connecting the **Loader1** and **Merge2** tool tiles; the connecting pipe is highlighted. Next, right-click on the pipe; a shortcut menu is displayed. Choose **Add Tool > Transform > DVE** from the menubar; the **DVE2** tool tile is inserted between the **Loader1** and **Merge2** tools.

7. In the **DVE2** tool control window, enter the values of the parameters as follows:

    Center
    X: **-0.63**   Y: **0.52**

    ZMove: **1.099**
    Pivot
    X: **0.39**   Y: **0.006**

    X Rotation: **27**   Y Rotation: **5.71**   Z Rotation: **211.43**

8. In the **Merge2** tool control window, enter **0.27** in the **Blend** edit box.

    After entering the values, the output of the **Merge2** tool is displayed, as shown in Figure 6-27. Figure 6-28 displays the network of tools in the **Flow** area.

9. Select the **DVE2** tool tile from the **Flow** area and then choose the **CC** button from the toolbar; the **ColorCorrector2** tool tile is inserted in the **Flow** area and a connection between the **DVE2**, **ColorCorrector2**, and **Merge2** tools is established.

Figure 6-27 *The output of the **Merge2** tool*

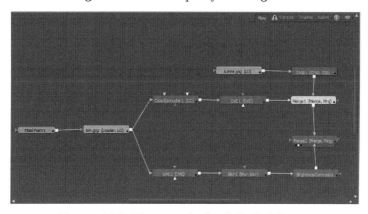

Figure 6-28 *The network of tools in the **Flow** area*

10. In the **ColorCorrector2** tool control window, enter **0** in the **Master-RGB-Gain** edit box.

Now, save the composition with the name *c06tut4* at the location *Documents > Fusion_7 > c06_tut > c06_tut_04*. Next, you need to render the composition. For rendering, refer to Tutorial 1 of Chapter 2. The output is shown in Figure 6-19. You can also view the final render of the composition by downloading the *c06_fusion_7_rndr.zip* file from *http://www. cadcim.com*. The path of the file is mentioned at the beginning of the chapter.

Self-Evaluation Test

Answer the following questions and compare them to those given at the end of this chapter:

1. The _____ tools are used to restrict the effect of the tool to specific areas of the image.

2. The _____ tool is used to create a mask based on the values from any of the color, alpha, hue, saturation, luminance, and auxiliary coverage channels of the image.

3. A mask tool consists of two input nodes. (T/F)

Review Questions

Answer the following questions:

1. Which of the following combinations of shortcut keys are used to create a group of tools in the **Flow** area?

    (a) CTRL+J   (b) CTRL+G
    (c) SHIFT+G   (d) ALT+G

2. The _____ button in the **Display View** toolbar is used to insert the **Polygon** tool in the **Flow** area.

3. The **Add an Ellipse Mask** button is used to create a circular mask. (T/F)

Answers to Self-Evaluation Test
1. Mask, **2. Bitmap**, **3.** T

Chapter 7

Color Tools

Learning Objectives

After completing this chapter, you will be able to:
- *Create a composition using the Color tools*
- *Change the color of an element in the image*
- *Create the sunset effect in the image*

INTRODUCTION

The Color tools are used to manipulate the output of a composition by changing the color information in the footage. These tools play a very important role in matching the colors of various components of the composition. In this chapter, you will color-correct the images using various Color tools.

TUTORIALS

The compositions created in this chapter can be downloaded from *http://www.cadcim.com*. These compositions are contained in the *c07_fusion_7_tut.zip* file. The path of the file is as follows:

> *Textbooks > Animation and Visual Effects > Fusion > Blackmagic Design Fusion 7 Studio: A Tutorial Approach*

Tutorial 1

In this tutorial, you will color-correct the composition by using the **Color Corrector** tool. The final output of the composition is shown in Figure 7-1.   **(Expected time: 15 min)**

Figure 7-1 *The final output of the composition*

The following steps are required to complete this tutorial:

a. Set the frame format.
b. Download and import the image.
c. Color-correct the image.
d. Adjust the brightness and contrast of the image.

Setting the Frame Format

In this section, you will specify the frame format settings.

1. Choose **File > New** from the menubar; a new composition is opened in the Fusion screen.

2. Choose **File > Preferences** from the menubar; the **Preferences** dialog box is displayed.

3. In this dialog box, select **Frame Format** from the **Composition#** preferences tree; various frame format settings are displayed on the right in the **Preferences** dialog box. Next, select

the **HDTV 720** option from the **Default format** drop-down list and then choose the **Save** button to save the changes made.

4. In the Time Ruler area, enter **0** in the **Global End Time** edit box.

Downloading and Importing the Image

In this section, you will download the image and then import it to the **Flow** area.

1. Open the following link: *http://www.rgbstock.com/image/mfjAjX6;* an image is displayed.

2. Download the image at */Documents/Fusion_7/c07_tut/c07_tut_01/Media_Files* with the name *street.jpg*.

 Note
Footage Courtesy : Ayla87 (http://www.rgbstock.com/gallery/Ayla87)

3. Choose the **LD** button from the toolbar; a dialog box is displayed. In this dialog box, choose **Documents > Fusion_7 > c07_tut > c07_tut_01 > Media_Files > street.jpg** and then choose the **Open** button; the **Loader1** tool tile is inserted in the **Flow** area.

4. Press 1; the output of the **Loader1** tool is displayed in the left Display View.

5. Choose the **Fit** button from the left **Display View** toolbar to fit the image into the Display View.

6. Select the **Loader1** tool tile from the **Flow** area and then choose the **Rsz** buttonfrom the toolbar; the **Resize1** tool tile is inserted in the **Flow** area and a connection between the **Resize1** and **Loader1** tool tiles is established.

7. Press 1; the output of the **Resize1** tool is displayed in the left Display View, as shown in Figure 7-2.

*Figure 7-2 The output of the **Resize1** tool*

Color-Correcting the Image

In this section, you will color-correct the image.

1. Make sure the **Resize1** tool tile is selected in the **Flow** area and choose the **CC** button from the toolbar; the **ColorCorrector1** tool tile is inserted in the **Flow** area and a connection between the **ColorCorrector1** and **Resize1** tool tiles is established.

    The **Color Corrector** tool is a powerful tool that is used to color-correct an image with the help of histogram, matching and equalizing functions, hue shifting, and color suppression. This tool has two inputs, orange input for attaching an input image and the green input for attaching a second image for histogram matching.

2. Press 2; the output of the **ColorCorrector1** tool is displayed in the right Display View. Next, choose the **Fit** button from the right **Display View** toolbar to fit the image into the Display View.

    Next, you will create an evening scene.

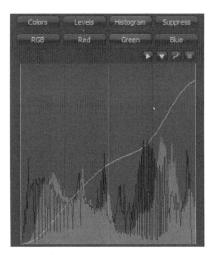

3. In the **ColorCorrector1** tool control window, choose the **Histogram** button; the histogram graph is displayed. This graph represents the distribution of color values in the composition. Next, choose the **Green** button and then choose the **Equalize** button; the pixel values for the green channel are evenly distributed and the histogram graph is updated, as shown in Figure 7-3.

    The **Equalize** button is used to evenly distribute colors (flatten histogram) in the input image.

Figure 7-3 The histogram graph updated

4. Clear the **Lock red/green/blue** check box and then set the following values:

    Equalize blue: **0.8**   Smooth out correction curve: **0.089**

    Next, you need to suppress yellow color from the image.

5. Choose the **Suppress** button from **ColorCorrector1** tool control window and then choose the **Shadows** button. Next, suppress the yellow color by entering **0.4** in the **Yellow** edit box.

    The **Suppress** button is used to remove the unwanted colors from an image.

    After entering the values, the output of the **ColorCorrector1** tool is displayed in the right Display View, as shown in Figure 7-4.

Figure 7-4 *The output of the **ColorCorrector1** tool*

Adjusting the Brightness and Contrast of the Image

In this section, you will adjust the brightness and contrast of the image by using the **Brightness/Contrast** tool.

1. Make sure the **ColorCorrector1** tool tile is selected in the **Flow** area and then choose the **BC** button from the toolbar; the **BrightnessContrast1** tool tile is inserted in the **Flow** area and a connection between the **ColorCorrector1** and **BrightnessContrast1** tool tiles is established.

2. Press 2; the output of the **BrightnessContrast1** tool is displayed in the right Display View.

3. In the **BrightnessContrast1** tool control window, clear the **Red** and **Green** check boxes and set the following parameters:

    Gain: **0.96**   Gamma: **0.54**

    Brightness: **0.11**   Saturation: **1.3**

    The **Brightness/Contrast** tool is used to adjust the brightness, contrast, gain, and gamma of an image. You can also reverse the output of the **BrightnessContrast1** tool by choosing the **Reverse** button from the **Direction** area of the **BrightnessContrast1** tool control window.

    Now, save the composition with the name *c07tut1* at the location *Documents > Fusion_7 > c07_tut > c07_tut_01*. Next, you need to render the composition. For rendering, refer to Tutorial 1 of Chapter 2. The output of the composition is shown in Figure 7-1. You can also view the final render of the composition by downloading the *c07_fusion_7_rndr.zip* file from *http://www.cadcim.com*. The path of the file is mentioned at the beginning of the chapter.

Tutorial 2

In this tutorial, you will change the color of an element in the image. The final output of the composition is shown in Figure 7-5.   **(Expected time: 15 min)**

Figure 7-5 *The final output of the composition*

The following steps are required to complete this tutorial:

a.   Set the frame format.
b.   Download and import the image.
c.   Change the color of the element.

Setting the Frame Format

In this section, you will specify the frame format settings.

1.   Choose **File > New** from the menubar; a new composition is opened in the Fusion screen.

2.   Choose **File > Preferences** from the menubar; the **Preferences** dialog box is displayed.

3.   In this dialog box, select **Frame Format** from the **Composition#** preferences tree; various frame format settings are displayed on the right in the **Preferences** dialog box. Next, select the **HDTV 720** option from the **Default format** drop-down list and then choose the **Save** button to save the changes made.

4.   In the Time Ruler area, enter **0** in the **Global End Time** edit box.

Downloading and Importing the Image

In this section, you will download the image and import it to the composition.

1.   Open the following link: *http://www.rgbstock.com/image/mHNmhyO;* an image is displayed.

2.   Download the image at the location */Documents/Fusion_7/c07_tut/c07_tut_02/ Media_Files* with the name *teapot.jpg.*

Note
*Footage Courtesy : **Ayla87** (http://www.rgbstock.com/gallery/Ayla87)*

3. Choose the **LD** button from the toolbar; a dialog box is displayed. In this dialog box, choose **Documents > Fusion_7 > c07_tut > c07_tut_02 > Media_Files > teapot. jpg** and then choose the **Open** button; the **Loader1** tool tile is inserted in the **Flow** area.

4. Press 1; the output of the **Loader1** tool is displayed in the left Display View.

5. Choose the **Fit** button from the left **Display View** toolbar to fit the image into the left Display View, refer to Figure 7-6.

*Figure 7-6 The output of the **Loader1** tool*

6. Select the **Loader1** tool tile from the **Flow** area and then choose the **Rsz** button from the toolbar; the **Resize1** tool tile is inserted in the **Flow** area and a connection between the **Resize1** and **Loader1** tools is established.

7. Press 1; the output of the **Resize1** tool is displayed in the left Display View.

Changing the Color of the Element

In this section, you will change the color of the element with the help of the **Channel Booleans** tool.

1. Make sure the **Resize1** tool tile is selected in the **Flow** area and then choose the **Bol** button from the toolbar; the **ChannelBooleans1** tool tile is inserted in the **Flow** area and a connection between the **Resize1** and **ChannelBooleans1** tool tiles is established, as shown in Figure 7-7.

2. In the **Resize1** tool control window, enter **900** in the **Height** edit box.

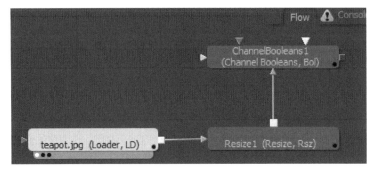

*Figure 7-7 The **Resize1** tool connected to the **ChannelBooleans1** tool*

The **Channel Booleans** tool is used to modify RGB channels of the input image by using the mathematical and logical operations.

3. Press 2; the output of the **ChannelBooleans1** tool is displayed in the right DisplayView . Next, choose the **Fit** button from the right **Display View** toolbar to fit the image into the right Display View.

4. In the **ChannelBooleans1** control window, select the **Green BG** option from the **To Red** drop-down list.

After entering the values, the output of the **ChannelBooleans1** tool is displayed in the right Display View, as shown in Figure 7-8.

*Figure 7-8 The output of the **ChannelBooleans1** tool*

The options in the **Operation** drop-down list are used to specify the mathematical method applied to the selected channels. The **Copy** option is used to copy the value from one channel to another channel.

Notice that in the **ChannelBooleans1** tool tile, no tool is connected to the green node (foreground). If the foreground input is not available, the **Channel Booleans** tool will use the background input color channels instead the tool tile no tool is connected to the green node (foreground). If the foreground input is not available, the **ChannelBooleans** tool will use the background input color channels instead.

Now, save the composition with the name *c07tut2* at the location *Documents > Fusion_7 > c07_tut > c07_tut_02*. Next, you need to render the composition. For rendering, refer to Tutorial 2 of Chapter 2. The output of the composition is shown in Figure 7-5. You can also view the final render of the composition by downloading the *c07_fusion_7_rndr.zip* file from *http://www.cadcim.com*. The path of the file is mentioned at the beginning of the chapter.

Tutorial 3

In this tutorial, you will change the color of an element in the image by using the **Hue Curves** tool. The final output of the composition is shown in Figure 7-9.   **(Expected time: 10 min)**

Figure 7-9 The final output of the composition at frames 350

The following steps are required to complete this tutorial:

a.   Set the frame format.
b.   Download and import the image.
c.   Change the color of the element.

Setting the Frame Format

In this section, you will specify the frame format settings.

1.   Choose **File > New** from the menubar; a new composition is opened in the Fusion screen.

2.   Choose **Files > Preferences** from the menubar; the **Preferences** dialog box is displayed.

3.   In this dialog box, select **Frame Format** from the **Composition#** preferences tree; various frame format settings are displayed on the right in the **Preferences** dialog box. Next, select the **HDTV 720** option from the **Default format** drop-down list and then choose the **Save** button to save the changes made.

Downloading and Importing the Image

In this section, you will download the image and import it to the composition.

1.   Open the following link: *http://www.freeimages.com/photo/1149337;* an image is displayed.

2.   Download the image at the location */Documents/Fusion_7/c07_tut/c07_tut_03/Media_Files* with the name *t-shirt.jpg*.

> **Note**
>
> *Footage Courtesy : **Bina Sveda** (http://www.freeimages.com/profile/binababy12)*

3.   Choose the **LD** button from the toolbar; a dialog box is displayed. In this dialog box, choose **Documents > Fusion_7 > c07_tut > c07_tut_03 > Media_Files > t-shirt. jpg** and then choose the **Open** button; the **Loader1** tool tile is inserted in the **Flow** area.

4.   Press 1; the output of the **Loader1** tool is displayed in the left Display View.

5.   Choose the **Fit** button from the left **Display View** toolbar to fit the image into the Display View, refer to Figure 7-10.

*Figure 7-10 The output of the **Loader1** tool*

6.   Make sure the **Loader1** tool tile is selected in the **Flow** area and then choose the**Rsz** button from the toolbar; the **Resize1** tool tile is inserted in the **Flow** area and a connection between the **Resize1** and **Loader1** tool tiles is established.

7.   Press 1; the output of the **Resize1** tool is displayed in the left Display View.

8.   In the **Resize1** tool control window, select the **Keep Frame Aspect** check box.

Changing the Color of the Element

In this section, you will change the color of the element using the **Hue Curves** tool.

1.   Select the **Resize1** tool tile from the **Flow** area and then choose the **HCv** button from

the toolbar; the **HueCurves1** tool tile is inserted in the **Flow** area and a connection between the **Resize1** and **HueCurves1** tool tiles is established.

2. Press 2; the output of the **HueCurves1** tool is displayed in the right Display View. Next, choose the **Fit** button from the right **Display View** toolbar to fit the image into the Display View.

   The **HueCurves** tool is used to adjust the color of an image by using multiple spline curves. These curves control the hue, saturation, luminance, and color channels of an image. You can also suppress the color channels by using these curves.

   Next, you will change the color of the t-shirt in the image.

3. In the **HueCurves1** tool control window, clear the **Sat** check box and then select the **Hue** and **Blue** check boxes.

4. Adjust the shape of the spline, as shown in Figure 7-11. After adjusting the shape, the output of the **HueCurves1** tool is displayed, as shown in Figure 7-12.

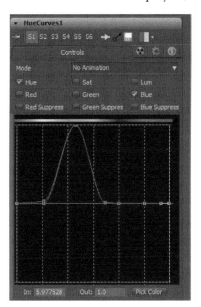

Figure 7-11 The **Hue** and **Blue** splines modified

Figure 7-12 The output of the **HueCurves1** tool

5. Make sure the **HueCurves1** tool tile is selected in the **Flow** area. Next, draw a polyline shape on the T-shirt using the **Add a Polyline Mask** button from the left Display View, refer to Figure 7-13.

Figure 7-13 *The polyline shape drawn in the left Display View*

6. Select the **HueCurves1** tool tile from the **Flow** area and then choose the **CC** tool from the toolbar; the **Color Corrector1** tool tile is inserted in the **Flow** area and a connection between the **HueCurves1** and **Color Corrector1** tool tiles is established.

7. Drag the white output node of the **Polygon1** tool tile to the purple node of the **ColorCorrector** tool tile in the **Flow** area.

    Next, you will animate the color of T-shirt.

8. Select the **ColorCorrector1** tool tile from the **Flow** area, if it is not selected. Now, animate the **Tint** and **Strength** controls in the **Correction** tab to create the keyframes by using the values given in the following table:

Frame	Tint	Strength
0	-0.420	0.529
200	-0.86	0.989
400	-1.266	0.994
600	-0.986	1
800	-1.086	1
1000	-1.635	1

Press SPACEBAR to view the animation in the Display View.

Now, save the composition with the name *c07tut3* at the location *Documents > Fusion_7 > c07_tut > c07_tut_03*. Next, you need to render the composition at frame 350. For rendering, refer to Tutorial 2 of Chapter 2. The output of the composition is shown in Figure 7-9. You can also view the final render of the composition by downloading the *c07_fusion_7_rndr.zip* file from *http://www.cadcim.com*. The path of the file is mentioned at the beginning of the chapter.

Tutorial 4

In this tutorial, you will create the sunset effect in the scene with the help of the **Color Curves** and **Hot Spot** tools. The final output of the composition is shown in Figure 7-14.

(Expected time: 25 min)

Figure 7-14 *The final output of the composition*

The following steps are required to complete this tutorial:

a.   Set the frame format.
b.   Download and import the images.
c.   Create the sunset effect.

Setting the Frame Format

In this section, you will specify the frame format settings.

1.   Choose **File > New** from the menubar; a new composition is opened in the Fusion screen.

2.   Choose **File > Preferences** from the menubar; the **Preferences** dialog box is displayed.

3.   In this dialog box, select **Frame Format** from the **Composition#** preferences tree; various frame format settings are displayed on the right in the **Preferences** dialog box. Next, select the **NTSC (Square Pixel)** option from the **Default format** drop-down list and then choose the **Save** button to save the changes made.

4.   In the Time Ruler area, enter **0** in the **Global End Time** edit box.

Downloading and Importing the Images

In this section, you will download the images and import them to the composition.

1. Open the following link: *http://www.freeimages.com/photo/1352219;* an image is displayed.

2. Download the image at the location */Documents/Fusion_7/c07_tut/c07_tut_04/Media_Files* with the name *beach.jpg*.

> **Note**
> *Footage Courtesy : **Auro Queiroz** (http://www.freeimages.com/profile/Auroqueiro)*

3. Open *beach.jpg* in the Photoshop and then separate the sky and ground in two layers. Save the sky and ground layers with the names *sky.png* and *scene.png*, respectively, at the location specified in the previous step.

4. Choose the **LD** button from the toolbar; a dialog box is displayed. In this dialog box, choose **Documents > Fusion_7 > c07_tut > c07_tut_04 > Media_Files > sky.png** and then choose the **Open** button; the **Loader1** tool is inserted in the **Flow** area.

5. Press 1; the output of the **Loader1** tool is displayed in the left Display View.

6. Make sure the **Loader1** tool tile is selected in the **Flow** area. In the **Loader1** tool control window, choose the **Import** tab and then select the **Post-Multiply by Alpha** check box.

7. Choose the **Fit** button from the left **Display View** toolbar to fit the image into the Display View, refer to Figure 7-15.

8. Click on the empty space in the **Flow** area and then load *scene.png*; the **Loader2** tool tile is inserted in the **Flow** area.

9. In the **Loader2** tool control window, choose the **Import** tab and then select the **Post-Multiply by Alpha** check box.

10. Press 2; the output of the **Loader2** tool is displayed in the left Display View. Choose the **Fit** button from the right **Display View** toolbar to fit the image into the Display View, refer to Figure 7-15.

*Figure 7-15 The output of the **Loader1** and **Loader2** tools*

Creating the Sunset Effect

In this section, you will create the sunset effect in the scene by using the **Color Curves** tool.

1. Select the **Loader1** tool tile from the **Flow** area and then choose the **CCv** button from the toolbar; the **ColorCurves1** tool tile is inserted in the **Flow** area and a connection between the **Loader1** and **ColorCurves1** tool tiles is established.

2. Press 1; the output of the **ColorCurves1** tool is displayed in the left Display View.

3. In the **ColorCurves1** tool control window, set the curves, as shown in Figure 7-16.

Note

You can edit the curves easily by selecting one channel check box at a time.

4. Select the **Loader2** tool tile from the **Flow** area and then choose the **CCv** button from the toolbar; the **ColorCurves2** tool tile is inserted in the **Flow** area and a connection between the **Loader2** and **ColorCurves2** tool tiles is established.

5. In the **ColorCurves2** tool control window, set the curves, as shown in Figure 7-17.

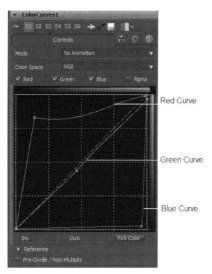

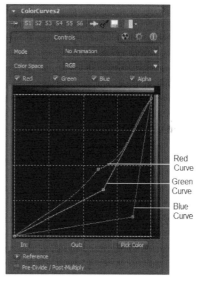

Figure 7-16 The ColorCurves1 tool control window

Figure 7-17 The ColorCurves2 tool control window

6. Select the **ColorCurves1** tool tile from the **Flow** area and then choose **Tools > Effect > Hot Spot** from the menubar; the **HotSpot1** tool tile is inserted in the **Flow** area and a connection between the **ColorCurves1** and **HotSpot1** tool tiles is established.

7. Press 1; the output of the **HotSpot1** tool is displayed in the left Display View.

8. In the **HotSpot1** tool control window, set the following values:

    Primary Center
    X: **0.48**   Y: **0.5**

    Primary Strength: **0.29**   HotSpot Size: **0.42**   Aspect Angle: **819.04**

    Secondary Strength: **0.702**   Secondary Size: **0.15**

    After entering the values, the output of the **HotSpot1** tool is displayed in the left Display
    View, as shown in Figure 7-18.

*Figure 7-18 The output of the **HotSpot1** tool*

9. Drag the red output node of the **ColorCurves2** tool tile to the red output node of the
    HotSpot1 tool tile; the **Merge1** tool tile is inserted in the **Flow** area and a connection between
    the **ColorCurves2**, **HotSpot1**, and **Merge1** tool tiles is established.

10. Press 2; the output of the **Merge1** tool is displayed in the right Display View, as shown in
    Figure 7-19

*Figure 7-19 The output of the **Merge1** tool*

11. Select the **Merge1** tool tile from the **Flow** area and then choose the **BC** button from the
    toolbar; the **BrightnessContrast1** tool tile is inserted in the **Flow** area and a connection
    between the **Merge1** and **BrightnessContrast1** tools is established.

12. Press 1; the output of the **BrightnessContrast1** tool is displayed in the left Display View.

13. In the **BrightnessContrast1** tool control window, set the following values:

    Gain: **1.04**   Contrast: **-0.01**   Brightness: **0.15**

14. Select the **BrightnessContrast1** tool tile from the **Flow** area and then choose the**Ply** button from the toolbar; the **Polygon1** tool tile is inserted in the **Flow** area and a connection between the **BrightnessContrast1** and **Polygon1** tool tiles is established.

15. Draw a polyline shape in the left Display View, as shown in Figure 7-20.

Figure 7-20 *The polyline shape drawn in the left Display View*

16. In the **Polygon1** tool control window, set the following values:

    Soft Edge: **0.17**   Border Width: **0.075**

    Center
    X: **0.56**   Y: **0.43**

17. Select the **BrightnessContrast1** tool tile from the **Flow** area and then choose the**BC** button from the toolbar; the **BrightnessContrast2** tool tile is inserted in the **Flow** area and a connection between the **BrightnessContrast1** and **BrightnessContrast2** tool tiles is established.

18. Press 2; the output of the **BrightnessContrast2** tool is displayed in the right Display View.

19. In the **BrightnessContrast2** tool control window, set the following values:

    Gain: **0.78**   Contrast: **-0.01**   Brightness: **-0.08**

20. Make sure the **BrightnessContrast2** tool tile is selected in the **Flow** area and choose the **Ply** button from the toolbar; the **Polygon2** tool tile is inserted in the **Flow** area and a connection between the **BrightnessContrast2** and **Polygon2** tool tiles is established.

21. Draw a polyline shape in the left Display View, as shown in Figure 7-21.

Figure 7-21 The polyline shape drawn in the left Display View

22. In the **Polygon2** tool control window, select the **Invert** check box and then set the following values:

Soft Edge: **0.17**   Border Width: **0.2**

Now, save the composition with the name *c07tut4* at the location *Documents > Fusion_7 > c07_tut > c07_tut_04*. Next, you need to render the composition. For rendering, refer to Tutorial 2 of Chapter 2. The output of the composition is shown in Figure 7-13. You can also view the final render of the composition by downloading the *c07_fusion_7_rndr.zip* file from *http://www.cadcim.com*. The path of the file is mentioned at the beginning of the chapter.

Self-Evaluation Test

Answer the following questions and then compare them to those given at the end of this chapter:

1. Which of the following tools is used to color-correct the composition?

    (a) **Mask**   (b) **Color Corrector**
    (c) **Creator**   (d) none of these

2. The _____ option in the **Color Corrector** tool control window is used to increase the gain of the image.

3. The _____ button in the toolbar is used to add the **Brightness/Contrast** tool tile in the **Flow** area.

4. The _____ tool is used to change the color of an image by using the spline curves.

5. The _____ button in the **Color Corrector** tool control window is used to evenly distribute colors in the input image.

Review Questions

Answer the following questions:

1. Which of the following tools does not belong to the Color category?

    (a) **Blur**   (b) **Channel Boolean**
    (c) **White Balance**   (d) none of these

2. The _____ tool category is used to change the final look of the composition.

3. The **Color Corrector** tool is used to adjust the gain and gamma of the image. (T/F)

4. The **Bol** button from the toolbar is used to add the **Channel Booleans** tool in the **Flow** area. (T/F)

Answers to Self-Evaluation Test
1. b, **2. Master-RGB-Gain**, **3. BC**, **4. Hue Curves**, **5. Equalize**

Chapter 8

Matte Tools

After completing this chapter, you will be able to:
- *Extract matte by using the Chroma Keyer tool*
- *Extract matte by using the Luma Keyer tool*
- *Extract matte by using the Ultra Keyer tool*

INTRODUCTION

The Matte tools are used to create an alpha channel (matte) by removing the selected color (or a color range) from an image sequence. The alpha channel can also be generated by using the luminance information of the pixels. Once the alpha channel (matte) is generated, the extracted image is composited over the background. In this chapter, you will learn various techniques of creating alpha channel.

TUTORIALS

The compositions created in this chapter can be downloaded from *http://www.cadcim.com*. These compositions are contained in the *c08_fusion_7_tut.zip* file. The path of the file is as follows:

> *Textbooks > Animation and Visual Effects > Fusion > Blackmagic Design Fusion 7 Studio: A Tutorial Approach*

Next, you need to extract the contents of the downloaded zip file to *\Documents\Fusion_7*.

Tutorial 1

In this tutorial, you will create a matte in a footage with the help of the **Chroma Keyer** tool and then compose the footage on a real environment. The final output of the composition at frame 69 is shown in Figure 8-1.   **(Expected time: 30 min)**

Figure 8-1 *The final output at frame 69*

The following steps are required to complete this tutorial:

a. Set the frame format.
b. Download and import images.
c. Extract the key.
d. Merge images.

Setting the Frame Format

In this section, you will specify the frame format settings.

1. Choose **File > New** from the menubar; a new composition is opened in the Fusion interface.

2. Choose **File > Preferences** from the menubar; the **Preferences** dialog box is displayed.

3. In this dialog box, select **Frame Format** from the **Composition#** preferences tree; various frame format settings are displayed on the right in the **Preferences** dialog box. Next, select the **HDTV 720** option from the **Default format** drop-down list and then choose the **Save** button to save the changes made and close the dialog box.

4. In the Time Ruler area, enter **69** in the **Global End Time** edit box.

Downloading and Importing the Images

In this section, you will download the images and then import them to the composition.

1. Open the following link: *http://www.rgbstock.com/image/mCN9dH2;* an image is displayed.

2. Download the image at the location */Documents/Fusion_7/c08_tut/c08_tut_01/Media_Files* and save it with the name *green.jpg*.

3. Open the following link: *http://www.hollywoodcamerawork.us/greenscreenplates.html;* a page is displayed. Download *hcw_godiva_medium.zip* from it and extract the contents of the zip file at the location */Documents/Fusion_7/c08_tut/c08_tut_01/Media_Files/girl*.

   Note
   *Footage Courtesy: **Ayla87** (http://www.rgbstock.com/gallery /Ayla87) **Hollywood Camera Work** (http://www.hollywoodcamerawork.us)*

4. Choose the **LD** button from the toolbar; the **Open File** dialog box is displayed. In this dialog box, choose **Documents >Fusion_7> c08_tut1 > c08_tut_01 > Media_Files > girl > hcw_godiva_medium.####.png(1-70)** and then choose the **Open** button; the **Loader1** tool tile is inserted in the **Flow** area.

5. Press 1; the output of the **Loader1** tool is displayed in the left Display View.

6. Choose the **Fit** button from the **Display View** toolbar to fit the image in the Display View, refer to Figure 8-2.

7. Click on the empty space in the **Flow** area and then load **green.jpg** in the **Flow** area; the **Loader2** tool tile is inserted in the **Flow** area.

8. Press 2; the output of the **Loader2** tool is displayed in the right Display View. Choose the **Fit** button from the **Display View** toolbar to fit the image in the Display View, refer to Figure 8-2.

Figure 8-2 *The output of the **Loader1** and **Loader2** tools*

9. Select the **Loader1** tool tile from the **Flow** area and then choose the **Rsz** button from the toolbar; the **Resize1** tool tile is inserted in the **Flow** area and a connection between the **Loader1** and **Resize1** tools is established.

10. Select the **Loader2** tool tile from the **Flow** area and then choose the **Rsz** button from the toolbar; the **Resize2** tool tile is inserted in the **Flow** area and a connection between the **Loader2** and **Resize2** tools is established.

Extracting the Key

In this section, you will extract the key to create an alpha channel by using the **Chroma Keyer** tool.

1. Select the **Resize1** tool tile from the **Flow** area and then choose **Tools > Matte > Chroma Keyer** from the menubar; the **ChromaKeyer1** tool tile is inserted in the **Flow** area and a connection between the **Resize1** and **ChromaKeyer1** tools is established.

2. Press 1; the output of the **ChromaKeyer1** tool is displayed in the left Display View.

    The **ChromaKeyer** tool is used to remove the selected color from the images.

3. In the left Display View, drag the cursor over the green area to create a small rectangular region, which is used to sample the color range from the image sequence; the transparency is displayed in the left Display View, refer to Figure 8-3.

 Note
You may need to sample the color range more than once to pick the required color. Make sure that you do not sample over the character.

4. In the **ChromaKeyer1** tool control window, select the **Lock Color Picking** check box.

5. Choose the **Image** tab in the **ChromaKeyer1** tool control window. Choose the **Green** button from the **Spill Color** area and then choose the **Well Done** button from the **Spill Method** tab; the green color disappears from the Display View and transparency is displayed in the Display View.

6. Click in the left Display View to make it active and then press A; the alpha channel created by the **ChromaKeyer1** tool is displayed, as shown in Figure 8-4.

Figure 8-3 *The output of the **ChromaKeyer1** tool*

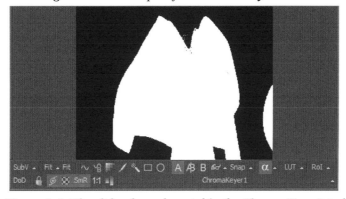

Figure 8-4 *The alpha channel created by the **ChromaKeyer1** tool*

7. In the **Matte** tab of the **ChromaKeyer1** tool control window, set the following values:

Matte Blur: **2.09**   Matte Contract/Expand: **-0.25**

Matte Gamma: **2.65**   Matte Threshold(High): **0.78**

The **Matte Blur** control is used to blur the edges of the matte by using the guassian blur.

The **Matte Gamma** control is used to control the values of the matte in the semi-transparent areas.

The **Matte Contract/Expand** control is used to shrink or expand the semi-transparent areas of the matte. The value specified lower than the value specified for **Matte Threshold** control becomes black and the value specified more than this value becomes white in the matte.

8. Click on the left Display View to make it active and then press C; the color channels are displayed in the Display View, as shown in Figure 8-5.

Figure 8-5 The color channels displayed in the Display View

9. In the **Image** tab of the **ChromaKeyer1** tool control window, set the following values:

Fringe Gamma: **0.81**   Fringe Size: **1.68**

Fringe Shape: **0.82**   Yellow Blue: **0.18**

The **Fringe Gamma** parameter is used to adjust the brightness of the fringe.

The **Fringe Size** parameter is used to expand or contract the size of the fringe.

The **Fringe Shape** parameter is used to expand the matte toward the external edge of the image. Alternatively, it is used to contract the matte toward the inner edge of the fringe.

The **Yellow/Blue** slider is used to color-correct the fringe. It is particularly useful for color-correcting the semi-transparent pixels.

Next, you will draw a garbage matte to remove the unwanted parts from the image.

10. Make sure the **ChromaKeyer1** tool tile is selected in the **Flow** area. Next, choose the **Add a Polyline Mask** button from the left toolbar; the **Polygon1** tool tile is inserted in the **Flow** area. Draw a polyline shape in the Display View, as shown in Figure 8-6.

By default, the **Polygon1** tool is connected to the purple effect mask node.

11. Switch the mask from the purple node to the white garbage matte node, refer to Figure 8-7.

Merging the Images
In this section, you will merge the images to composite them.

1. Drag the red output node of the **ChromaKeyer1** tool tile to the red output node of the **Resize2** tool tile in the **Flow** area; the **Merge1** tool tile is inserted in the **Flow** area and a connection between the **Resize2**, **ChromaKeyer1**, and **Merge1** tools is established.

Figure 8-6 *The polyline shape drawn in the left Display View*

Figure 8-7 The **Polygon1** tool connected to white garbage matte node of the **ChromaKeyer1** tool

2. Press 2; the output of the **Merge1** tool is displayed in the right Display View.

3. Select the **Merge1** tool tile from the **Flow** area and then choose the **CC** button from the toolbar; the **ColorCorrector1** tool tile is inserted in the **Flow** area and a connection between the **ColorCorrector1** and **Merge1** tools is established.

4. Press 2; the output of the **ColorCorrector1** tool is displayed in the right Display View.

5. In the **ColorCorrector1** tool control window, enter the values of the parameters as follows:

Tint: **0.34**   Strength: **0.06**

Master-RGB-Gain: **1.16**

Press SPACEBAR to start the playback of the composition. The output of the **ColorCorrector1** tool at frame 69 is shown in Figure 8-8.

Now, save the composition with the name *c08tut1* at the location *Documents > Fusion_7 > c08_tut > c08_tut_01*. Next, you need to render the composition. For rendering, refer to Tutorial 2 of Chapter 2. You can also view the final render of the composition by downloading the *c08_fusion_7_rndr.zip* file from *http://www.cadcim.com*. The path of the file is mentioned at the beginning of this tutorial.

Figure 8-8 *The output of the **ColorCorrector1** tool at frame 69*

Tutorial 2

In this tutorial, you will extract the matte from an image by using the **Luma Keyer** tool. The final output of the composition is shown in Figure 8-9. **(Expected time: 20 min)**

Figure 8-9 *The final output of the composition*

The following steps are required to complete this tutorial:

a. Set the frame format.
b. Download and import images.
c. Extract the key.
d. Merge the images.

Setting the Frame Format

In this section, you will specify the frame format settings.

1. Choose **File > New** from the menubar; a new composition is opened in the Fusion interface.

2. Choose **File > Preferences** from the menubar; the **Preferences** dialog box is displayed.

3. In this dialog box, select **Frame Format** from the **Composition#** preferences tree; various frame format settings are displayed on the right in the **Preferences** dialog box. Next, select the **HDTV 720** option from the **Default format** drop-down list and then choose the **Save** button to save the changes made and close the dialog box.

4. In the Time Ruler area, enter **0** in the **Global End Time** edit box.

Downloading and Importing the Images

In this section, you will download the images and then import them to the composition.

1. Open the following link: *http:///www.freeimages.com/photo/1200551*; an image is displayed.

2. Download the image at the location */Documents/Fusion_7/c08_tut/c08_tut_02/Media_Files* and save it with the name *church.jpg*.

3. Open *church.jpg* in the Photoshop application and then erase everything from it except the window glasses. Next, save the file with the name *church.tga* at the location specified in the previous step.

> **Note**
> *Footage Courtesy : **Michal Zacharzewski** (http:///www.freeimages.com/profile/mzacha).*

4. Choose the **LD** button from the toolbar; the **Open File** dialog box is displayed. In this dialogbox, choose **Documents > Fusion_7 > c08_tut > c08_tut_02 > Media_Files > church.jpg** and then choose **Open** button; the **Loader1** tool tile is inserted in the **Flow** area.

5. Press 1; the output of the **Loader1** tool is displayed in the left Display View.

6. Choose the **Fit** button from the left **Display View** toolbar to fit the image into the left Display View, refer to Figure 8-10.

7. Click on the empty space in the **Flow** area and then load *church.tga* in the **Flow** area; the **Loader2** tool tile is inserted in the **Flow** area.

8. Press 2 to view the output in the right Display View. Choose the **Fit** button from the **Display View** toolbar to fit the image into the Display View, refer to Figure 8-10.

9. Make sure the **Loader2** tool tile is selected in the **Flow** area. In the **Loader2** tool control window, choose the **Import** tab and then select the **Post-Multiply by Alpha** check box.

Figure 8-10 *The output of the **Loader1** and **Loader2** tools*

10. Select the **Loader1** tool tile from the **Flow** area and then choose the **Rsz** buttonfrom
    the toolbar; the **Resize1** tool tile is inserted in the **Flow** area and a connection between
    the **Loader1** and **Resize1** tools is established.

11. Select the **Loader2** tool tile from the **Flow** area and then choose the **Rsz** button from the
    toolbar; the **Resize2** tool tile is inserted in the **Flow** area and a connection between the
    Loader2 and **Resize2** tools is established.

12. In the **Resize1** and **Resize2** tool control windows, select the **Keep Frame Aspect** check box.

Extracting the Key

In this section, you will extract the key from the image using the **Luma Keyer** tool.

1. Select the **Resize1** tool tile from the **Flow** area. Next, choose **Tools > Matte > Luma Keyer**
    from the menubar; the **LumaKeyer1** tool tile is inserted in the **Flow** area and a connection
    between the **Resize1** and **LumaKeyer1** tools is established.

    The **Luma Keyer** tool creates an alpha channel by using the overall luminance of the image.

2. Press 1; the output of the **Lumakeyer1** tool is displayed in the left Display View.

3. In the **LumaKeyer1** tool control window, enter **0.94** in the **Low** edit box. Next, select the
    Invert check box.

4. Select the **Lumakeyer1** tool tile from the **Flow** area and then choose the **CC** button
    from the toolbar; the **ColorCorrector1** tool tile is inserted in the **Flow** area and a
    connection between the **LumaKeyer1** and **ColorCorrector1** tools is established.

5. Press 2; the output of the **ColorCorrector1** tool is displayed in the right Display View.

6. Choose the **Show Checker Underlay** button from the **Display View** toolbar to disable the
    transparency in the Display View, refer to Figure 8-11.

7. Enter **0.48** in the **Master-RGB-Gain** edit box of the **ColorCorrector1** tool control window.

8. Choose the **BC** button from the toolbar; the **BrightnessContrast1** tool tile is inserted in the
    Flow area and a connection between the **BrightnessContrast1** and **ColorCorrector1**
    tools is established.

9. Press 2; the output of the **BrightnessContrast1** tool is displayed in the right Display View.

10. In the **BrightnessContrast1** tool control window, set the following values:

Gain: **0.63**   Gamma: **0.76**   Contrast: **0.083**

After entering the values, the output of the **BrightnessContrast1** tool is displayed, as shown in Figure 8-12.

Figure 8-11 *The output of the **LumaKeyer1** tool*

Figure 8-12 *The output of the **BrightnessContrast1** tool*

Merging the Images

In this section, you will merge the images.

1. Drag the red output node of the **Resize2** tool tile to the red output node of the **BrightnessContrast1** tool tile; the **Merge1** tool tile is inserted in the **Flow** area and a connection between the **BrightnessContrast1**, **Resize2** and **Merge1** tools is established.

2. Press 2; the output of the **Merge1** tool is displayed in the right Display View, as shown in Figure 8-13.

3. Select the **Resize2** tool tile from the **Flow** area and then choose the **CC** button from the toolbar; the **ColorCorrector2** tool tile is inserted in the **Flow** area and a connection between the **Resize2** and **ColorCorrector2** tools is established.

4. In the **ColorCorrector2** tool control window, set the following values:

Tint: **0.12**   Strength: **0.49**   Master-RGB-Gain: **1.42**

5. Choose **Tools > Blur > Soft Glow** from the menubar; the **SoftGlow1** tool tile is inserted in the **Flow** area and a connection between the **ColorCorrector2** and **SoftGlow1** tools is established.

6. In the **SoftGlow1** tool control window, set the following values:

Gain: **4.08**   Glow Size: **29.84**

After entering the values, the output of the **SoftGlow1** tool is displayed, as shown in Figure 8-14.

Figure 8-13 *The output of the* ***Merge1*** *tool*

Figure 8-14 *The output of the* ***SoftGlow1*** *tool*

Now, save the composition with the name *c08tut2* at the location *Documents > Fusion_7 > c08_tut > c08_tut_02*. Next, you need to render the composition. For rendering, refer to Tutorial 2 of Chapter 2. You can also view the final render of the composition by downloading the *c08_fusion_7_rndr.zip* file from *http://www.cadcim.com*. The path of the file is mentioned at the beginning of the chapter.

Tutorial 3

In this tutorial, you will extract the matte from a footage by using the **Ultra Keyer** tool. The final output of the composition at frame 10 is shown in Figure 8-15.   **(Expected time: 25 min)**

The following steps are required to complete this tutorial:

a. Set the frame format.
b. Download and import images.
c. Extract the key.
d. Merge images.

Figure 8-15 *The final output of the composition at frame 10*

Setting the Frame Format

In this section, you will specify the frame format settings.

1. Choose **File > New** from the menubar; a new composition is opened in the Fusion interface.

2. Choose **File > Preferences** from the menubar; the **Preferences** dialog box is displayed.

3. In this dialog box, select **Frame Format** from the **Composition#** preferences tree; various frame format settings are displayed on the right in the **Preferences** dialog box. Next, select the **HDTV 720** option from the **Default format** drop-down list and then choose the **Save** button to save the changes made and close the dialog box.

4. In the Time Ruler area, enter **50** in the **Global End Time** edit box.

Downloading and Importing the Images

In this section, you will download the images and then import them to the composition.

1. Open the following link: *http://freeimages.com/photo/368787*; an image is displayed.

2. Download the image at the location */Documents/Fusion_7/c08_tut/c08_tut_01/Media_Files* with the name *building.jpg*.

3. Open the following link: *http://www.hollywoodcamerawork.us/greenscreenplates.html;* an image is displayed. Download *hcw_garden_walk.zip* from it and extract the contents of the zip file at the location */Documents/Fusion_7/c08_tut/c08_tut_03/Media_Files/Garden Walk*.

Note
*Footage Courtesy : **Steve Knight** (http://freeimages.com/profile/stevekrh19)*
***Hollywood Camera Work** (http://www.hollywoodcamerawork.us)*

4. Choose the **LD** button from the toolbar; the **Open File** dialog box is displayed. In this dialog box, choose **Documents > Fusion_7 > c08_tut > c08_tut_03 > Media_Files > building.jpg**; the **Loader1** tool tile is inserted in the **Flow** area.

5. Press 1; the output of the **Loader1** tool is displayed in the left Display View.

6. Choose the **Fit** button from the **Display View** toolbar to fit the image into the Display View, refer to Figure 8-16.

7. Click on the empty space in the **Flow** area and then load **hcw_garden_walk.####.png (0-50)** in the **Flow** area; the **Loader2** tool tile is inserted in the **Flow** area, refer to Figure 8-16.

8. Press 2; the output of the **Loader2** tool is displayed in the right Display View. Next, choose the **Fit** button from the **Display View** toolbar to fit the image into the Display View, refer to Figure 8-16.

*Figure 8-16 The output of the **Loader1** and **Loader2** tools*

9. Select the **Loader1** tool tile from the **Flow** area and then choose the **Rsz** button from the toolbar; the **Resize1** tool tile is inserted in the **Flow** area and a connection between the **Loader1** and **Resize1** tools is established.

10. Select the **Loader2** tool tile from the **Flow** area and then choose the **Rsz** button from the toolbar; the **Resize2** tool tile is inserted in the **Flow** area and a connection between the **Loader2** and **Resize2** tools is established.

Extracting the Key

In this section, you will extract the key from the image by using the **Ultra Keyer** tool.

1. Select the **Resize2** tool tile from the **Flow** area and then choose **Tools > Matte > Ultra Keyer** from the menubar; the **UltraKeyer1** tool tile is inserted in the **Flow** area and a connection between the **UltraKeyer1** and **Resize1** tools is established.

2. Press 1; the output of the **Ultra Keyer1** tool is displayed in the left Display View. Next, press 2; the output of the **UltraKeyer1** tool is displayed in the right Display View. Make sure the right Display View is active. Press A to view the alpha channel.

3. In the **UltraKeyer1** tool control window, choose the **Green** button and set the following values:

Background Correction: **0.089**   Matte Separation: **0.031**   Pre-Matte Size: **1.31**

The **Background Correction** parameter works in combination with the background color selected for keying. It allows the **Ultra Keyer** tool to interactively merge the pre-keyed image over the background color selected from the **Color Background** area.

The **Matte Separation** parameter is used to separate/extract the selected color from the footage. This parameter runs a pre-process on the image to separate the foreground from the background before the color selection.

The **Pre Matte Size** parameter is used to close the holes in the matte that are created by spill in the semi-transparent areas.

4. Select the **Lock Color Picking** check box to lock the sampled color range.

5. Choose the **Well Done** button from the **Image** tab and then enter **0.854** in the **Fringe Gamma** edit box.

6. Choose the **Matte** tab and set the following values:

Matte Threshold
Low: **0.55**   High: **0.841**

Matte Blur: **0.366**   Matte Contract/Expand: **0.042**   Matte Gamma: **1.125**

After entering the values, the output of the **UltraKeyer1** tool is displayed in the left and right Display Views, as shown in Figure 8-17.

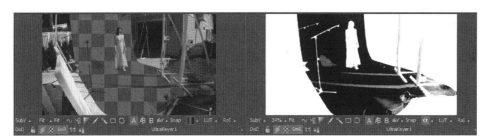

Figure 8-17 *The output of the **UltraKeyer1** tool*

7. Select the **UltraKeyer1** tool tile from the **Flow** area and then choose the **Add a Polyline Mask** button from the toolbar; the **Polygon1** tool tile is inserted in the **Flow** area.

8. Draw a polyline shape in the left Display View, as shown in Figure 8-18.

9. Disconnect the connection between the **Polygon1** and **UltraKeyer1** tools.

10. Drag the red output node of the **Polygon1** tool tile to the white node (garbage matte) of the **UltraKeyer1** tool tile; a connection is established between **Polygon1** and **UltraKeyer1** tools.

Figure 8-18 *The polyline shape drawn in the left Display View*

11. Select the **Invert** check box from the **Polygon1** tool control window. The output of the **UltraKeyer1** tool is displayed in the left and right Display Views, refer to Figure 8-19.

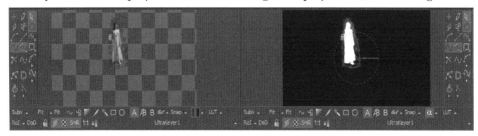

Figure 8-19 *The output of the **UltraKeyer1** tool*

12. Select the **UltraKeyer1** tool tile from the **Flow** area and choose the **CC** button from the toolbar; the **ColorCorrector1** tool tile is inserted in the **Flow** area and a connection between the **UltraKeyer1** and **ColorCorrector1** tools is established.

13. Click on the right Display View to make it active and then press C; the color channels are displayed. Next, press 2; the output of the **ColorCorrector1** tool is displayed in the right Display View.

    Next, you will desaturate the image.

14. In the **ColorCorrector1** tool control window, choose the **Suppress** button and enter the following values:

    Red: **0**   Yellow: **0**   Green: **0**
    Cyan: **0**   Blue: **0**   Magenta: **0**

15. Make sure the **ColorCorrector1** tool tile is selected in the **Flow** area and choose **Tools > Transform > DVE** from the menubar; the **DVE1** tool tile is inserted in the **Flow** area and a connection between the **ColorCorrector1** and **DVE1** tools is established. Next, press 1; the output of the **DVE1** tool is displayed in the left Display View.

16. In the **DVE1** tool control window, enter **38.1** in the **Y Rotation** edit box.

    Next, you will create a shadow of the character.

17. Click on the empty space in the **Flow** area to deselect the selected tool tile, if any. Choose **Tools > Transform > DVE** from the menubar; the **DVE2** tool tile is inserted in the **Flow** area.

18. Drag the red output node of the **ColorCorrector1** tool tile to the orange output node of the **DVE2** tool tile, refer to Figure 8-20. Press 2; the output of the **DVE2** tool is displayed in the right Display View.

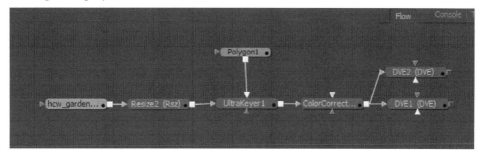

*Figure 8-20 The **DVE2** tool connected to the **ColorCorrector1** tool*

19. In the **DVE2** tool control window, set the following values:

    Center
    X: **0.46**   Y: **0.48**

    X Rotation: **65**   Z Rotation: **61**

20. Make sure the **DVE2** tool tile is selected in the **Flow** area and then choose the **CC**button [CC] from the toolbar; the **ColorCorrector2** tool tile is inserted in the **Flow** area and a connection between the **DVE2** and **ColorCorrector2** tools is established. Press 2; the output of the **ColorCorrector2** tool is displayed in the right Display View.

21. Enter **0** in the **Maser-RGB-Gain** in the **ColorCorrector2** tool control window.

22. Choose the **Show Checker Underlay** button from the right **Display View** toolbar to enable transparency in the Display View, if it is not already chosen, refer to Figure 8-11.

23. Make sure the **ColorCorrector2** tool tile is selected in the **Flow** area and choose the **Blur** button from the toolbar; the **Blur1** tool tile is inserted in the **Flow** area and a connection between the **Blur1** and **ColorCorrector2** tools is established. Press 2; the output of the **Blur1** tool is displayed in the right Display View.

24. Enter **5** in the **Blur Size** edit box in the **Blur1** tool control window.

25. Drag the red output node of the **DVE1** tool tile to the red output node of the **Blur1** tool tile; the **Merge1** tool tile is inserted in the **Flow** area and a connection between the **DVE1**, **Blur1**, and **Merge1** tools is established, refer to Figure 8-21. Press 2; the output of the **Merge1** tool is displayed in the right Display View, as shown in Figure 8-22.

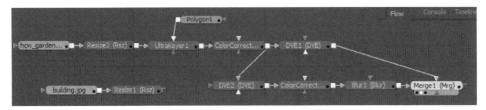

Figure 8-21 *A connection between* ***DVE1***, ***Blur1***, *and* ***Merge1*** *tools established*

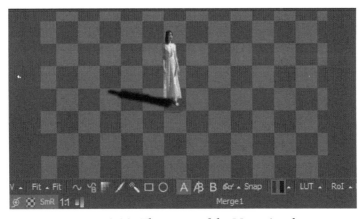

Figure 8-22 *The output of the* ***Merge1*** *tool*

26. Drag the red output node of the **Merge1** tool tile to the red output node of the **Resize1** tool tile; the **Merge2** tool tile is inserted in the **Flow** area and a connection between the **Resize1**, **Merge1**, and **Merge2** tools is established.

27. Press 2; the output of the **Merge2** tool is displayed in the right Display View. Next, in the **Merge2** tool control window, set the following values:

Center
X: **0.18**   Y: **0.18**

Size: **0.56**

After entering the values, the output of the **Merge2** tool is displayed in the right Display View, as shown in Figure 8-23.

Figure 8-23 *The output of the* ***Merge2*** *tool*

Now, save the composition with the name *c08tut3* at the location *Documents > Fusion_7 > c08_tut > c08_tut_03*. Next, you need to render the composition. For rendering, refer to Tutorial 2 of Chapter 2. You can also view the final render of the composition by downloading the *c08_fusion_7_rndr.zip* file from *http://www.cadcim.com*. The path of the file is mentioned at the beginning of the chapter.

Self-Evaluation Test

Answer the following questions and then compare them to those given at the end of this chapter:

1. Which of the following tool categories is used to generate alpha channel by extracting the selected colors from the composition?

   (a) **Warp**   (b) **Matte**
   (c) **Mask**   (d) **Creator**

2. The white node of the **Chroma Keyer** tool is called _____.

3. The **Luma Keyer** tool only extracts matte based on the luminance channel. (T/F)

4. The **Matte Gamma** option is used to make edges in the matte transparent. (T/F)

Review Questions

Answer the following questions:

1. The _____ tool is optimized for extracting mattes from images using the bluescreen or the greenscreen.

2. The _____ tool is used to extract matte based on different channels.

3. The _____ option in all matte tools is used to blur the edges of the matte.

Answers to Self-Evaluation Test
1. b, **2.** Garbage Matte, **3.** F, **4.** T

Chapter 9

Tracking

Learning Objectives

After completing this chapter, you will be able to:
- *Track a footage*
- *Track and composite the foreground image*
- *Stabilize the footage*

INTRODUCTION

Tracking means detecting and following a pixel pattern across the frames in an image sequence. You can detect and measure the movement of patterns that takes place from one frame to another by using the **Tracker** tool. This tool also generates a motion path from the pattern movement that can be used for match-moving, image stabilization, reverse stabilization, sign replacement, and so on. In this chapter, you will learn the tracking process in Fusion.

TUTORIALS

Before you start the tutorials of this chapter, you need to download *c09_fusion_7_tut.zip* file from *http://www.cadcim.com*. The path of the file is as follows:

> *Textbooks > Animation and Visual Effects > Fusion > Blackmagic Design Fusion 7 Studio: A Tutorial Approach*

Next, you need to extract the contents of the downloaded zip file to *\Documents\Fusion_7*.

Tutorial 1

In this tutorial, you will track a footage by using the **Tracker** tool and then superimpose a foreground image over it. The final output of the composition at frame 100 is shown in Figure 9-1.   **(Expected time: 20 min)**

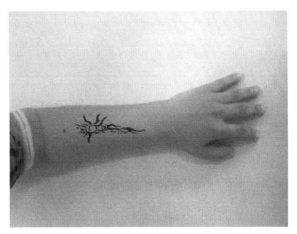

Figure 9-1 *The final output of the composition at frame 100*

The following steps are required to complete this tutorial:

a. Set the frame format.
b. Import the footage.
c. Crop the footage.
d. Track the footage.
e. Color-correct the composition.

Setting the Frame Format

In this section, you will specify the frame format settings.

1. Choose **File > New** from the menubar; a new composition is displayed in the Fusion screen.

2. Choose **File > Preferences** from the menubar; the **Preferences** dialog box is displayed.

3. In this dialog box, select **Frame Format** from the **Composition#** preferences tree; various frame format settings are displayed on the right in the **Preferences** dialog box. Next, select the **NTSC (Square Pixel)** option from the **Default format** drop-down list and then choose the **Save** button to save the changes made and close the dialog box.

Importing the Footage

In this section, you will import the footage.

1. Choose the **LD** button from the toolbar; a dialog box is displayed. In this dialog box, choose **Documents > Fusion_7 > c09_tut > c09_tut_01 > Media_Files > hand.mov** and then choose the **Open** button; the **Loader1** tool tile is inserted in the **Flow** area.

2. Press 1; the output of the **Loader1** tool is displayed in the left Display View.

3. Choose the **Fit** button from the left **Display View** toolbar to fit the footage into the left Display View, refer to Figure 9-2. Next, choose the **Show Checker Underlay** button from the **Display View** toolbar.

4. Press 2; the output of the **Loader2** tool is displayed in the right Display View.

5. In the Time Ruler area, enter **30** in the **Global Start Time** edit box and **100** in the **Global End Time** edit box.

6. Now, import *tattoo.tga* to the **Flow** area; the **Loader2** tool tile is inserted in the **Flow** area.

7. In the control window of the **Loader2** tool, choose the **Import** tab and then select the **Post-Multiply by Alpha** check box.

8. Choose the **Fit** button from the right **Display View** toolbar to fit the image into the right Display View, refer to Figure 9-2.

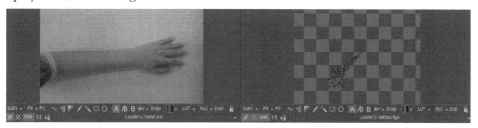

*Figure 9-2 The output of the **Loader1** and **Loader2** tools*

Cropping the Footage

In this section, you will crop the footage.

1. Select the **Loader2** tool tile from the **Flow** area and then choose **Tools > Transform > Crop** from the menubar; the **Crop1** tool tile is inserted in the **Flow** area and a connection between the **Loader2** and **Crop1** tools is established.

2. Press 2; the output of the **Crop1** tool is displayed in the right Display View.

3. In the **Crop1** tool control window, set the values of the parameters as follows:

   X Offset: **400**   Y Offset: **145**

   X Size: **800**   Y Size: **700**

Tracking the Footage

In this section, you will track the footage with the help of the **Tracker** tool.

1. Select the **Loader1** tool tile from the **Flow** area and then choose **Tools > Tracking > Tracker** from the menubar; the **Tracker1** tool tile is inserted in the **Flow** area and a connection between the **Loader1** and **Tracker1** tools is established.

2. Press 1; the output of the **Tracker1** tool is displayed in the left Display View. Also, a solid green rectangular pattern is displayed in the Display Views.

   A pattern is a region of pixels. These pixels are selected for tracking an image. The pattern is visible in the Display Views, only if the tool is active, refer to Figure 9-3. When you hover the cursor over the pattern, an outer rectangle is displayed which represents the search area, refer to Figure 9-4. You can resize the search area by dragging the corners of the rectangle.

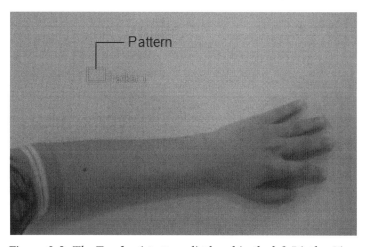

*Figure 9-3 The **Tracker1** pattern displayed in the left Display View*

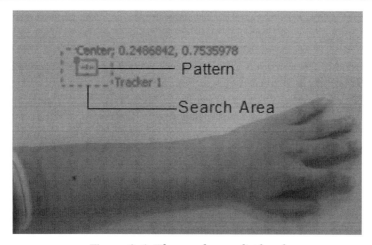

Figure 9-4 The search area displayed

3. Hover the cursor over the pattern in the Display View; a small square box is displayed in the top-left corner of the pattern. By dragging the box, you can zoom the pixels underneath the pattern. Now, drag the box over the tracking marker on the hand, refer to Figure 9-5.

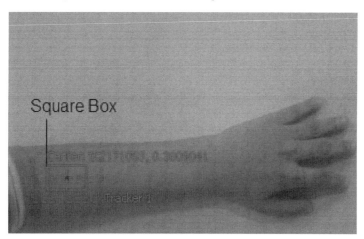

*Figure 9-5 The **Tracker1** placed on the tracking marker*

4. In the **Tracker1** tool control window, choose the **Track forward from currenttime** button; the tracking process is started. On the completion of process, the **Composition1** message box is displayed with the message that the rendering process is completed, as shown in Figure 9-6. Next, choose the **OK** button to close the message box. Notice that a path is created by **Tracker1**, as shown in Figure 9-7.

Figure 9-6 *The* ***Composition1*** *message box displayed*

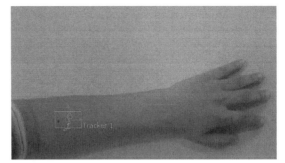

Figure 9-7 *Path displayed in the Display View*

Notice that in the **Tracker1** tool control window, colored bars are displayed in the **Show** area, as shown in Figure 9-8. The green bar indicates a higher degree of accuracy, yellow bar indicates lesser accuracy, and red bar indicates no accuracy.

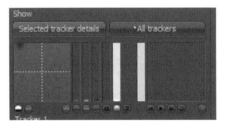

Figure 9-8 *The* ***Show*** *area showing green bar*

You can also add more tracker points by choosing the **+Add** button from the control window. To delete the tracker points, select the tracker that you want to delete from the **Tracker List** area in the **Tracker** tool control window and then choose the **x Delete** button.

5. Choose the **Operations** tab in the **Tracker1** tool control window and then choose the **Match Move** button.

On choosing the **Match Move** button, various options are displayed in the **Tracker1** tool control window. These options are used to match the position, rotation, and scale of the footage. You can also use these options for match moving another element in the scene.

Note
Whenever the ***Tracker*** *tool generates a path, it also creates key points on the path for each frame. If you want to see all the key points for all the frames on the path, you need to select the* ***Tracker1*** *tool tile from the* ***Flow*** *area and then select the path in the Display View. On doing so, the* ***Polyline*** *toolbar will appear on left of the Display View. Choose the* ***Show Key Points*** *button from the toolbar or press SHIFT+K, refer to Figure 9-9.*

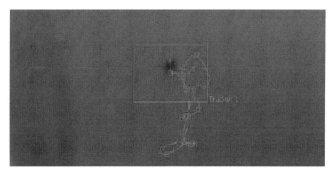

Figure 9-9 *Keypoints on the path in the Display View*

6. Drag the red output node of the **Crop1** tool tile to the green node of the **Tracker1** tool tile in the **Flow** area; the output of the **Crop1** tool is superimposed over the hand, refer to Figure 9-10.

Figure 9-10 *The output of the **Crop1** tool is superimposed over the hand*

7. Select the **Crop1** tool tile from the **Flow** area and then choose the **Xf** button on the toolbar; the **Transform1** tool tile is inserted in the **Flow** area and a connection between the **Crop1**, **Tracker1**, and **Transform1** tools is established.

8. In the **Transform1** tool control window, set the values of the parameters as follows:

   Center
   X: **0.4**   Y: **0.45**

   Size: **0.22**   Aspect: **1**   Angle: **-51**

9. In the **Operations** tab of the **Tracker1** tool control window, select the **Overlay** option from the **Apply Mode** drop-down list.

   After setting the values, the output of the **Tracker1** tool is shown in Figure 9-11.

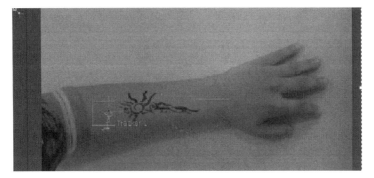

Figure 9-11   *The output of the **Tracker1** tool*

Color-Correcting the Composition

In this section, you will color-correct the composition.

1. Select the **Tracker1** tool tile from the **Flow** area and then choose the **CC** button from the toolbar; the **ColorCorrector1** tool tile is inserted in the **Flow** area and a connection between the **Tracker1** and **ColorCorrector1** tools is established.

2. Press 2; the output of the **ColorCorrector1** tool is displayed in the right Display View.

3. In the **Color Corrector1** tool control window, set the values of the parameters as follows:

Tint: **0.1**   Strength: **0.081**   Master-RGB-Gain: **1.54**

After setting the values of the parameters in the **ColorCorrector1** tool control window, the output of the **ColorCorrector1** tool is displayed in the right Display View, as shown in Figure 9-12.

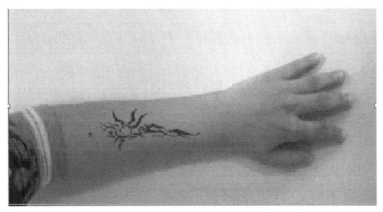

Figure 9-12   *The output of the **ColorCorrector1** tool*

Start the playback of the composition. You will notice that the tatoo image is locked to the position of the marker on the hand. Next, you need to render the composition. For rendering, refer to Tutorial 2 of Chapter 2. The final output is shown in Figure 9-1.

Now, save the composition with the name *c09tut1* at the location *Documents > Fusion_7 > c09_tut > c09_tut_01*. Next, you need to render the composition. For rendering, refer to Tutorial 2 of Chapter 2. The output of the composition at frame 100 is shown in Figure 9-1. You can also view the final render of the composition by downloading the *c09_fusion_7_rndr.zip* from *http://www.cadcim.com*. The path of the file is mentioned at the beginning of the chapter.

Tutorial 2

In this tutorial, you will stabilize a footage by using the **Tracker** tool. The final output of the composition at frame 102 is shown in Figure 9-13.   **(Expected time: 15 min)**

Figure 9-13 *The final output of the composition at frame 102*

The following steps are required to complete this tutorial:

a. Set the frame format.
b. Import the footage.
c. Stabilize the footage.

Setting the Frame Format

In this section, you will specify the frame format settings.

1. Choose **File > New** from the menubar; a new composition is displayed in the Fusion screen.

2. Choose **File > Preferences** from the menubar; the **Preferences** dialog box is displayed.

3. In this dialog box, select **Frame Format** from the **Composition#** preferences tree; various frame format settings are displayed on the right of the **Preferences** dialog box. Next, select the **HDTV 720** option from the **Default format** drop-down list and then choose the **Save** button to save the changes made.

Importing the Footage

In this section, you will import the footage.

1. Choose the **LD** button from the toolbar; a dialog box is displayed. In this dialog box, choose **Documents > Fusion_7 > c09_tut_02 > Media_Files > shot_#####.jpg(0..194)** and then choose the **Open** button; the **Loader1** tool is inserted in the **Flow** area.

2. Press 1; the output of the **Loader1** tool is displayed in the left Display View.

3. Choose the **Fit** button from the **Display View** toolbar to fit the footage into the Display View, refer to Figure 9-14.

Figure 9-14 *The output of the **Loader1** tool*

Stabilizing the Footage

In this section, you will stabilize the footage.

1. Select the **Loader1** tool tile from the **Flow** area and then choose **Tools > Tracking > Tracker** from the menubar; the **Tracker1** tool tile is inserted in the **Flow** area and a connection between the **Tracker1** and **Loader1** tools is established.

2. Press 1; the output of the **Tracker1** tool is displayed in the left Display View; a pattern is displayed in the Display View.

3. Hover the cursor over the pattern in the Display View; a square box is displayed in the top-left corner of the pattern.

4. Drag the square box over the door handle in the footage, as discussed in Tutorial 1 of this chapter, refer to Figure 9-15.

5. Choose the **+Add** button from the **Tracker1** tool control window; the **Tracker 2** pattern is displayed with a square in the Display View. Next, drag the **Tracker2** tool small box to the top right corner of the door, as shown in Figure 9-16.

Figure 9-15 The **Tracker 1** placed on the door handle

Figure 9-16 The **Tracker2** tool placed on the top right corner of the door

6. Choose the **Track forward** button; the tracking process starts. On completion of the tracking process, the **Composition #** message box is displayed. Choose the **OK** button to close the message box.

7. Choose the **Operation** tab from the **Tracker1** tool control window. Next, choose the **Match Move** button and then choose the **BG only** button from the **Merge** area.

   Start the playback of the composition. You will notice that the footage is stabilized around the two track points. Also, the transparent area becomes visible, as shown in Figure 9-17.

8. Select the **Tracker1** tool tile from the **Flow** area and then choose the **Xf** button from the toolbar; the **Transform1** tool tile is inserted in the **Flow** area and a connection between the **Tracker1** and **Transform1** tools is established.

9. Press 2; the output of the **Transform1** tool is displayed in the right Display View.

10. Enter **1.8** in the **Size** edit box of the **Transform1** tool control window.

After entering the value, the output of the **Transform1** tool is displayed in the right Display View. Figure 9-18 shows the output of the **Transform1** tool at frame 102. Start the playback of the composition. You will notice that the footage is now stabilized.

Figure 9-17 *The transparent area in the left Display View at frame 102*

Figure 9-18 *The output of the* ***Transform1*** *tool at frame 102*

Now, save the composition with the name *c09tut2* at the location *Documents > Fusion_7 > c09_tut > c09_tut_02*. Next, you need to render the composition. For rendering, refer to Tutorial 2 of Chapter 2. The output of the composition at frame 102 is shown in Figure 9-13. You can also view the final render of the composition by downloading the *c09_fusion_7_rndr.zip* file from *http://www.cadcim.com*. The path of the file is mentioned at the beginning of the chapter.

Tutorial 3

In this tutorial, you will track a sign board by using the **Corner Positioning** option in the **Tracker** tool. The final output of the composition is shown in Figure 9-19.   **(Expected time: 20 min)**

The following steps are required to complete this tutorial:

a. Set the frame format.
b. Import the footage.
c. Track the footage.
d. Adjust the brightness of the footage.

Figure 9-19 *The final output of the composition*

Setting the Frame Format

In this section, you will specify the frame format settings.

1. Choose **File > New** from the menubar; a new composition is displayed in the Fusion screen.

2. Choose **File > Preferences** from the menubar; the **Preferences** dialog box is displayed.

3. In this dialog box, select **Frame Format** from the **Composition#** preferences tree; various frame format settings are displayed on the right of the **Preferences** dialog box. Next, select the **HDTV 720** option from the **Default format** drop-down list and then choose the **Save** button to save the changes made.

Importing the Footage

In this section, you will import the footage.

1. Choose the **LD** button from the toolbar; a dialog box is displayed. In this dialog box, choose **Documents > Fusion_7 > c09_tut > c09_tut_03 > Media_Files > road_###.jpg(0..16)** and then choose the **Open** button; the **Loader1** tile tool is inserted in the **Flow** area.

2. Press 1; the output of the **Loader1** tool is displayed in the left Display View.

3. Choose the **Fit** button from the **Display View** toolbar to fit the footage into the Display View, refer to Figure 9-20.

4. In the Time Ruler area, enter **30** in the **Global End Time** edit box.

5. Click on the empty space in the **Flow** area to deselect the selected tool tile, if any. Import *direction.jpg* to the **Flow** area; the **Loader2** tool tile is inserted in the **Flow** area.

6. Press 2; the output of the **Loader2** tool is displayed in the right Display View. Choose the **Fit** button from the **Display View** toolbar to fit the image into the Display View, refer to Figure 9-20.

Figure 9-20 *The output of the* **Loader1** *and* **Loader2** *tools*

Tracking the Footage

In this section, you will track the footage.

1. Select the **Loader1** tool tile from the **Flow** area and then choose **Tools > Tracking > Tracker** from the menubar; the **Tracker1** tool tile is inserted in the **Flow** area and a connection between the **Loader1** and **Tracker1** tools is established.

2. Drag the red output node of the **Loader2** tool tile to the green node of the **Tracker1** tool tile; a connection between the **Loader2** and **Tracker1** tools is established.

3. Make sure that the **Tracker1** tool tile is selected in the **Flow** area. Press 1; the output of the **Tracker1** tool is displayed in the left Display View.

   Notice that a pattern is displayed in the left Display View, as shown in Figure 9-21.

Figure 9-21 *The pattern displayed in the left Display View*

4. Hover the cursor over the pattern in the Display View; a small square box is displayed at the top-left corner of the pattern. Next, drag the square box to the top left of the "No Parking" sign board, as shown in Figure 9-22.

Figure 9-22 *The square moved to top left of the "No Parking'" sign board*

5. Choose the **+Add** button from the **Tracker1** tool control window; the **Tracker 2**
    pattern is displayed in the Display View. Now, drag the small square box to the
    top right of the "No Parking" sign board, as shown in Figure 9-23.

Figure 9-23 *The square moved to top right of the "No Parking" sign board*

6. Choose the **+Add** button from the **Tracker1** tool control window; the **Tracker 3** pattern is
    displayed. Next, drag the small square box to the bottom left of the "No Parking" board to
    be tracked, as shown in Figure 9-24.

Figure 9-24 *The square moved to bottom left of the "No Parking" sign board*

7. Choose the **+Add** button from the **Tracker1** tool control window; the **Tracker 4** pattern is displayed. Next, drag the square box to the bottom right of the board, as shown in Figure 9-25.

Figure 9-25 The square moved to bottom right of the No Parking sign board

8. Choose the **Trackers** tab from the **Tracker1** tool control window, and then choose the **Track forward** button; the tracking process starts. On the completion of tracking process, the **Composition#** message box is displayed. Choose the **OK** button to close the message box.

9. Choose the **Operation** tab from the **Tracker1** tool control window and then choose the **Corner Positioning** button from the **Operation** area; the "No Parking" board is replaced by the output of the **Loader2** tool.

Adjusting the Brightness of the Footage

In this section, you will adjust the brightness of the footage.

1. Select the **Loader2** tool tile from the **Flow** area and then choose the **BC** button from the toolbar; the **BrightnessContrast1** tool tile is inserted in the **Flow** area and a connection between the tools **Loader2** and **BrightnessContrast1** tools is established.

2. In the **BrightnessContrast1** tool control window, set the values of the parameters as follows:

    Gain: **0.77**   Gamma: **1.21**   Contrast: **0.08**   Saturation: **0.94**

    After setting the values, the output of the **Tracker1** tool is displayed in the left Display View. Figure 9-26 shows the output of the **Tracker1** tool at frame 14.

    Start the playback of the composition. You will notice that the output of the **Loader2** tool is superimposed over the "No Parking" sign board.

    Now, save the composition with the name *c09tut3* at the location *Documents > Fusion_7 > c09_tut > c09_tut_03*. Next, you need to render the composition. For rendering, refer to Tutorial 2 of Chapter 2. The output of the composition at frame 14 is shown in Figure 9-26. You can also view the final render of the composition by downloading the *c09_fusion_7_rndr.zip* file from *http://www.cadcim.com*. The path of the file is mentioned at the beginning of the chapter.

Figure 9-26 *The output of the **Tracker1** tool at frame 14*

Self-Evaluation Test

Answer the following questions and then compare them to those given at the end of this chapter:

1. Which of the following tools is used to detect and follow a pixel pattern across the frames in a video?

    (a) **Effect**   (b) **Transform**
    (c) **Creator**   (d) **Tracker**

2. Which of the following combinations of shortcut keys is used to display keys of the tracking path in the Display View?

    (a) SHIFT+P   (b) SHIFT+S
    (c) SHIFT+K   (d) CTRL+L

3. The _____ tool is used to detect and measure the movement of patterns that takes place from one frame to another.

4. You can add tracker by choosing the _____ button to add tracker from the **Tracker** tool control window in the Display View.

5. The red bar in the **Show** area of the **Tracker** tool control window indicates that there is no accuracy. (T/F)

Review Questions

Answer the following questions:

1. The _____ mode is used to stabilize an image.

2. A green bar displayed in tracking process indicates _____ accuracy.

3. A yellow bar in the **Tracker** tool control window indicates less accuracy. (T/F)

Answers to Self-Evaluation Test
1. d, **2.** c, **3. Tracker**, **4. +Add**, **5.** T

Chapter 10

Effect Tools

Learning Objectives

After completing this chapter, you will be able to:

- *Create the highlight effect*
- *Create the lens flare effect*
- *Create the shadow effect*
- *Create the ghost effect*

INTRODUCTION

The Effect tools are used to create various effects in a composition. These effects help add realism to the composition. In this chapter, you will learn how to create various effects such as highlight, shadow, lens flare, and so on in a composition.

TUTORIALS

The compositions created in this chapter can be downloaded from *http://www.cadcim.com*. These compositions are contained in the *c10_fusion_7_tut.zip* file. The path of the file is as follows:

Textbooks > Animation and Visual Effects > Fusion > Blackmagic Design Fusion 7 Studio: A Tutorial Approach

Next, extract the contents of the zip file to *\Documents\Fusion_7*.

Tutorial 1

In this tutorial, you will create sparkling stars by using the **Highlight** tool. The final output of the composition is shown in Figure 10-1.   **(Expected time: 15 min)**

Figure 10-1 The final output of the composition at frame 10

The following steps are required to complete this tutorial:

a. Set the frame format.
b. Download and import the image.
c. Create the highlight effect.

Setting the Frame Format

In this section, you will specify the frame format settings.

1. Choose **File > New** from the menubar; a new composition is displayed in the Fusion screen.

2. Choose **File > Preferences** from the menubar; the **Preferences** dialog box is displayed.

3. In this dialog box, select **Frame Format** from the **Composition#** preferences tree; various frame format settings are displayed on the right in the **Preferences** dialog box. Next, select the **HDTV 720** option from the **Default format** drop-down list and then choose the **Save** button to save the changes made.

4. In the Time Ruler area, enter **50** in the **Global End Time** edit box.

Downloading and Importing the Image

In this section, you will download and import the image.

1. Open the following link: *http://www.freeimages.com/photo/430366*; an image is displayed.

2. Download the image to */Documents/Fusion_7/c10_tut/c10_tut_01/Media_Files* and save it with the name *christmas tree.jpg*.

 Note
*Footage Courtesy: **Johannes Wienke** (http://www.freeimages.com/profile/languitar).*

3. Choose the **LD** button from the toolbar; the **Open File** dialog box is displayed. In this dialog box, choose **Documents > Fusion_7 > c10_tut > c10_tut_01 > Media_Files > christmas tree.jpg** and then choose the **Open** button; the **Loader1** tool is inserted in the **Flow** area.

4. Press 1; the output of the **Loader1** tool is displayed in the left Display View.

5. Choose the **Fit** button from the left **Display View** toolbar to fit the image into the left Display View, refer to Figure 10-2.

Creating the Highlight Effect

In this section, you will create the highlight effect by using the **Highlight** tool.

1. Select the **Loader1** tool tile from the **Flow** area and then choose **Tools > Effect > Highlight** from the menubar; the **Highlight1** tool tile inserted in the **Flow** area and a connection between the **Loader1** and **Highlight1** tools is established.

2. Press 2; the output of the **Highlight1** tool is displayed in the right Display View. Choose the **Fit** button from the right **Display View** toolbar to fit the image into the right Display View.

Figure 10-2 *The output of the **Loader1** tool*

3. In the **Highlight1** tool control window, set the values of the parameters as follows:

Low: **0.87**   Curve: **0.65**

The **Highlight** tool is used to create highlights in the brighter areas of the image. The **Low** and **High** parameters are used to define the range of luminance level. The brighter areas having luminance value less than the value specified in the **Low** parameter will not receive highlights, whereas the area having luminance value lower than the value specified in the **High** parameter will receive full highlights.

Next, you will animate the highlights.

4. In the **Highlight1** tool control window, create keyframes for the **Length** control by using the following values:

Frame	Length
0	0.22
10	0.89
20	0.28
30	0.86
40	0.61
50	0.87

Press SPACEBAR to start the playback of the composition. The output of the **Higlight1** tool at frame 10 is shown in Figure 10-3.

Now, save the composition with the name *c10tut1* at the location *Documents > Fusion_7 > c10_tut > c10_tut_01*. Next, you need to render the composition. For rendering, refer to Tutorial 2 of Chapter 2. You can also view the final render of the composition by downloading the *c10_fusion_7_rndr.zip* from *http://www.cadcim.com*. The path of the file is mentioned at the beginning of the chapter.

Figure 10-3 *The output of the **Highlight1** tool at frame 10*

Tutorial 2

In this tutorial, you will create the lens flare effect by using the **Hot Spot** tool. The final output of the composition is shown in Figure 10-4. **(Expected time: 15 min)**

Figure 10-4 *The final output of the composition*

The following steps are required to complete this tutorial:

a. Set the frame format.
b. Download and import the image.
c. Create the lens flare effect.

Setting the Frame Format

In this section, you will specify the frame format settings.

1. Choose **File > New** from the menubar; a new composition is displayed in the Fusion screen.

2. Choose **File > Preferences** from the menubar; the **Preferences** dialog box is displayed.

3. In this dialog box, select **Frame Format** from the **Composition#** preferences tree; various frame format settings are displayed on the right in the **Preferences** dialog box. Next, select

the **NTSC (Square Pixel)** option from the **Default format** drop-down list and then choose the **Save** button to save the changes made.

4. In the Time Ruler area, enter **0** in the **Global End Time** edit box.

Downloading and Importing the Image

In this section, you will download the image and import it to the composition.

1. Open the following link: *http://www.freeimages.com/photo/633050*; an image is displayed.

2. Download the image to */Documents/Fusion_7/c06_tut/c10_tut_02/Media_Files* and save it with the name *sun.jpg*.

Note

Footage Courtesy: **Daniel Duchon** *(http://www.freeimages.com/profile/dduchon)*

3. Choose the **LD** button from the toolbar; a dialog box is displayed. In this dialog box, choose **Documents > Fusion_7 > c10_tut > c10_tut_02 > Media_Files > sun.jpg** and then choose the **Open** button; the **Loader1** tool tile is inserted in the **Flow** area.

4. Press 1; the output of the **Loader1** tool is displayed in the left Display View.

5. Choose the **Fit** button from the left **Display View** toolbar to fit the image into the left Display View, refer to Figure 10-5.

Figure 10-5 *The output of the **Loader1** tool*

6. Select the **Loader1** tool tile from the **Flow** area and choose the **Rsz** button from the toolbar; the **Resize1** tool tile is inserted in the **Flow** area and a connection between the **Loader1** and **Resize1** tools is established.

7. Press 1; the output of the **Resize1** tool is displayed in the left Display View.

Creating the Lens Flare Effect

In this section, you will create the lens flare effect by using the **Hot Spot** tool.

1. Make sure the **Resize1** tool tile is selected in the **Flow** area. Next, choose **Tools > Effect > Hot Spot** from the menubar; the **HotSpot1** tool tile is inserted in the **Flow** area and a connection between the **Resize1** and **HotSpot1** tools is established.

2. Press 2; the output of the **HotSpot1** tool is displayed in the right Display View.

    The **HotSpot** tool is used to create the lens flare and spotlight effects in the composition.

3. In the **HotSpot1** tool control window, set the values of the parameters as follows:

    Primary Center
    X: **0.254**   Y: **0.513**

    Primary Strength: **0.26**   HotSpot Size: **0.09**   Aspect: **0.97**

    Aspect Angle: **220.95**   Secondary Strength: **0.51**   Secondary Size: **0.53**

    Apply Mode: **Add (Burn)**   Lens Aberration: **Out**   Aberration: **2.63**

Primary Center is used to set the position of the primary hotspot. The **Primary Strength** parameter is used to control the brightness of the primary hotspot. **HotSpot Size** is used to set the size of the hotspot. **Aspect Angle** is used to set the rotation of the hotspot. The **Secondary Strength** parameter is used to set the brightness of the secondary hotspot. The **Secondary Size** parameter is used to set the size of the secondary hotspot. The **Apply Mode** option controls how hotspot will affect the image underneath it. The **Lens Aberration** option is used to control the shape of the primary and secondary hotspots. The **Aberration** option is used to control the overall strength of the lens aberration effect.

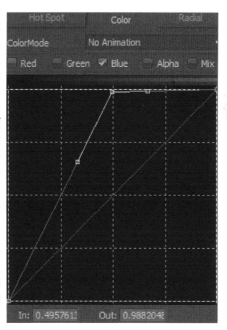

4. In the **HotSpot1** tool control window, choose the **Color** tab and then clear the **Red**, **Green**, **Alpha**, and **Mix** check boxes located below the **ColorMode** drop-down list. Next, modify the blue spline, as shown in Figure 10-6.

Figure 10-6 *The blue spline modified in the Color tab*

5. In the **HotSpot1** tool control window, choose the **Radial** tab and then enter **57.14** in the **Length Angle** edit box.

6. Choose the **L1** tab and then select the **Lens Reflc 1** check box. In this tab, set the values of the parameters as follows:

Element Strength: **0.97**   Element Size: **0.48**   Element Position: **0.61**

7. Choose the **L2** tab and then select the **Lens Reflc 2** check box. In this tab, set the value of the parameter as follows:

Element Size: **0.65**

8. In the **Lens** area, set the values of the parameters as follows:

R: **0.4**   G: **0.4**   B: **1.0**

9. Choose the **L3** tab and then select the **Lens Reflc 3** check box. In this tab, set the values of the parameters as given next:

Element Strength: **0.11**   Element Size: **0.67**   Element Position: **1.2**

10. Choose the **NGon Solid** button and then set the values of the parameters as follows:

NGon Angle: **400**   NGon Sides: **6**   NGon Starryness: **0.12**

11. In the **Lens** area, set the values of the parameters as follows:

R: **0.11**   G: **0.15**   B: **0.72**

After entering the values, the output of the **HotSpot1** tool is displayed in the right Display View, as shown in Figure 10-7.

*Figure 10-7 The final output of the **HotSpot1** tool*

Now, save the composition with the name *c10tut2* at the location *Documents > Fusion_7 > c10_tut > c10_tut_02*. Next, you need to render the composition. For rendering, refer to Tutorial 1 of Chapter 2. You can also view the final render of the composition by downloading the *c10_fusion_7_rndr.zip* file from *http://www.cadcim.com*. The path of the file is mentioned at the beginning of the chapter.

Tutorial 3

In this tutorial, you will create the shadow of an object by using the **Shadow** tool. The final output of the composition is shown in Figure 10-8.   **(Expected time: 20 min)**

Figure 10-8 *The final output of the composition*

The following steps are required to complete this tutorial:

a.   Set the frame format.
b.   Download and import the image.
c.   Create a shadow.

Setting the Frame Format

In this section, you will specify the frame format settings.

1.   Choose **File > New** from the menubar; a new composition is displayed in the Fusion screen.

2.   Choose **File > Preferences** from the menubar; the **Preferences** dialog box is displayed.

3.   In this dialog box, select **Frame Format** from the **Composition#** preferences tree; various frame format settings are displayed on the right in the **Preferences** dialog box. Next, select the **NTSC (Square Pixel)** option from the **Default format** drop-down list and then choose the **Save** button to save the changes made.

4.   In the Time Ruler area, enter **0** in the **Global End Time** edit box.

Downloading and Importing the Image

In this section, you will download the image and import them to the composition.

1.   Open the following link: *http://www.freeimages.com/photo/1161750*; an image is displayed.

2.   Download the image to */Documents/Fusion_7/c10_tut/c10_tut_03/Media_Files* and save it with the name *street.jpg*.

Note

*Footage Courtesy: **Mattox** (http://www.freeimages.com/profile/Mattox)*

3. Choose the **LD** button from the toolbar; a dialog box is displayed. In this dialog box, choose **Documents > Fusion_7 > c10_tut > c10_tut_03 > Media_Files > street.jpg** and then choose the **Open** button; the **Loader1** tool tile is inserted in the **Flow** area.

4. Press 1; the output of the **Loader1** tool is displayed in the left Display View.

5. Choose the **Fit** button from the left **Display View** toolbar to fit the image into the left Display View, refer to Figure 10-9.

6. Click on the empty space in the **Flow** area to deselect the selected tool tile, if any. Similarly, load *girl.tga* in the **Flow** area; the **Loader2** tool tile is inserted in the **Flow** area.

7. Press 2; the output of the **Loader2** tool is displayed in the right Display View.

8. Choose the **Fit** button from the right **Display View** toolbar to fit the image into the right Display View.

9. In the **Loader2** tool control window, choose the **Import** tab and then select the **Post-Multiply by Alpha** check box. The output after selecting the **Post-Multiply by Alpha** check box is displayed in the right Display View, refer to Figure 10-9.

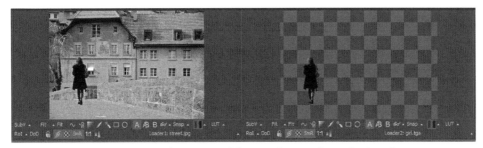

*Figure 10-9 The output of the **Loader1** and **Loader2** tools*

10. Select the **Loader1** tool tile in the **Flow** area and then choose the **Rsz** button from the toolbar; the **Resize1** tool is inserted in the **Flow** area.

Creating a Shadow

In this section, you will create a shadow by using the **Shadow** tool.

1. Drag the red output node of the **Loader2** tool tile to the red output node of the **Resize1** tool tile; the **Merge1** tool tile is inserted in the **Flow** area and a connection between the **Resize1**, **Loader2**, and **Merge1** tools is established.

2. Press 2; the output of the **Merge1** tool is displayed in the right Display View.

3. Select the **Loader2** tool tile from the **Flow** area and choose **Tools > Effect > Shadow** from the menubar; the **Shadow1** tool tile is inserted in the **Flow** area and a connection between the **Loader2** and **Shadow1** tools is established.

4. Drag the white output node of the **Loader2** tool tile to the green node of the **Shadow1** tool tile; a connection between the **Loader2** and **Shadow1** tools is established, as shown in Figure 10-10.

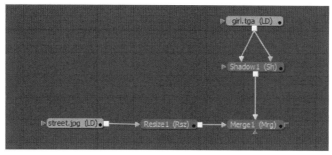

*Figure 10-10 The **Shadow1** tool connected to the **Loader2** tool*

5. In the **Shadow1** tool control window, set the values of the parameters as follows:

Shadow Offset
X: **0.59**   Y: **0.39**

Softness: **0.004**

Shadow Color
R: **0.48**   G: **0.48**   C: **0.48**

Light Distance: **0.71**   Z Map Channel: **Alpha**   Output: **Shadow Only**

After entering the values, the output of the **Merge1** tool is displayed, as shown in Figure 10-11.

*Figure 10-11 The output of the **Merge1** tool*

6. Make sure the **Shadow1** tool tile is selected in the **Flow** area and then choose **Tools > Transform > DVE** from the menubar; the **DVE1** tool tile is inserted in the **Flow** area and a connection between the **Shadow1** and **DVE1** tools is established.

7. In the **DVE1** tool control window, set the values of the parameters as follows:

Center
X: **0.46**   Y: **0.52**   Z Move: **1.31**

Pivot
X: **0.29**   Y: **0.07**   Z Pivot: **0.07**

X Rotation: **59**   Z Rotation: **182.1**

The output of the **Merge1** tool after adjusting the shadow is shown in Figure 10-12.

Figure 10-12 *The output of the **Merge1** tool after adjusting the shadow*

Now, save the composition with the name *c10tut3* at the location *Documents > Fusion_7 > c10_tut > c10_tut_03*. Next, you need to render the composition. For rendering, refer to Tutorial 1 of Chapter 2. The output of the composition is shown in Figure 10-8. You can also view the final render of the composition by downloading the *c10_fusion_7_rndr.zip* file from *http://www.cadcim.com*. The path of the file is mentioned at the beginning of the chapter.

Tutorial 4

In this tutorial, you will create a ghost effect by using the **Trails** tool. The final output of the composition at frame 15 is shown in Figure 10-13.   **(Expected time: 25 min)**

The following steps are required to complete this tutorial:

a. Set the frame format.
b. Download and import the images.

c. Color-correct the composition.
d. Create a ghost effect.

Figure 10-13 *The final output of the composition at frame 15*

Setting the Frame Format

In this section, you will specify the frame format settings.

1. Choose **File > New** from the menubar; a new composition is displayed in the Fusion screen.

2. Choose **File > Preferences** from the menubar; the **Preferences** dialog box is displayed.

3. In this dialog box, select **Frame Format** from the **Composition#** preferences tree; various frame format settings are displayed on the right in the **Preferences** dialog box. Next, select the **NTSC (Square Pixel)** option from the **Default format** drop-down list and then choose the **Save** button to save the changes made.

4. In the Time Ruler area, enter **25** in the **Global End Time** edit box.

Downloading and Importing the Images

In this section, you will download the images and import them to the composition.

1. Open the following link: *http://www.freeimages.com/photo/1109484*; an image is displayed.

2. Download the image to */Documents/Fusion_7/c10_tut/c10_tut_04/Media_Files* and save it with the name *graveyard.jpg*.

Note
Footage Courtesy: **Yuri Nemkin** *(http://www.freeimages.com/profile/sardinelly)*

3. Choose the **LD** button from the toolbar; a dialog box is displayed. In this dialog box, choose **Documents > Fusion_7 > c10_tut > c10_tut_04 > Media_Files > graveyard.jpg** and then choose the **Open** button; the **Loader1** tool is inserted in the **Flow** area.

4. Press 1; the output of the **Loader1** tool is displayed in the left Display View.

5. Choose the **Fit** button from the left **Display View** toolbar to fit the image into the left Display View, refer to Figure 10-14.

6. Click on the empty space in the **Flow** area and then import *run####.tga(0..100)*; the **Loader2** tool tile is inserted in the **Flow** area.

7. Press 2; the output of the **Loader2** tool is displayed in the right Display View.

8. Choose the **Fit** button from the right **Display View** toolbar to fit the image into the right Display View, refer to Figure 10-14.

Figure 10-14 *The output of the **Loader1** and **Loader2** tools*

9. In the **Loader2** tool control window, choose the **Import** tab and then select the **Post-Multiply by Alpha** check box.

10. Select the **Loader1** tool tile from the **Flow** area and then choose the **Rsz** button from the toolbar; the **Resize1** tool tile is inserted in the **Flow** area and a connection between the **Loader1** and **Resize1** tools is established.

Color-Correcting the Composition

In this section, you will color-correct the composition.

1. Select the **Resize1** tool tile from the **Flow** area and choose the **CC** button from the toolbar; the **ColorCorrector1** tool tile is inserted in the **Flow** area and a connection between the **Resize1** and **ColorCorrector1** tools is established.

2. Press 1; the output of the **ColorCorrector1** tool is displayed in the left Display View.

3. Enter **0.14** in the **Master-RGB-Gain** edit box of the **ColorCorrector1** tool control window. Next, choose the **Suppress** tab and set the values of the parameters as follows:

Red: **0**	Yellow: **0**	Green: **0**
Cyan: **0**	Blue: **0**	Magenta: **0**

4. Select the **Loader2** tool tile from the **Flow** area and choose the **CC** button from the toolbar; the **ColorCorrector2** tool tile is inserted in the **Flow** area and a connection between the **Loader2** and **ColorCorrector2** tools is established.

5. Press 2; the output of the **ColorCorrector2** tool is displayed in the right Display View.

6. In the **ColorCorrector2** tool control window, enter **0.99** in the **Master-RGB-Gain** edit box. Next, choose the **Suppress** tab and set the values of the parameters as follows:

Red: **0**	Yellow: **0**	Green: **0**
Cyan: **0**	Blue: **0**	Magenta: **0**

The output of the **ColorCorrector2** tool after specifying all parameters is shown in Figure 10-15.

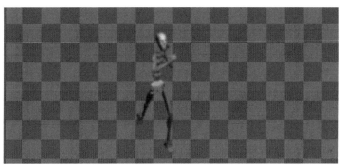

Figure 10-15 *The output of the **ColorCorrector2** tool*

Creating a Ghost Effect

In this section, you will create a ghost effect by using the **Trails** tool.

1. Select the **ColorCorrector2** tool tile from the **Flow** area and choose **Tools > Effect > Trails** from the toolbar; the **Trails1** tool tile is inserted in the **Flow** area and a connection between the **ColorCorrector1** and **Trails1** tools is established.

2. Press 2; the output of the **Trails1** tool is displayed in the right Display View.

3. In the **Trails1** tool control window, set the values of the parameters as follows:

Gain: **0.86**   Blur Size: **2.5**   X Offset: **-0.001**

Now, play the simulation to see the output of the **Trails1** tool.

4. Drag the red output node of the **Trails1** tool tile to the red output node of the **ColorCorrector1** tool tile; the **Merge1** tool tile is inserted in the **Flow** area and a connection between the **Trails1**, **ColorCorrector1**, and **Merge1** tools is established.

5. Press 2; the output of the **Merge1** tool is displayed in the right Display View.

6. In the **Merge1** tool control window, set the values of the parameters as follows:

    Center
    X: **0.44**   Y: **0.023**

    Size: **2.08**

7. Select the **Trails1** tool tile from the **Flow** area and then choose **Tools > Effect > Highlight** from the menubar; the **Highlight1** tool tile is inserted in the **Flow** area and a connection between the **Trails1** and **Highlight1** tools is established.

8. In the **Highlight1** tool control window, set the values of the parameters as follows:

    Low: **0.8**   Curve: **0.9**   Length: **0.58**

    Press SPACEBAR to start the playback of the composition. Figure 10-16 shows the output of **Merge1** tool at frame 15. Figure 10-17 shows the network of tools in the composition.

Figure 10-16 *The output of the **Merge1** tool at frame 15*

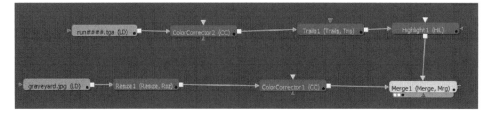

Figure 10-17 *The network of tools in the composition*

Note
*Before playing the animation, you need to choose the **Restart** button in the **Trails** tool control window to clear the image buffer and display a clean frame.*

Now, save the composition with the name *c10tut4* at the location *Documents > Fusion_7 > c10_tut > c10_tut_04*. Next, you need to render the composition. For rendering, refer to Tutorial 2 of Chapter 2. You can also view the final render of the composition by downloading the *c10_fusion_7_rndr.zip* file from *http://www.cadcim.com*. The path of the file is mentioned at the beginning of the chapter.

Self-Evaluation Test

Answer the following questions and then compare them to those given at the end of this chapter:

1. Which of the followings tools is used to create highlight in the brighter areas of an image?

   (a) **FastNoise**   (b) **Highlight**
   (c) **Hot Spot**   (d) **Trails**

2. The _____ tool is used to create the lens flare effect in the composition.

3. The _____ tool is used to create the shadow in the composition.

4. The **Trails** tool is used to create the trailing ghost effect. (T/F)

Review Questions

Answer the following questions:

1. The _____ is used to set the _____ of the hotspot.

2. The _____ is used to set the brightness of the secondary hotspot.

3. The **Highlight** tool is a part of the **Matte** tool category. (T/F)

Answers to Self-Evaluation Test
1. b, **2. Hot Spot**, **3. Shadow**, **4.** T

Chapter 11

Deep Pixel and Position Tools

Learning Objectives

After completing this chapter, you will be able to:
- *Create the fog effect*
- *Control the texture mapping*
- *Control the lighting and reflection mapping of a 3D image*
- *Create the depth-of-field effect*
- *Create the volume fog effect*

INTRODUCTION

The Deep Pixel tool category contains four tools: **Depth Blur**, **Fog**, **Shader**, and **Texture**. These tools are used to generate depth effects, simulated fog effects, lighting effects, and texture mapping. The **Deep Pixel** and **Position** tools are dependant on the presence of Auxiliary channels such as UV maps, XYZ Normal maps, and Z channel in a 3D rendered image. In this chapter, you will create various depth based effects by using the Deep Pixel and Position tools.

TUTORIALS

Before you start the tutorials of this chapter, you need to download the *c11_fusion_7_tut.zip* file from *http://www.cadcim.com*. The path of the file is as follows:

Textbooks > Animation and Visual Effects > Fusion > Blackmagic Design Fusion 7 Studio: A Tutorial Approach

Next, extract the contents of the zip file to *\Documents\Fusion_7*.

Tutorial 1

In this tutorial, you will create fog by using the **Fog** tool on a 3D rendered image. The final output of the composition at frame 22 is shown in Figure 11-1.   **(Expected time: 25 min)**

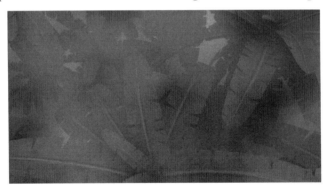

Figure 11-1 *The final output of the composition at frame 22*

The following steps are required to complete this tutorial:

a. Set the frame format.
b. Import the images.
c. Simulate fog.

Setting the Frame Format

In this section, you will specify the frame format settings.

1. Choose **File > New** from the menubar; a new composition is opened in the Fusion screen.

2. Choose **File > Preferences** from the menubar; the **Preferences** dialog box is displayed.

3. In this dialog box, select **Frame Format** from the **Composition#** preferences tree; various frame format settings are displayed on the right of the **Preferences** dialog box.

4. Now, choose the **New** button in the **Settings** area; the **Enter the name for the new image format** dialog box is displayed. Enter **640x360** in the edit box displayed in this dialog box and then choose the **OK** button to close it. Next, set the values of the parameters in the **Preferences** dialog box as follows:

Settings
Width: **640**   Height: **360**

Frame rate: **24**   Aspect ratio: **1:1**

5. Choose the **Save** button to save the changes made.

6. In the Time Ruler area, enter **79** in the **Global End Time** edit box.

Importing the Images
In this section, you will import images in the composition.

1. Choose the **LD** button from the toolbar; the **Open File** dialog box is displayed. In this dialog box, choose **Documents > Fusion_7 > c11_tut > c11_tut_01 > Media_Files > jungle. mov** and then choose the **Open** button; the **Loader1** tool tile is inserted in the **Flow** area.

2. Press 1; the output of the **Loader1** tool is displayed in the left Display View. Next, choose the **Fit** button from the left **Display View** toolbar to fit the image into the left Display View.

3. Activate the left Display View and then press Z; a big red cross is displayed in the viewport along with a message informing that Z channel is not present in the image, as shown in Figure 11-2. Next, press C to view the color channels in the Display View.

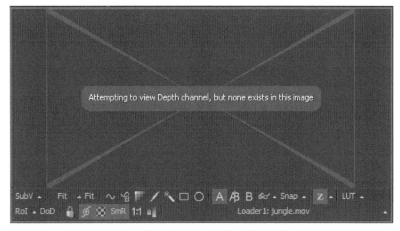

Figure 11-2 The red cross in the left Display View

4. Click on the empty space in the **Flow** area to deselect the selected tool tile, if any. Now, load the *DZP.##.iff (1..80)* file from the */Media_Files/jungleDepthPass* folder in the **Flow** area; the **Loader2** tool tile is inserted in the **Flow** area.

5. Press 2; the output of the **Loader2** tool is displayed in the right Display View. Next, choose the **Fit** button from the right **Display View** toolbar to fit the image into the right Display View.

   Notice the greyscale pixels in the output of the **Loader2** tool shown in Figure 11-3. You need to map these pixels to the Auxiliary Z channel to create depth planes. The Z channel will be used to simulate the fog effect.

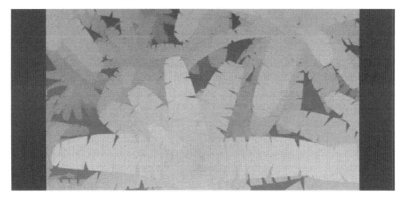

Figure 11-3 *The output of the **Loader2** tool*

Simulating Fog

The **Fog** tool is used to simulate the fog effect in a 3D rendered image. This tool relies on a valid Z-buffer channel. The placement of fog is controlled by using the Z channel planes. It can be specified using the **Fog** tool control window. If the Z channel is not present in the 3D rendered image, you can use the **Channel Boolean** tool to map the luminance of the image to the Z-Auxiliary channel, provided you have a luminance version of the 3D rendered image such as Luminance pass.

Next, you will generate the Z channel by using the **Channel Booleans** tool and then connect the **Fog** tool with the **Channel Booleans** tool to simulate the fog.

1. Select the **Loader1** tool tile from the **Flow** area and choose **Tools > Color > Channel Booleans**; the **ChannelBooleans1** tool tile is inserted in the **Flow** area and a connection between the **Loader1** and **ChannelBooleans1** tools is established.

2. Drag the red output node of the **Loader2** tool tile to the green node of the **ChannelBooleans1** tool tile; a connection between the **Loader2** and **ChannelBooleans1** tools is established, as shown in Figure 11-4.

3. Press 2; the output of the **ChannelBooleans1** tool is displayed in the right Display View.

4. In the **Color Channels** tab of the **ChannelBooleans1** tool control window, select **Do Nothing**

in the **To Red**, **To Green**, **To Blue**, and **To Alpha** drop-down lists, as shown in Figure 11-5.

As **Do Nothing** is selected in the drop-down lists, there will be no effect on the RGBA channels.

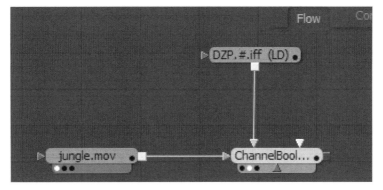

*Figure 11-4 The **ChannelBooleans1** tool connected to the **Loader2** tool*

*Figure 11-5 The **ChannelBooleans1** tool control window*

5. Choose the **Aux Channels** tab and select the **Enable Extra channels** check box. Next, select **Lightness FG** from the **To Z Buffer** drop-down list; the lightness (luminance values) from the **Loader2** tool is mapped on to the Z channel.

   In the **To Z Buffer** drop-down list, the **Lightness BG** option is also available but the **Lightness FG** option is selected in Step 4 as the luminance data (**Loader2** tool) is connected to the **Foreground** input of the **ChannelBooleans1** tool.

6. Activate the right Display View and then press Z; the Z channel is displayed in the right Display View, as shown in Figure 11-6. Next, press C; the color channels are displayed in the Display View.

7. Right-click on the **ChannelBooleans1** tool; a shortcut menu is displayed. Next, choose **Insert Tool > Deep Pixel > Fog** from the shortcut menu; the **Fog1** tool tile is inserted in the **Flow** area and a connection between the **ChannelBoolean1** and **Fog1** tools is established, as shown in Figure 11-7.

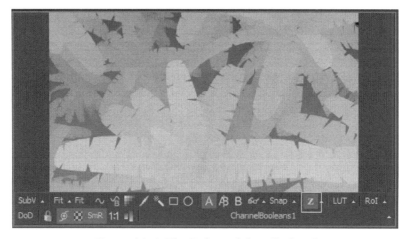

Figure 11-6 *The Z channel data displayed*

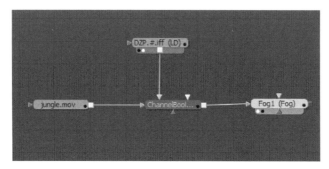

Figure 11-7 *The **Fog1** tool inserted in the **Flow** area*

8. Press 1; the output of the **Fog1** tool is displayed in the left Display View, as shown in Figure 11-8.

Figure 11-8 *The output of the **Fog1** tool*

9. In the **Fog1** tool control window, click-drag the **Pick** button located on the left of the **Z Near Plane** slider to an area on the image where you want to locate the near plane in the Z buffer. On doing so, a tooltip showing the information of RGBA and Z channels is displayed, as

shown in Figure 11-9. The value in the **Z Near Plane** edit box will change as you drag and move the cursor on the Display View.

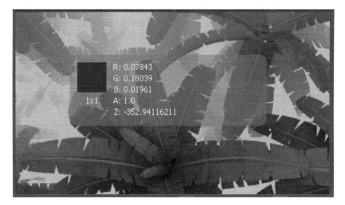

Figure 11-9 *Information of the RGBA and Z channels displayed in the tooltip*

10. Enter **-768** in the **Z Far Plane** edit box in the **Fog1** tool control window.

The **Z Near Plane** parameter is used to specify the plane in the Z buffer where fog would disappear. The **Z Far Plane** parameter is used to specify the plane in the Z buffer where fog would become opaque.

The green Fog input on the **Fog** tool is used to connect to the external source of the fog. For example, if you have rendered the fog using a 3D application, you can connect the rendered image sequence to the green fog input of the **Fog** tool. If you connect an image sequence to the fog input of the **Fog** tool, the color specified in the **Fog Color** area of the **Fog** tool control window will be overridden.

Next, you will create the animated fog by using the **FastNoise** tool.

11. Click on the empty space of the **Flow** area to deselect the selected tool tile, if any. Choose **Tools > Creator > FastNoise** from the menubar; the **FastNoise1** tool tile is inserted in the **Flow** area.

12. Drag the green node of the **Fog1** tool tile to the red output node of the **FastNoise1** tool tile; a connection between the **FastNoise1** and **Fog1** tools is established, as shown in Figure 11-10.

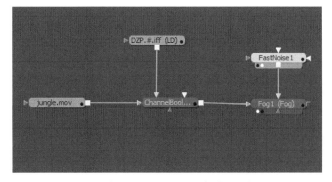

Figure 11-10 *The **FastNoise1** tool tile in the **Flow** area*

13. Press 2; the output of the **FastNoise1** tool is displayed in the right Display View.

14. In the **Noise** tab of the **FastNoise1** tool control window, set the values of the parameters as follows:

Detail: **2.14**   Brightness: **-0.29**   Contrast: **0.88**
Scale: **2.2**   Angle: **80**

The output of the **Fog1** and **FastNoise1** tools is displayed in the left and right Display Views, respectively, refer to Figure 11-11.

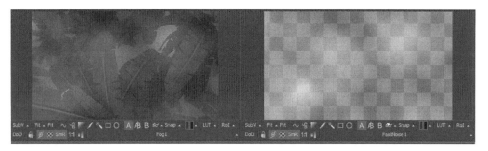

Figure 11-11 *The output of the* ***Fog1*** *and* ***FastNoise1*** *tools*

15. Enter **0.2** in the **Seethe Rate** edit box. Now, start the playback of the composition and notice the automatic drift in the noise animation.

    The **Seethe Rate** parameter is used to change the noise map over time. The value specified for this parameter determines the speed at which the noise map will change over time.

16. Move the cursor over the pipe connecting the **FastNoise1** and **Fog1** tool tiles; the pipe is highlighted in the blue color. Right-click on the pipe; a shortcut menu is displayed. Next, choose **Add Tool > Film > Grain** from the shortcut menu; the **Grain1** tool tile is connected to the **Fog1** and **FastNoise1** tools.

    The **Grain** tool is used to generate simulated grain into an image sequence.

17. In the **Grain** tab of the **Grain1** tool control window, enter **3** in the **Power** edit box.

    The **Power** parameter is used to specify the strength of the grain. Higher the value of this parameter, more visible will be the grain.

    Press SPACEBAR to start the playback of the composition.

    Now, save the composition with the name *c11tut1* at the location *Documents > Fusion_7 > c11_tut > c11_tut_01*. Next, you need to render the composition. For rendering, refer to Tutorial 2 of Chapter 2. You can also view the final render of the composition by downloading the *c11_fusion_7_rndr.zip* from *http://www.cadcim.com*. The path of the file is mentioned at the beginning of the chapter.

Tutorial 2

In this tutorial, you will control the texture mapping of a 3D rendered image by using the **Texture** tool. The final output of the composition is shown in Figure 11-12. **(Expected time: 30 min)**

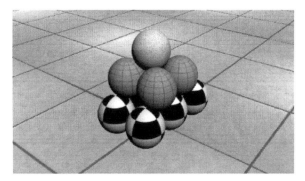

Figure 11-12 *The final output of the composition*

The following steps are required to complete this tutorial:

a. Set the frame format.
b. Import images.
c. Change the texture.

Setting the Frame Format

In this section, you will specify the frame format settings.

1. Choose **File > New** from the menubar; a new composition is opened in the Fusion screen.

2. Choose **File > Preferences** from the menubar; the **Preferences** dialog box is displayed.

3. In this dialog box, select **Frame Format** from the **Composition#** preferences tree; various frame format settings are displayed on the right of the **Preferences** dialog box.

4. Now, choose the **New** button in the **Settings** area; the **Enter the name for the new image format** dialog box is displayed. Enter **640x360** in the edit box displayed in this dialog box and then choose the **OK** button to close it. Next, set the values of the parameters in the **Preferences** dialog box as follows:

Settings
Width: **640**   Height: **360**
Frame rate: **24**   Aspect ratio: **1:1**

5. Choose the **Save** button in the **Preferences** dialog box to save the changes made.

6. In the Time Ruler area, enter **0** in the **Global End Time** edit box.

Importing Images

In this section, you will import images in the composition.

1. Choose **Tools > I/O > Loader** from the menubar; the **Open File** dialog box is displayed. In this dialog box, choose **Documents > Fusion_7 > c11_tut > c11_tut_02> Media_Files > spheres.rpf** and then choose the **Open** button; the **Loader1** tool tile is inserted in the **Flow** area.

Note

The RPF (Rich Pixel Format) image format supports the Auxiliary image channels. The channels stored in this format are Z, Material Effects, Object, UV Coordinates, Normal, Non-Clamped Color, Coverage, Node Render ID, Color, Transparency, Velocity, Sub-Pixel Weight, and Sub-Pixel Mask.

2. Press 1; the output of the **Loader1** tool is displayed in the left Display View. Next, choose the **Fit** button in the left **Display View** toolbar to fit the image into the left Display View, refer to Figure 11-13.

3. Click on the empty space of the **Flow** area to deselect the **Loader1** tool tile. Next, choose **Tools > I/O > Loader** from the menubar; the **Open File** dialog box is displayed. In this dialog box, choose **Documents > Fusion_7 > c11_tut_02 > Media_Files > tiles.jpg** and then choose the **Open** button; the **Loader2** tool tile is inserted in the **Flow** area.

4. Press 2; the output of the **Loader2** tool is displayed in the right Display View. Next, choose the **Fit** button from the right **Display View** toolbar to fit the image into the right Display View, refer to Figure 11-13.

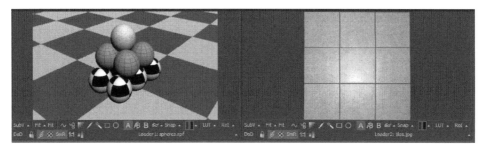

*Figure 11-13 The output of the **Loader1** and **Loader2** tools displayed*

Changing the Texture

In this section, you will change the texture of the floor.

1. Click in the empty space of the **Flow** area to deselect the selected tool tile, if any. Next, choose **Tools > Deep Pixel > Texture** from the menubar; the **Texture1** tool is inserted in the **Flow** area.

   The **Texture** tool is used to control the texture mapping of the elements in a 3D rendered image. This tool can be used only when the U and V map channels are present in the rendered image.

Note
*You must use a 32 bit float UV map image to eliminate artifacts in the final output. If you see a pixelated output, make sure that you choose the **HiQ** button located below the timeruler. Also, avoid the use of pre-multiplied UV channels while using the **Texture** tool as it produces artifacts. To get rid of these artifacts, divide the UV data with the alpha channel by using the **ChannelBooleans** tool.*

2. Drag the orange input node of the **Texture1** tool tile to the red output node of the **Loader1** tool tile. Similarly, connect the green input of the **Texture1** tool tile to the red output node of the **Loader2** tool tile; a connection between the **Loader1**, **Loader2** and **Texture1** tools is established, as shown in Figure 11-14.

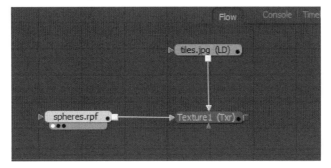

*Figure 11-14 A connection established between the **Loader1**, **Loader2**, and **Texture1** tools*

3. Make sure the **Texture1** tool tile is selected in the **Flow** area. Press 2; the output of the **Texture1** tool is displayed in the right Display View, as shown in Figure 11-15.

Notice that *tiles.jpg* is wrapped around all the elements in the rendered image, refer to Figure 11-15. To restrict the texturing to specific elements, you can create an effect mask based on the alpha channel or the Object or Material ID channel of the element. The *spheres.rpf* used in this tutorial contains the Object ID channel.

Figure 11-15 The texture map wrapped around all objects

Next, you will create an effect mask using the Object ID channel.

4. In the **Common Controls** tab of the **Texture1** tool, select the **Use Object** check box; the **Object/Material** area is displayed, refer to Figure 11-16.

*Figure 11-16 The **Object/Material** area*

5. Click-drag the **Pick** button to an area on the image where you want texture to be remapped; a tooltip with the information about the channels and colors is displayed along with the Object IDs, as shown in Figure 11-17. In this case, drop the **Pick** button over the red and yellow checker floor; the value **1** is displayed in the **O** edit box in the **Object/Material** area. This is because the **Object ID** of checker pattern object is stored as 1 in the *spheres.rpf*.

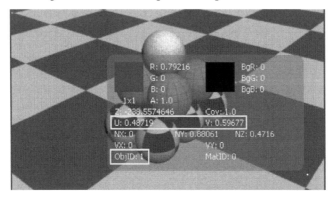

Figure 11-17 The tooltip displayed in the Display View

Notice that in the right Display View, the *tiles.jpg* is wrapped around the floor, as shown in Figure 11-18.

Figure 11-18 The tile.jpg wrapped around the floor

6. In the **Texture** tab of the **Texture1** tool control window, set the **U Scale** and **V Scale** parameters to **4**. Figure 11-19 shows the scaled U and V coordinates.

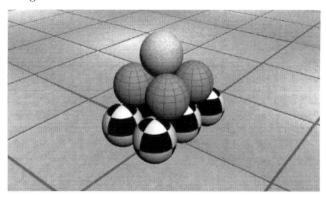

Figure 11-19 *The scaled texture displayed*

The **U Scale** and **V Scale** parameters are used to scale the U and V coordinates. These coordinates are used to map the texture. You can enlarge or shrink the texture map by using these parameters. The **U Offset** and **V Offset** parameters are used to offset the U and V coordinates. You can use these parameters to animate the texture. The **Swap UV** check box is used to swap the U and V channels of the source image. The **Flip Horiz** and **Flip Vert** parameters are used to flip the texture image horizontally and vertically, respectively.

Now, save the composition with the name *c11tut2* at the location *Documents > Fusion_7 > c11_tut > c11_tut_02*. Next, you need to render the composition. For rendering, refer to Tutorial 1 of Chapter 2. The output of the composition is shown in Figure 11-12. You can also view the final render of the composition by downloading the *c11_fusion_7_rndr.zip* file from *http://www.cadcim.com*. The path of the file is mentioned at the beginning of the chapter.

Tutorial 3

In this tutorial, you will control the lighting, reflection mapping, and 3D shading of a 3D rendered image by using the **Shader** tool. The final output of the composition is shown in Figure 11-20.   **(Expected time: 20 min)**

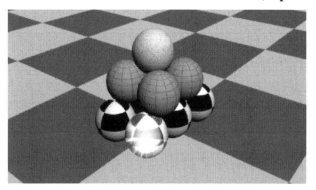

Figure 11-20 *The final output of the composition*

The following steps are required to complete this tutorial:

a. Set the frame format.
b. Import images.
c. Change the lighting of the element.

Setting the Frame Format

In this section, you will specify the frame format settings.

1. Choose **File > New** from the menubar; a new composition is opened in the Fusion screen.

2. Choose **File > Preferences** from the menubar; the **Preferences** dialog box is displayed.

3. In this dialog box, select **Frame Format** from the **Composition#** preferences tree; various frame format settings are displayed on the right of the **Preferences** dialog box.

4. Now, choose the **New** button in the **Settings** area; the **Enter the name for the new image format** dialog box is displayed. Enter **640x360** in the edit box displayed in this dialog box and then choose the **OK** button to close it. Next, set the values of the parameters in the **Preferences** dialog box as follows:

    Settings
    Width: **640**   Height: **360**
    Frame rate: **24**   Aspect ratio: **1:1**

5. Choose the **Save** button in the **Preferences** dialog box to save the changes made.

6. In the Time Ruler area, enter **0** in the **Global End Time** edit box.

Importing Images

In this section, you will import the images in the composition.

1. Choose the **LD** button from the toolbar; the **Open File** dialog box is displayed. In this dialog box, choose **Documents > Fusion_7 > c11_tut > c11_tut_03 > Media_Files > spheres.rpf** and then choose the **Open** button; the **Loader1** tool is inserted in the **Flow** area.

2. Press 1; the output of the **Loader1** tool is displayed in the left Display View, refer to Figure 11-21.

3. Click on the empty space in the **Flow** area to deselect the **Loader1** tool tile. Choose **Tools > I/O > Loader** from the menubar; the **Open File** dialog box is displayed. In this dialog box, choose **Documents > Fusion_7 > c11_tut > c11_tut _03 > Media_Files > reflectionMap.jpg** and then choose the **Open** button; the **Loader2** tool tile is inserted in the **Flow** area.

4. Press 2; the output of the **Loader2** tool is displayed in the right Display View, refer to

Figure 11-21.

Figure 11-21 *The output of the **Loader1** and **Loader2** tools in Display Views*

Changing the Lighting of the Element

In this section, you will change the lighting of an element in the image.

1. Click on the empty space of the **Flow** area to deselect the selected tool tile, if any. Next, choose **Tools > Deep Pixel > Shader** from the menubar; the **Shader1** tool tile is inserted in the **Flow** area.

    The **Shader** tool is used to control the lighting, reflection mapping, and 3D shading in a 3D rendered image. Make sure the X, Y, and Z normal map channels are present in the image. This tool has an additional green **Environment Reflection Map** input, which can be used to project the image onto the objects in a 3D rendered image.

2. Drag the orange input node of the **Shader1** tool tile to the red output node of the **Loader1** tool tile. Similarly, connect the green input node of the **Shader1** tool tile to the **Loader2** tool tile; the connection between the **Loader1**, **Loader2** and **Shader1** tools is established, as shown in Figure 11-22.

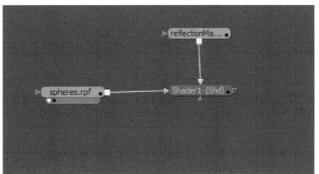

Figure 11-22 *The **Shader1** tool connected with the **Loader** tools*

3. Press 2; the output of the **Shader1** tool is displayed in the right Display View. To restrict the effect of the **Shader1** tool, you can create an effect mask, as discussed in Tutorial 2.

    Next, you will create an effect mask by using the Object ID channel 9, refer to Figure 11-23.

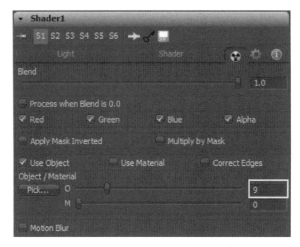

Figure 11-23 The Object ID channel set to 9

4.   In the **Light** tab of the **Shader1** tool control window, set the values of the parameters as follows:

Ambient: **0.5**   Diffuse: **0.42**   Specular: **0.9**

Reflection: **0.72**   Equator Angle: **0.74**   Polar Height: **0.8**

Next, choose the **Spherical** button; the reflection map is now wrapped around the sphere, as shown in Figure 11-24.

Figure 11-24 The reflection map wrapped around the sphere

The **Ambient, Diffuse**, and **Specular** parameters are used to control the amount of ambient, diffuse, and specular colors present in the scene for the selected object. The ambient color is added to all pixels evenly in the shadowed area, thus giving them a flat look. The diffuse color is the normal color of the element in the scene. This color is reflected equally in all directions. The specular color controls the amount of reflection on the element. The **Equator Angle** parameter is used to control the left-to-right angle of light and the **Polar Height** parameter is used to control the top-to-bottom angle of light.

The **Reflection Type** area has three buttons: **Screen**, **Spherical**, and **Refraction**. These buttons are used to specify the type of reflection mapping.

5. Choose the **Shader** tab in the **Shader1** tool control window. It is used to control the shader curves of the **Shader** tool. Next, change the curves, as shown in Figure 11-25.

 Tip: *You can fine-tune the shader curves by right-clicking on the spline graph and then choosing the required option from the shortcut menu displayed.*

6. In the **Specular Color** area of the **Shader1** tool control window, set the values of the parameters as follows:

R: **0.92**   G: **0.75**   B: **0.3**

The **Edit Diffuse** and **Edit Specular** check boxes are used to individually edit the diffuse and specular curves. The **In** and **Out** parameters are used to display the value of the selected edit point on the curve. The **Specular Color** area is used to specify the color of specular highlights.

Now, save the composition with the name *c11tut3* at the location *Documents > Fusion_7 > c11_tut > c11_tut_03*. Next, you need to render the composition. For rendering, refer to Tutorial 1 of Chapter 2. You can also view the final render of the composition by downloading the *c11_fusion_7_rndr.zip* file from *http://www.cadcim.com*. The path of the file is mentioned at the beginning of the chapter.

*Figure 11-25 Shader curves in the **Shader1** tool controls area*

Tutorial 4

In this tutorial, you will map the normal pass to the X, Y, and Z Normal Auxiliary channels and then use the **Shader** tool to change the lighting of the elements in a rendered image, refer to Figure 11-26.   **(Expected time: 20 min)**

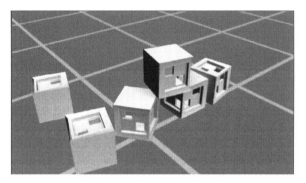

Figure 11-26 *The final output*

The following steps are required to complete this tutorial:

a.   Set the frame format.
b.   Import images.
c.   Change the lighting.

Setting the Frame Format

In this section, you will specify the frame format settings.

1.   Choose **File > New** from the menubar; a new composition is opened in the Fusion screen.

2.   Choose **File > Preferences** from the menubar; the **Preferences** dialog box is displayed.

3.   In this dialog box, select **Frame Format** from the **Composition#** preferences tree; various frame format settings are displayed on the right of the **Preferences** dialog box.

4.   Now, choose the **New** button in the **Settings** area; the **Enter the name for the new image format** dialog box is displayed. Enter **640x360** in the edit box displayed in this dialog box and then choose the **OK** button to close it. Next, set the values of the parameters in the **Preferences** dialog box as follows:

Settings
Width: **640**   Height: **360**
Frame rate: **24**   Aspect ratio: **1:1**

5.   Choose the **Save** button in the **Preferences** dialog box to save the changes made.

6.   In the Time Ruler area, enter **88** in the **Global End Time** edit box.

Importing the Images
In this section, you will import the images in the composition.

1. Choose **Tools > I/O > Loader** from the menubar; the **Open File** dialog box is displayed. In this dialog box, choose **Documents > Fusion_7 > c11_tut> c11_tut_04 > Media_Files > flrDiffuse > flrDiffuse.1.tif** and then choose the **Open** button; the **Loader1** tool tile is inserted in the **Flow** area.

2. Press 1; the output of the **Loader1** tool is displayed in the left Display View. Choose the **Fit** button from the left **Display View** toolbar to fit the image into the left Display View.

3. Click on the empty space of the **Flow** area to deselect the selected tool tile, if any. Next, choose **Tools > I/O > Loader** from the menubar; the **Open File** dialog box is displayed. In this dialog box, choose **Documents > Fusion_7 > c11_tut > c11_tut_04 > Media_Files > cubeDiffuse > cubeDiffuse.1-89.tif** and then choose the **Open** button; the **Loader2** tool tile is inserted in the **Flow** area.

4. Press 2; the output of the **Loader3** tool is displayed in the right Display View. Choose the **Fit** button from the right **Display View** toolbar to fit the image into the right Display View, refer to Figure 11-27.

5. Click on the empty space of the **Flow** area to deselect the selected tool tile, if any. Next choose **Tools > I/O > Loader** from the menubar; the **Open File** dialog box is displayed. In this dialog box, choose **Documents > Fusion_7 > c11_tut > c11_tut_04> Media_Files > cubeNormal > Normal.1-89.tif** and then choose the **Open** button; the **Loader3** tool tile is inserted in the **Flow** area.

6. Press 2; the output of the **Loader3** tool is displayed in the right Display View, refer to Figure 11-27.

Figure 11-27 *The output of the **Loader3** tool displayed in right Display View*

7. Drag the red output node of the **Loader2** tool tile to the red output node of the **Loader1** tool tile; the **Merge1** tool tile is inserted in the **Flow** area and a connection between the **Loader1**, **Loader2**, and **Merge1** tools is established, refer to Figure 11-28.

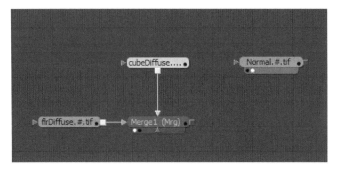

*Figure 11-28 The **Merge1** tool inserted in the **Flow** area*

8.   Press 1; the output of the **Merge1** tool is displayed in the left Display View.

Changing the Lighting

In this section, you will map the normal pass image to Normal Auxiliary channels and then change the lighting of the scene.

1.   Make sure the **Merge1** tool tile is selected in the **Flow** area and then choose **Tools > Color > Channel Booleans** from the toolbar, the **ChannelBooleans1** tool tile is inserted in the **Flow** area and a connection between the **Merge1** and **ChannelBooleans1** tools is established.

2.   Drag the green node of the **ChannelBooleans1** tool tile and drop the connection over the **Loader3** tool tile; a connection is established between the **ChannelBooleans1** and **Loader3** tools, as shown in Figure 11-29.

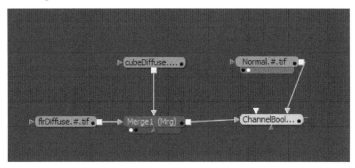

*Figure 11-29 The **ChannelBooleans1** tool connected to the **Loader3** tool*

3.   Press 1; the output of the **ChannelBooleans1** tool is displayed in the left Display View.

4.   Select **Do Nothing** from the **To Red**, **To Green**, **To Blue**, and **To Alpha** drop-down lists in the **Color Channels** tab of the **ChannelBooleans1** tool. The output of the **ChannelBoolean1** tool is displayed in the left Display view, as shown in Figure 11-30.

5.   In the **Aux Channels** tab of the **ChannelBooleans1** tool control window, select the **Enable Extra channels** check box. Now, select the parameters in the **Aux Channels** tab as follows:

To X Normal: **Red FG**   To Y Normal: **Green FG**   To Z Normal: **Blue FG**

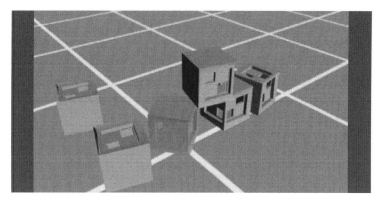

Figure 11-30 *The output of the **ChannelBooleans1** tool*

6. Make sure the **ChannelBooleans1** tool tile is selected in the **Flow** area and then choose **Tools > Deep Pixel > Shader** from the toolbar; the **Shader1** tool tile is inserted in the **Flow** area and a connection is established between the **Shader1** and **ChannelBooleans1** tools, as shown in Figure 11-31.

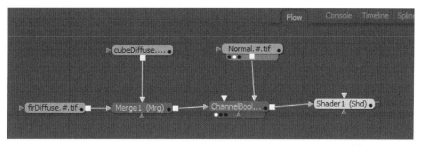

Figure 11-31 *A connection established between the **ChannelBooleans1** and **Shader1** tools*

7. Press 2; the output of the **Shader1** tool is displayed in the right Display View, as shown in Figure 11-32.

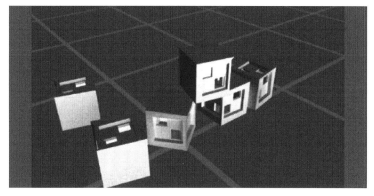

Figure 11-32 *The output of the **Shader1** tool*

8. In the **Light** tab of the **Shader1** tool control window, set the values of the parameters as follows:

Ambient: **0.82**   Diffuse: **0.45**   Specular: **0.72**

Equator Angle: **132**   Polar Height: **-45**

The output of the **Shader1** tool after specifying all parameters is shown in Figure 11-33.

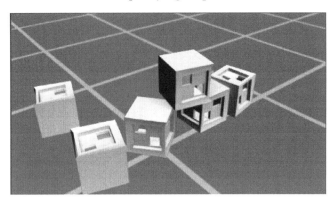

*Figure 11-33 The final output of the **Shader1** tool*

Now, save the composition with the name *c11tut4* at the location *Documents > Fusion_7 > c11_tut > c11_tut_04*. Next, you need to render the composition. For rendering, refer to Tutorial 2 of Chapter 2. You can also view the final render of the composition by downloading the *c11_fusion_7_rndr.zip* file from *http://www.cadcim.com*. The path of the file is mentioned at the beginning of the chapter.

Tutorial 5

In this tutorial, you will create the depth-of-field effect using the **Depth Blur** tool. The final output of the composition at frame 50 is shown in Figure 11-34.   **(Expected time: 20 min)**

Figure 11-34 The final output of the composition at frame 50

The following steps are required to complete this tutorial:

a.   Set the frame format.
b.   Import the images.
c.   Create the depth-of-field effect.

Setting the Frame Format

In this section, you will specify the frame format settings.

1. Choose **File > New** from the menubar; a new composition is opened in the Fusion screen.

2. Choose **File > Preferences** from the menubar; the **Preferences** dialog box is displayed.

3. In this dialog box, select **Frame Format** from the **Composition#** preferences tree; various frame format settings are displayed on the right of the **Preferences** dialog box.

4. Now, choose the **New** button in the **Settings** area; the **Enter the name for the new image format** dialog box is displayed. Enter **640x360** in the edit box displayed in this dialog box and then choose the **OK** button to close it. Next, set the values of the parameters in the **Preferences** dialog box as follows:

   Settings
   Width: **640**   Height: **360**

   Frame rate: **24**   Aspect ratio: **1:1**

5. Choose the **Save** button in the **Preferences** dialog box to save the changes made.

6. In the Time Ruler area, enter **88** in the **Global End Time** edit box.

Importing the Images

In this section, you will import the images in the composition.

1. Choose **Tools > I/O > Loader** from the menubar; the **Open File** dialog box is displayed. In this dialog box, choose **Documents > Fusion_7 > c11_tut > c11_tut_05 > Media_Files > diffPass.mov** and then choose the **Open** button; the **Loader1** tool tile is inserted in the **Flow** area.

2. Press 1; the output of the **Loader1** tool is displayed in the left Display View. Next, choose the **Fit** button from the left **Display View** toolbar to fit the image into the left Display View, refer to Figure 11-35.

3. Click on the empty space of the **Flow** area. Next, choose **Tools > I/O > Loader** from the menubar; the **Open File** dialog box to load the file is displayed. In this dialog box, choose **Documents > Fusion_7 > c11_tut_05 > Media_Files > lumPass.mov**; the **Loader2** tool tile is inserted in the **Flow** area.

4. Press 2; the output of the **Loader2** tool is displayed in the right Display View.

5. Choose the **Fit** button from the right **Display View** toolbar to fit the image into the right Display View, refer to Figure 11-35.

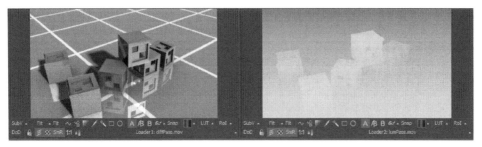

Figure 11-35 *The output of the **Loader1** and **Loader2** tools*

Creating the Depth-of-Field Effect

In this section, you will create the depth-of-field effect using the **Channel Booleans** and **Depth Blur** tools.

1. Select the **Loader1** tool tile in the **Flow** area and then choose **Tools > Color > Channel Booleans** from the menubar; the **ChannelBooleans1** tool tile is inserted in the **Flow** area and it gets connected to the **Background** input of the **ChannelBooleans1** tool.

2. Drag the green node of the **ChannelBooleans1** tool tile to the red output node of the **Loader2** tool tile; a connection between the **Loader2** and **ChannelBooleans1** tools is established, as shown in Figure 11-36.

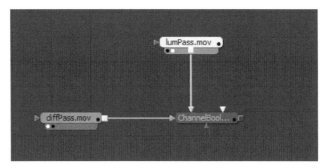

Figure 11-36 *The **ChannelBooleans1** tool connected with the **Loader2** tool*

3. Press 2; the output of the **ChannelBooleans1** tool is displayed in the right Display View.

4. In the **Color Channels** tab of the **ChannelBooleans1** tool control window, select **Do Nothing** from the **To Red**, **To Green**, **To Blue**, and **To Alpha** drop-down lists, refer to Figure 11-37.

    As **Do Nothing** is selected in all drop-down lists, there in no effect on the RGBA channels.

5. Choose the **Aux Channels** tab and then select the **Enable Extra channels** check box. Next, select **Lightness FG** from the **To Z Buffer** drop-down list; the lightness from the **Loader2** tool is mapped to the Z channel.

Figure 11-37 The **ChannelBooleans1** tool control window

6. Activate the right Display View and then press Z; the Z channel is displayed in the right Display View, as shown in Figure 11-38. Next, press C; the color channels are displayed in the Display View.

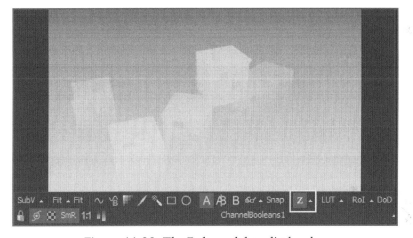

Figure 11-38 The Z channel data displayed

7. Right-click on the **ChannelBooleans1** tool; a shortcut menu is displayed. Next, choose **Insert Tool > Deep Pixel > Depth Blur** from the shortcut menu; the **DepthBlur1** tool tile is inserted in the **Flow** area and it also gets connected with the **ChannelBooleans1** tool, as shown in Figure 11-39.

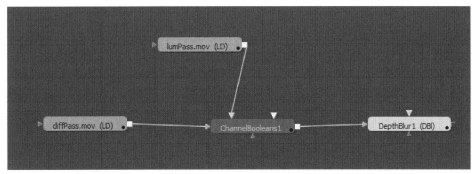

Figure 11-39 The **DepthBlur1** tool connected to the **ChannelBooleans1** tool

The **Depth Blur** tool is used to create depth-of-field effect. It is dependent on the Z channel data that is embedded in the image. If the image does not contain the Z channel data, you can use the luminance pass image to map the lightness values to the Z channel.

8. Press 1; the output of the **DepthBlur1** tool is displayed in the left Display View.

9. In the **Controls** tab of the **DepthBlur1** tool control window, set the values of the parameters as follows:

Blur Size: **5**   Focal Point: **-100**   Depth of Field: **6**
Z Scale: **320**

The output of the **DepthBlur1** tool at frame 50 after specifying all parameters is shown in Figure 11-40.

Figure 11-40 *The output of the **DepthBlur1** tool at frame 50*

The **Focal Point** parameter is used to specify the simulated focal length. This option is available only when the **Z** button is chosen in the **Blur Channel** section. The **Blur Size** parameter is used to control the blurriness on the image. The **Depth of Field** parameter is used to control the depth of the area in focus. The **Z Scale** parameter is used to scale the Z buffer value.

Now, save the composition with the name *c11tut5* at the location *Documents > Fusion_7 > c11_tut > c11_tut_05*. Next, you need to render the composition. For rendering, refer to Tutorial 2 of Chapter 2. You can also view the final render of the composition by downloading the *c11_fusion_7_rndr.zip* file from *http://www.cadcim.com*. The path of the file is mentioned at the beginning of the chapter.

Self-Evaluation Test

Answer the following questions and then compare them to those given at the end of this chapter:

1. The _____ tools are used to generate depth effects, simulated fog effects, and texture mapping.

2. The _____ parameter is used to specify the near plane in the Z-buffer where fog disappears.

3. The _____ tool is used to control lighting, reflection mapping, and 3D shading in a 3D rendered image.

4. The **U Scale** and **V Scale** parameters are used to scale the U and V coordinates. (T/F)

5. The **Flip Horizontal** and **Flip Vertical** parameters are used to flip the texture image to the horizontal and vertical directions, respectively. (T/F)

Review Questions

Answer the following questions:

1. The **Depth Blur** tool is used to create _____ effects.

2. The **Z Scale** parameter is used to scale _____ value.

3. The _____ tool is used to create simulated _____ in a 3D rendered image.

4. The diffuse color is the normal color of the element in a scene. (T/F)

5. The **Depth of Field** parameter is used to specify the depth of the area in focus. (T/F)

Answers to Self-Evaluation Test
1. Deep Pixel, **2. Z Near Plane**, **3. Shader**, **4.** T, **5.** T

Chapter 12

Paint Tool

Learning Objectives

After completing this chapter, you will be able to:

• *Remove the unwanted objects from the footage*
• *Attach a brush stroke to a path*

INTRODUCTION

The **Paint** tool is a powerful and flexible tool that is used for removing wire and rig as well as for cloning, and creating masks. It consists of a series of brush strokes that are called vector shapes. These shapes can be converted to editable polylines shapes that can be animated over time.

TUTORIAL

The compositions created in this chapter can be downloaded from *http://www.cadcim.com*. These compositions are contained in the *c12_fusion_7_tut.zip* file. The path of the file is as follows:

> *Textbooks > Animation and Visual Effects > Fusion > Blackmagic Design Fusion 7 Studio: A Tutorial Approach*

Next, extract the contents of the file at *\Documents\Fusion_7*.

Tutorial 1

In this tutorial, you will remove unwanted objects from the footage by using the **Paint** tool. The final output of the composition at frame 30 is shown in Figure 12-1.   **(Expected time: 20 min)**

Figure 12-1 *The final output of the composition at frame 30*

The following steps are required to complete this tutorial:

a.   Set the frame format.
b.   Import the footage.
c.   Track the objects.
d.   Remove the objects from the footage.
e.   Adjust the brightness and contrast of the composition.

Setting the Frame Format

In this section, you will specify the frame format settings.

1.   Choose **File > New** from the menubar; a new composition is displayed in the Fusion screen.

2.   Choose **File > Preferences** from the menubar; the **Preferences** dialog box is displayed.

3. In this dialog box, select **Frame Format** from the **Composition#** preferences tree; various frame format settings are displayed on the right in the **Preferences** dialog box. Next, select the **HDTV 720** option from the **Default format** drop-down list and then choose the **Save** button to save the changes made.

4. In the Time Ruler area, enter **30** in both the **Global End Time** edit box.

Importing the Footage
In this section, you will import the footage to be cleaned by using the **Paint** tool.

1. Choose the **LD** button from the toolbar; a dialog box is displayed. In this dialog box, choose **Documents > Fusion_7 > c12_tut > c12_tut_01 > Media_Files > floor_#####.jpg(0..30) and then choose the Open button**; the **Loader1** tool tile is inserted in the **Flow** area.

2. Press 1; the output of the **Loader1** tool is displayed in the left Display View.

3. Choose the **Fit** button from the left **Display View** toolbar to fit the footage into the left Display View, refer to Figure 12-2.

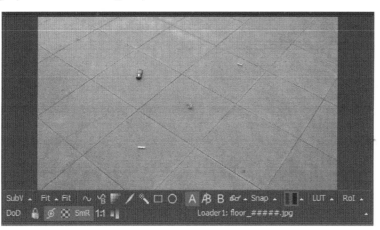

Figure 12-2 *The output of the **Loader1** tool*

Tracking the Objects
In this section, you will track the objects by using the **Tracker** tool.

1. Select the **Loader1** tool tile from the **Flow** area and choose **Tools > Tracking > Tracker** from the menubar; the **Tracker1** tool tile is inserted in the **Flow** area and a connection between the **Tracker1** and **Loader1** tools is established.

2. Press 1; the output of the **Tracker1** tool is displayed in the left Display View.

   Now, you will notice that a green rectangle is displayed in the left Display View that represents **Tracker 1** track point, as shown in Figure 12-3.

*Figure 12-3 The **Tracker 1** track point displayed in the left Display View*

3. Hover the cursor over the **Tracker1** track point; a small box square appears on it. Drag this small square box to the cell phone in the footage, as shown in Figure 12-4. Next, release the left-mouse button.

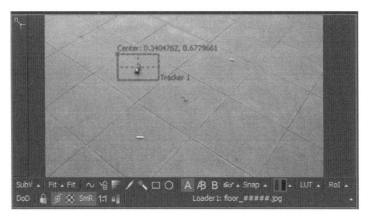

*Figure 12-4 The **Tracker 1** track point placed over the cell phone*

4. In the **Tracker1** tool control window, choose the **Best match** button and then choose the **Track forward** button; the tracking process starts. After the completion of the tracking process, the **Composition1** message box is displayed, as shown in Figure 12-5.

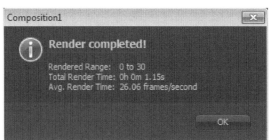

*Figure 12-5 The **Composition1** message box*

This message box displays information about the completion of tracking process and the time taken to complete it. Next, choose the **OK** button to close the message box.

Removing the Objects from the Footage

In this section, you will remove the unwanted objects from the footage by using the **Paint** tool.

1. Select the **Tracker1** tool tile from the **Flow** area and then choose **Tools > Paint > Paint** from the menubar; the **Paint1** tool tile is inserted in the **Flow** area and a connection between the **Tracker1** and **Paint1** tools is established.

2. Press 2; the output of the **Paint1** tool is displayed in the right Display View. Next, choose the **Fit** button from the right **Display View** toolbar to fit the image into the right Display View.

3. Choose the **Stroke** tool from the **Tool** toolbar which is displayed on the right side of the right Display View, as shown in Figure 12-6.

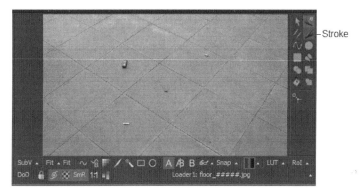

*Figure 12-6 Choosing the **Stroke** tool from the **Tool** toolbar*

4. In the **Paint1** tool control window, choose the **Clone** button from the **Apply** **Controls (Apply Mode)** area to set the apply mode to clone, refer to Figure 12-7.

 Tip: *To change the size of the brush interactively, press and hold CTRL and then drag the cursor in the Display View.*

In Fusion, there are eight types of apply modes such as **Color**, **Clone**, **Emboss**, **Erase**, **Merge**, **Smear**, **Stamp**, and **Wire**, refer to Figure 12-8. The **Color** apply mode is used to paint the color strokes on the screen. The **Clone** apply mode is used to clone areas from one place to another. The **Emboss** apply mode is used to emboss the area of the image covered by the brush strokes. The **Erase** apply mode is used to erase the brush strokes. The **Merge** apply mode is used to blend the brush strokes with the underlying image. The **Smear** brush stroke is used to smear the image along the direction of the brush strokes. The **Stamp** apply mode is used to stamp the brush stroke onto the image. The **Wire** apply mode is used to remove wires and rigs from the footage.

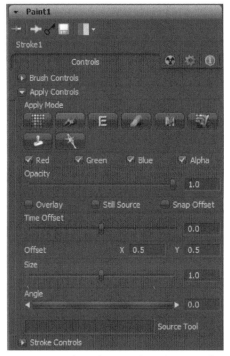

Figure 12-7 *Selecting the* ***Clone*** *apply*
mode in the ***Paint1*** *tool control window*

5. Press and hold ALT and then click on the area near the cell phone in the right Display View, as shown in Figure 12-9. Move the cursor slightly away; you will notice a red cross displayed on the screen. It indicates the area to be cloned.

Figure 12-8 *The* ***Apply Controls*** *(Apply*
Mode*) area in the* ***Paint1*** *tool control window*

Figure 12-9 *Area to be cloned*

6. Press and hold the left mouse button and draw brush strokes over the cell phone; the cell phone disappears from the screen as the neighboring area is cloned over it, as shown in Figure 12-10.

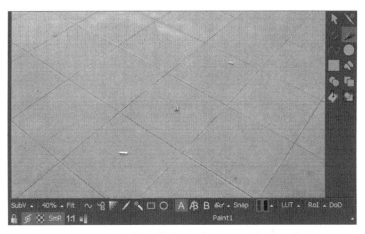

Figure 12-10 *The cellphone disappeared after cloning*

7. Similarly, remove all unwanted objects from the footage. As a result, all objects disappear from the footage, as shown in Figure 12-11.

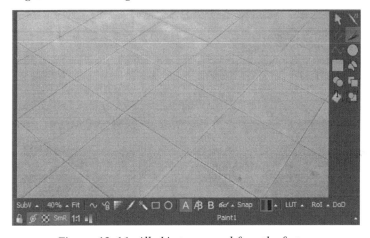

Figure 12-11 *All objects removed from the footage*

Each stroke you draw has its own set of controls. You can access these controls from the **Modifiers** tab of the **Paint** tool control window. Next, you will attach strokes to the path generated by the **Tracker1** tool. Once the strokes are attached to the path, they will be merged with the footage seamlessly.

8. Choose the **Modifiers** tab from the **Paint1** tool control window; all strokes are displayed as tabs in the control window, as shown in Figure 12-12. You can expand a tab by clicking on its name.

9. Right-click on the **Stroke1** modifier; a shortcut menu is displayed. Next, move the cursor over the **Script** option; a cascading menu is displayed. Next, choose the **Attach Mask-XF-Stroke to Path-Keep Position TOOL** from the cascading menu, refer to Figure 12-13; the **Select Your Path** dialog box is displayed, as shown in Figure 12-14. Next, choose the **OK** button to close the dialog box; the stroke is attached to the path generated by the **Tracker** tool.

Figure 12-12 *The **Modifiers** tab showing all strokes*

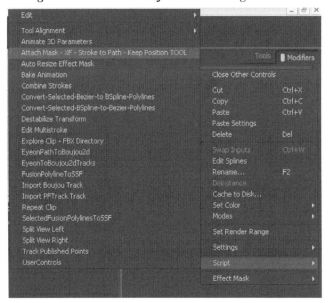

Figure 12-13 *Choosing the **Attach Mask- XF - Stroke**
to Path - Keep Position TOOL from the cascading menu*

Figure 12-14 *The **Select Your Path** dialog box*

10. Repeat the process followed in step 9 to attach all strokes to the path generated by the **Tracker1** tool.

Adjusting the Brightness and Contrast of the Composition

In this section, you will adjust the brightness and contrast of the composition.

1. Select the **Paint1** tool tile from the **Flow** area and choose the **BC** button from the toolbar; the **BrightnessContrast1** tool tile is inserted in the **Flow** area and a connection between the **Paint1** and **BrightnessContrast1** tools is established.

2. Press 2; the output of the **BrightnessContrast1** tool is displayed in the right Display View.

3. In the **BrightnessContrast1** tool control window, make sure the **Controls** tab is chosen. Next, set the parameters as follows:

Gain: **1.21**   Gamma: **0.71**

Brightness: **0.052**   Saturation: **0.91**

After entering the values, the final output of the composition is displayed. Figure 12-15 shows the final output of the composition at frame 5.

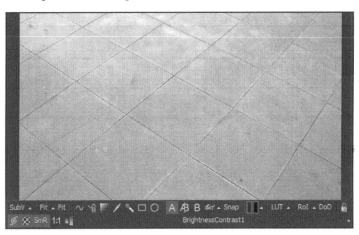

Figure 12-15 *The final output of the composition at frame 5*

Now, save the composition with the name *c12tut1* at the location *Documents > Fusion_7 > c12_tut > c12_tut_01*. Next, you need to render the composition. For rendering, refer to Tutorial 2 of Chapter 2. You can also view the final render of the composition by downloading the *c12_fusion_7_rndr.zip* file from *http://www.cadcim.com*. The path of the file is mentioned at the beginning of the chapter.

Self-Evaluation Test

Answer the following questions and then compare them to those given at the end of this chapter:

1. The _____ tool is used for removing the wire and rig from the footage.

2. The _____ apply mode is used to emboss the area of the image that is covered by by the brush.

3. The **Color** apply mode in the **Paint** tool is used to paint color strokes on the screen. (T/F)

4. The **Stamp** apply mode is used to clone the brush stroke onto an image. (T/F)

Review Questions

Answer the following questions:

1. The _____ apply mode is used to smear the image along the direction of brush strokes.

2. To change the size of the brush interactively, press and hold _____ and then drag the cursor in the Display View.

3. After the completion of the tracking process, the _____ message box is displayed.

4. You can apply a series of brush strokes using the **Paint** tool. (T/F)

Answers to Self-Evaluation Test
1. Paint, 2. Emboss, 3. T, **4.** F

Chapter 13

3D Tools and Stereo 3D

Learning Objectives

After completing this chapter, you will be able to:

- *Understand the 3D environment of Fusion*
- *Create the 3D model of a bench by using the 3D tools*
- *Create the 3D model of a window*
- *Apply materials and textures to the 3D models*
- *Merge 3D objects in a real environment*
- *Create the stereoscopic effect*

INTRODUCTION

The advanced OpenGL accelerated 3D environment of Fusion allows you to create a 3D composition. This environment also supports texts, primitives, and particles. You can use the 3D environment of Fusion to convert a 2D image into a 3D image plane and import the FBX scene and cameras from popular 3D applications such as Maya, Max, and Softimage. You can also create primitive geometry, 3D particle system, shadows, and realistic looking surfaces in this environment. This 3D environment can also be used to match camera with 3D match moving applications such as Boujou or PF Track. You cannot use a 2D tool within the network of 3D tools.

This chapter explains how to set up a 3D scene in Fusion, and how to add objects, lights, and cameras in the 3D workspace. You will also learn how to texture objects and transform objects and cameras.

TUTORIALS

Before you start the tutorials of this chapter, you need to download the *c13_fusion_7_tut.zip* file from *http://www.cadcim.com*. The path of the file is as follows:

> *Textbooks > Animation and Visual Effects > Fusion > Blackmagic Design Fusion 7 Studio: A Tutorial Approach*

> Next, extract the contents of the zip file to *\Documents\Fusion_7*.

Tutorial 1

In this tutorial, you will create a 3D object by using the 3D tools. The final output of the composition is shown in Figure 13-1. **(Expected time: 25 min)**

Figure 13-1 *The final output of the composition*

The following steps are required to complete this tutorial:

a. Set the frame format.
b. Create the 3D bench model.

c. Create the ground in the scene.

d. Add light to the scene.

Setting the Frame Format

In this section, you will specify the frame format settings.

1. Choose **File > New** from the menubar; a new composition is opened in the Fusion screen.

2. Choose **File > Preferences** from the menubar; the **Preferences** dialog box is displayed.

3. In this dialog box, select **Frame Format** from the **Composition#** preferences tree; various frame format settings are displayed on the right in the **Preferences** dialog box. Next, select the **HDTV 720** option from the **Default format** drop-down list and then choose the **Save** button to save the changes made.

4. In the Time Ruler area, enter **0** in the **Global End Time** edit box.

Creating the 3D Bench Model

In this section, you will create the model of a 3D bench by using the **Shape 3D** tool.

1. Choose **Tools > 3D > Shape 3D** from the menubar; the **Shape3D1** tool tile is inserted in the **Flow** area.

2. Press 1; the output of the **Shape3D1** tool is displayed in the left Display View, as shown in Figure 13-2.

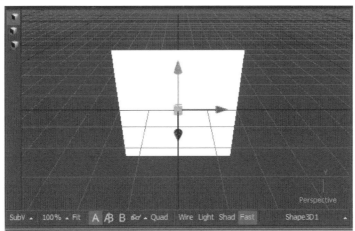

*Figure 13-2 The output of the **Shape3D1** tool*

By default, the output of the **Shape3D1** tool is displayed as a plane in the Display View. Next, you will change the shape of the model to that of the cube.

3. Choose the **Cube** button from the **Shape3D1** tool control window; the shape of the model changes to a cube in the Display View, as shown in Figure 13-3.

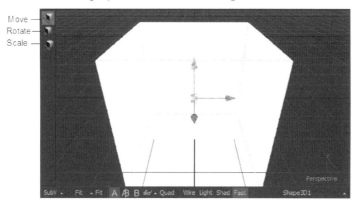

Figure 13-3 Model changed into a cube

Tip: *Panning and zooming in a 3D environment is identical to the 2D navigation of images in the Display Views. However, to rotate the view, press ALT+MMB. You can also use the following shortcut keys for transformation of objects in the Display Views, refer to Figure 13-3.*

Move - Q, Rotate - W, and Scale - E.

4. In the **Controls** tab of **Shape3D1** tool control window, clear the **Lock Width/Height/ Depth** check box and enter the values of the parameters as follows:

Width: **5.32**   Height: **0.26**   Depth: **1.52**

5. Choose the **Fit** button from the **Display View** toolbar to fit the image into the Display View.

Next, you will change the color of the cube.

6. Choose the **Materials** tab of the **Shape3D1** tool control window and enter the values of the parameters as follows:

Diffuse (Diffuse Color)
R: **0.5**   G: **0.25**   B: **0**

7. Choose the **3D Controls** tab of the **Shape3D1** tool control window and enter the values of the parameters as follows:

Translation
X Offset: **0.67**   Y Offset:**7.9**

Scale
Scale: **8.5**

8. Choose the **Fit** button from the left **Display View** toolbar to fit the image into the left Display View. The seat of the bench is created, as shown in Figure 13-4.

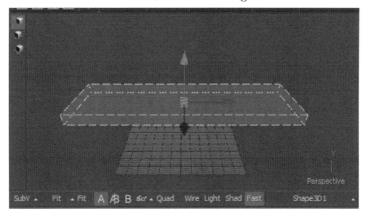

Figure 13-4 *The seat of the bench created*

9. Make sure the **Shape3D1** tool tile is selected in the **Flow** area and choose **Tools > 3D > Merge 3D** from the menubar; the **Merge3D1** tool tile is inserted in the **Flow** area and a connection between the **Shape3D1** and **Merge3D1** tools is established.

10. Press 1; the output of the **Merge3D1** tool is displayed in the left Display View.

Next, you will create the back support of the bench.

11. Select the **Shape3D1** tool tile in the **Flow** area and press CTRL+C. Next, click on the empty space in the **Flow** area and press CTRL+V; the **Shape3D1_1** tool tile is inserted in the **Flow** area.

12. Press 2; the output of the **Shape3D1_1** tool is displayed in the right Display View.

13. Choose the **Fit** button from the right **Display View** toolbar to fit the 3D object into the right Display View. Drag the red output node of the **Shape3D1_1** tool tile to the green node **Merge3D1** tool tile; a connection between the **Shape3D1_1** and **Merge3D1** tools is established.

14. Choose the **Controls** tab of **Shape3D1_1** tool control window, if it is not already chosen and enter the values of the parameters as follows:

Width: **5.76**   Height: **0.428**   Depth: **0.68**

15. Choose the **3D Controls** tab of the **Shape3D1_1** tool control window and enter the values of the parameters as follows:

Translation
X Offset: **0.56**   Y Offset: **21.56**   Z Offset: **-5.07**

Scale
Clear the **Lock X/Y/Z** check box.
X Scale: **8.5**   Y Scale: **8.5**   Z Scale: **2.0**

16. Select the **Merge3D1** tool tile in the **Flow** area and then press 2; the output of the **Merge3D1** tool is displayed in the right Display View.

    The back support of the bench is created, as shown in Figure 13-5.

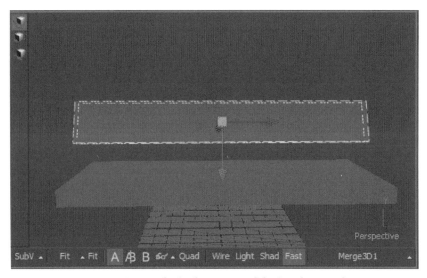

Figure 13-5 The back support of the bench created

Next, you will create the legs of the bench.

17. Click on the empty space in the **Flow** area to deselect the selected tool tile, if any. Next, choose **Tools > 3D > Shape 3D** from the menubar; the **Shape3D2** tool tile is inserted in the **Flow** area.

18. Press 2; the output of the **Shape3D2** tool is displayed in the right Display View. Next, choose the **Fit** button from the **Display View** toolbar to fit the image into the Display View.

19. Drag the red output node of the **Shape3D2** tool tile to the pink output node of the **Merge3D1** tool tile; a connection between the **Shape3D2** and **Merge3D1** tools is established.

20. In the **Shape3D2** tool control window, choose the **Cube** button from the **Shape** area. Next, clear the **Lock Width/Height/Depth** check box and enter the values of the parameters as given next:

    Width: **1.26**   Height: **15**

21. Choose the **3D Controls** tab of the **Shape3D2** tool control window and enter the values of the parameters as given next:

Translation
X Offset: **-20**   Y Offset: **3.89**   Z Offset: **4.7**

Scale
Scale: **1.26**

22. In the **Materials** tab of the **Shape3D2** tool control window, choose the **Pick** button in the **Diffuse** area; the **Color** dialog box is displayed. Select the grey color swatch in this dialog box and then choose the **OK** button to close it.

The first leg of the bench is created, as shown in Figure 13-6.

Figure 13-6 *The first leg of the bench created*

23. Click on the empty space in the **Flow** area to deselect the selected tool tile, if any. Next, choose **Tools > 3D > Shape 3D** from the menubar; the **Shape3D3** tool tile is inserted in the **Flow** area.

24. Press 2; the output of the **Shape3D3** tool is displayed in the right Display View. Next, choose the **Fit** button from the right **Display View** toolbar to fit the image into the right Display View.

25. Drag the red output node of the **Shape3D3** tool tile to the red output node of the **Merge3D1** tool tile; a connection between the **Shape3D3** and **Merge3D1** tools is established.

26. In the **Shape3D3** tool control window, choose the **Cube** button from the **Shape** area. Next, clear the **Lock Width/Height/Depth** check box and enter **17** in the **Height** edit box.

27. In the **3D Controls** tab of the **Shape3D3** tool control window, enter the values of the parameters as follows:

Translation
X Offset: **-20**   Y Offset: **8.77**   Z Offset: **-5.536**

Scale
Scale: **1.0**

28. In the **Materials** tab of the **Shape3D3** tool control window, choose the **Pick** button; the **Color** dialog box is displayed. In this dialog box, select the grey color swatch and then choose the **OK** button to close the dialog box.

The other leg of the bench is created, as shown in Figure 13-7.

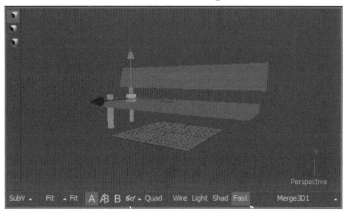

Figure 13-7 *The other leg of the bench created*

 Tip: *You can also display the perspective and orthographic views in a Display View by choosing the **Quad** button from the **Display View** toolbar. Alternatively, you can press CTRL+Q to switch to the quad view. The quad view of the output of the **Merge3D1** tool is shown in Figure 13-8.*

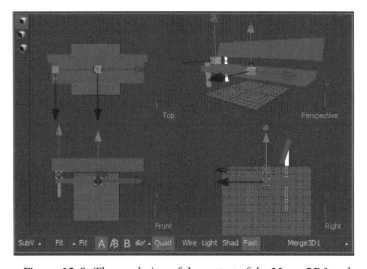

Figure 13-8 *The quad view of the output of the **Merge3D1** tool*

29. Select the **Merge3D1** tool tile from the **Flow** area and choose **Tools > 3D > Renderer 3D** from the menubar; the **Renderer3D1** tool tile is inserted in the **Flow** area and a connection between the **Renderer3D1** and **Merge3D1** tools is established.

The **Renderer3D** tool is used to convert a 3D scene into a 2D image by using the default perspective camera, if a camera is not available in the scene.

30. Press 2; the output of the **Renderer3D1** tool is displayed in the right Display View.

Next, you will add camera to the scene to get a clear view.

31. Select the **Merge3D1** tool tile from the **Flow** area and choose **Tools > 3D > Camera 3D** from the menubar; the **Camera3D1** tool tile is inserted in the **Flow** area and a connection between the **Camera3D1** and **Merge3D1** tools is established.

32. Make sure the **Camera3D1** tool tile is selected in the **Flow** area. In the **Controls** tab of the **Camera3D1** tool control window, enter the values of the parameters as follows:

Angle of View: **36.66**   Focal Length: **22.77**

The **Angle of View** option is used to view the specified area through camera. The **Focal Length** option is used to measure the distance between the center of the lens and the point of interest.

33. In the **3DControls** tab of the **Camera3D1** tool control window, enter the values of the parameters as follows:

Translation
X Offset: **10.77**   Y Offset: **23.33**   Z Offset: **54.9**

Rotation
X Rotation: **-13.03**   Y Rotation: **7.24**   Z Rotation: **-1.75**

The output of the **Merge3D1** and **Renderer3D1** tools is shown in Figure 13-9.

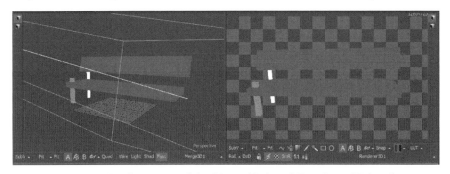

Figure 13-9 *The output of the **Merge3D1** and **Renderer3D1** tools*

34. Select the **Merge3D1** tool tile from the **Flow** area and choose **Tools > 3D > Shape3D** from the menubar; the **Shape3D4** tool tile is inserted in the **Flow** area and a connection between the **Shape3D4** and **Merge3D1** tools is established.

35. Select the **Shape3D4** tool tile from the **Flow** area. In the **Shape3D4** tool control window, choose the **Cube** button from the **Shape** area and clear the **Lock Width/Height/Depth** check box and then enter the values of the parameters as follows:

Width: **1.68**   Height: **1.82**   Depth: **10**

36. In the **3D Controls** tab of the **Shape3D4** tool control window, enter the values of the parameters as follows:

Translation
X Offset: **-20**   Y Offset: **11.07**   Z Offset: **0.12**

37. In the **Materials** tab of the **Shape3D4** tool control window, choose the **Pick** button; the **Color** dialog box is displayed. In this dialog box, select the grey color swatch and then choose the **OK** button to close it.

The left arm of the bench is created, as shown in Figure 13-10.

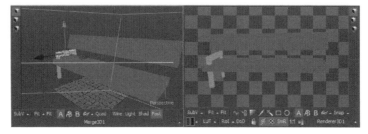

Figure 13-10 *The left arm of the bench created*

38. Select the **Shape3D2** tool tile from the **Flow** area and press CTRL+C to copy the tool tile. Click on the empty space in the **Flow** area and press CTRL+V; the **Shape3D2_1** tool tile is inserted in the **Flow** area. Next, drag the red output node of the **Shape3D2_1** tool to the **Merge3D1** tool tile; a connection is established between the **Shape3D2_1** and **Merge3D1** tools.

39. In the **3D Controls** tab of the **Shape3D2_1** tool control window, enter the values of the parameters as follows:

Translation
X Offset: **21.3**

The third leg of the bench is created, as shown in Figure 13-11.

40. Select the **Shape3D3** tool tile from the **Flow** area and press CTRL+C. Click on the empty space in the **Flow** area and press CTRL+V; the **Shape3D3_1** tool tile is inserted in the **Flow** area.

41. Drag the red output node of the **Shape3D3_1** tool tile to the **Merge3D1** tool tile; a connection between the **Shape3D3_1** and **Merge3D1** tools is established.

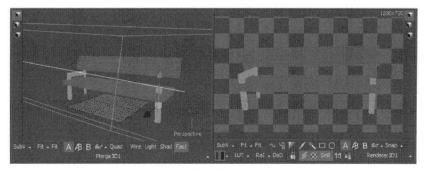

Figure 13-11 *The third leg of the bench created*

42. In the **3D Controls** tab of the **Shape3D3_1** tool control window, enter the values of the parameters as follows:

Translation
X Offset: **21.2**

The fourth leg of the bench is created, as shown in Figure 13-12.

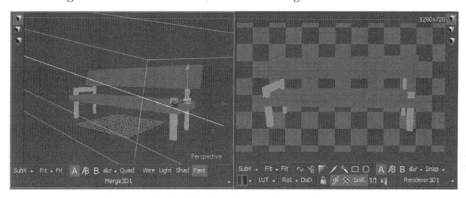

Figure 13-12 *The fourth leg of the bench created*

43. Select the **Shape3D4** tool tile from the **Flow** area and press CTRL+C. Click on the empty space in the **Flow** area and press CTRL+V; the **Shape3D4_1** tool tile is inserted in the **Flow** area.

44. Drag the red output node of the **Shape3D4_1** tool tile to the **Merge3D1** tool tile; a connection between the **Shape3D4_1** and **Merge3D1** tools is established.

45. In the **3D Controls** tab of the **Shape3D4_1** tool control window, enter the value of the following parameter:

Translation
X Offset: **21.3**

The right arm of the bench is created, as shown in Figure 13-13.

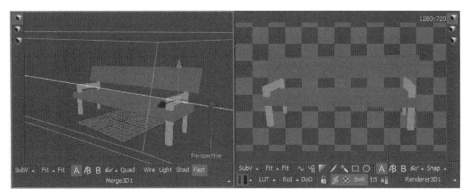

Figure 13-13 *The right arm of the bench created*

Creating the Ground in the Scene

In this section, you will create the ground in the scene.

1. Click on the empty space in the **Flow** area to deselect the selected tool tile, if any and then choose **Tools > 3D > Image Plane 3D** from the menubar; the **ImagePlane3D1** tool tile is inserted in the **Flow** area.

2. Choose the **LD** button from the toolbar; a dialog box is displayed. In this dialog box, choose **Documents > Fusion_7 > c13_tut > c13_tut_01 > Media_Files > grass.jpg** and then choose the **Open** button; the **Loader1** tool tile is inserted in the **Flow** area.

3. Drag the red output node of the **Loader1** tool tile to the green node of the **ImagePlane3D1** tool in the **Flow** area; a connection between the **Loader1** and **ImagePlane3D1** tools is established.

4. Make sure the **ImagePlane3D1** tool tile is selected in the **Flow** area and then press 1; the output of the **ImagePlane3D1** tool is displayed in the left Display View, as shown in Figure 13-14.

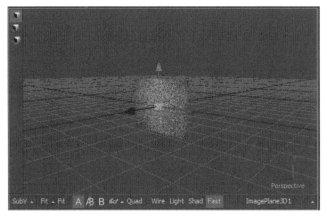

Figure 13-14 *The output of the **ImagePlane3D1** tool*

Next, choose the **Fit** button from the left **Display View** toolbar to fit the image in the left Display View.

5. Drag the red output node of the **ImagePlane3D1** tool tile to the **Merge3D1** tool tile; a connection between the **ImagePlane3D1** and **Merge3D1** tools is established.

6. In the **3D Controls** tab of the **ImagePlane3D1** tool control window, enter the values of the parameters as follows:

Translation
X Offset: **-5**

Rotation
Rotation Order
X Rotation: **-90**

Scale
Scale: **108**

7. Choose the **Fit** button from the **Display View** toolbar to fit the image into the Display View.

The rotated view of the output of the **ImagePlane3D1** tool is shown in Figure 13-15. The merged view of the output of the **ImagePlane3D1** tool and bench is displayed in the Display View, as shown in Figure 13-16.

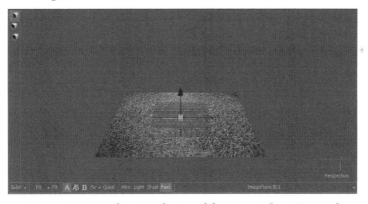

Figure 13-15 *The rotated view of the **Imageplane3D1** tool*

Adding the Light to the Scene

In this section, you will add light to the scene by using the **Spot Light** tool.

1. Click on the empty space in the **Flow** area to deselect the selected tool tile, if any, and then choose **Tools > 3D > Light > Spot Light** from the menubar; the **SpotLight1** tool tile is inserted in the **Flow** area. Drag the red output node of the **SpotLight1** tool tile to the **Merge3D1** tool tile in the **Flow** area; a connection between the **SpotLight1** and **Merge3D1** tools is established.

Figure 13-16 *The merged view of the **Imageplane3D1** tool and bench*

Next, you will enable the light and shadow options in the **Renderer3D1** tool control window to view the effect of the light in the scene.

2. Choose the **Display scene using lights** button from the left Display View toolbar; the light effect is displayed in the right Display View. Select the **Renderer3D1** tool tile from the **Flow** area. Next, in the **Controls** tab of the **Renderer3D1** tool control window, expand the **Lighting** area and then select the **Enable Lighting** and **Enable Shadows** check boxes.

3. Select the **SpotLight1** tool tile in the **Flow** area. Next, in the **Controls** tab of the **SpotLight1** tool control window, enter the values of the parameters as follows:

Intensity: **1.2**   Cone Angle: **90**   Penumbra Angle: **2**

Next, expand the **Shadows** area and enter the value as follows:

Shadow
Density: **0.7**

The **Intensity** parameter is used to set the intensity of the light. The **Cone Angle** of the light refers to the width of the cone where the light is emitted with full intensity. Larger the angle wider the cone angle. The maximum limit of the cone angle is 90 degrees. The **Penumbra Angle** determines the area beyond the **Cone Angle** where the intensity of light falls off towards 0. A larger **Penumbra Angle** defines a larger falloff, while a value of 0 generates a hard edged light. The **Density** parameter is used to control the transparency of the shadows.

4. Choose the **Constant** button from the **Softness** area.

There are three buttons in the **Softness** area namely, **None**, **Constant**, and **Variable**. If you choose the **None** button, shadows produced by the **Spot Light** tool will have hard edges. When the **Constant** button is chosen, the **Constant Softness** sliders will appear. As a result, the edges of the shadow will have a constant softness. When the **Variable** button is chosen, the softness of the shadow edges grows as the distance between shadow receiver and shadow caster increases.

5. In the **3D Controls** tab of the **SpotLight1** tool control window, select the **Use Target** check box and then enter the values of the parameters as follows:

    Translation
    X Offset: **3.19**   Y Offset: **122**   Z Offset: **94.6**

6. Choose the **Show Checker Underlay** button from the right Display View toolbar. The final output of the **Renderer3D1** tool after adding light is shown in Figure 13-17.

Figure 13-17 *The final output of the **Renderer3D1** tool after adding light*

Now, save the composition with the name *c13tut1* at the location *Documents > Fusion_7 > c13_tut > c13_tut_01*. Next, you need to render the composition. For rendering, refer to Tutorial 1 of Chapter 2. You can also view the final render of the composition by downloading the *c13_fusion_7_rndr.zip* from *http://www.cadcim.com*. The path of the file is mentioned at the beginning of the chapter.

Tutorial 2

In this tutorial, you will create a glass window texture by using the **3D** and **Texture** tools. The final output of the composition is shown in Figure 13-18.   **(Expected time: 25 min)**

Figure 13-18 *The final output of the composition*

The following steps are required to complete this tutorial:

a. Set the frame format.
b. Download and import the image.
c. Create a window.
d. Apply the material.
e. Add reflection to the window.

Setting the Frame Format
In this section, you will specify the frame format settings.

1. Choose **File > New** from the menubar; a new composition is opened in the Fusion screen.

2. Choose **File > Preferences** from the menubar; the **Preferences** dialog box is displayed.

3. In this dialog box, select **Frame Format** from the **Composition#** preferences tree; various frame format settings are displayed on the right in the **Preferences** dialog box. Next, select the **HDTV 720** option from the **Default format** drop-down list and then choose the **Save** button to save the changes made.

4. In the Time Ruler area, enter **0** in the **Global End Time** edit box.

Downloading and Importing the Image
In this section, you will download and import the image.

1. Open the following link: *http://www.freeimages.com/photo/1103730*; an image is displayed.

2. Download the image at the location */Documents/Fusion_7/c013_tut/c13_tut_02/ Media_Files* and save it with the name *bg.jpg*.

 Note
Footage Courtesy: **Dimitri Castrique** *(http://www.freeimages.com/profile/dimitri_c)*

3. Choose the **LD** button from the toolbar; a dialog box is displayed. In this dialog box, choose **Documents > Fusion_7 > c13_tut > c13_tut_02 > Media_Files > glass.jpg** and then choose the **Open** button; the **Loader1** tool is inserted in the **Flow** area.

Creating the Window
In this section, you will create a window by using the **3D** tools.

1. Click on the empty space in the **Flow** area to deselect the selected tool tile, if any. Choose **Tools > 3D > Shape 3D** from the menubar; the **Shape3D1** tool tile is inserted in the **Flow** area.

2. Select the **Shape3D1** tool tile from the **Flow** area. Next, press 1; the output of the **Shape3D1** tool is displayed in the left Display View.

3. In the **Shape3D1** tool control window, choose the **Cylinder** button from the **Shape** area and enter the values of the parameters as follows:

Radius: **0.05**   Height: **4**

4. Choose the **Fit** button from the left **Display View** toolbar to fit the image into the left Display View.

5. In the **Shape3D1** tool control window, choose the **3D Controls** tab and set the values of the parameters as follows:

Translation
X Offset: **0.15**   Y Offset: **1.81**

6. In the **Materials** tab of the **Shape3D1** tool control window, choose the **Pick** button and select the black color swatch in the **Color** dialog box and then close it.

7. Make sure the **Shape3D1** tool tile is selected in the **Flow** area and choose **Tools > 3D > Merge 3D** from the menubar; a connection between the **Shape3D1** and **Merge3D1** tools is established.

8. Press 1; the output of the **Merge3D1** tool is displayed in the left Display View, as shown in Figure 13-19.

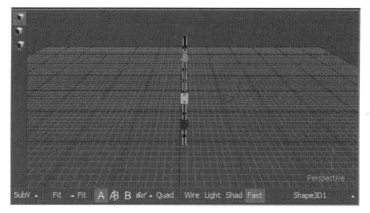

Figure 13-19 *The output of the **Merge3D1** tool*

9. Select the **Shape3D1** tool tile from the **Flow** area and choose **Tools > 3D > Duplicate 3D** from the menubar; the **Duplicate3D1** tool tile is inserted in the **Flow** area and a connection between the **Shape3D1** and **Duplicate3D1** tools is established.

The **Duplicate3D** tool is used to create a duplicate copy of the 3D object in the scene.

10. Press 2; the output of the **Duplicate3D1** tool is displayed in the right Display view. Choose the **Fit** button from the right **Display View** toolbar to fit the image into the right Display View.

11. In the **Duplicate3D1** tool control window, enter the values of the parameters as follows:

Last Copy: **5**

Translation
X Offset: **1**

The **Last Copy** option is used to specify the number of copies that you will create in the scene. The copies of the **Shape3D1** tool are created, as shown in Figure 13-20.

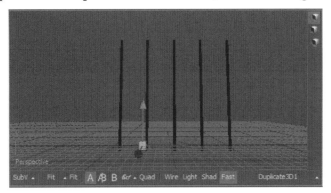

*Figure 13-20 The copies of the **Shape3D1** tool created*

12. Make sure the **Duplicate3D1** tool tile is selected in the **Flow** area. Next, choose **Tools > 3D > Duplicate3D** from the menubar; the **Duplicate3D2** tool tile is inserted in the **Flow** area and a connection between the **Duplicate3D1** and **Duplicate3D2** tools is established.

13. Press 2; the output of the **Duplicate3D2** tool is displayed in the right Display view.

14. In the **Controls** tab of the **Duplicate3D2** tool control window, enter the values of the parameters as follows:

Translation
X Offset: **0.37**   Y Offset: **4**

Rotation
Z Rotation: **-90**

The output of the **Duplicate3D2** tool is shown in Figure 13-21.

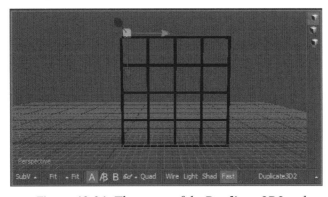

*Figure 13-21 The output of the **Duplicate3D2** tool*

15. Select the **Merge3D1** tool tile in the **Flow** area and then choose **Tools > 3D > Shape3D** from the menubar; the **Shape3D2** tool tile is inserted in the **Flow** area.

16. Press 2; the output of the **Shape3D2** tool is displayed in the right Display view.

17. In the **Controls** tab of the **Shape3D2** tool control window, enter **4** in the **Size** edit box.

18. In the **3D Controls** area of the **Shape3D2** tool control window, enter the values of the parameters as follows:

    Translation
    X Offset: **2.12**   Y Offset: **1.83**   Z Offset: **-0.007**

19. In the **Materials** tab of the **Shape3D2** tool control window, choose the **Pick** button and select the black color swatch in the **Color** dialog box and then close it. Next, enter **0.5** in the **Opacity** edit box of the **Shape3D2** tool control window.

20. Select the **Merge3D1** tool in the **Flow** area and then choose **Tools > 3D > Shape 3D** from the menubar; the **Shape3D3** tool tile is inserted in the **Flow** area and a connection is established between the **Merge3D1** and **Shape3D3** tools.

21. Press 2; the output of the **Shape3D3** tool is displayed in the right Display view.

22. Select the **Shape3D3** tool tile in the **Flow** area. Next, choose the **Cylinder** button from the **Shape** area and enter the values of the parameters as follows:

    Radius: **0.09**   Height: **4**

23. In the **3D Controls** tab of the **Shape3D3** tool control window, enter the values of the parameters as follows:

    Translation
    X Offset: **0.11**   Y Offset: **1.86**

24. In the **Materials** tab of the **Shape3D3** tool control window, choose the **Pick** button and select the black color swatch in the **Color** dialog box and then close it.

25. Make sure the **Shape3D3** tool tile is selected from the **Flow** area. Next, choose **Tools > 3D > Duplicate 3D** from the menubar; the **Duplicate3D3** tool tile is inserted in the **Flow** area and a connection between the **Shape3D3** and **Duplicate3D3** tools is established.

26. Press 2; the output of the **Duplicate3D3** tool is displayed in the right Display view.

27. In the **Duplicate3D3** tool control window, make sure the **Controls** tab is chosen. Next, enter the values of the parameters as follows:

    Translation
    X Offset: **3.99**   Y Offset: **-0.01**

The output of the **Merge3D1** tool after adding material is shown in Figure 13-22.

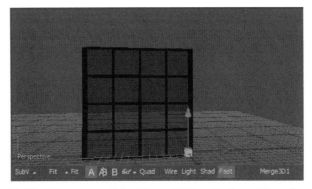

*Figure 13-22 The output of the **Merge3D1** tool after adding the material*

28. Make sure the **Merge3D1** tool tile is selected in the **Flow** area and then choose **Tools > 3D > Shape3D** from the menubar; the **Shape3D4** tool tile is inserted in the **Flow** area and a connection is established between the **Merge3D1** and **Shape3D4** tools.

29. Select the **Shape3D4** tool tile in the **Flow** area. In the **Shape3D4** tool control window, choose the **Cube** button from the **Shape** area and then enter **0.2** in the **Size** edit box.

30. In the **Shape3D4** tool control window, choose the **Materials** tab and enter the values of the parameters as follows:

    Diffuse Color (Diffuse)
    R: **0**   G: **0**   B: **0**

31. Choose the **3D Controls** tab and enter the values of the parameters as follows:

    X Offset: **1.17**   Y Offset: **0.85**   Z Offset: **0.06**

32. Make sure the **Shape3D4** tool tile is selected in the **Flow** area. Next, choose **Tools > 3D > Duplicate3D** from the menubar; the **Duplicate3D4** tool tile is inserted in the **Flow** area and a connection between the **Shape3D4** and **Duplicate3D4** tools is established.

33. In the **Duplicate3D4** tool control window, choose the **Controls** tab and enter the values of the parameters as follows:

    Last Copy: **3**

    Translation
    X Offset: **1.01**

34. Make sure the **Duplicate3D4** tool tile is selected in the **Flow** area and then choose **Tools > 3D > Duplicate3D** from the menubar; the **Duplicate3D5** tool tile is inserted in the **Flow** area and a connection between the **Duplicate3D4** and **Duplicate3D5** tools is established.

35. In the **Duplicate3D5** tool control window, choose the **Controls** tab and enter the values of the parameters as follows:

Last Copy: **3**

Translation
X Offset: **-0.02**   Y Offset: **1.02**

The final window pane is created, as shown in Figure 13-23.

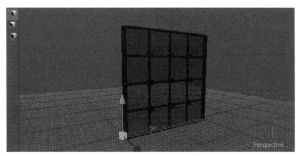

Figure 13-23 *The final window pane created*

Applying the Material

In this section, you will apply a material to the window glass.

1. Select the **Loader1** tool tile in the **Flow** area and then choose **Tools > 3D > Material > Blinn** from the menu bar; the **Blinn1** tool tile is inserted in the **Flow** area and a connection is established between the **Blinn1** and **Loader1** tools.

2. Drag the red output node of the **Blinn1** tool tile to the green node of the **Shape3D2** tool tile; a connection is established between the **Blinn1** and **Shape3D2** tools.

The output of the **Merge3D1** tool after adding **Blinn** material is shown in Figure 13-24.

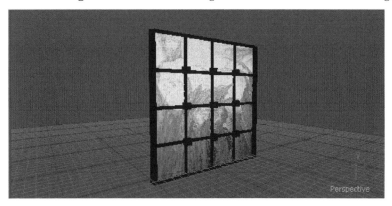

Figure 13-24 *The output of the **Merge3D1** tool after adding the **Blinn** material*

3. In the **Controls** tab of the **Blinn1** tool control window, enter **0.9** in the **Opacity** edit box of the **Blinn1** tool control window.

4. Press 2; the output of the **Blinn1** tool is displayed in the right Display View, as shown in Figure 13-25.

Figure 13-25 *The output of the* **Binn1** *tool*

When you display the output of a material tool in a Display View, the corresponding Display View changes to Material Viewer. By default, Fusion applies the material to lit a 3D sphere and displays the OpenGL rendered output. You cannot pan and scale the Material Viewer. However, Material Viewer can be rotated around an axis. To do so, press and hold ALT and then drag the middle-mouse button to rotate the view. You can use the middle-mouse button to change the position of the light. The light can be turned off by choosing the **Light** button from the **Display View** toolbar. The 3D geometry displayed in the Material Viewer can be changed by choosing the **Sphere** button in the **Display View** toolbar, refer to Figure 13-26.

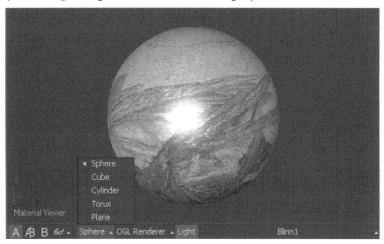

Figure 13-26 *The Material Viewer*

5. Click on the empty space in the **Flow** area and then choose **Tools > Color > Color Corrector** from the menu bar; the **ColorCorrector1** tool tile is inserted in the **Flow** area.

6. Drag the red output node of the **Loader1** tool tile to the orange node of the **ColorCorrector1** tool tile; a connection is established between the **Loader1** and **ColorCorrector1** tools.

7. Press 2; the output of the **ColorCorrector1** node is displayed in the right Display View.

8. Enter **0** in the **Master-Saturation** edit box of the **ColorCorrector1** tool control window; the greyscale image is displayed in the Display View.

9. Make sure the **ColorCorrector1** tool tile is selected in the **Flow** area and then choose **Tools > 3D > Texture > BumpMap** from the menu bar; the **BumpMap1** tool tile is inserted in the **Flow** area and a connection is established between the **ColorCorrector1** and **BumpMap1** tools.

   The **BumpMap** tool is used to create a bump map for the objects in the scene.

10. Enter **2.5** in the **Height Scale** edit box in the **BumpMap1** tool control window.

    The higher the value of the **Scale** parameter, the greater will be the visibility of the bump.

11. Drag the red output node of the **BumpMap1** tool tile to the Bump node of the **Blinn1** tool tile; a connection is established between the **BumpMap1** and **Blinn1** tools.

12. Select the **Blinn1** tool tile in the **Flow** area and press 2; the output of the **Blinn1** tool with the bump map added is displayed in the right Display View, as shown in Figure 13-27. Notice that now the bump is visible on the surface of the sphere.

*Figure 13-27   The output of the **Blinn1** tool with the bumpmap added*

Adding Reflection to the Window

In this section, you will add reflection to the window.

1. Click on the empty space in the **Flow** area and then import *bg.jpg* to it; the **Loader2** tool tile is inserted in the **Flow** area.

2. Make sure the **Loader2** tool tile is selected in the **Flow** area and then choose **Tools > 3D > Texture > SphereMap** from the menubar; the **SphereMap1** tool tile is inserted in the **Flow** area and a connection is established between the **Loader2** and **SphereMap1** tools.

3. Select the **Blinn1** tool tile from the **Flow** area and then choose **Tools > 3D > Material > Reflect** from the menubar; the **Reflect1** tool tile is inserted in the **Flow** area and a connection is established between the **Blinn1** and **Reflect1** tools.

4. Drag the red output node of the **SphereMap1** tool tile to the **Reflection Color Material** node of the **Reflect1** tool tile and a connection is established between the **SphereMap1** and **Reflect1** tools, as shown in Figure 13-28.

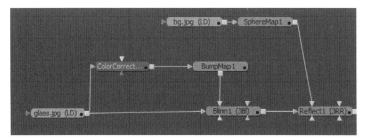

*Figure 13-28 The **SphereMap1** tool connected to the **Reflect1** tool*

5. In the **Reflect1** tool control window, choose the **Constant** button and then enter **0.6** in the **Constant Strength** edit box.

6. Press 2; the output of the **Reflect1** tool is displayed in the right Display View, as shown in Figure 13-29. Figure 13-30 shows the output of the **Merge3D1** tool after adding the reflection.

*Figure 13-29 The output of the **Reflect1** tool displayed*

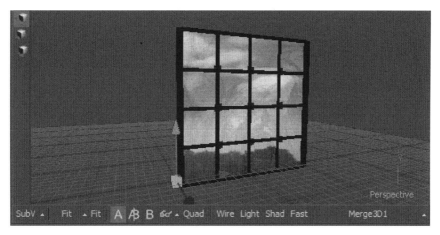

*Figure 13-30 The output of the **Merge3D1** tool after adding reflection*

Now, you need to add **Camera3D** and **Renderer3D** tools to the **Flow** area to render the final output, refer to Tutorial 1.

Now, save the composition with the name *c13tut2* at the location *Documents > Fusion_7 > c13_tut > c13_tut_02*. Next, you need to render the composition. For rendering, refer to Tutorial 1 of Chapter 2. The output of the composition is shown in Figure 13-18. You can also view the final render of the composition by downloading the *c13_fusion_7_rndr.zip* from *http://www.cadcim.com*. The path of the file is mentioned at the beginning of the chapter.

Tutorial 3

In this tutorial, you will compose 3D objects in a 2D environment. The final output of the composition is shown in Figure 13-31.   **(Expected time: 30 min)**

Figure 13-31 The final output of the composition

The following steps are required to complete this tutorial:

a.   Set the frame format.
b.   Import images.
c.   Add a rug to the scene.

d.   Add a lamp to the scene.

e.   Add a vase to the scene.

f.   Add light to the scene.

Setting the Frame Format

In this section, you will specify the frame format settings.

1.   Choose **File > New** from the menubar; a new composition is opened in the Fusion screen.

2.   Choose **File > Preferences** from the menubar; the **Preferences** dialog box is displayed.

3.   In this dialog box, select **Frame Format** from the **Composition#** preferences tree; various frame format settings are displayed on the right in the **Preferences** dialog box. Next, select the **HDTV 720** option from the **Default format** drop-down list and then choose the **Save** button to save the changes made.

4.   In the Time Ruler area, enter **0** in the **Global End Time** edit box.

Importing the Images

In this section, you will import the images.

1.   Choose the **LD** button from the toolbar; the **Open File** dialog box is displayed. In this dialog box, choose **Documents > Fusion_7 > c13_tut > c13_tut_03 > Media_Files > living room. jpg** and then choose the **Open** button; the **Loader1** tool is inserted in the **Flow** area.

2.   Press 1; the output of the **Loader1** tool is displayed in the left Display View.

3.   Choose the **Fit** button from the left **Display View** toolbar to fit the image into the left Display View, refer to Figure 13-32.

Figure 13-32   *The output of the **Loader1** tool*

4.   Click in the empty space of the **Flow** area to deselect the selected tool tile, if any and then choose **Tools > 3D > Image Plane 3D** from the menubar; the **ImagePlane3D1** tool tile is inserted in the **Flow** area.

5. Drag the red output of the **Loader1** tool tile to the green node of the **ImagePlane3D1** tool tile.

6. Make sure the **ImagePlane3D1** tool tile is selected in the **Flow** area. Next, press 1; the output of the **ImagePlane3D1** tool is displayed in the left Display View, as shown in Figure 13-33.

Figure 13-33 *The output of the **ImagePlane3D1** tool*

Adding a Rug to the Scene

In this section, you will add a rug to the scene.

1. Click on the empty space in the **Flow** area to deselect the selected tool tile, if any and then choose **Tools > 3D > Shape 3D** from the menubar; the **Shape3D1** tool tile is inserted in the **Flow** area.

2. Rename the **Shape3D1** tool tile as **Rug**, by pressing F2.

3. Press 2; the output of the **Rug** tool is displayed in the right Display View.

4. Choose the **Cube** button from the **Shape** area in the **Rug** tool control window.

5. In the **Rug** tool control window, clear the **Lock Width/Height/Depth** check box and set the values of parameters as follows:

    Width: **0.27**   Height: **0.27**   Depth: **0.005**

6. Click on the empty space in the **Flow** area to deselect the selected tool tile, if any. Next, choose **Tools > 3D > Merge 3D** from the menubar; the **Merge3D1** tool tile is inserted in the **Flow** area.

7. Press 1; the output of the **Merge3D1** tool is displayed in the left Display View.

8. Drag the red output of the **ImagePlane3D1** tool tile to the orange node of the **Merge 3D1** tool tile; a connection between the **ImagePlane3D1** and **Merge3D1** tools is established.

9. Drag the red output of the **Rug** tool tile to the green node of the **Merge 3D1** tool tile; a connection between the **Rug** and **Merge3D1** tools is established.

The output of the **Merge3D1** tool after adding the plane is displayed, as shown in Figure 13-34.

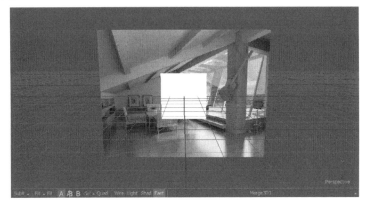

*Figure 13-34 The output of the **Merge3D1** tool after adding the plane*

10. Choose the **3D Controls** tab in the **Rug** tool control window and then enter the values of the parameters as follows:

Translation
X Offset: **0.102**   Y Offset: **-0.202**   Z Offset: **0.111**

Rotation
Rotation Order: **YZX**

X Rotation: **100.544**   Y Rotation: **1.99**   Z Rotation: **-36.19**

Next, clear the **Lock X/Y/Z** check box in the **Scale** area and enter the values of the parameters as follows:

X Scale: **0.387**   Y Scale: **0.744**   Z Scale: **0.58**

The positioning of **ImagePlane3D1** tool is shown in Figure 13-35.

*Figure 13-35 The positioning of **ImagePlane3D1** tool*

11. Select the **Merge3D1** tool tile from the **Flow** area and choose **Tools > 3D > Renderer 3D** from the menubar; the **Renderer3D1** tool tile is inserted in the **Flow** area and a connection between the **Merge3D1** and **Renderer3D1** tools is established.

12. Press 2; the output of the **Renderer3D1** tool is displayed in the right Display View.

13. Choose the **Fit** button from the **Display View** toolbar to fit the image into the Display View.

14. Click in the empty space of the **Flow** area to deselect the selected tool tile, if any. Next, choose **Tools > 3D > Camera 3D** from the menubar; the **Camera3D1** tool tile is inserted in the **Flow** area.

15. Drag the red output node of the **Camera3D1** tool tile to the **Merge3D1** tool tile; a connection between the **Camera3D1** and **Merge3D1** tools is established.

16. Enter **24.33** in the **Angle of View** edit box in the **Camera3D1** tool control window.

17. Choose the **3D Controls** tab in the **Camera3D1** tool control window and enter the value of the following parameter:

    Translation
    Z Offset: **1.3**

18. Select the **Rug** tool tile and then choose the **Materials** tab from the **Rug** tool control window and enter the values of the parameters as follows:
    Diffuse Color(Diffuse)
    R: **0.22**   G: **0.004**   B: **0.027**

    Now, you need to add the shadow to the Rug.

19. Make sure the **Rug** tool tile is selected in the **Flow** area is selected and then press CTRL+C. Next, click in the empty space of the **Flow** area and press CTRL+V; the **Rug_1** tool is inserted in the **Flow** area. Rename the **Rug_1** as **Rug_shadow**.

20. Drag the red output of the **Rug_shadow** tool tile to the **Merge 3D1** tool; a connection between the **Rug_shadow** and **Merge3D1** tools is established.

21. In the **3D Controls** tab of the **Rug_shadow** tool control window, enter the values of the parameters as follows:

    Translation
    X Offset: **0.102**   Y Offset: **-0.203**   Z Offset: **0.111**

22. Choose the **Materials** tab of the **Rug_shadow** tool control window and enter the values of the parameters as follows:

    Diffuse Color (Diffuse)
    R: **-0.121**   G: **0.08**   B: **0.05**

The output of the **Merge3D1** and **Renderer3D1** tools after adding the rug is shown in Figure 13-36.

Figure 13-36 *The output of the* ***Merge3D1*** *and* ***Renderer3D1*** *tools after adding rug*

Adding a Lamp to the Scene

In this section, you will add a lamp to the scene.

1. Click on the empty space in the **Flow** area and choose the **LD** button from the toolbar; the **Open File** dialog box is displayed. In this dialog box, choose **Documents > Fusion_7 > c13_tut > c13_tut_03 > Media_Files > lamp.tga** and then choose the **Open** button; the **Loader2** tool tile is inserted in the **Flow** area.

2. Press 1; the output of the **Loader2** tool is displayed in the left Display View.

3. In the control window of the **Loader2** tool, choose the **Import** tab and then select the **Post-Multiply by Alpha** check box.

4. Click on the empty space in the **Flow** area and choose the **Ply** button from the toolbar; the **Polygon1** tool is inserted in the **Flow** area.

5. Click and draw a polyline in the left Display View, as shown in Figure 13-37.

Figure 13-37 *The polyline drawn in the left Display View*

6. Drag the red output node of the **Polygon1** tool tile to the purple node of the **Loader2** tool tile; a connection between the **Polygon1** and **Loader2** tools is established.

7. Select the **Invert** check box from the **Polygon1** tool control window. The output of the **Loader2** tool is shown in Figure 13-38.

*Figure 13-38 The output of the **Loader2** tool*

8. Click on the empty space in the **Flow** area and choose **Tools > 3D > Image Plane 3D** from the menubar; the **ImagePlane3D2** tool tile is inserted in the **Flow** area.

9. Drag the red output of the **Loader2** tool tile to the green node of the **ImagePlane3D2** tool tile; a connection between the **Loader2** and **ImagePlane3D2** tools is established.

10. Press 1; the output of the **ImagePlane3D2** tool is displayed in the left Display View.

11. Drag the red output of the **ImagePlane3D2** tool tile to the **Merge 3D1** tool; a connection between the **ImagePlane3D2** and **Merge3D1** tools is established.

12. Choose the **3D Controls** tab from the **ImagePlane3D2** tool control window and enter the values of the parameters as follows:

Translation
X Offset: **-0.2**   Y Offset: **-0.04**   Z Offset: **0.013**

Y Rotation: **185**

Scale
Scale: **0.33**

13. Select the **Merge3D1** tool in the **Flow** area and then press 1; the output of the **Merge3D1** tool is displayed in the left Display View. Also, the output of the **Renderer3D1** tool after adding the lamp is displayed in the right Display View, as shown in Figure 13-39.

Adding a Vase to the Scene
In this section, you will a add vase to the scene.

1. Click on the empty space in the **Flow** area and choose the **LD** button from the toolbar; the **Open File** dialog box is displayed. In this dialog box, choose **Documents >**

Fusion_7 > c13_tut > c13_tut_03 > Media_Files > vase.tga and then choose the **Open** button; the **Loader3** tool tile is inserted in the **Flow** area.

Figure 13-39 *The output of the **Renderer3D1** tool after adding the lamp*

2. In the control window of the **Loader3** tool, choose the **Import** tab and then select the **Post-Multiply by Alpha** check box.

3. Click on the empty space in the **Flow** area and choose **Tools > 3D > Image Plane 3D** from the menubar; the **ImagePlane3D3** tool tile is inserted in the **Flow** area.

4. Drag the red output of the **Loader3** tool tile to the green node of the **ImagePlane3D3** tool tile; a connection between the **Loader3** and **ImagePlane3D3** tools is established.

5. Drag the red output node of the **ImagePlane3D3** tool tile to the **Merge3D1** tool tile; a connection between the **ImagePlane3D3** and **Merge3D1** tools is established.

6. Select the **Loader3** tool tile from the **Flow** area and then choose the **CC** button from the toolbar; the **ColorCorrector1** tool tile is inserted in the **Flow** area and a connection between the **Loader3**, **ColorCorrector1**, and **ImagePlane3D3** tools is established.

7. Enter **0.77** in the **Master-RGB-Gain** in the **ColorCorrector1** tool control window.

8. Select the **ImagePlane3D3** tool tile from the **Flow** area and choose the **3D Controls** tab from the **ImagePlane3D3** tool control window and enter the values of the parameters as follows:

Translation
X Offset: **-0.54**   Y Offset: **-0.14**   Z Offset: **0.06**

Next, you will add reflection to the vase.

9. Select the **Loader3**, **ColorCorrector1,** and **ImagePlane3D3** tool tiles from the **Flow** area and press CTRL+C. Next, click on the empty space in the **Flow** area and then press CTRL+V; the **Loader3_1**, **ColorCorrector1_1**, and **ImagePlane3D3_1** tools are inserted in the **Flow** area.

10. Drag the red output of the **ImagePlane3D3_1** tool tile to the **Merge3D1** tool tile; a connection between the **Merge3D1** and **ImagePlane3D3_1** tools is established.

11. Enter **0.57** in the **Opacity** edit box of the **Materials** tab in the **ImagePlane3D3_1** tool control window.

12. Choose the **3D Controls** tab in the **ImagePlane3D3_1** tool control window and enter the values of the parameters as follows:

Translation
X Offset: **-0.54**   Y Offset: **-0.32**   Z Offset: **0.05**

Rotation
X Rotation: **185**

The output of the **Renderer3D1** tool after adding the vase is shown in Figure 13-40.

Figure 13-40 *The output of the **Renderer3D1** tool after adding the vase*

Adding a Light to the Scene
In this section, you will add a light to the scene.

1. Click on the empty space in the **Flow** area and choose the **LD** button from the toolbar; the **Open File** dialog box is displayed. In this dialog box, choose **Documents > Fusion_7 > c13_tut > c13_tut_03 > Media_Files > light.tga** and then choose the **Open** button; the **Loader4** tool tile is inserted in the **Flow** area.

2. Press 1; the output of the **Loader4** tool is displayed in the left Display View.

3. Make sure the **Loader4** tool tile is selected in the **Flow** area. In the control window of the **Loader4** tool, choose the **Import** tab and then select the **Post-Multiply by Alpha** check box.

4. Click on the empty space in the **Flow** area. Choose **Tools > 3D > Image Plane 3D** from the menubar; the **ImagePlane3D4** tool tile is inserted in the **Flow** area.

5.   Drag the red output node of the **Loader4** tool tile to the green node of the **ImagePlane3D4** tool tile; a connection between the **Loader4** and **ImagePlane3D4** tools is established.

6.   Drag the red output of the **ImagePlane3D4** tool tile to the **Merge3D1** tool tile; a connection between the **ImagePlane3D4** and **Merge3D1** tools is established.

7.   Make sure the **ImagePlane3D4** tool tile is selected in the **Flow** area. Press 1; the output of the **ImagePlane3D4** tool is displayed in the left Display View.

8.   Choose the **3D Controls** tab from the **ImagePlane3D4** tool control window and enter the values of the parameters as follows:

Translation
X Offset: **0.06**   Y Offset: **0.017**   Z Offset: **0.361**

Rotation
X Rotation: **10.94**   Y Rotation: **8.04**

Scale
Scale: **0.36**

The output of the **Renderer3D1** tool after adding the light is shown in Figure 13-41.

*Figure 13-41 The output of the **Renderer3D1** tool after adding the light*

Now, save the composition with the name *c13tut3* at the location *Documents > Fusion_7 > c13_tut > c13_tut_03*. Next, you need to render the composition. For rendering, refer to Tutorial 1 of Chapter 2. The output of the composition is shown in Figure 13-31. You can also view the final render of the composition by downloading the *c13_fusion_7_rndr.zip* from *http://www.cadcim.com*. The path of the file is mentioned at the beginning of the chapter.

Tutorial 4

In this tutorial, you will compose 3D objects in a 2D environment. The final output of the composition is shown in Figure 13-42.   **(Expected time: 35 min)**

Figure 13-42 *The final output of the composition*

The following steps are required to complete this tutorial:

a. Set the frame format.
b. Download and import the image.
c. Convert the 2D image into a 3D scene.
d. Add lights to the scene.
e. Import the 3D objects.
f. Add shadows to the scene.

Setting the Frame Format

In this section, you will specify the frame format settings.

1. Choose **File > New** from the menubar; a new composition is opened in the Fusion screen.

2. Choose **File > Preferences** from the menubar; the **Preferences** dialog box is displayed.

3. In this dialog box, select **Frame Format** from the **Composition#** preferences tree; various frame format settings are displayed on the right in the **Preferences** dialog box. Next, select the **HDTV 720** option from the **Default format** drop-down list and then choose the **Save** button to save the changes made.

4. In the Time Ruler area, enter **0** in the **Global End Time** edit box.

Downloading and Importing the Image

In this section, you will download the image and import it to the composition.

1. Open the following link: *http://www.freeimages.com/photo/1147288;* an image is displayed.

2. Download the image at the location: *Documents/Fusion_7/c013_tut/c13_tut_04/ Media_Files* and save it with the name *snow.jpg*.

Note

*Footage Courtesy: **Juliane Riedl** (http://www.freeimages.com/profile/GermanGirl)*

3. Choose the **LD** button from the toolbar; the **Open File** dialog box is displayed. In this dialog box, choose **Documents > Fusion_7 > c13_tut > c13_tut_04 > Media_Files > snow.jpg** and then choose the **Open** button; the **Loader1** tool tile is inserted in the **Flow** area.

4. Press 1; the output of the **Loader1** tool is displayed in the left Display View.

5. Choose the **Fit** button from the left **Display View** toolbar to fit the image into the left Display View, as shown in Figure 13-43.

6. Make sure the **Loader1** tool tile is selected in the **Flow** area and then choose the **CC** button from the toolbar; a connection between the **Loader1** and **ColorCorrector1** tools is established.

7. Press1; the output of the **ColorCorrector1** tool is displayed in the left Display View.

8. In the **ColorCorrector1** tool control window, enter the values of the parameters as follows:

Tint: **0.16**   Strength: **0.21**

Figure 13-43 *The output of the **Loader1** tool*

The output of the **ColorCorrector1** tool is shown in Figure 13-44.

Figure 13-44 *The output of the* *ColorCorrector1* *tool*

Converting the 2D Image into a 3D Scene

In this section, you will convert the 2D image into a 3D scene.

1. Click on the empty space in the **Flow** area to deselect the selected tool tile, if any. Next, choose **Tools > 3D > ImagePlane 3D** from the menubar; the **ImagePlane3D1** tool tile is inserted in the **Flow** area.

2. Drag the red output node of the **ColorCorrector1** tool tile to the green node of the **ImagePlane3D1** tool tile; a connection between the **ColorCorrector1** and **ImagePlane3D1** tools is established.

3. Press 1; the output of the **ImagePlane3D1** tool is displayed in the left Display View.

4. In the **3D Controls** tab, enter **1** in the **Y Offset** edit box of the **ImagePlane3D1** tool control window.

5. Enter **2.9** in the **Scale** edit box of the **3D Controls** tab of the **ImagePlane3D1** tool control window.

   The output of the **ImagePlane3D1** tool is displayed in the left Display View, as shown in Figure 13-45.

6. Select the **ImagePlane3D1** tool tile from the **Flow** area and choose **Tools > 3D > Merge 3D** from the menubar; the **Merge3D1** tool tile is inserted in the **Flow** area and a connection between the **ImagePlane3D1** and **Merge3D1** tools is established.

7. Press 1; the output of the **Merge3D1** tool is displayed in the left Display View.

Adding Lights to the Scene

In this section, you will add lights to the scene.

1. Select the **Merge3D1** tool tile from the **Flow** area and then choose the **3Rn** button from the toolbar; the **Renderer3D1** tool tile is inserted in the **Flow** area and a connection between the **Merge3D1** and **Renderer3D1** tools is established. Next, press 2; the output of the **Renderer3D1** tool is displayed in the right Display View.

Figure 13-45 *The output of the **ImagePlane3D1** tool*

2. Choose the **Fit** button from the left **Display View** toolbar to fit the image into the left Display View.

3. Select the **Merge3D1** tool tile from the **Flow** area and choose the **3Cm** button from the toolbar; the **Camera3D1** tool tile is inserted in the **Flow** area.

4. In the **Camera3D1** tool control window, enter the value of the following parameter:

   Angle of View: **27.4**

5. In the **Camera3D1** tool control window, choose the **3D Controls** tab and enter the value of the parameters as follows:

   Translation
   Y Offset: **1.05**   Z Offset: **3**

6. Click on the empty space in the **Flow** area to deselect the selected tool tile, if any. Choose **Tools > 3D > Light > Ambient Light** from the menubar; the **AmbientLight1** tool tile is inserted in the **Flow** area.

7. Select the **Renderer3D1** tool tile from the **Flow** area. In the **Renderer3D1** tool control window, select the **Enable Lighting** and **Enable Shadows** check boxes in the **Lighting** area to view the output of the light tools.

8. Drag the red output node of the **Ambient Light1** tool tile to the **Merge3D1** tool tile.

9. Select the **Ambient Light1** tool tile in the **Flow** area and then enter **2.0** in the **Intensity** edit box of the **Ambient Light1** tool control window.

   The **Intensity** parameter is used to adjust the brightness of the light.

10. In the **AmbientLight1** tool control window, choose the **3D Controls** tab, enter the value of the following parameters:

Translation
Y Offset: **0.873**   Z Offset:**3.71**

The output of the **Merge3D1** and **Renderer3D1** tools after specifying the values is shown in Figure 13-46.

*Figure 13-46 The output of the **Merge3D1** and **Renderer3D1** tools*

11. Click on the empty space in the **Flow** area to deselect selected tool tile, if any. Next, choose **Tools > 3D > Light > Point Light** from the menubar; the **PointLight1** tool tile is inserted in the **Flow** area.

12. Drag the red output node of the **PointLight1** tool tile to the **Merge3D1** tool tile; a connection between the **PointLight1** and **Merge3D1** is established.

13. In the **PointLight1** tool control window, enter the value of the parameter as follows:

Intensity: **5**

14. In the **3D Controls** tab of the **PointLight1** tool control window, enter the values of the parameters as follows:

Translation
X Offset: **0.7**   Y Offset: **0.93**   Z Offset: **0.006**

The output of the **Merge3D1** tool and **Renderer3D1** tools after adding the point light is shown in Figure 13-47.

Importing 3D Objects
In this section, you will import 3D objects to the scene.

1. Click on the empty space in the **Flow** area to deselect any selected tool. Next, choose **File > Import > FBX Scene** from the menubar; the **Open File** dialog box is displayed. Choose **Documents > Fusion_7 > c13_tut > c13_tut_04 > Media_Files > bench.FBX** and then choose the **Open** button; the **FBX Importer** dialog box is displayed.

2. Clear all the check boxes accept **Meshes** and **Materials** check boxes and then choose the **OK** button to close the dialog box; the **Default**, **bench(FBX)**, and **Transform 3D1** tool tiles are inserted in the **Flow** area.

*Figure 13-47 The output of the **Merge3D1** and **Renderer3D1** tools after adding the point light*

3. Drag the red output node of the **Transform 3D1** tool tile to the **Merge3D1** tool tile. Make sure the **Merge3D1** tool tile is selected in the **Flow** area. Press 1; the output of the **Merge3D1** tool is displayed in the left Display View.

4. Choose the **Fit** button from the left **Display View** toolbar to fit the 3D scene into the Display View. The output of the **Merge3D1** tool after importing 3D bench is displayed, as shown in Figure 13-48.

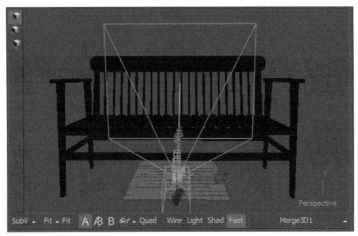

*Figure 13-48 The output of the **Merge3D1** tool after importing the 3D bench*

Next, you will scale down the object.

5. Select the **bench(FBX)** tool tile from the **Flow** area and enter **0.002** in the **Size** edit box of the **bench(FBX)** tool control window.

6. Select the **bench(FBX)** tool tile from the **Flow** area In the **3D Controls** tab of the **bench(FBX)** tool control window, enter the values of the parameters as follows:

Translation
X Offset: **-0.336**   Y Offset: **-0.207**   Z Offset: **0.053**

Rotation

X Rotation: **-90**   Y Rotation: **151.8**

Positioning of 3D Bench in the scene is shown in Figure 13-49.

Figure 13-49 *Positioning of 3D bench in the scene*

Now, you will import a street lamp to the scene.

7. Choose **File > Import > FBX Scene** from the menubar; the **Open File** dialog box is displayed. Choose **Documents > Fusion_7 > c13_tut > c13_tut_04 > Media_Files > lampstreet.FBX** and then choose the **Open** button; the **FBX Importer** dialog box is displayed, as shown in Figure 13-50.

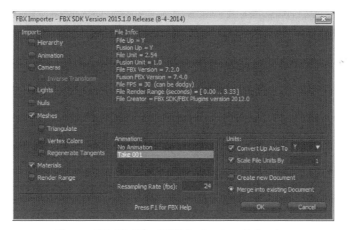

Figure 13-50 *The **FBX Importer** dialog box*

8. Clear all the check boxes accept the **Null**, **Mesh**, **Material**, and **Hierachy** check boxes. Next, choose the **OK** button to close the dialog box; a network of 10 tool tiles are inserted in the **Flow** area.

9. Drag the red output node of the **RootNode** tool tile to the **Merge3D1** tool tile; a connection between the **RootNode** and **Merge3D1** tools is established.

10. Select the **RootNode** tool tile from the **Flow** area. In the **3D Controls** tab of the **RootNode** tool control window, enter the values of the parameters as follows:

    Translation
    X Offset: **0.04**   Y Offset: **0.88**   Z Offset: **2.4**

    Expand the **Scale** area, select the **LockX/Y/Z** check box and set the **Scale** value as follows:

    Scale: **0.001**

11. Select the **Material4802** tool tile in the **Flow** area. In the **Controls** tab of the **Material4802** tool control window, enter the values of the parameters as follows:
    R: **0**   G: **0**   B: **0**

    Clear the **Receives Lighting** check box.

12. Select the **Material4801** tool tile in the **Flow** area. In the **Controls** tab of the **Material4801** tool control window, enter the values of the parameters as follows:

    R: **1**   G: **1**   B: **1**

    Opacity: **0.0386**

    After entering the values, the output of the **Merge3D1** and **Renderer3D1** tools after importing the street lamp is shown in Figure 13-51.

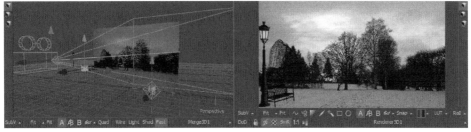

Figure 13-51 *The output of the **Merge3D1** and **Renderer3D1** tool after importing street lamp*

Now, you will import the fence to the scene.

13. Choose **File > Import > FBX Scene** from the menubar; the **Open File** dialog box is displayed. Choose **Documents > Fusion_7 > c13_tut > c13_tut_04 > Media_Files > Fence.FBX** and then choose the **Open** button; the **FBX Importer** dialog box is displayed.

14. Choose the **OK** button to close the dialog box; a network of six tools is inserted in the **Flow** area.

15. Drag the red output node of the **fencelrg1m001** tool tile to the **Merge3D1** tool tile; a connection between the **fencelrg1m001** and **Merge3D1** tools is established.

16. Select the **fencelrg1m001** tool tile from the **Flow** area. In the **fencelrg1m001** tool control window, choose the **3D Controls** tab and enter the values of the parameters as follows:

Translation
X Offset: **0.088**   Y Offset: **0.59**   Z Offset: **0.128**

Rotation
X Rotation: **35**   Z Rotation: **90**

Enter **0.05** to the **Scale** edit box.

17. Select the **Default** tool tile in **Flow** area. In the **Default** tool control window, enter the values of the parameters as follows:

R: **0**   G: **0**   B: **0**

18. Select the **fencelrg1m001** tool tile from the **Flow** area and choose **Tools > 3D > Duplicate 3D** from the menubar; the **Duplicate3D1** tool tile is inserted in the **Flow** area and a connection between the **Fencelrg1m001** and **Duplicate3D1** tools is established.

19. In the **Controls** tab of the **Duplicate3D1** tool control window, enter the values of the parameters as follows:

Last Copy: **20**

Translation
X Offset: **0.03**   Y Offset: **-0.004**   Z Offset: **-0.13**

Rotation
Y Rotation: **8.48**

The output of the **Merge3D1** and **Renderer3D1** tools after adding 3D fence is shown in Figure 13-52.

Adding Shadows to the Scene

In this section, you will add shadows of the bench and the street lamp to the scene.

1. Click on the empty space in the **Flow** area to deselect the selected tool tile, if any. Choose **Tools > 3D > Light > Spot Light** tool from the menubar; the **SpotLight1** tool tile is inserted in the **Flow** area.

2. Drag the red output node of the **SpotLight1** tool tile to the **Merge3D1** tool tile.

Figure 13-52   *The output of the* **Merge3D1** *and* **Renderer3D1** *tools after adding 3D fence*

3. In the **Controls** tab of the **SpotLight1** tool control window, enter the values of the parameters as follows:

Color
R: **0.41**   G: **0.63**   B: **0.54**

Intensity: **0.2**   Penumbra Angle: **15.08**

4. Expand the **Shadows** area, enter the values of the parameters as follows:

Density: **2.5**   Shadow Map Size: **2057**

Shadow Map Proxy: **0.54**

Multiplicative Bias: **13.4**

5. In the **3D Controls** of the **SpotLight1** tool control window, enter the values of the parameters as follows:

Translation
X Offset: **0.022**   Y Offset: **1.1**   Z Offset: **3.1**

Rotation
Y Rotation: **4.02**

Pivot
Select the **Use Target** check box.

Target
X Target Position: **-0.027**   Y Target Position: **0.45**   Z Target Position: **1.63**

The output of the **Merge3D1** and **Renderer3D1** tools after adding spot light is shown in Figure 13-53.

*Figure 13-53 The output of the **Merge3D1** and **Renderer3D1** tools after adding spot light*

Now, save the composition with the name *c13tut4* at the location *Documents > Fusion_7 > c13_tut > c13_tut_04*. Next, you need to render the composition. For rendering, refer to Tutorial 1 of Chapter 2. The output of the composition is shown in Figure 13-46. You can also view the final render of the composition by downloading the *c13_fusion_7_rndr.zip* from *http://www.cadcim.com*. The path of the file is mentioned at the beginning of the chapter.

Tutorial 5

In this tutorial, you will create the stereoscopic effect in an image by using the **Stereo Mix** and **Anaglyph** tools. The final output of the composition at frame 50 is shown in Figure 13-54.

(Expected time: 25 min)

Figure 13-54 The final output of the composition at frame 50

The following steps are required to complete this tutorial:

a. Set the frame format.
b. Import images.
c. Create the stereoscopic effect.

Setting the Frame Format

In this section, you will specify the frame format settings.

1. Choose **File > New** from the menubar; a new composition is opened in the Fusion screen.

2. Choose **File > Preferences** from the menubar; the **Preferences** dialog box is displayed.

3. In this dialog box, select **Frame Format** from the **Composition#** preferences tree; various frame format settings are displayed on the right in the **Preferences** dialog box. Next, select the **HDTV 720** option from the **Default format** drop-down list and then choose the **Save** button to save the changes made.

4. In the Time Ruler area, enter **100** in the **Global End Time** edit box.

Importing the Images

In this section, you will import the images in the **Flow** area.

1. Choose the **LD** button from the toolbar; the **Open File** dialog box is displayed. In this dialog box, choose **Documents > Fusion_7 > c13_tut > c13_tut_05 > Media_Files > left eye. jpg** and then choose the **Open** button; the **Loader1** tool is inserted in the **Flow** area.

2. Press 1; the output of the **Loader1** tool is displayed in the left Display View.

3. Choose the **Fit** button from the left **Display View** toolbar to fit the image into the left Display View, refer to Figure 13-55.

4. Click on the empty space in the **Flow** area and load the *right eye.jpg* in the **Flow** area; the **Loader2** tool tile is inserted in the **Flow** area.

5. Press 2; the output of the **Loader2** tool is displayed in the right Display View.

6. Choose the **Fit** button from the right Display View toolbar to fit the image into the right Display View, refer to Figure 13-55.

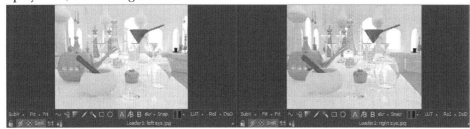

*Figure 13-55 The output of the **Loader1** and **Loader2** tools*

Creating the 3D Stereo Effect

In this section, you will create a stereoscopic effect.

1. Select the **Loader1** tool tile from the **Flow** area and choose **Tools > 3D > Material > Stereo Mix** from the menubar; the **StereoMix1** tool tile is inserted in the **Flow** area and a connection between the **Loader1** and **StereoMix1** tools is established.

2. Drag the red output node of the **Loader2** tool tile to the green node of the **StereoMix1** tool tile; a connection between the **Loader1**, **Loader2**, and **StereoMix1** tools is established.

3. Press 1; the output of the **StereoMix1** tool is displayed in the left Display View, as shown in Figure 13-56.

    The **StereoMix** tool is used to apply separate materials to the left eye and right eye in a stereo pair.

    The output of the **Stereo Mix** tool is displayed on a sphere which can be changed by choosing the **Sphere** option in the **Display View** toolbar, refer to Figure 13-56.

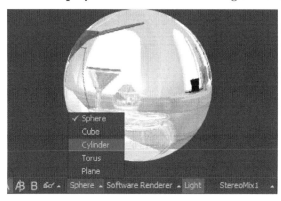

*Figure 13-56 The output of the **StereoMix1** tool*

4. Click on the empty space in the **Flow** area and choose the **3Im** button from the toolbar; the **ImagePlane3D1** tool tile is inserted in the **Flow** area.

5. Drag the red output of the **StereoMix1** tool tile to the green node of the **ImagePlane3D1** tool tile; a connection between the **StereoMix1** and **ImagePlane3D1** tools is established.

6. Press 2; the output of **ImagePlane3D1** tool is displayed in the right Display View, as shown in Figure 13-57.

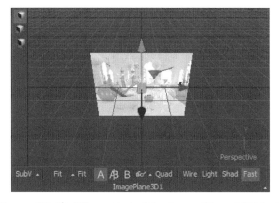

*Figure 13-57 The output of the **ImagePlane3D1** tool*

7. Choose the **Enable Stereo 3D** button from the right **Display View** toolbar; the output of the **ImagePlane3D1** tool is displayed in the right Display View, as shown in Figure 13-58.

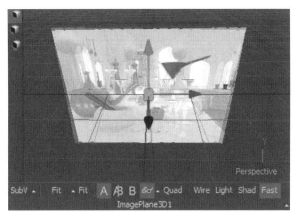

*Figure 13-58 The output of the **ImagePlane3D1** tool after choosing the **Enable Stereo 3D** button*

The **Enable Stereo 3D** button is used to view the Stereo 3D effect in a 2D image. By default, the Red/Cyan colors are displayed in a 2D image. You can modify the colors by clicking on the small triangle located next to the **Enable Stereo 3D** button. On doing so, a flyout with a group of options will be displayed, as shown in Figure 13-59.

8. Click on the empty space in the **Flow** area and choose the **3Cm** button from the toolbar; the **Camera3D1** tool tile is inserted in the **Flow** area.

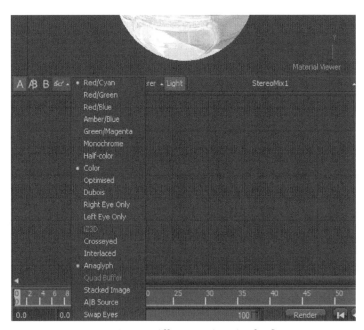

Figure 13-59 Different options in the flyout

9. Drag the red output node of the **Camera3D1** tool tile to the red output node of the **ImagePlane3D1** tool tile; the **Merge3D1** tool tile is inserted in the **Flow** area and a connection between the **ImagePlane3D1**, **Camera3D1**, and **Merge3D1** tools is established. Press 1; the output of the **Merge3D1** tool is displayed in the left Display View.

10. In the **Controls** tab of the **Camera3D1** tool control window, enter the values of the parameters as follows:

    Angle of View: **10.26**   Focal Length: **84.029**   Plane of Focus: **3.68**

11. In the **Camera3D1** tool control window, choose the **3D Controls** tab and enter **2.9** in the **Z Offset** edit box.

12. Click on the empty space in the **Flow** area to deselect any selected tool tile. Next, choose **Tools > 3D > Renderer 3D** tool from the menubar; the **Renderer3D1** tool tile is inserted in the **Flow** area.

13. Drag the red output node of the **Merge3D1** tool tile and then drag the cursor to the orange node of the **Renderer3D1** tool tile; a connection between the **Merge3D1** and **Renderer3D1** tools is established.

14. In the **Renderer3D1** tool control window, choose the **Left** button in the **Eye** area.

15. Make sure the **Renderer3D1** tool tile is selected in the **Flow** area and press CTRL+C. Next, click in the empty space of the **Flow** area and press CTRL+V; the **Renderer3D1_1** tool tile is inserted in the **Flow** area. Rename **Renderer3D1_1** tool as **Renderer3D2** by pressing F2.

16. Drag the red output node of the **Merge3D1** tool tile to the orange input node of the **Renderer3D2** tool tile.

17. In the **Renderer3D2** tool control window, choose the **Right** button in the **Eye** area.

18. Click on the empty space in the **Flow** area to deselect selected tool tile, if any. Next, choose **Tools > Stereo > Anaglyph** tool from the menubar. Alternatively, choose the **Ana** button from the toolbar; the **Anaglyph1** tool is inserted in the **Flow** area.

19. Click on the red output node of the **Renderer3D1** tool. Next, press ALT and then drag the cursor to the **Anaglyph1** tool; a flyout is displayed, refer to Figure 13-60. Choose the **Left** option from it; a connection between the **Renderer3D1**and **Anaglyph1** tools is established.

20. Click on the red output node of the **Renderer3D2** tool. Next, press ALT and then drag the cursor to the **Anaglyph1** tool; a flyout is displayed, refer to Figure 13-61. Choose the **Right** option from it; a connection between the **Renderer3D2** and **Anaglyph1** tools is established.

Figure 13-60 *The **Left** option chosen from the flyout*

Figure 13-61 *The **Right** option chosen from the flyout*

21. Make sure the **Anaglyph1** tool tile is selected in the **Flow** area and then press 2; the output of the **Anaglyph1** tool is displayed in the right Display View, as shown in Figure 13-62.

Figure 13-62 *The output of the **Anaglyph1** tool*

22. Choose the **Dubois** option from the **Method** drop-down list in the **Anaglyph1** tool control window.

    The **Dubois** option is used to reduce the color effect to produce a better anaglyph.

    Figure 13-63 shows the output of the **Anaglyph1** tool after choosing the **Dubois** option.

Figure 13-63 *The output of the **Anaglyph1** tool after choosing **Dubois** option*

23. In the **Camera3D1** tool control window, choose the **3DControls** tab and right-click on the **Z Offset** parameter; a flyout is displayed. Next, animate the **Z Offset** to create the keyframe by using the values given in the table below:

Frames	Z Offset
50	2.12
100	2.9

Now, save the composition with the name *c13tut5* at the location *Documents > Fusion_7 > c13_tut > c13_tut_05*. Next, you need to render the composition. For rendering, refer to Tutorial 2 of Chapter 2. You can also view the final render of the composition by downloading the *c13_fusion_7_rndr.zip* from *http://www.cadcim.com*. The path of the file is mentioned at the beginning of the chapter.

Self-Evaluation Test

Answer the following questions and then compare them to those given at the end of this chapter:

1. Which of the following tools is used to create 3D shapes in a composition?

    (a) **Merge3D**   (b) **Material3D**
    (c) **Shape3D**   (d) **Renderer3D**

2. The _____ button in the toolbar is used to add a spotlight in the composition.

3. The _____ tool is used to view a 3D scene from a 3D camera.

4. The _____ tool is used to create a copy of the 3D object in the composition.

5. The _____ tool is used to apply separate materials to the left eye and right eye in a stereo pair.

Review Questions

Answer the following questions:

1. The _____ button is used to view the 3D effect in a 2D image.

2. The _____ button in the toolbar is used to add the **Camera3D** tool in the **Flow** area.

3. You can import 3D objects, hierarchy, animation, and camera in a Fusion composition. (T/F)

Chapter 14

Particles

INTRODUCTION

Particles are computer generated points that are used to create a wide variety of visual effects such as rain, snow, fireworks, fire, and so on. In this chapter, you will create various effects using particles. These effects add realism to a scene.

TUTORIALS

The compositions created in this chapter can be downloaded from *http://www.cadcim.com*. These compositions are contained in the *c14_fusion_7_tut.zip* file. The path of the file is as follows:

> *Textbooks > Animation and Visual Effects > Fusion > Blackmagic Design Fusion 7 Studio: A Tutorial Approach*

Tutorial 1

In this tutorial, you will create the rain effect in the scene using the **Particle** tools. The final output of the composition at frame 100 is shown in Figure 14-1.   **(Expected time: 20 min)**

Figure 14-1 *The final output of the composition at frame 100*

The following steps are required to complete this tutorial:

a. Set the frame format.
b. Download and import the image.
c. Create rain in the scene.

Setting the Frame Format

In this section, you will specify the frame format settings.

1. Choose **File > New** from the menubar; a new composition is displayed in the Fusion screen.

2. Choose **File > Preferences** from the menubar; the **Preferences** dialog box is displayed.

3. In this dialog box, select **Frame Format** from the **Composition#** preferences tree; various frame format settings are displayed on the right in the **Preferences** dialog box. Next, select the **HDTV 720** option from the **Default format** drop-down list and then choose the **Save** button to save the changes made.

4. In the Time Ruler area, enter **100** in the **Global End Time** edit box.

Downloading and Importing the Image

In this section, you will download the image and import it to the composition.

1. Open the following link: *http://www.freeimages.com/photo/979013*; an image is displayed.

2. Download the image to */Documents/Fusion_7/c14_tut/c14_tut_01/Media_Files* and save it with the name *rain.jpg*.

Note
*Footage Courtesy: **Jekaterina Vitkauskiene** (http://www.freeimages.com/profile/jek_ka)*

3. Choose the **LD** button from the toolbar; a dialog box is displayed. In this dialog box, choose **Documents >Fusion_7 > c14_tut > c14_tut_01 > Media_Files > street.jpg and then choose the Open button**; the **Loader1** tool tile is inserted in the **Flow** area.

4. Press 1; the output of the **Loader1** tool is displayed in the left Display View. Next, choose the **Fit** button from the left **Display View** toolbar to fit the image in the left Display View, as shown in Figure 14-2.

5. Click on the empty space in the **Flow** area and then choose **Tools > 3D > Image Plane3D** from the menubar; the **ImagePlane3D1** tool tile is inserted in the **Flow** area.

6. Drag the red output node of the **Loader1** tool tile to the green node of the **ImagePlane3D1** tool tile; a connection between the **Loader1** and **ImagePlane3D1** tools is established.

7. Press 1; the output of the **ImagePlane3D1** tool is displayed in the left Display View, as shown in Figure 14-3.

Figure 14-2 *The output of the* ***Loader1*** *tool*

Figure 14-3 *The output of the* ***ImagePlane3D1*** *tool*

8. Click on the empty space in the **Flow** area to deselect the selected tool tile, if any. Next, choose **Tools > 3D > Camera 3D** from the menubar; the **Camera3D1** tool tile is inserted in the **Flow** area.

9. Click on the empty space in the **Flow** area to deselect the selected tool tile, if any. Next, choose **Tools > 3D > Merge3D** from the menubar; the **Merge3D1** tool tile is inserted in the **Flow** area. Next, drag the red output node of the **ImagePlane3D1** tool tile to the orange node of the **Merge3D1** tool tile; a connection between the **ImagePlane3D1** and **Merge3D1** tools is established.

10. Drag the red output node of the **Camera3D1** tool tile to the green node of the **Merge3D1** tool tile; a connection between the **Camera3D1** and **Merge3D1** tools is established.

11. Select the **Merge3D1** tool tile from the **Flow** area and then choose **Tools > 3D > Renderer 3D** from the menubar; the **Renderer3D1** tool tile is inserted in the **Flow** area.

12. Press 2; the output of the **Renderer3D1** tool is displayed in the right Display View. Notice that the image is not displayed in the Display View as both the camera and the image plane are placed at the origin, refer to Figure 14-4.

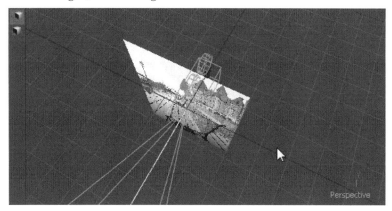

Figure 14-4 *The camera and image plane placed at the origin*

Next, you will adjust the position of the camera.

13. In the **Camera3D1** tool control window, choose the **3D Controls** tab. Next, enter **3.01** in the **Z Offset** edit box in the **Translation** area; the image is now visible in the Display View.

14. In the **Renderer3D1** tool control window, select **OGL Renderer** from the **Renderer Type** drop-down list.

The **OGL Renderer** option is used to produce fast and quality results. However, you must have a graphics card installed on your system.

Creating Rain in the Scene
In this section, you will create rain in the scene.

1. Click on the empty space in the **Flow** area to deselect the selected tool tile, if any. Next, choose **Tools > Particles > pEmitter** from the menubar; the **pEmitter1** tool tile is inserted in the **Flow** area.

2. Make sure the **pEmitter1** tool tile is selected in the **Flow** area and choose **Tools > Particles > pRender** from the menubar; the **pRender1** tool tile is inserted in the **Flow** area and a connection between the **pEmitter1** and **pRender1** tools is established.

3. Press 1; the output of the **pRender1** tool is displayed in the left Display View.

The **pEmitter** tool is used to emit particles in a scene. The **pRender** tool is used to produce a 2D image from a particle system.

4. In the **Renderer3D1** tool control window, choose the **Image** tab and enter **450** and **600** in the **Width** and **Height** parameters, respectively.

5. In the **pEmitter1** tool control window, choose the **Region** tab and then select **Rectangle** from the **Region** drop-down list. Next, set the values of the parameters as follows:

Translation
X Offset: **0.07**   Y Offset: **1.11**   Z Offset: **0.14**

Rotation
X Rotation: **95.76**   Y Rotation: **0.41**   Z Rotation: **6.64**

Width: **3**   Height: **1.5**

The parameters available in the **Region** tab are used to define the area of the image that will emit particles. Only one region can be defined in a particle system to emit particles. The **Rectangle** option in the **Region** drop-down list is used to create a rectangular region for particle emission. This region can also be transformed into the Z space.

6. Choose the **Style** tab and then select **Line** from the **Style** drop-down list. Expand the **Color Controls** area and set the values of the parameters as follows:

R: **0.54**   G: **0.54**   B: **0.54**

The parameters in the **Style** tab are used to control the appearance of the particles. You can animate controls in this tab to change the appearance of the particles over time.

7. In the **Controls** tab of the **pEmitter1** tool control window, set the values of the parameters as follows:

Number: **90**   Lifespan: **94**   Position Variance: **0.012**

Velocity Controls
Velocity: **2**   Velocity Variance: **0.65** Angle: **-90**

8. In the **Rotation Controls** area, select the **Rotation relative to motion** option from the **Rotation Mode** drop-down list. Next, clear the **Always Face Camera** check box.

The **Number** parameter is used to specify the number of new particles to be created at each frame. The **Lifespan** parameter defines the life of the particles. The **Position Variance** parameter is used to specify whether the particles will be generated outside the boundary of the specified region defined in the **Region** tab. The default value of this parameter is zero. The **Velocity** parameter controls the initial velocity of the particles. The **Velocity Variance** parameter is used to randomize the initial velocity of the particles. The **Rotation relative to motion** option is used to orient particles in the direction in which they are moving.

9. Select the **pEmitter1** tool tile from the **Flow** area and choose **Tools > Particles > pBounce** from the menubar; the **pBounce1** tool tile is inserted in the **Flow** area and a connection between the **pEmitter1**, **pBounce1**, and **pRender1** tools is established.

The **pBounce** tool is used to create a region from where the particles will bounce if they come to its contact.

10. Drag the red output node of the **pRender1** tool tile to the pink node of the **Merge3D1** tool tile; a connection between the **pRender1** and **Merge3D1** tools is established.

11. In the **Controls** tab of the **pBounce1** tool control window, set the values of the parameters as follows:

Variance: **0.2**   Spin: **-2.0**   Roughness: **3.46**

The **Variance** parameter is used to provide a degree of variation to the angle of reflection of the particles. The **Spin** parameter is used to impart spin to the particles based on the angle of reflection from the bouncing region. The **Roughness** parameter is used to slightly randomize direction of the particles.

12. In the **Region** tab of the **pBounce1** tool control window, set the values of the parameters as follows:

Start
Start X Offset: **-28.3**   Start Y Offset: **-6.95**   Start Z Offset: **16.6**

End
End X Offset: **23.3**   End Y Offset: **-6.78**   End Z Offset: **13.83**

13. Enter **50** in the **Current Time** edit box; the output of the **Renderer3D1** tool is displayed in the right Display View, as shown in Figure 14-5.

14. Select the **Renderer3D1** tool tile from the **Flow** area and then choose the **Blur** button from the toolbar; the **Blur1** tool tile is inserted in the **Flow** area and a connection between the **Renderer3D1** and **Blur1** tools is established.

15. Press 2; the output of the **Blur1** tool is displayed in the right Display View.

16. Enter **1.5** in the **Blur Size** edit box in the **Blur1** tool control window.

Now, save the composition with the name *c14tut1* at the location *Documents > Fusion_7 > c14_tut > c14_tut_01*. Next, you need to render the composition. For rendering, refer to Tutorial 2 of Chapter 2. The output of the composition is shown in Figure 14-1. You can also view the final render of the composition by downloading the *c14_fusion_7_rndr.zip* from *http://www.cadcim.com*. The path of the file is mentioned at the beginning of the chapter.

Figure 14-5 *The output of the* ***Renderer3D1*** *tool*

Tutorial 2

In this tutorial, you will create the effect of snowfall in an image by using the Particle tools. The final rendered output of the composition at frame 90 is shown in Figure 14-6.

(Expected time: 20 min)

Figure 14-6 *The final rendered output of the composition at frame 90*

The following steps are required to complete this tutorial:

a.   Set the frame format.
b.   Download and import the image.
c.   Create snowfall in the scene.

Setting the Frame Format
In this section, you will specify the frame format settings.

1.   Choose **File > New** from the menubar; a new composition is displayed in the Fusion screen.

2.   Choose **File > Preferences** from the menubar; the **Preferences** dialog box is displayed.

3.   In this dialog box, select **Frame Format** from the **Composition#** preferences tree; various frame format settings are displayed on the right of the **Preferences** dialog box. Next, select the **HDTV 720** option from the **Default format** drop-down list and then choose the **Save** button to save the changes made.

4.   In the Time Ruler area, enter **350** in the **Global End Time** edit box.

Downloading and Importing the Image
In this section, you will download the image and import it to the composition.

1.   Open the following link: *http://www.freeimages.com/photo/1322953*; an image is displayed.

2.   Download the image to */Documents/Fusion_7/c14_tut/c14_tut_02/Media_Files* and save it with the name *snow.jpg*.

   Note
   Footage Courtesy: **Colin Brough** *(http://www.freeimages.com/profile/ColinBroug)*

3.   Choose the **LD** button from the toolbar; a dialog box is displayed. In this dialog box, choose **Documents > Fusion_7 > c14_tut > c14_tut_02 > Media_Files > snow.jpg and then choose the Open button**; the **Loader1** tool tile is inserted in the **Flow** area.

4.   Press 1; the output of the **Loader1** tool is displayed in the left Display View. Next, choose the **Fit** button from the left **Display View** toolbar to fit the image into the Display View, as shown in Figure 14-7.

5.   Choose the **3Im** button from the toolbar; the **ImagePlane3D1** tool is inserted in the **Flow** area.

6.   Drag the red output node of the **Loader1** tool tile to the green node of the **ImagePlane3D1** tool tile in the **Flow** area.

7.   Press 2; the output of the **ImagePlane3D1** tool is displayed in the right Display View, as shown in Figure 14-8.

Figure 14-7 *The output of the **Loader1** tool*

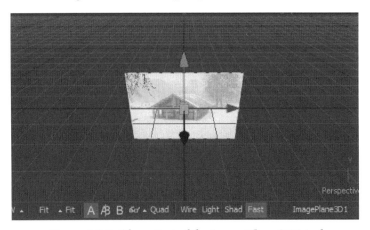

Figure 14-8 *The output of the **ImagePlane3D1** tool*

8. In the **ImagePlane3D1** tool control window, choose the **3D Controls** tab. Next, enter **15.7** in the **Scale** edit box of the **Scale** area. Next, choose the **Fit** button from the **Display View** toolbar to fit the image into the Display View.

Creating Snowfall in the Scene

In this section, you will create snowfall in the scene by using Particle tools.

1. Click on the empty space in the **Flow** area to deselect the selected tool tile, if any. Next, choose the **pEm** button and then the **pRn** button from the toolbar; the **pEmitter1** and **pRender1** tool tiles are inserted in the **Flow** area and a connection is established between them.

2. Click on the empty space in the **Flow** area to deselect the selected tool tile, if any. Next, choose **Tools > 3D > Camera3D** from the menubar; the **Camera3D1** tool tile is inserted in the **Flow** area.

3. Drag the red output node of the **Camera3D1** tool tile to the red output node of the **ImagePlane3D1** tool tile; the **Merge3D1** tool tile is inserted in the **Flow** area and a connection between the **Camera3D1** and **ImagePlane3D1** tools is established.

4. Press 1; the output of the **Merge3D1** tool is displayed in the left Display View, as shown in Figure 14-9.

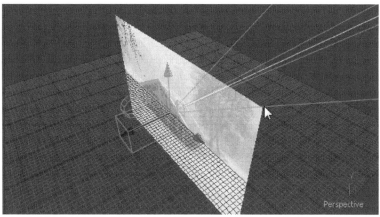

*Figure 14-9 The output of the **Merge3D1** tool*

5. Make sure the **Merge3D1** tool tile is selected in the **Flow** area and choose **Tools > 3D > Renderer3D** from the menubar; the **Renderer3D1** tool tile is inserted in the **Flow** area and a connection between the **Merge3D1** and **Renderer3D1** tools is established.

6. Press 2; the output of the **Renderer3D1** tool is displayed in the right Display View.

7. In the **Camera3D1** tool control window, enter **1059.7** in the **Far Clip** edit box.

8. Choose the **3D Controls** tab and then enter **19.22** in the **Z Offset** edit box.

9. Select the **pRender1** tool tile in the **Flow** area and press 1; the output of the **pRender1** tool is displayed in the left Display View.

10. In the **Region** tab of the **pEmitter1** tool control window, select **Cube** from the **Region** drop-down list and set the values of the parameters as follows:

Translation
X Offset: **-0.256**   Y Offset: **5.5**   Z Offset: **3.6**

Rotation
X Rotation: **127.08**   Y Rotation: **-1.44**   Z Rotation: **-1.8**

Pivot
Y Pivot: **0.16**

Width: **15**   Height: **10**

11. Choose the **Fit** button from the right **Display View** toolbar to fit the image into the right Display View.

12. Choose the **Style** tab from the **pEmitter1** tool control window. Next, select **Blob** from the **Style** drop-down list.

13. In the **Controls** tab of the **pEmitter1** tool control window, set the values of the parameters as follows:

    Number: **20**   Number Variance: **2**

    Life Span: **26.18**   Lifespan Variance: **3.67**

    Position Variance: **0.021**

14. Expand the **Velocity Controls** area and then set the values of the parameters as follows:

    Velocity: **2**   Velocity Variance: **0.45**

    Angle: **-90**   Angle Z: **123**

15. In the **Style** tab, expand the **Color Controls** area and then set the values of the parameters as follows:

    R: **0.75**   G: **0.82**   B: **0.89**

16. Expand the **Size Controls** area and then enter **0.15** in the **Size** edit box.

17. Modify the **Size Over Life** graph, as shown in Figure 14-10.

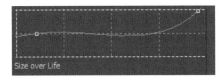

*Figure 14-10 The **Size Over Life** graph*

18. Enter **0.3** in the **Noise** edit box.

19. In the **Controls** tab, expand the **Rotation Controls** area and then select the **Rotation relative to motion** option from the **Rotation Mode** drop-down list. Next, expand the **Rotation** area and then set the values of the parameters as follows:

    Rotation X(3D Only): **-2.13**   Rotation Y(3D Only): **-17.04**

    Rotation Z(3D Only): **296**

20. Expand the **Spin** area and then set the values of the parameters as follows:

Spin X(3D Only): **38.34**   Rotation Y(3D Only): **36.21**

Rotation Z(3D Only): **127.8**

21. Expand the **Spin Variance** area and then set the values of the parameters as follows:

Spin X Variance (3D Only): **129.94**   Spin Y Variance (3D Only): **36.21**

Spin Z Variance: **117.8**

After entering the values, play the simulation; the output of the **pRender1** tool is displayed in the left Display View. Figure 14-11 shows the output of the **pRender1** tool at frame 50.

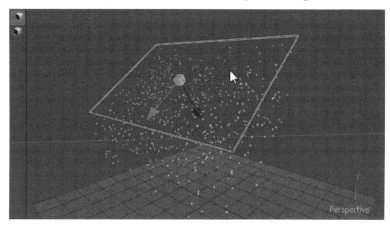

Figure 14-11 *The output of the **pRender1** tool at frame 50*

22. Drag the red output node of the **pRender1** tool tile to the pink node of the **Merge3D1** tool tile; a connection between the **pRender1** and **Merge3D1** tools is established.

23. Play the simulation; the output of the **Renderer3D1** tool is displayed in the right Display View. Figure 14-12 shows the output of the **Renderer3D1** tool at frame 190.

Now, save the composition with the name *c14tut2* at the location *Documents* > *Fusion_7* > *c14_tut* > *c14_tut_02*. Next, you need to render the composition. For rendering, refer to Tutorial 2 of Chapter 2. The output of the composition at frame 90 is shown in Figure 14-6. You can also view the final render of the composition by downloading the *c14_fusion_7_rndr.zip* from *http://www.cadcim.com*. The path of the file is mentioned at the beginning of the chapter.

Figure 14-12 *The output of the* ***Renderer3D1*** *tool at frame 190*

Tutorial 3

In this tutorial, you will create fireworks in a scene using the **Particle** tools. The final rendered output of the composition at frame 100 is shown in Figure 14-13.   **(Expected time: 25 min)**

Figure 14-13 *The final rendered output of the composition at frame 100*

The following steps are required to complete this tutorial:

a.   Set the frame format.
b.   Download and import the image.
c.   Create fireworks in the scene.

Setting the Frame Format

In this section, you will specify the frame format settings.

1. Choose **File > New** from the menubar; a new composition is displayed in the Fusion screen.

2. Choose **File > Preferences** from the menubar; the **Preferences** dialog box is displayed.

3. In this dialog box, select **Frame Format** from the **Composition#** preferences tree; various frame format settings are displayed on the right in the **Preferences** dialog box. Next, select the **NTSC (Square Pixel)** option from the **Default format** drop-down list and then choose the **Save** button to save the changes made.

4. In the Time Ruler area, enter **200** in both the **Render End Time** and **Global End Time** edit boxes.

Downloading and Importing the Image

In this section, you will download the image and import it to the composition.

1. Open the following link: *http:///www.freeimages.com/photo/1247596*; an image is displayed.

2. Download the image to */Documents/Fusion_7/c14_tut/c14_tut_03/Media_Files* and save it with the name *night city.jpg*.

Note

Footage Courtesy: **Mike Munchel** *(http:///www.freeimages.com/profile/merlin1075)*

3. Choose the **LD** button from the toolbar; a dialog box is displayed. In this dialog box, choose **Documents > Fusion_7 > c14_tut > c14_tut_03 > Media_Files > night city.jpg** and then choose the **Open** button; the **Loader1** tool tile is inserted in the **Flow** area.

4. Press 1; the output of the **Loader1** tool is displayed in the left Display View. Next, choose the **Fit** button from the **Display View** toolbar to fit the image into the Display View, as shown in Figure 14-14.

Creating Fireworks in the Scene

In this section, you will create fireworks in the scene.

1. Click in the empty space in the Flow area to deselect the selected tool tile, if any. Choose the **pEm**button from the toolbar; the **pEmitter1** tool is inserted in the **Flow** area.

2. Choose the **pRn** button from the toolbar; the **pRender1** tool tile is inserted in the **Flow** area and a connection between the **pEmitter1** and **pRender1** tools is established.

*Figure 14-14 The output of the **Loader1** tool*

3. Choose the **2D** button from the **pRender1** tool control window.

4. In the **pEmitter1** tool control window, choose the **Region** tab and then set the values of the parameters as follows:

    Region: **Line**

    Start
    Start X Offset: **-0.49**   Start Y Offset: **-0.034**

    End
    End X Offset: **0.51**   End Y Offset: **0.15**

5. Select the **pRender1** tool tile in the **Flow** area and then press 2; the output of the **pRender1** tool is displayed in the right Display View.

6. Choose the **Style** tab from the **pEmitter1** tool control window. Next, expand the **Color Controls** area and then set the values of the parameters as follows:

    R: **0.97**   G: **0.61**   B: **0.33**

7. Choose the **Controls** tab and then set the values of the parameters as follows:

    Number: **0.25**   Lifespan: **80**   Lifespan Variance: **10**

8. Expand the **Velocity Controls** area and set the values of the parameters as follows:

    Velocity: **0.06**   Velocity Variance: **0.03**   Angle: **90**

    Angle Variance: **15**

9. Expand the **Rotation Controls** area and then select the **Rotation Relative to motion** option from the **Rotation Mode** drop-down list.

10. Select the **Loader1** tool tile in the **Flow** area and then choose the **Rsz** button from the toolbar; the **Resize1** tool is inserted in the **Flow** area and a connection between **Loader1** and **Resize1** tools is established.

11. Drag the red output node of the **pRender1** tool tile to the red output node of the **Resize1** tool tile; the **Merge1** tool tile is inserted in the **Flow** area and a connection between the **Resize1**, **pRender**, and **Merge1** tools is established.

12. Press 2; the output of the **Merge1** tool is displayed in the right Display View.

13. Select the **pEmitter1** tool tile from the **Flow** area and choose **Tools > Particles > pDirectionalForce** from the menubar; the **pDirectionalForce1** tool tile is inserted in the **Flow** area and a connection between the **pDirectionalForce1**, **pEmitter1**, and **pRender1** tools is established.

    The **pDirectionalForce1** tool is used to pull the particles in the direction specified by the **Direction** and **Direction Z** parameters.

14. In the **pDirectionalForce1** tool control window, set the values of the parameters as follows:

    Strength: **0.006**   Direction: **-95**

    After entering the values, the output of the **Merge1** tool at frame 90 is displayed in the right Display view, as shown in Figure 14-15.

Figure 14-15 *The output of the **Merge1** tool at frame 90*

Next, you will spawn the particles that were generated by the **pEmitter1** tool. The spawned particles will create a spark burst in the sky.

15. Make sure the **pDirectionalForce** tool tile is selected in the **Flow** area and then choose **Tools > Particles > pSpawn** from the menubar; the **pSpawn1** tool tile is inserted in the **Flow** area and a connection between the **pSpawn1**, **pDirectionalForce1**, and **pRender1** tools is established.

    The **pSpawn** tool is used to emit particles from the particles generated by another source. The original particle exists till the end of its lifespan. The spawned particles become independent of the original particle.

16. Choose the **Style** tab from the **pSpawn1** tool control window and then select **Line** from the **Style** drop-down list.

17 In the **Color Controls** area of the **pSpawn1** tool control window, set the values of the parameters as follows:

R: **0.56** G: **0.83** B: **0.64**

18. In the **Size Controls** area, enter **1** in the **Size** edit box in the **pSpawn1** tool control window.

19. In the **Controls** tab of the **pSpawn1** tool control window, set the values of the parameters as follows:

Number: **300** Lifespan: **35**

20. In the **Velocity Controls** area of the **Controls** tab in the **pSpawn1** tool control window, set the values of the parameters as follows:

Velocity: **0.015** Velocity Variance: **0.015** Angle Variance: **360**
Angle Z Variance: **360** Velocity Transfer: **0.0**

21. Choose the **Rotation Relative to motion** option from the **Rotation Mode** drop-down list in the **Rotation Controls** area of the **pSpawn1** tool control window.

22. Choose the **Conditions** tab. Next, enter **0.99** and **0.99** in the **Start Age** and **End Age** edit boxes, respectively.

After entering the values, the output of the **Merge1** tool is displayed in the right Display View. Figure 14-16 shows the output of the **Merge1** tool at frame 100.

Figure 14-16 *The output of the **Merge1** tool at frame 100*

23. Select the **pRender1** tool tile from the **Flow** area and choose **Tools > Blur > Glow** from the menubar; the **Glow1** tool tile is inserted in the **Flow** area and a connection between the **pRender1**, **Merge1**, and **Glow1** tools is established.

24. In the **Glow1** tool control window, set the values of the parameters as follows:

Glow Size: **8.38**   Glow: **0.15**

Now, save the composition with the name *c14tut3* at the location *Documents > Fusion_7 > c14_tut > c14_tut_03*. Next, you need to render the composition. For rendering, refer to Tutorial 2 of Chapter 2. The output of the composition at frame 100 is shown in Figure 14-13. You can also view the final render of the composition by downloading the *c14_fusion_7_rndr.zip* from *http://www.cadcim.com*. The path of the file is mentioned at the beginning of the chapter.

Tutorial 4

In this tutorial, you will create the effect of fire in a scene using the **Particles** tools. The final rendered output of the composition at frame 100 is shown in Figure 14-17.

(Expected time: 25 min)

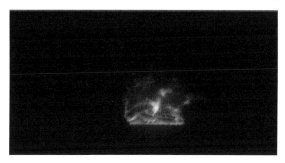

Figure 14-17 The final rendered output of the composition at frame 100

The following steps are required to complete this tutorial:

a.   Set the frame format.
b.   Create the fire effect.

Setting the Frame Format
In this section, you will specify the frame format settings.

1.   Choose **File > New** from the menubar; a new composition is displayed in the Fusion screen.

2.   Choose **File > Preferences** from the menubar; the **Preferences** dialog box is displayed.

3.   In this dialog box, select **Frame Format** from the **Composition#** preferences tree; various frame format settings are displayed on the right in the **Preferences** dialog box. Next, select the **HDTV 720** option from the **Default format** drop-down list and then choose the **Save** button to save the changes made.

4.   In the Time Ruler area, enter **300** in the **Global End Time** edit box.

Creating the Fire Effect

In this section, you will create fire effect.

1. Choose the **pEm** button from the toolbar; the **pEmitter1** tool is inserted in the **Flow** area.

2. Choose the **pRn** button from the toolbar; the **pRender1** tool is inserted in the **Flow** area and a connection between the **pEmitter1** and **pRender1** tools is established.

3. Choose the **2D** button from the **pRender1** tool control window.

4. Press 1; the output of the **pRender1** tool is displayed in the left Display View.

5. In the **pEmitter1** tool control window, choose the **Region** tab. Next, select **Line** from the **Region** drop-down list and then set the values of the parameters as follows:

Start
Start X Offset: **-0.055**   Start Y Offset: **-0.16**

End
End X Offset: **0.143**   End Y Offset: **-0.16**

After entering the values, the output of the **pRender1** tool is displayed in the left Display View, as shown in Figure 14-18.

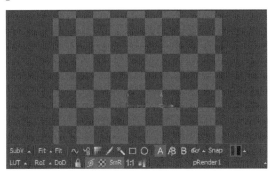

Figure 14-18 *The output of the pRender1 tool*

6. In the **Style** tab, expand the **Color Controls** area and then expand the **Color over Life Controls** area. Next, click on the extreme right of the **Color Over Life** gradient; a triangle is displayed. Next, set the **A** slider to **0**, refer to Figure 14-19.

7. In the **Style** tab of the **pEmitter1** tool control window, select **Merge** from the **Apply Mode** drop-down list and then select the **Sub-Pixel Rendered** check box.

The **Apply Mode** drop-down list is used to control the behavior of the overlapping particles. The options in this drop-down list only affect the 2D particle system. The **Merge** option is used to merge the overlapping particles. The **Sub-Pixel Rendered** check box is selected to ensure that the particles are rendered with Sub Pixel precision which produces smooth results. This option only works with **Point** and **Point Cluster** style option in the **Style** drop-down list.

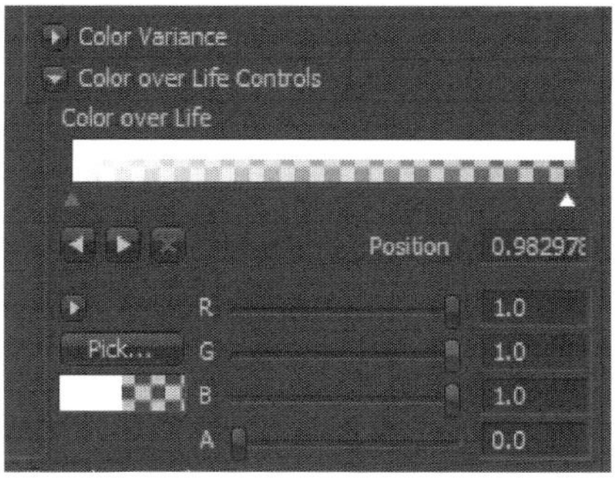

*Figure 14-19   Partial view of the **pEmitter1** tool control window*

8. In the **Controls** tab of the **pEmitter1** tool control window, set the values of the parameters as follows:

Number: **500**   Lifespan: **90**   Lifespan Variance: **25.13**

9. Expand the **Rotation Controls** area and select the **Rotation relative to motion** option from the **Rotation Mode** drop-down list.

10. Make sure the **pEmitter1** tool tile is selected in the **Flow** area and choose **Tools > Particles > pTurbulence** from the menubar; the **pTurbulence1** tool tile is inserted in the **Flow** area and a connection between the **pTurbulence1** and **pEmitter1** tools is established.

The **pTurbulence** tool is used to provide uneven motion to the particles. It does so by affecting the position of the particles.

11. In the **pTurbulence1** tool control window, set the values of the parameters as follows:

X Strength: **0.05**   Y Strength: **0.05**   Z Strength: **0.05**

12. Make sure the **pTurbulence1** tool tile is selected in the **Flow** area and choose **Tools > Particles > pTurbulence** from the menubar; the **pTurbulence2** tool tile is inserted in the **Flow** area and a connection between the **pTurbulence1**, **pTurbulence2**, and **pRender1** tools is established.

13. In the **pTurbulence2** tool control window, set the values of the parameters as follows:

Z Strength: **0.2**   Density: **26**

The **Density** parameter is used to produce detailed variations in the turbulence produced by the **pTurbulence** tool.

14. Make sure the **pTurbulence2** tool tile is selected in the **Flow** area and choose **Tools > Particles > pDirectionalForce** from the menubar; the **pDirectionalForce1** tool tile is

inserted in the **Flow** area and a connection between the **pTurbulence2, pDirectionalForce1, pRender1** tools is established.

15. In the **pDirectionalForce1** tool control window, set the values of the parameters as follows:

    Strength: **0.01**   Direction: **90**

    After entering the values, the output of the **pRender1** tool at frame 100 is displayed in the left Display View, as shown in Figure 14-20.

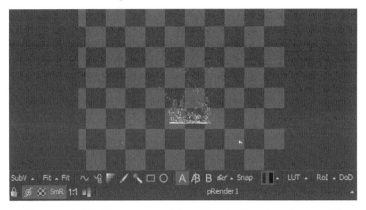

Figure 14-20 *The output of the **pRender1** tool at frame 100*

16. Select the **pRender1** tool tile from the **Flow** area and choose **Tools > Blur > Blur** from the menubar; the **Blur1** tool tile is inserted in the **Flow** area and a connection between the **Blur1** and **pRender1** tools is established.

17. Press 2; the output of the **Blur1** tool is displayed in the right Display View.

18. Enter **2.09** in the **Blur Size** edit box in the **Blur1** tool control window.

19. Choose the **Blur** button from the toolbar; the **Blur2** tool is inserted in the **Flow** area.

20. Drag the red output node of the **Blur1** tool tile to the orange node of the **Blur2** tool tile in the **Flow** area; a connection between **Blur1** and **Blur2** tools is established.

21. Enter **1.5** in the **Blur Size** edit box in the **Blur2** tool control window.

22. Click on the empty space in the **Flow** area and choose **Tools > Warp > Displace** from the menubar; the **Displace1** tool is inserted in the **Flow** area.
    The **Displace** tool is used to displace or refract an image.

23. Drag the white output node of the **Blur1** tool tile to the orange node of the **Displace1** tool tile. Next, Drag the red output node of the **Blur2** tool tile to the green node of the **Displace1** tool tile in the **Flow** area, refer to Figure 14-21.

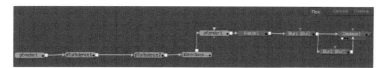

Figure 14-21 *The **Displace1** tool inserted and connected to the **Blur1** and **Blur2** tools*

24. Press 1; the output of the **Displace1** tool is displayed in the left Display View.

25. Enter **0.56** in the **Refraction Strength** edit box in the **Displace1** tool control window.

26. Select the **Displace1** tool tile from the **Flow** area and choose **Tools > Warp > Vector Distortion** from the menubar; the **VectorDistortion1** tool tile is inserted in the **Flow** area and a connection between the **VectorDistortion1** and **Displace1** tools is established.

    The **Vector Distortion** tool is used to distort the input image based on the vector channel data of the input image or a channel from another image.

27. Press 1; the output of the **VectorDistortion1** tool is displayed in the left Display View.

28. In the **VectorDistortion1** tool control window, set the values of the parameters as follows:

    Scale: **0.21**   Glow: **0.22**

    The output of the **VectorDistortion1** tool at frame 120 after specifying all parameters is shown in Figure 14-22.

Figure 14-22 *The output of the **VectorDistortion1** tool at frame 120*

Next, you will set the color of the fire.

29. Make sure the **VectorDistortion1** tool tile is selected in the **Flow** area and choose the **CC** button from the toolbar; the **ColorCorrector1** tool tile is inserted in the **Flow** area and a connection between the **ColorCorrector1** and **VectorDistortion1** tools is established.

30. Press 2; the output of the **ColorCorrector1** tool is displayed in the right Display View.

31. Choose the **Show Checker Underlay** button from the **Display View** toolbar.

32. In the **ColorCorrector1** tool control window, choose the **Highlights** tab and set the values of the parameters as follows:

    Tint: **0.15**   Strength: **0.86**

33. Choose the **Midtones** button and set the values of the parameters as follows:

    Tint: **0.11**   Strength: **0.8**   Midtones-RGB-Gain:**1.6**

34. Choose the **Shadows** button and set the values of the parameters as follows:

    Tint: **0.070**   Shadows-RGB-Gain: **1.67**

    After entering the values, the output of the **ColorCorrector1** tool at frame 200 is displayed in the right Display View, as shown in Figure 14-23. Figure 14-24 displays all tools used in the composition.

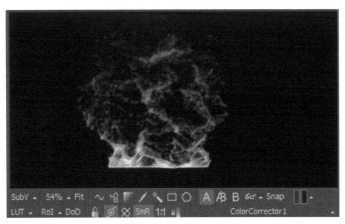

Figure 14-23 *The output of the **ColorCorrector1** tool at frame 200*

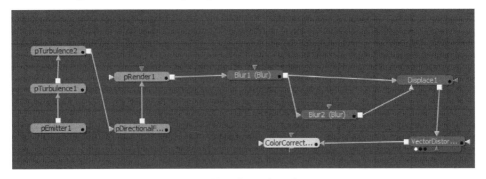

Figure 14-24 *All tools used in the composition*

Now, save the composition with the name *c14tut4* at the location *Documents > Fusion_7 > c14_tut > c14_tut_04*. Next, you need to render the composition. For rendering, refer to Tutorial 2 of Chapter 2. The output of the composition at frame 100 is shown in Figure 14-18. You can also view the final render of the composition by downloading the *c14_fusion_7_rndr.zip* file from *http://www.cadcim.com*. The path of the file is mentioned at the beginning of the chapter.

Tutorial 5

In this tutorial, you will extract the color of the flower using the **Particle** tools. Figure 14-25 is shows before and after image of the flower.   **(Expected time: 25 min)**

Figure 14-25 Before and after image of the flower

The following steps are required to complete this tutorial:

a.   Set the frame format.
b.   Download and import the image.
c.   Extract the color.

Setting the Frame Format

In this section, you will specify the frame format settings.

1.   Choose **File > New** from the menubar; a new composition is displayed in the Fusion screen.

2.   Choose **File > Preferences** from the menubar; the **Preferences** dialog box is displayed.

3.   In this dialog box, select **Frame Format** from the **Composition#** preferences tree; various frame format settings are displayed on the right of the **Preferences** dialog box.

4.   Make sure the **2K Full Aperture (Super 35)** option is selected in the **Default format** drop-down list and then choose the **Save** button.

5.   In the Time Ruler area, enter **500** in the **Global End Time** edit box.

Downloading and Importing the Image

In this section, you will download the image and import it to the composition.

1. Download the image to */Documents/Fusion_7/c14_tut/c14_tut_05/Media_Files*.

2. Choose the **LD** button from the toolbar; a dialog box is displayed. In this dialog box, choose **Documents > Fusion_7 > c14_tut > c14_tut_05 > Media_Files > flower.jpg** and then choose the **Open** button; the **Loader1** tool tile is inserted in the **Flow** area.

3. Press 1; the output of the **Loader1** tool is displayed in the left Display View. Next, choose the **Fit** button from the **Display View** toolbar to fit the image into the Display View, refer to Figure 14-26.

Figure 14-26 *The output of the loader1 tool in the left Display view*

Extracting the Color

In this section, you will extract the color of the flower using particle.

1. Choose **Tools > Particles > pEmitter** from the menubar; the **pEmitter1** tool tile is inserted in the **Flow** area.

2. Make sure the **pEmitter1** tool tile is selected in the **Flow** area. In the control window of the **pEmitter1** tool, choose the **Region** tab and select **Bitmap** from the **Region** drop-down list. Notice that the orange node is displayed in the **pEmitter1** tool tile in the **Flow** area.

3. Drag the red output node of the **Loader1** tool tile to the orange node of the **pEmitter1** tool tile in the **Flow** area. a connection between the **Loader1** and **pEmitter1** tools is established.

4. Make sure the **pEmitter1** tool tile is selected in the **Flow** area. Choose **Tools > Particles > pRender** from the menubar; the **pRender1** tool tile is inserted in the **Flow** area and a connection between **pEmitter1** and **pRender1** tools is established.

5. In the **pRender1** control window, select the **2D** button in the **Output Mode** area. Make sure the **Controls** tab is chosen. Now, enter **68** in the **Pre-Generates Frame** edit box.

6. Press 2; the output of the **Render 1** tool is displayed in the right Display View. Press SPACEBAR to view the animation at frame 180, as shown in Figure 14-27. Next, choose the **Fit** button from the **Display View** toolbar to fit the image into the Display View.

Figure 14-27 *The output of the **Render 1** tool at frame 180 in the right Display view*

7. Select the **pEmitter1** tool tile from the **Flow** area. In the control window of the **pEmitter1** tool, choose the **Controls** tab and then enter the values of the parameters as follows.

   Random Seed: **27220**   Number: **200**   Number Variance: **11.90**

   Lifespan: **795.23**

8. Choose the **Use Color from Region** option from the **Color** drop-down list. In the **Velocity Controls** area, enter **0.08** and **0.46** in the **Velocity** and **Velocity Variance** edit boxes.

9. In the control window of the **pEmitter1** tool, choose the **Style** tab. choose the **Blob** from the **Style** drop-down list.

10. Expand the **Size Controls** area in the **pEmitter1** control window and then set the parameters as follows:

    Size: **0.0025**   Size Variance: **0.1125**

    Next, you will animate the size of the particles.

11. In the control window of the **pEmitter1** tool, animate **Size** to create keyframes by using the values given next.

Frame	Size
100	0.22
200	0.4
300	0.6
400	0.7
500	0

12. Select the **Loader 1** tool tile is elected in the **Flow** area and then choose **Add a B-Splin e Mask** button from the **Display View** toolbar; the **BSpline1** tool tile is inserted in the **Flow** area and a connection is established between the **Loader1** and **BSpline1** tools.

13. In the control window of the **BSpline1,** select the **Invert** check box. Next, draw a polyline shape in the left Display viewport. Now, clear the   check box in the **BSpline1** tool control window.

Figure 14-28 shows the output of the **BSpline1** tool in the left Dispaly view.

*Figure 14-28 The output of the **BSpline1** tool in the right Display view*

14. Select the **pEmitter1** tool tile from the Flow area and then choose **Tools > Particles > pTurbulence** from the menubar; the **pTurbulence 1** tool tile is inserted in the **Flow** area and a connection between the **pEmitter1** and **pTurbulence 1** tools is established.

15. Make sure the **pTurbulence 1** tool tile is selected in the Flow area. In the **pTurbulence 1** tool control window, enter **259** in the **Random Seed** edit box.

16. Select the **pRender1** tool tile from the **Flow** area and then press SPACEBAR to play the animation.

17. Select the **pTurbulence 1** tool tile from the Flow area. Next, choose **Tools > Particles > pVortex** from the menubar; the **pVortex 1** tool tile is inserted in the **Flow** area and a connection between the **pTurbulence 1** and **pVortex 1** tools is established.

18. Make sure the **pVortex1** tool tile is selected in the Flow area. In the **pVortex1** tool control window, make sure the **Controls** tab is chosen and then enter the values of the parameters as follows.

    Strength: **3.82**   Power: **2.76**

    Next, you will animate the size in the control window of the **pVortex1** tool.

19. Enter **0** in the **Current Time** edit box; the current time indicator (CTI) moves to the beginning of the timeline.

20. Right-click on the **Size** control; a shortcut menu is displayed. Choose the **Animate** option from the shortcut menu; a keyframe is added at frame 0.

21. Animate the **Size** control of the **pVortex** tool by using the values given next.

Frame	Size
0	0
500	0.6

22. Select the **pRender1** tool tile from the **Flow** area and then press SPACEBAR to view the animation. Next, choose **Tools > Composite > Merge** from the menubar; the **Merge1 tool** tile is inserted in the **Flow** area.

23. Select the **Loader1** tool tile from the **Flow** area and press CTRL+C and then click on the empty space in the **Flow** area; a **Loader1_1** tool tile is inserted in the Flow area.

24. Drag the red output node of the **Loader1_1** tool tile to the orange node of the **Merge1** tool tile in the **Flow** area; a connection is established between **Loader1_1** and **Merge1** tools.

25. Select the **Merge1** tool tile from the **Flow** area and then choose **Tools > Composite > Merge** from the menubar; the **Merge2** tool tile is inserted in the **Flow** area and a connection between **Merge1** and **Merge2** tools is established.

26. Click on the empty space in the **Flow** area and choose the **LD** button from the toolbar; the **Open File** dialog box is displayed. In this dialog box, choose **Documents > Fusion_7 > c14_tut > c14_tut_05 > Media_Files > d_flower.jpg** and then choose the **Open** button; the **Loader2** tool tile is inserted in the **Flow** area. Now, select the **Merge2** tool tile and then press 2; the output of the **Merge2** tool is displayed in the right Display View.

27. Make sure the CTI is set at frame 0. In **Merge2** tool control window, enter **0** in the **Blend** edit box. Right-click on the **Blend** control; a shortcut menu is displayed. Choose the **Animation** option from the shorcut menu; a key frame is added at frame 0.

28. Move the CTI at frame 500. Now, enter **1** in the **Blend** edit box. Right-click on the **Blend** control; a shortcut menu is displayed. Choose the **Set Key** option from the shorcut menu; a key frame is added at frame 500. Press SPACEBAR to view the animation.

Now, save the composition with the name *c14tut5* at the location *Documents > Fusion_7 > c14_tut > c14_tut_05*. Next, you need to render the composition. For rendering, refer to Tutorial 2 of Chapter 2. The output of the composition at frame 500 is shown in Figure 14-29. You can also view the final render of the composition by downloading the *c14_fusion_7_rndr.zip* file from *http://www.cadcim.com*. The path of the file is mentioned at the beginning of the chapter.

Figure 14-29 *The output of the* **composition at frame 500**

Self-Evaluation Test

Answer the following questions and then compare them to those given at the end of this chapter:

1. Which of the following buttons in the toolbar is used to add particle emitter in a scene?

   (a) **pRn**   (b) **pEm**
   (c) **3Cm**   (d) **3SL**

2. _____ are computer generated points that are used to create a wide variety of effects.

3. The _____ tool is used to create more particles from the existing particles.

4. The _____ renderer uses system's graphics card to produce fast and quality results.

5. The **Displace** tool is used to displace or refract an image. (T/F)

6. The **pDirectionalForce** tool allows the particles to move in the specified direction. (T/F)

7. The **Turbulence** tool is used to provide even motion to particles. (T/F)

8. The **pEmitter** tool is used to emit particles in the composition. (T/F)

9. The default value of the **Position Variance** parameter in the **pEmitter** tool control window is 1. (T/F)

10. The **Lifespan** parameter is used to define the life of the particles. (T/F)

Review Questions

Answer the following questions:

1. Which of the following options in the **Style** drop-down list in the **pEmitter3D** tool control window is used to create snow in the scene?

    (a) **Point Cluster**   (b) **NGon**
    (c) **Blob**   (d) **Point**

2. The _____ button in the **pRender** tool control window is used to switch to 2D particle system.

3. The _____ parameter is used to produce detailed variations in the turbulence produced by the **pTurbulence** tool.

4. The **pRn** button from the toolbar is used to insert the **pRender** tool in the **Flow** area. (T/F)

5. The parameters in the _____ tab are used to control the appearance of particles.

Answer to Self-Evaluation Test
1. b, **2. Particles**, **3. pSpawn**, **4. OGL**, **5.** T, **6.** T, **7.** F, **8.** T, **9.** F, **10.** T

Project 1

Converting a Day Scene into a Night Scene

PROJECT DESCRIPTION

In this project, you will convert a day scene into a night scene and then simulate moving clouds and street lights in the scene. Also, you will add star and moon in the sky. The final rendered output of Project 1 is shown in Figure Prj1-1.

Figure Prj1-1 *The final rendered output of Project 1*

Downloading Composition

Before starting the project, you need to download the *prj1_fusion_7.zip* file from *http://www.cadcim.com*. The path of the file is as follows:

Textbooks > Animation and Visual Effects > Fusion > Blackmagic Design Fusion 7 Studio: A Tutorial Approach

Next, extract the contents of the file at *\Documents\Fusion_7*.

Setting the Frame Format

In this section, you will specify the frame format settings.

1. Choose **File > New** from the menubar; a new composition is displayed on the Fusion screen.

2. Choose **File > Preferences** from the menubar; the **Preferences** dialog box is displayed.

3. In this dialog box, select **Frame Format** from the **Composition#** preferences tree; various frame format settings are displayed on the right in the **Preferences** dialog box. Next, select the **NTSC (Square Pixel)** option from the **Default format** drop-down list and then choose the **Save** button to save the changes made.

4. In the Time Ruler area, enter **300** in the **Global End Time** edit box.

Importing the Images

In this section, you will import the images.

1. Choose the **LD** button from the toolbar; a dialog box is displayed. In this dialog box, choose **Documents > Fusion_7 > prj_01 > Media Files > building.tga** and then choose the **Open** button; the **Loader1** tool tile is inserted in the **Flow** area.

2. Press 1; the output of the **Loader1** tool is displayed in the left Display View.

3. Choose the **Fit** button from the left **Display View** toolbar to fit the image into the left Display View.

4. In the **Loader1** tool control window, choose the **Import** tab and then select the **Post-Multiply by Alpha** check box; the output of the **Loader1** tool is displayed in the left Display View, refer to Figure Prj1-2.

5. Similarly, load the *blue_sky.jpg* in the **Flow** area; the **Loader2** tool tile is inserted in the **Flow** area.

6. Press 2; the output of the **Loader2** tool is displayed in the right Display View, refer to Figure Prj1-2.

7. Choose the **Fit** button from the right **Display View** toolbar to fit the image into the right Display View.

*Figure Prj1-2 The output of **Loader1** and **Loader2** tools*

Adjusting Contrast of the Image

In this section, you will adjust the contrast of the image.

1. Select the **Loader1** tool tile from the **Flow** area and then choose the **CC** button from the toolbar; the **ColorCorrector1** tool tile is inserted in the **Flow** area and a connection between the **Loader1** and **ColorCorrector1** tools is established.

2. Press 1; the output of the **ColorCorrector1** tool is displayed in the left Display View.

3. In the **ColorCorrector1** tool control window, choose the **Suppress** button and then enter the values of the parameters as follows:

    Red: **0**   Cyan: **0**   Blue: **0**

4. Choose the **BC** button from the toolbar; the **BrightnessContrast1** tool tile is inserted in the **Flow** area and a connection between the **Loader1**, **ColorCorrector1**, and **BrightnessContrast1** tools is established.

5. Press 1; the output of the **BrightnessContrast1** tool is displayed in the left Display View.

6. In the **BrightnessContrast1** tool control window, enter the values of the parameters as follows:

    Gain: **0.72**   Gamma: **0.22**

    The output of the **BrightnessContrast1** tool after specifying all the parameters is displayed in the left Display View, refer to Figure Prj1-3.

7. Select the **Loader2** tool tile from the **Flow** area and then choose the **CC** buttonfrom the toolbar; the **ColorCorrector2** tool tile is inserted in the **Flow** area and a connection between the **Loader2** and **ColorCorrector2** tools is established.

8. Press 2; the output of the **ColorCorrector2** tool is displayed in the right Display View.

9. In the **ColorCorrector2** tool control window, choose the **Suppress** button and then enter the values of the parameters as follows:

    Cyan: **0**   Blue: **0**

10. Choose the **BC** button from the toolbar; the **BrightnessContrast2** tool tile is inserted in the **Flow** area and a connection between the **Loader2**, **ColorCorrector2**, and **BrightnessContrast2** tools is established.

11. Press 2; the output of the **BrightnessContrast2** tool is displayed in the right Display View.

12. In the **BrightnessContrast2** tool control window, enter the values of the parameters as follows:

Gain: **0.2**   Gamma: **0.84**

After entering the values, the output of the **BrightnessContrast2** tool is displayed, refer to Prj1-3.

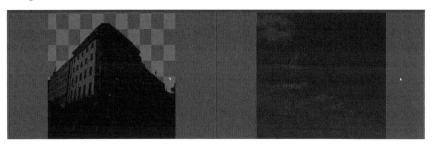

Figure Prj1-3 *The output of the* ***BrightnessContrast1*** *and* ***BrightnessContrast2*** *tools*

Creating the Moving Clouds Effect

In this section, you will create the moving clouds effect.

1. Make sure the **BrightnessContrast2** tool is selected in the **Flow** area. Next, choose **Tools > Transform > Crop** from the menubar; the **Crop1** tool tile is inserted in the **Flow** area and a connection between the **Crop1** and **BrightnessContrast2** tools is established.

2. Press 2; the output of the **Crop1** tool is displayed in the right Display View.

3. Now, create keyframes by using the values given in the table below:

Frame	X Offset
0	0
200	615

Press SPACEBAR to start the playback of the composition. Notice the moving clouds effect in the right Display View.

4. Click on the empty space in the **Flow** area to deselect the selected tool tile, if any. Next, choose **Tools > Transform > Crop** from the menubar; the **Crop2** tool tile is inserted in the **Flow** area.

5. Drag the white output node of the **BrightnessContrast2** tool tile to the orange node of the **Crop2** tool tile; a connection between the **BrightnessContrast2** and **Crop2** tools is established, as shown in Figure Prj1-4.

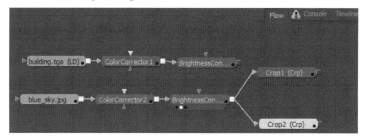

*Figure Prj1-4 The **Crop2** tool connected to the **BrightnessContrast2** tool*

6. Press 2; the output of the **Crop2** tool is displayed in the right Display View.

7. Now, create keyframes by using the values given in the table below:

Frame	X Offset
0	0
200	1000

8. Drag the red output node of the **Crop1** tool tile to the red output node of the **Crop2** tool tile; the **Merge1** tool tile is inserted in the **Flow** area and a connection between the **Crop1**, **Crop2**, and **Merge1** tools is established.

9. Press 2; the output of the **Merge1** tool is displayed in the right Display View, as shown in Figure Prj1-5.

*Figure Prj1-5 The output of the **Merge1** tool*

10. Drag the red output node of the **BrightnessContrast1** tool tile to the red output node of the **Merge1** tool tile; the **Merge2** tool tile is inserted in the **Flow** area and a connection between the **BrightnessContrast1**, **Merge1**, and **Merge2** tools is established.

11. Press 1; the output of the **Merge2** tool is displayed in the left Display View.

12. Enter **0.8** in the **Size** edit box of the **Merge2** tool control window. The output of the **Merge2** tool after specifying all the parameters is shown in Figure Prj1-6.

Figure Prj1-6 *The output of the **Merge2** tool*

Adding Traffic Lights to the Scene

In this section, you will add traffic lights to the scene.

1. Click on the empty space in the **Flow** area to deselect the selected tool tile, if any. Next, choose the **BG** button from the toolbar; the **Background1** tool tile is inserted in the **Flow** area. Next, press 1; the output of the **Background1** tool is displayed in the left Display View.

2. In the **Background1** tool control window, choose the **Pick** button; the **Color** dialog box is displayed. Select the red color swatch in this dialog box and then choose the **OK** button to close it.

3. Make sure the **Background1** tool tile is selected in the **Flow** area. Next, choose the **Elp** button from the toolbar; the **Ellipse1** tool tile is inserted in the **Flow** area and a connection between the **Background1** and **Ellipse1** tools is established.

4. Drag the red output node of the **Background1** tool tile to the red output node of the **Merge2** tool tile; the **Merge3** tool is inserted in the **Flow** area and a connection between the **Background1**, **Merge2**, and **Merge3** tools is established.

5. Press 2; the output of the **Merge3** tool is displayed in the right Display View.

6. Select the **Ellipse1** tool tile in the **Flow** area. Next, enter the following parameters in the **Ellipse1** tool control window:

   Soft Edge: **0.004**

Center
X: **0.47**   Y: **0.32**

Width: **0.19**   Height: **0.19**

7. Select the **Background1** tool tile from the **Flow** area. Next, choose **Tools > Transform > DVE** from the menubar; the **DVE1** tool tile is inserted in the **Flow** area and a connection between the **DVE1**, **Background1**, and **Merge3** tools is established.

8. Enter **-27** in the **Y Rotation** edit box of the **DVE1** tool control window.

9. Make sure the **DVE1** tool tile is selected in the **Flow** area and choose **Tools > Blur > Glow** from the menubar; the **Glow1** tool tile is inserted in the **Flow** area and a connection between the **DVE1**, **Glow1**, and **Merge3** tools is established.

10. Enter **11.5** in the **Glow Size** edit box of the **Glow1** tool control window.

The output of the **Merge3** tool after specifying all the parameters is shown in Figure Prj1-7.

*Figure Prj1-7 The output of the **Merge3** tool*

Next, you will add green light to the scene.

11. Click on the empty space in the **Flow** area to deselect the selected tool tile, if any. Next, choose the **BG** button from the toolbar; the **Background2** tool tile is inserted in the **Flow** area.

12. In the **Background2** tool control window, enter the values of the parameters as follows:

Color
R: **0**   G: **1**   B: **0**

13. Make sure the **Background2** tool tile is selected in the **Flow** area. Next, choose the **Elp** button from the toolbar; the **Ellipse2** tool tile is inserted in the **Flow** area and a connection between the **Background2** and **Ellipse2** tools is established.

14. Select the **Background2** tool tile and then press 1; the output of the **Background2** tool is displayed in the left Display View.

15. Drag the red output node of the **Background2** tool tile to the red output node of the **Merge3** tool tile; the **Merge4** tool tile is inserted in the **Flow** area and a connection between the **Background2**, **Merge3**, and **Merge4** tools is established.

16. Press 2; the output of the **Merge4** tool is displayed in the right Display View.

17. Select the **Ellipse2** tool tile in the **Flow** area and then enter the values of the following parameters in the **Ellipse2** tool control window:

    Center
    X: **0.47**   Y: **0.28**

    Width: **0.011**   Height: **0.013**

18. In the **Merge4** tool control window, enter the values of the parameters as follows:

    Center
    Y: **0.49**

19. Select the **Background2** tool tile from the **Flow** area. Next, choose **Tools > Transform > DVE** from the menubar; the **DVE2** tool tile is inserted in the **Flow** area and a connection between the **Background2** and **DVE2** tools is established.

20. Enter **-36** in the **Y Rotation** edit box of the **DVE2** tool control window.

21. Make sure the **DVE2** tool tile is selected in the **Flow** area. Next, choose **Tools > Blur > Glow** from the menubar; the **Glow2** tool tile is inserted in the **Flow** area and a connection between the **DVE2**, **Glow2**, and **Merge4** tools is established.

22. Enter **11.5** in the **Glow Size** edit box of the **Glow2** tool control window.

    The output of the **Merge4** tool after specifying all the parameters is shown in Figure Prj1-8.

Adding Street Lights to the Scene
In this section, you will add street lights to the scene.

1. Click on the empty space in the **Flow** area to deselect the selected tool tile, if any. Next, choose the **BG** button from the toolbar; the **Background3** tool tile is inserted in the **Flow** area.

Figure Prj1-8 *The output of the **Merge4** tool*

2. In the **Background3** tool control window, enter the values of the parameters as follows:

    R: **1**   G: **1**   B: **1**

3. Make sure the **Background3** tool tile is selected in the **Flow** area. Next, choose the **Elp** button from the toolbar; a connection between the **Background3** and **Ellipse3** tools is established.

4. Press 1; the output of the **Background3** tool is displayed in the left Display View.

5. Drag the red output node of the **Background3** tool tile to the red output node of the **Merge4** tool tile; the **Merge5** tool tile is inserted in the **Flow** area and a connection between the **Background3**, **Merge4**, and **Merge5** tools is established.

6. Press 2; the output of the **Merge5** tool is displayed in the right Display View.

7. Select the **Ellipse3** tool tile in the **Flow** area and then enter the values of the following parameters in the **Ellipse3** tool control window:

    Soft Edge: **0.002**

    Center
    X: **0.2**   Y: **0.39**

    Width: **0.02**   Height: **0.02**

8. Select the **Background3** tool tile from the **Flow** area. Next, choose **Tools > Transform > DVE** from the menubar; the **DVE3** tool tile is inserted in the **Flow** area and a connection between the **Background3**, **DVE3**, and **Merge5** tools is established.

9. In the **DVE3** tool control window, enter the values of the parameters as follows:

Center
X: **0.47**   Y: **0.46**

Rotation
X Rotation: **62.9**

10. Make sure the **DVE3** tool tile is selected in the **Flow** area. Next, choose **Tools > Blur > Glow** from the menubar; the **Glow3** tool tile is inserted in the **Flow** area and a connection between the **DVE3**, **Glow3**, and **Merge5** tools is established.

11. In the **Glow3** tool control window, enter the values of the parameters as follows:

Glow Size: **58**   Glow: **0.98**

The output of the **Merge5** tool after specifying all the parameters is shown in Figure Prj1-9.

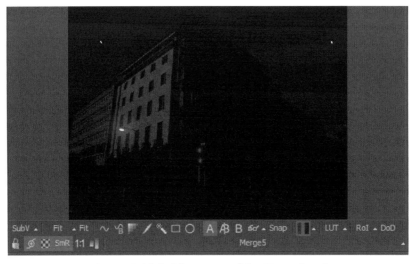

Figure Prj1-9 *The output of the **Merge5** tool*

12. Click on the empty space in the **Flow** area to deselect the selected tool tile, if any. Next, choose the **BG** button from the toolbar; the **Background4** tool tile is inserted in the **Flow** area.

13. Press 1; the output of the **Background4** tool is displayed in the left Display View.

14. In the **Background4** tool control window, enter the values of the parameters as follows:

R: **1**   G: **1**   B: **1**

15. Click on the empty space in the **Flow** area to deselect the selected tool tile, if any. Next, choose the **Elp** button from the toolbar; the **Ellipse4** tool tile is inserted in the **Flow** area.

16. Drag the red output node of the **Ellipse4** tool tile to the purple node of the **Background4** tool tile; a connection between the **Background4** and **Ellipse4** tools is established.

17. Drag the red output node of the **Background4** tool tile to the red output node of the **Merge5** tool tile; the **Merge6** tool tile is inserted in the **Flow** area and a connection between the **Background4**, **Merge5**, and **Merge6** tools is established.

18. Press 2; the output of the **Merge6** tool is displayed in the right Display View. Select the **Ellipse4** tool tile in the **Flow** area. Next, enter the values of the following parameters in the **Ellipse4** tool control window:

Soft Edge: **0.002**

Width: **0.02**   Height: **0.02**

19. Select the **Merge6** tool tile in the **Flow** area. In the **Merge6** tool control window, enter the values of the parameters as follows:

Center
X: **0.08**   Y: **0.4**

20. Select the **Background4** tool tile from the **Flow** area and then choose **Tools > Transform > DVE** from the menubar; the **DVE4** tool tile is inserted in the **Flow** area and a connection between the **Background4** and **DVE4** tools is established.

21. In the **DVE4** tool control window, enter the values of the parameters as follows:

Center
X: **0.47**   Y: **0.46**

X Rotation: **62.9**

22. Make sure the **DVE4** tool tile is selected in the **Flow** area. Next, choose **Tools > Blur > Glow** from the menubar; the **Glow4** tool tile is inserted in the **Flow** area and a connection between the **DVE4**, **Glow4**, and **Merge6** tools is established.

23. In the **Glow4** tool control window, set the values of the parameters as follows:

Glow Size: **58**   Glow: **0.98**
The output of the **Merge6** tool after specifying all parameters is shown in Figure Prj1-10.

24. Click on the empty space in the **Flow** area to deselect the selected tool tile, if any. Next, choose the **BG** button from the toolbar; the **Background5** tool tile is inserted in the **Flow** area.

25. Press 1; the output of the **Background5** tool is displayed in the left Display View.

Figure Prj1-10 *The output of the Merge6 tool*

26. In the **Background5** tool control window, enter the values of the parameters as follows:

    R: **1**   G: **1**   B: **1**

27. Make sure the **Background5** tool tile is selected in the **Flow** area . Next, choose the
    Elp button from the toolbar; the **Ellipse5** tool is inserted in the **Flow** area and a
    connection between the **Background5** and **Ellipse5** tools is established.

28. Drag the red output node of the **Background5** tool tile to the red output node of the **Merge6**
    tool tile; the **Merge7** tool tile is inserted in the **Flow** area and a connection between the
    Background5, **Merge6**, and **Merge7** tools is established.

29. Press 2; the output of the **Merge7** tool is displayed in the right Display View.

30. Select the **Ellipse5** tool tile in the **Flow** area. Next, enter the values of the following
    parameters in the **Ellipse5** tool control window:

    Soft Edge: **0.2**

    Width: **0.05**   Height: **0.09**

31. In the **Merge7** tool control window, enter the values of the parameters as follows:
    Center
    X: **0.41**   Y: **0.49**

32. Select the **Background5** tool tile from the **Flow** area. Next, choose **Tools > Transform >
    DVE** from the menubar; the **DVE5** tool tile is inserted in the **Flow** area and a connection
    between the **Background5**, **DVE5**, and **Merge7** tools is established.

33. In the **DVE5** tool control window, enter the values of the parameters as follows:

Center
X: **0.08**   Y: **0.09**

X Rotation: **-102.9**

34. Make sure the **DVE5** tool tile is selected in the **Flow** area. Next, choose **Tools > Blur >** **Glow** from the menubar; the **Glow5** tool tile is inserted in the **Flow** area and a connection between the **DVE5, Glow5**, and **Merge7** tools is established.

35. Enter **44.5** in the **Glow Size** edit box of the **Glow5** tool control window.

The output of the **Merge7** tool after specifying all the parameters is shown in Figure Prj1-11.

Figure Prj1-11 *The output of the Merge7 tool*

36. Click on the empty space in the **Flow** area to deselect the selected tool tile, if any. Next, choose the **BG** button from the toolbar; the **Background6** tool tile is inserted in the **Flow** area.

37. Press 1; the output of the **Background6** tool is displayed in the left Display View.

38. In the **Background6** tool control window, enter the values of the parameters as follows:
Color
R: **1**   G: **1**   B: **1**

39. Make sure the **Background6** tool tile is selected in the **Flow** area. Next, choose the **Elp** button from the toolbar; the **Ellipse6** tool is inserted in the **Flow** area and a connection between the **Background6** and **Ellipse6** tools is established.

40. Drag the red output node of the **Background6** tool tile to the red output node of the **Merge7** tool tile; the **Merge8** tool tile is inserted in the **Flow** area and a connection between the **Background6, Merge7**, and **Merge8** tools is established.

41. Press 2; the output of the **Merge8** tool is displayed in the right Display View.

42. Select the **Ellipse6** tool tile in the **Flow** area. Next, enter the values of the following parameters in the **Ellipse6** tool control window:

    Soft Edge: **0.2**

    Width: **0.2**   Height: **0.18**

43. In the **Merge8** tool control window, enter the values of the parameters as follows:

    Center
    X: **0.54**   Y: **0.5**

    Size: **1.125**

44. Select the **Background6** tool tile from the **Flow** area. Next, choose **Tools > Transform > DVE** from the menubar; the **DVE6** tool tile is inserted in the **Flow** area and a connection between the **Background6**, **DVE6**, and **Merge8** tools is established.

45. In the **DVE6** tool control window, enter the values of the parameters as follows:

    Center
    X: **0.08**   Y: **0.09**

    X Rotation: **-102.9**

46. Make sure the **DVE6** tool tile is selected in the **Flow** area. Next, choose **Tools > Blur > Glow** from the menubar; the **Glow6** tool tile is inserted in the **Flow** area and a connection between the **DVE6**, **Glow6**, and **Merge8** tools is established.

47. Enter **44.5** in the **Glow Size** edit box of the **Glow6** tool control window.

    The output of the **Merge8** tool after specifying all the parameters is shown in Figure Prj1-12.

Figure Prj1-12 *The output of the **Merge8** tool*

48. Click on the empty space in the **Flow** area to deselect the selected tool tile, if any. Next, choose the **BG** button from the toolbar; the **Background7** tool tile is inserted in the **Flow** area.

49. Press 1; the output of the **Background7** tool is displayed in the left Display View.

50. In the **Background7** tool control window, enter the values of the parameters as follows:

    R: **1**   G: **1**   B: **1**

51. Make sure the **Background7** tool tile is selected in the **Flow** area. Next, choose the **Elp** button from the toolbar; the **Ellipse7** tool tile is inserted in the **Flow** area and a connection between the **Background7** and **Ellipse7** tools is established.

52. Drag the red output node of the **Background7** tool tile to the red output node of the **Merge8** tool tile; the **Merge9** tool tile is inserted in the **Flow** area and a connection between the **Background7**, **Merge8**, and **Merge9** tools is established.

53. Press 2; the output of the **Merge9** tool is displayed in the right Display View.

54. Select the **Ellipse7** tool tile in the **Flow** area. Next, enter the following values in the **Ellipse7** tool control window:

    Soft Edge: **0.02**

    Center
    X: **0.66**   Y: **0.27**

    Width: **0.02**   Height: **0.03**

    Angle: **0.08**

55. In the **Merge9** tool control window, enter the values of the parameters as follows:

    Center
    X: **0.54**   Y: **0.38**

    Size: **0.6**

56. Select the **Background7** tool tile from the **Flow** area. Next, choose **Tools > Transform > DVE** from the menubar; the **DVE7** tool tile is inserted in the **Flow** area and a connection between the **Background7**, **DVE7**, and **Merge9** tools is established.

57. In the **DVE7** tool control window, enter the values of the parameters as follows:

    Center
    X: **0.52**   Y: **0.36**

Rotation
X Rotation: **69**

58. Make sure the **DVE7** tool tile is selected in the **Flow** area. Next, choose **Tools > Blur > Glow** from the menubar; the **Glow7** tool tile is inserted in the **Flow** area and a connection between the **DVE7**, **Glow7**, and **Merge9** tools is established.

59. In the **Glow7** tool control window, enter the values of the parameters as follows:

Glow Size: **22**   Glow: **0.92**   Blend: **0.09**

The output of the **Merge9** tool after specifying all the parameters is shown in Figure Prj1-13.

Figure Prj1-13   *The output of the **Merge9** tool*

60. Click on the empty space in the **Flow** area to deselect the selected tool tile, if any. Next, choose the **BG** button from the toolbar; the **Background8** tool tile is inserted in the **Flow** area.

61. Press 1; the output of the **Background8** tool is displayed in the left Display View.

62. In the **Background8** tool control window, enter the values of the parameters as follows:

R: **1**   G: **1**   B: **1**

63. Make sure the **Background8** tool tile is selected in the **Flow** area. Next, choose the **Elp** button from the toolbar; the **Ellipse8** tool is inserted in the **Flow** area and a connection between the **Background8** and **Ellipse8** tools is established.

64. Drag the red output node of the **Background8** tool to the red output node of the **Merge9** tool tile; the **Merge10** tool tile is inserted in the **Flow** area and a connection between the **Background8**, **Merge9**, and **Merge10** tools is established.

65. Press 2; the output of the **Merge10** tool is displayed in the right Display View.

66. Select the **Ellipse8** tool tile in the **Flow** area and enter values of the following parameters in the **Ellipse8** tool control window:

Soft Edge: **0.08**

Center
X: **0.66**   Y: **0.27**

Width: **0.09**   Height: **0.08**

Angle: **0.09**

67. In the **Merge10** tool control window, enter the values of the parameters as follows:

Center
X: **0.49**   Y: **0.2**

Blend: **0.53**

68. Select the **Background8** tool tile from the **Flow** area and choose **Tools > Transform > DVE** from the menubar; the **DVE8** tool tile is inserted in the **Flow** area and a connection between the **Background8**, **DVE8**, and **Merge10** tools is established.

69. In the **DVE8** tool control window, enter the values of the parameters as follows:

Center
X: **0.52**   Y: **0.36**

Rotation
X Rotation: **78**

70. Make sure the **DVE8** tool tile is selected in the **Flow** area. Next, choose **Tools > Blur > Glow** from the menubar; the **Glow8** tool tile is inserted in the **Flow** area and a connection between the **DVE8**, **Glow8**, and **Merge10** tools is established.

71. In the **Glow8** tool control window, enter the values of the parameters as follows:

Glow Size: **6.28**   Glow: **0.77**

The output of the **Merge10** tool after specifying all the parameters is shown in Figure Prj1-14.

72. Click on the empty space in the **Flow** area to deselect the selected tool tile, if any. Next, choose the **BG** button from the toolbar; the **Background9** tool tile is inserted in the **Flow** area.

73. Press 1; the output of the **Background9** tool is displayed in the left Display View.

Figure Prj1-14 *The output of the Merge10 tool*

74. In the **Background9** tool control window, choose the **Pick** button; the **Color** dialog box is displayed. Select the red color swatch in this dialog box and then choose the **OK** button to close it.

75. Make sure the **Background9** tool tile is selected in the **Flow** area and then choose the **Elp** button from the toolbar; the **Ellipse9** tool is inserted in the **Flow** area and a connection between the **Ellipse9** and **Background9** tools is established.

76. Drag the red output node of the **Background9** tool tile to the red output node of the **Merge10** tool tile; the **Merge11** tool tile is inserted in the **Flow** area and a connection between the **Background9**, **Merge10**, and **Merge11** tools is established.

77. Press 2; the output of the **Merge11** tool is displayed in the right Display View.

78. Select the **Ellipse9** tool tile from the **Flow** area and then enter the values of the following parameters in the **Ellipse9** tool control window:

Soft Edge: **0.005**

Width: **0.011**   Height: **0.011**

79. In the **Merge11** tool control window, enter the values of the parameters as follows:

Center
X: **0.85**   Y: **0.53**

80. Select the **Background9** tool tile from the **Flow** area. Next, choose **Tools > Transform > DVE** from the menubar; the **DVE9** tool tile is inserted in the **Flow** area and a connection between the **Background9** and **DVE9** tools is established.

81. Enter **130** in the **Y Rotation** edit box of the **DVE9** tool control window.

The output of the **Merge11** tool after specifying all the parameters is shown in Figure Prj1-15.

Figure Prj1-15 *The output of the Merge11 tool*

Creating Moon in the Scene

In this section, you will create moon in the scene.

1. Click on the empty space in the **Flow** area to deselect the selected tool tile, if any. Choose the **BG** button from the toolbar; the **Background10** tool tile is inserted in the **Flow** area.

2. Press 1; the output of the **Background10** tool is displayed in the left Display View.

3. In the **Background10** tool control window, enter the values of the parameters as follows:
   R: **1**   G: **1**   B: **1**

4. Make sure the **Background10** tool tile is selected in the **Flow** area. Next, choose the **Elp** button from the toolbar; the **Ellipse10** tool tile is inserted in the **Flow** area and a connection between the **Background10** and **Ellipse10** tools is established.

5. Drag the red output node of the **Background10** tool tile to the red output node of the **Merge11** tool; the **Merge12** tool tile is inserted in the **Flow** area and a connection between the **Background10**, **Merge11**, and **Merge12** tools is established.

6. Press 2; the output of the **Merge12** tool is displayed in the right Display View.

7. Select the **Ellipse10** tool tile in the **Flow** area and then enter the values of the following parameters in the **Ellipse10** tool control window:

   Center
   X: **0.45**   Y: **0.32**

   Width: **0.19**   Height: **0.26**

8. Make sure the **Ellipse10** tool tile is selected in the **Flow** area. Next, choose the **Elp** button from the toolbar; the **Ellipse11** tool tile is inserted in the **Flow** area and a connection between the **Background10**, **Ellipse10** and **Ellipse11** tools is established.

9. Select the **Ellipse11** tool tile in the **Flow** area and then enter the values of the following parameters in the **Ellipse11** tool control window:

Paint Mode: **Subtract**

Center
X: **0.45**   Y: **0.54**

Width: **0.27**   Height: **0.52**

10. In the **Merge12** tool control window, enter the values of the parameters as follows:

Center
X: **0.03**   Y: **0.72**

Size: **0.08**   Angle: **394.2**   Blend: **0.49**

The output of the **Merge12** tool after specifying all the parameters is shown in Figure Prj1-16.

*Figure Prj1-16 The output of the **Merge12** tool*

Creating the Star in the Scene

In this section, you will create a star in the scene.

1. Click on the empty space in the **Flow** area to deselect the selected tool tile, if any. Choose the **BG** button from the toolbar; the **Background11** tool tile is inserted in the **Flow** area.

2. Press 1; the output of the **Background11** tool is displayed in the left Display View.

3. In the **Background11** tool control window, enter the values of the parameters as follows:

R: **1**   G: **1**   B: **1**

4. Select the **Background11** tool tile from the **Flow** area. Next, choose the **Ply** button from the toolbar; the **Polygon1** tool tile is inserted in the **Flow** area and a connection between the **Polygon1** and **Background11** tools is established.

5. Press 1; the output of the **Polygon1** tool is displayed in the left Display View.

6. Create the shape of a star in the left Display View, as shown in Figure Prj1-17.

Figure Prj1-17 *Star shape created in left Display View*

7. Enter **0.03** in the **Soft Edge** edit box of the **Polygon1** tool control window.

8. Drag the red output node of the **Background11** tool and then drag the cursor to the red output node of the **Merge12** tool tile; the **Merge13** tool tile is inserted in the **Flow** area and a connection between the **Background11**, **Merge12**, and **Merge13** tools is established.

9. Press 2; the output of the **Merge13** tool is displayed in the right Display View.

10. In the **Merge13** tool control window, enter the values of the parameters as follows:

    Center
    X: **0.97**   Y: **0.88**

    Size: **0.05**

11. Select the **Background11** tool tile from the **Flow** area and choose **Tools > Blur > Glow** from the menubar; the **Glow9** tool tile is inserted in the **Flow** area and a connection between the **Background11** and **Glow9** tools is established.

12. Enter **85.34** in the **Glow Size** edit box of the **Glow9** tool control window. The output of the **Merge13** tool after specifying all parameters is shown in Figure Prj1-18.

Figure Prj1-18 *The output of the* **Merge13** *tool*

Adding More Lights in the Scene

In this section, you will add more lights in the scene.

1. Click on the empty space in the **Flow** area to deselect the selected tool tile, if any. Next, choose the **BG** button from the toolbar; the **Background12** tool tile is inserted in the **Flow** area.

2. Press 1; the output of the **Background12** tool is displayed in the left Display View.

3. In the **Background12** tool control window, enter the values of the parameters as follows:

   R: **1**   G: **1**   B: **1**

4. Make sure the **Background12** tool tile is selected in the **Flow** area. Next, choose the **Elp** button from the toolbar; the **Ellipse12** tool tile is inserted in the **Flow** area and a connection between the **Ellipse12** and **Background12** tools is established.

5. Drag the red output node of the **Background12** tool tile to the red output node of the **Merge13** tool tile; the **Merge14** tool tile is inserted in the **Flow** area and a connection between the **Background12**, **Merge13**, and **Merge14** tools is established.

6. Press 2; the output of the **Merge14** tool is displayed in the right Display View.

7. Select the **Ellipse12** tool tile in the **Flow** area and enter the values of the following parameters in the **Ellipse12** tool control window:

   Soft Edge: **0.004**

   Center
   X: **0.46**   Y: **0.46**

   Width: **0.021**   Height: **0.021**

8. In the **Merge14** tool control window, enter the values of the parameters as follows:

Center
X: **0.74**   Y: **0.29**

9. Select the **Background12** tool tile from the **Flow** area. Next, choose **Tools > Transform > DVE** from the menubar; the **DVE10** tool tile is inserted in the **Flow** area and a connection between the **Background12** and **DVE10** tools is established.

10. In the **DVE10** tool control window, enter the values of the parameters as follows:

Center
X: **0.62**

X Rotation: **78**

The output of the **Merge14** tool after specifying all the parameters is shown in Figure Prj1-19.

Figure Prj 1-19 *The output of the **Merge14** tool*

11. Click on the empty space of the **Flow** area to deselect the selected tool tile, if any. Next, choose the **BG** button from the toolbar; the **Background13** tool is inserted in the **Flow** area.

12. Press 1; the output of the **Background13** tool is displayed in the left Display View.

13. In the **Background13** tool control window, enter the values of the parameters as follows:

R: **1**   G: **1**   B: **1**

14. Select the **Background13** tool tile from the **Flow** area. Next, choose the **Elp** button from the toolbar; the **Ellipse13** tool is inserted in the **Flow** area and a connection between the **Ellipse13** and **Background13** tools is established.

15. Drag the red output node of the **Background13** tool tile to the red output node of the **Merge14** tool tile; the **Merge15** tool tile is inserted in the **Flow** area and a connection between the **Background13**, **Merge14**, and **Merge15** tools is established.

16. Press 2; the output of the **Merge15** tool is displayed in the right Display View.

17. Select the **Ellipse13** tool tile in the **Flow** area and then enter the values of the following parameters in the **Ellipse13** tool control window:

    Soft Edge: **0.08**

    Center
    X: **0.67**   Y: **0.27**

    Width: **0.09**   Height: **0.08**

18. In the **Merge15** tool control window, enter the values of the parameters as follows:
    Center
    X: **0.67**   Y: **0.22**

    Blend: **0.23**

19. Select the **Background13** tool tile from the **Flow** area. Next, choose **Tools > Transform > DVE** from the menubar; the **DVE11** tool tile is inserted in the **Flow** area and a connection between the **Background13** and **DVE11** tools is established.

20. In the **DVE11** tool control window, enter the values of the parameters as follows:

    Center
    X: **0.52**   Y: **0.37**

    Rotation Order: **XYZ**   X Rotation: **102**   Perspective: **165**

21. Select the **DVE11** tool tile from the **Flow** area. Next, choose **Tools > Blur > Glow** from the menubar; the **Glow10** tool tile is inserted in the **Flow** area and a connection between the **DVE11** and **Glow10** tools is established.

22. In the **Glow10** tool control window, enter the values of the parameters as follows:

    Glow Size: **6.29**   Glow: **0.77**

    The output of the **Merge15** tool after specifying all the parameters is shown in Figure Prj1-20.

23. Click on the empty space in the **Flow** area to deselect the selected tool tile, if any. Next, choose the **BG** button from the toolbar; the **Background14** tool tile is inserted in the **Flow** area.

24. Press 1; the output of the **Background14** tool is displayed in the left Display View.

25. In the **Background14** tool control window, enter the values of the parameters as follows:

    R: **1**   G: **1**   B: **1**

*Figure Prj1-20 The output of the **Merge15** tool*

26. Select the **Background14** tool tile from the **Flow** area and then choose the **Ply**button from the toolbar; the **Polygon2** tool tile is inserted in the **Flow** area and a connection between the **Polygon2** and **Background14** tools is established.

27. Press 1; the output of the **Polygon2** tool is displayed in the left Display View.

28. Create a shape in the right Display View, as shown in Figure Prj1-21.

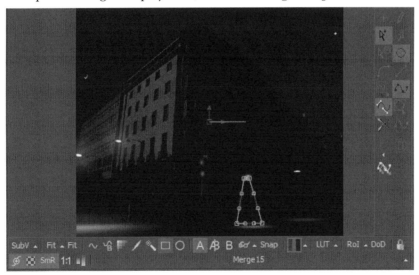

Figure Prj1-21 The shape drawn in the right Display View

29. Drag the red output node of the **Background14** tool tile to the red output node of the **Merge15** tool tile; the **Merge16** tool tile is inserted in the **Flow** area and a connection between the **Background14**, **Merge15**, and **Merge16** tools is established.

30. Press 2; the output of the **Merge16** tool is displayed in the right Display View.

31. In the **Polygon2** tool control window, enter the values of the parameters as follows:

Soft Edge: **0.05**   X Rotation: **17**

32. In the **Merge16** tool control window, enter the values of the parameters as follows:

Center
X: **0.45**   Y: **0.63**
Size: **1.33**   Blend: **0.042**

The output of the **Merge16** tool after specifying all parameters is shown in Figure Prj1-22.

Figure Prj1-22 *The output of the **Merge16** tool*

33. Click on the empty space in the **Flow** area to deselect the selected tool tile, if any. Next, choose the **BG** button from the toolbar; the **Background15** tool tile is inserted in the **Flow** area.

34. Press 1; the output of the **Background15** tool is displayed in the left Display View.

35. In the **Background15** tool control window, enter the values of the parameters as follows:

R: **1**   G: **1**   B: **1**

36. Select the **Background15** tool tile from the **Flow** area. Next, choose the **Ply** button from the toolbar; the **Polygon3** tool tile is inserted in the **Flow** area and a connection between the **Polygon3** and **Background15** tools is established.

37. Create a shape of the **Polygon3** in the right Display View, as shown in Figure Prj1-23.

*Figure Prj1-23 The shape of **Polygon3** drawn in the right Display View*

38. Drag the red output node of the **Background15** tool tile to the red output node of the **Merge16** tool tile; the **Merge17** tool tile is inserted in the **Flow** area and a connection between the **Background15**, **Merge16**, and **Merge17** tools is established.

39. Press 2; the output of the **Merge17** tool is displayed in the right Display View.

40. In the **Polygon3** tool control window, enter the values of the parameters as follows:

Soft Edge: **0.05**   X Rotation: **17**

41. In the **Merge17** tool control window, enter the values of the parameters as follows:

Center
X: **0.47**   Y: **0.49**

Blend: **0.042**

The output of the **Merge17** tool after specifying all the parameters is shown in Figure Prj1-24.

Creating the Window Panes
In this section, you will create window panes.

1. Click on the empty space in the **Flow** area to deselect the selected tool tile, if any. Next, choose the **BG** button from the toolbar; the **Background16** tool tile is inserted in the **Flow** area.

2. Press 1; the output of the **Background16** tool is displayed in the left Display View.

3. In the **Background16** tool control window, enter the values of the parameters as follows:

R: **0.8**   G: **0.62**

Figure Prj1-24 *The output of the **Merge17** tool*

4. Make sure the **Background16** tool tile is selected in the **Flow** area. Next, choose the
    Rct button from the toolbar; the **Rectangle1** tool tile is inserted in the **Flow** area
    and a connection between the **Rectangle1** and **Background16** tools is established.

5. Drag the red output node of the **Background16** tool tile to the red output node of the
    Merge17 tool tile; the **Merge18** tool tile is inserted in the **Flow** area and a connection be-
    tween the **Background16**, **Merge17**, and **Merge18** tools is established.

6. Press 2; the output of the **Merge18** tool is displayed in the right Display View.

7. In the **Rectangle1** tool control window, enter the values of the parameters as follows:

    Center
    X: **0.55**   Y: **0.65**

    Width: **0.055**   Height: **0.095**

8. Press 1; the shape of **Rectangle1** is displayed in the left Display View, is shown in
    Figure Prj1-25.

9. In the **Merge18** tool control window, enter the values of the parameters as follows:

    Center
    X: **0.46**   Y: **0.57**

    Size: **0.57**   Blend: **0.5**

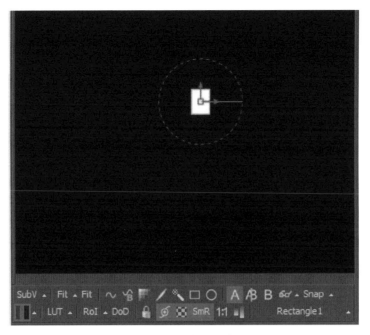

Figure Prj1-25 *The shape of* **Rectangle1**

10. Select the **Background16** tool tile from the **Flow** area. Next, choose **Tools > Transform > DVE** from the menubar; the **DVE12** tool tile is inserted in the **Flow** area and a connection between the **Background16**, **DVE12**, and **Merge18** tools is established.

11. In the **DVE12** tool control window, enter the values of the parameters as follows:

    Z Move: **1.15**   Y Rotation: **63**

12. Select the **DVE12** tool tile from the **Flow** area. Next, choose the **Blur** button from the toolbar; the **Blur1** tool tile is inserted in the **Flow** area and a connection between the **DVE12**, **Blur1**, and **Merge18** tools is established.

13. In the **Blur1** tool control window, enter the value of the following parameter:

    Blur Size: **5**

    The output of the **Merge18** tool after specifying all the parameters is shown in Figure Prj1-26.

14. Click on the empty space in the **Flow** area to deselect the selected tool tile, if any. Next, choose the **BG** button from the toolbar; the **Background17** tool tile is inserted in the **Flow** area.

15. Press 1; the output of the **Background17** tool is displayed in the Display View.

16. In the **Background17** tool control window, enter the values of the parameters as follows:

      R: **1**   G: **0.46**

Figure Prj1-26   *The output of the **Merge18** tool*

17. Make sure the **Background17** tool tile is selected in the **Flow** area. Next, choose the **Ply** button from the toolbar; the **Polygon4** tool tile is inserted in the **Flow** area and a connection between the **Polygon4** and **Background17** tools is established.

18. Create a shape in the right Display View, as shown in Figure Prj1-27.

Figure Prj1-27   *The shape drawn in the right Display View*

19. Drag the red output node of the **Background17** tool tile to the red output node of the **Merge18** tool tile; the **Merge19** tool tile is inserted in the **Flow** area and a connection between the **Background17**, **Merge18**, and **Merge19** tools is established.

20. Press 2; the output of the **Merge19** tool is displayed in the right Display View.

21. In the **Merge19** tool control window, enter the values of the parameters as follows:

Center
X: **0.53**

Size: **0.72**   Blend: **0.19**

22. Select the **Background17** tool tile from the **Flow** area. Next, choose the **Blur** button from the toolbar; the **Blur2** tool tile is inserted in the **Flow** area and a connection between the **Background17**and **Blur2** tools is established.

23. In the **Blur2** tool control window, enter the value of the following parameter:

Blur Size: **2.6**

The output of the **Merge19** tool after specifying all the parameters is shown in Figure Prj1-28.

24. Click on the empty space in the **Flow** area to deselect the selected tool tile, if any. Choose the **BG** button from the toolbar; the **Background18** tool tile is inserted in the **Flow** area.

25. Press 1; the output of the **Background18** tool is displayed in the left Display View.

26. In the **Background18** tool control window, enter the values of the parameters as follows:

R: **1**   G: **0.82**

Figure Prj1-28 *The output of the **Merge19** tool*

27. Make sure the **Background18** tool tile is selected in the **Flow** area. Next, choose the **Ply** button from the toolbar; the **Polygon5** tool tile is inserted in the **Flow** area and a connection between the **Polygon5** and **Background18** tools is established.

28. Create a shape in the right Display View, as shown in Figure Prj1-29.

29. Drag the red output node of the **Background18** tool tile to the red output node of the **Merge19** tool tile; the **Merge20** tool is inserted in the **Flow** area and a connection between the **Background18**, **Merge19**, and **Merge20** tools is established.

30. Press 2; the output of the **Merge20** tool is displayed in the right Display View.

31. In the **Merge20** tool control window, enter the values of the parameters as follows:

Center
X: **0.53**   Y: **0.55**

Size: **0.86**   Blend: **0.18**

Figure Prj1-29 *The shape drawn in the right Display View*

32. Select the **Background18** tool tile from the **Flow** area. Next, choose the **Blur** button  from the toolbar; the **Blur3** tool is inserted in the **Flow** area and a connection between the **Background18**, **Blur3**, and **Merge20** tools is established.

33. Enter **4.19** in the **Blur Size** edit box of the **Blur3** tool control window.

The output of the **Merge20** tool after specifying all the parameters is shown in Figure Prj1-30.

Figure Prj1-30 *The output of the **Merge20** tool*

Creating the Blinking Light Effect

In this section, you will create blinking light effect.

1. Select the **Merge13** tool tile from the **Flow** area and then create keyframes by using the values given next.

Frame	Blend
0	1
15	0
30	1
45	0
60	1
75	0
100	1
125	0
150	1
200	0
225	1
250	0
275	1
300	0

Next, you will animate the traffic lights.

2. Select the **Merge3** tool tile from the **Flow** area and then create keyframes by using the values given next.

Frames	Blend
0-29	1
30-59	0
60-89	1
90-119	0
120-149	1
150-179	0
180-199	1

Note

*To set a keyframe without changing the values of the **Blend** parameter, right-click on it; a shortcut menu will be displayed. Next, choose the **Set Key** option from the shortcut menu.*

3. Select the **Merge4** tool tile from the **Flow** area and then create the keyframes by using the values given next.

Frames	Blend
0-29	0
30-59	1
60-89	0
90-119	1
120-149	0
150-179	1
180-199	0

4. Play the composition to view the blinking light effect.

Now, save the composition with the name *Prj01* at the location *Documents > Fusion_7 > Prj > Prj01*. Next, you need to render the composition. For rendering, refer to Tutorial 2 of Chapter 2. The output of the composition is shown in Figure Prj1-1. You can also view the final render of the composition by downloading the *prj01_fusion_7_rndr.zip* from *http://www.cadcim.com*. The path of the file is mentioned at the beginning of the project.

Project 2

Compositing Render Passes

PROJECT DESCRIPTION

In this project, you will create a composite using render passes. Rendering a scene in passes is the process in which rendering of different attributes of a scene such as color, shadow, specular, shading, and reflection are done separately. Render passes allows you to fine tune the projects in conjunction with the compositing package. The final rendered output of Project 2 is shown in Figure Prj2-1.

Figure Prj2-1 *The final rendered output of Project2*

Downloading Composition

Before starting the project, you need to download the *prj2_fusion_7.zip* file from *http://www.cadcim.com*. The path of the file is as follows:

> *Textbooks > Animation and Visual Effects > Fusion > Blackmagic Design Fusion 7 Studio: A Tutorial Approach*

Next, extract the contents of the file at *Documents\Fusion_7*.

Setting the Frame Format

In this section, you will specify the frame format settings.

1. Choose **File > New** from the menubar; a new composition is displayed in the Fusion screen.

2. Choose **File > Preferences** from the menubar; the **Preferences** dialog box is displayed.

3. In this dialog box, select **Frame Format** from the **Composition#** preferences tree; various frame format settings are displayed on the right in the **Preferences** dialog box.

4. Choose the **New** button from the right pane in the **Settings** area in the **Preferences** dialog box; the **Enter a name for the new image format** dialog box is displayed. In this dialog box, enter **640*360** in the edit box. In the **Settings** area, enter **640** and **360** in the **Width** and **Height** edit boxes.

5. Enter **24** in the **Frame rate** edit box. Next, choose the **Save** button to save the changes made.

6. In the Time Ruler area, enter **0** in the **Global End Time** edit box.

Compositing the Render Passes

In this section, you will composite the render passes.

1. Choose the **LD** button from the toolbar; the **Open File** dialog box is displayed. In this dialog box, choose **Documents > Fusion_7 > prj_02 > Media_Files > candleDiffuse.tif** and then choose the **Open** button; the **Loader1** tool tile is inserted in the **Flow** area.

2. Press 1; the output of the **Loader1** tool is displayed in the left Display View. Next, choose the **Fit** button from the left **Display View** toolbar to fit the image into the left Display View, refer to Figure Prj2-2.

3. Click on the empty space in the **Flow** area and then choose the **LD** button from the toolbar; a dialog box is displayed. In this dialog box, choose **Documents > Fusion_7 > prj_02 > Media Files > candleShadow.tif**; the **Loader2** tool tile is inserted in the **Flow** area.

4. Press 2; the output of the **Loader2** tool is displayed in the right Display View. Next, choose the **Fit** button from the right **Display View** toolbar to fit the image into the right Display View, refer to Figure Prj2-2.

Figure Prj2-2 *The output of the **Loader1** and **Loader2** tools*

Now, you need to composite the diffuse and shadow passes. The diffuse pass (sometimes also referred to as beauty pass or color pass) is a full color rendering of the scene. It contains diffuse illumination, color, and color maps, excluding highlights, shadows, and reflection. The shadow pass only produces the shadow component of the render in the alpha channel. If a scene contains overlapping shadows, then render them in separate passes to have better control over the post application.

5. Drag the red output node of the **Loader2** tool tile to the red output node of the **Loader1** tool tile; the **Merge1** tool tile is inserted in the **Flow** area and a connection between the **Loader1**, **Loader2**, and **Merge1** tools is established.

6. Press 2; the output of the **Merge1** tool is displayed in the right Display View, as shown in Figure Prj2-3.

*Figure Prj2-3 The output of the **Merge1** tool*

Next, you will compose the ambient pass. The ambient pass displays the textures and color information only. It does not include diffuse shading, specular highlights, shadows, or reflections. The objects appear flat in this pass.

7. Click on the empty space in the **Flow** area to deselect the selected tool tile, if any. Choose the **LD** button from the toolbar; the **Open File** dialog box is displayed. In this dialog box, choose **Documents > Fusion_7 > prj_02 > Media_Files > candleAmbient.tif** and then choose the **Open** button; the **Loader3** tool tile is inserted in the **Flow** area.

8. Drag the red output node of the **Loader3** tool tile to the red output node of the **Merge1** tool tile; the **Merge2** tool tile is inserted in the **Flow** area and a connection between the **Merge1**, **Loader3**, and **Merge2** tools is established.

9. Press 2; the output of the **Merge2** tool is displayed in the right Display View.

10. Select the **Screen** option from the **Apply Mode** drop-down list in the **Merge2** tool control window.

The **Screen** option is used to merge the images based on the multiplication of their color values. As a result, brightness of the image is increased.

11. Enter **0.3** in the **Blend** edit box of the **Merge2** tool control window. The output of the **Merge2** tool after specifying all parameters is shown in Figure Prj2-4.

Figure Prj2-4 *The output of the* **Merge2** *tool*

Next, you will compose the occlusion pass. This pass is also sometimes referred to as dirt pass. It allows you to create better contact shadows.

12. Click on the empty space in the **Flow** area to deselect the selected tool tile, if any. Choose the **LD** button from the toolbar; the **Open File** dialog box is displayed. In this dialog box, choose **Documents > Fusion_7 > prj_02 > Media_Files > candleOcclusion.tif** and then choose the **Open** button; the **Loader4** tool tile is inserted in the **Flow** area.

13. Drag the red output node of the **Loader4** tool tile to the red output node of the **Merge2** tool tile; the **Merge3** tool tile is inserted in the **Flow** area and a connection between the **Loader4**, **Merge2**, and **Merge3** tools is established.

14. Press 2; the output of the **Merge3** tool is displayed in the right Display View.

15. Select the **Multiply** option from the **Apply Mode** drop-down list of the **Merge3** tool control window.

The **Multiply** option is used to multiply the values of the color channel and thus, if you use this option, the image will be darkened. However, if you use the **Multiply** option with white color, the color will remain same.

16. Enter **0.37** in the **Blend** edit box of the **Merge3** tool control window. The output of the **Merge3** tool is shown in Figure Prj2-5.

Next, you will compose the reflection pass. This pass allows you to fine tune the reflections in the scene. A reflection pass contains self-reflection, reflection of other elements, or reflection of the environment.

17. Click on the empty space in the **Flow** area to deselect the selected tool tile, if any. Choose the **LD** button from the toolbar; the **Open File** dialog box is displayed. In this dialog box,

choose **Documents > Fusion_7 > prj_02 > Media_Files > candleReflection.tif** and then choose the **Open** button; the **Loader5** tool tile is inserted in the **Flow** area.

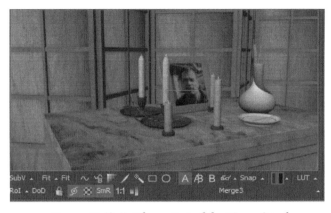

Figure Prj2-5 *The output of the* **Merge3** *tool*

18. Drag the red output node of the **Loader5** tool tile and to the red output node of the **Merge3** tool tile; the **Merge4** tool tile is inserted in the **Flow** area and a connection between the **Loader5**, **Merge3**, and **Merge4** tools is established.

19. Press 2; the output of the **Merge4** tool is displayed in the right Display View.

20. Select the **Screen** option from the **Apply Mode** drop-down list of the **Merge4** tool control window.

21. Enter **0.49** in the **Blend** edit box in the **Merge4** tool control window.

22. Select the **Loader5** tool tile from the **Flow** area and choose the **BC** button from the toolbar; the **BrightnessContrast1** tool tile is inserted in the **Flow** area and a connection between the **Loader5**, **BrightnessContrast1**, and **Merge4** tools is established.

23. Enter **1.5** in the **Gain** edit box of the **BrightnessContrast1** tool control window. The output of the **Merge4** tool is shown in Figure Prj2-6.

Figure Prj2-6 *The output of the* **Merge4** *tool*

Next, you will merge the specular pass.

24. Click on the empty space in the **Flow** area to deselect the selected tool tile, if any. Choose the **LD** button from the toolbar; the **Open File** dialog box is displayed. In this dialog box, choose **Documents > Fusion_7 > prj_02 > Media_Files > candleSpecular.tif** and then choose the **Open** button; the **Loader6** tool tile is inserted in the **Flow** area.

25. Drag the red output node of the **Loader6** tool tile to the red output node of the **Merge4** tool tile; the **Merge5** tool tile is inserted in the **Flow** area and a connection between the **Loader6**, **Merge4**, and **Merge5** tools is established.

26. Press 2; the output of the **Merge5** tool is displayed in the right Display View.

27. Select the **Color Dodge** option from the **Apply Mode** drop-down list of the **Merge5** tool control window.

    The **Color Dodge** option is used to brighten the image using the color values of the foreground.

28. Select the **Loader6** tool tile from the **Flow** area. Next, choose the **BC** button from the toolbar; the **BrightnessContrast2** tool tile is inserted in the **Flow** area and a connection between the **Loader6**, **BrightnessContrast2**, and **Merge5** tools is established.

29. Enter **3** in the **Gain** edit box of the **BrightnessContrast2** tool control window.

    The output of the **Merge5** tool is shown in Figure Prj2-7. Next, you will brighten the picture in the photo frame.

Figure Prj2-7 *The output of the **Merge5** tool*

30. Click on the empty space in the **Flow** area to deselect the selected tool tile, if any. Choose the **LD** button from the toolbar; the **Open File** dialog box is displayed. In this dialog box, choose **Documents > Fusion_7 > prj_02 > Media_Files > candlePic.tif** and then choose the **Open** button; the **Loader7** tool tile is inserted in the **Flow** area.

31. Drag the red output node of the **Loader7** tool tile and then drag the cursor to the red output node of the **Merge5** tool tile; the **Merge6** tool tile is inserted in the **Flow** area and a connection between the **Loader7**, **Merge5**, and **Merge6** tools is established.

32. Press 2; the output of the **Merge6** tool is displayed in the right Display View.

33. Select the **Lighten** option from the **Apply Mode** drop-down list of the **Merge6** tool control window.

    The **Lighten** option is used to check the color information in background and foreground images and then select the lighter color from the images.

34. Enter **0.8** in the **Blend** edit box of the **Merge6** tool control window.

    The output of the **Merge6** tool is shown in Figure Prj2-8.

*Figure Prj2-8 The output of the **Merge6** tool*

Next, you will add flames to the candles.

35. Click on the empty space in the **Flow** area to deselect the selected tool tile, if any. Choose the **LD** button from the toolbar; the **Open File** dialog box is displayed. In this dialog box, choose **Documents > Fusion_7 > prj_02 > Media_Files > candleFlame.tif** and then choose the **Open** button; the **Loader8** tool tile is inserted in the **Flow** area.

36. Drag the red output node of the **Loader8** tool tile to the red output node of the **Merge6** tool tile; the **Merge7** tool tile is inserted in the **Flow** area and a connection between the **Loader8**, **Merge6**, and **Merge7** tools is established.

37. Press 2; the output of the **Merge7** tool is displayed in the right Display View.

38. Select the **Loader8** tool tile from the **Flow** area. Next, choose **Tools > Blur > Soft Glow** button from the toolbar; the **SoftGlow1** tool tile is inserted in the **Flow** area and a connection between the **Loader8**, **SoftGlow1**, and **Merge7** tools is established.

39. Enter **2.36** in the **Gain** edit box of the **SoftGlow1** tool control window.

The output of the **Merge7** tool is shown in Figure Prj2-9.

Figure Prj2-9 *The output of the* **Merge7** *tool*

40. Select the **Merge7** tool tile from the **Flow** area. Next, choose the **CC** button from the toolbar; the **ColorCorrector1** tool tile is inserted in the **Flow** area and a connection between the **Merge7** and **ColorCorrector1** tools is established.

41. Press 2; the output of the **ColorCorrector1** tool is displayed in the right Display View.

42. In the **ColorCorrector1** tool control window, enter the values of the parameters as follows:

Tint: **0.12**   Strength: **0.18**   Master-RGB-Gain: **1.29**

The final output of the composition is displayed in the right Display View, refer to Figure Prj2-1.

Now, save the composition with the name *Prj02* at the location *Documents > Fusion_7 > Prj > Prj02*. Next, you need to render the composition. For rendering, refer to Tutorial 1 of Chapter 2. The output of the composition is shown in Figure Prj2-1. You can also view the final render of the composition by downloading the *prj02_fusion_7_rndr.zip* from *http://www.cadcim.com*. The path of the file is mentioned at the beginning of the project.

Index

Symbols

3D Tools 1-5

A

Add a Polyline Mask 8-6
Add a Rectangle Mask 3-4
Ambient Light 1-6
Anaglyph 1-22
Audio Enable 1-4
Auto Domain 1-19
Auto Gain 1-11

B

Background 1-13
Bender 3D 1-8
Bitmap 1-17, 6-22
Blinn 1-7
Blur 1-11
Blur Tools 1-10
Brightness / Contrast 1-12
BSpline 1-17
BumpMap 1-7, 13-23

C

Camera 3D 1-8
Camera Shake 1-22
Catcher 1-8
Change Depth 1-19
Channel Boolean 1-7
Channel Booleans 1-12, 7-8
Chat Tab 1-4
Chroma Keyer 1-18, 8-4
Cineon Log 1-15
Color Corrector 1-12, 2-8
Color Curves 1-12
Color Gain 1-12

Color Matrix 1-12
Color Space 1-12
Color Tools 1-11
Combiner 1-22
Comments Tab 1-4
Composite Tools 1-13
Console Tab 1-3
Control area 1-3
CookTorrance 1-7
Coordinate Space 1-23
Copy Metadata 1-18
Corner Positioner 1-23
Corner Positioning 9-16
Creator Tools 1-13
Crop 1-22, 4-4
Cube 3D 1-8
CubeMap 1-8
Custom Tool 1-19

D

DaySky 1-13, 3-28
Deep Pixel Tools 1-14
Defocus 1-11
Dent 1-23, 5-18
Depth Blur 1-14, 11-26
Difference Keyer 1-18
Directional Blur 1-11
Directional Light 1-6
Displace 1-23, 5-25
Displace 3D 1- 9
Display View area 1-3
Display Views Keys 1-26
Dissolve 1-13
Drip 1-23
Dubois 13-50
Duplicate 3D 1-9, 13-17
DVE 1-22

E

Effect Tools 1- 14
Ellipse 1-17
Enable Stereo 3D 13-48

F

Falloff 1-8
FastNoise 1-13, 3-21
FBX Exporter 1-9
FBX Mesh 3D 1-9
Fields 1-19
File LUT 1-15
Film Grain 1-15
Film Tools 1-15
Filter Tools 1-16
Flow Tab 1-3
Flow area Keys 1-16
Flow Tools 1-16
Fog 3D 1-9
Frame Format 2-4
Function Keys 1-25
Fuse Tools 1-16
Fusion INTERFACE 1-3

G

Gamut 1-12
General HotKeys 1-25
Global Start Time and Global End Time 1-4
Glow 1-11
Gradient 3-3
Grain 1-15, 11-8
Grid Warp 1-23
Grouping the Tools 6-6

H

Highlight 10-4
Hot Spot 1-15, 10-7
HueCurves 7-11

I

Image Plane 3D 1-9
I/O Tools 1-17

L

Letterbox 1-22
Light 1-6
Light Trim 1-16
Loader 1-17
Locator 3D 1-10
Luma Keyer 1-18, 8-10

M

Macro Tools 1-17
Mandelbrot 1-14
Mask Paint 1-17, 6-26
Mask Tools 1-17
Material 1-7
Matte Control 1-18
Matte Tools 1-18
Menubar 1-3
Merge 1-13
Merge 3D 1-10
Merging the Images 2-12
Metadata Tools 1-18
Miscellaneous Tools 1-19
Mtl Merge 1-8

O

OpenCL Tools 1-19
Override 3D 1-10
OCIO CDLTransform 1-12
OCIO ColorSpace 1-12
OCIO File Transform 1-13

P

Paint 12-5
Paint Tool 1-19
Particles 14-2
pAvoid 1-20
pBounce 1-20, 14-7
pChangeStyle 1-20
pCustom 1-20
pDirectionalForce 1-20, 14-17
pEmitter 1-20, 14-5
Perspective Positioner 1-23
pFlock 1-20
pFriction 1-20

pGradientForce 1-20
Phong 1-7
pImageEmitter 1-20
pKill 1-20
Plasma 1-14, 3-25
Playback Controls 1-4
pMerge 1-20
PointCloud 3D 1-9
Point Light 1-6, 13-39
Polygon 1-17
pPointForce 1-21
Preferences 2-3
pRender 1-21
Primatte Tool 1-21
Projector 3D 1-9
Pseudo Color 1-15
pSpawn 1-21, 14-17
pTangent Force 1-21
pTurbulence 1-21, 14-22
pVortex 1-21

Q

Quality Controls 1-4

R

Ranges 1-17
Rank Filter 1-16
Rectangle 1-17
Reflect 1-7
Remove Noise 1-15
Render Button 1-4
Renderer 3D 1-9
Render Settings dialog box 2-16
Render Start Time and Render End Time 1-4
Replace Material 3D 1-10
Resize 1-22
RunCommand 1-19
Replace Normal 3D 1-10
Replicate 3D 1-10
Ribbon 3D 1-10

S

Saver 1-16
Scale 1-23, 3-22
Set Canvas Color 1-13
Set Domain 1-19

Set Metadata 1-18
Shader 1-14, 11-15
Shadow 1-15
Shape 3D 1-10, 13-3
Sharpen 1-11
Show Checker Underlay button 3-21
SoftClip 1-10
Soft Glow 1-11
SphereMap 1-8
Spline Tab 1-4
Splitter 1-22
Spot Light 1-6, 13-14
Stereo Mix 1-7, 13-47
Stereo Tools 1-22
Sticky Note 1-16

T

Text+ 1-14
Text 3D 1-10
Texture 1-14, 11-10
Texture 2D 1-8
Texture Transform 1-6
Timeline Tab 1-4
Time Ruler 1-4
Time Ruler Keys 1-27
Time Speed 1-19
Time Stretcher 1-19
Tracker 9-6
Tracking 9-2
Tracking Tool 1-21
Trails 1-15, 10-16
Transform 1-22
Transform 3D 1-11
Transform Tools 1-22
Triangle 1-17

U

UltraKeyer 8-15
Underlay 1-16

Unsharp Mask 1-12
UV Map 3D 1-10

V

VariBlur 1-11
Vector Distortion 1-23, 5-5
Vector Motion Blur 1-11
View1 2-6
Vortex 1-24, 5-13

W

Wand 1-17
Ward 1-7
Warp Tools 1-23
White Balance 1-13
Work area 1-3
Working with the Layout 1-5

Other Publications by CADCIM Technologies

The following is the list of some of the publications by CADCIM Technologies. Please visit *www.cadcim.com* for the complete listing.

3ds Max Textbooks
- Autodesk 3ds Max 2016: A Comprehensive Guide, 16th Edition
- Autodesk 3ds Max 2016 for Beginners: A Tutorial Approach, 16th Edition
- Autodesk 3ds Max 2015: A Comprehensive Guide, 15th Edition
- Autodesk 3ds Max 2014: A Comprehensive Guide
- Autodesk 3ds Max 2013: A Comprehensive Guide
- Autodesk 3ds Max 2012: A Comprehensive Guide

Autodesk Maya Textbooks
- Autodesk Maya 2016: A Comprehensive Guide, 8th Edition
- Autodesk Maya 2015: A Comprehensive Guide, 7th Edition
- Character Animation: A Tutorial Approach
- Autodesk Maya 2014: A Comprehensive Guide
- Autodesk Maya 2013: A Comprehensive Guide
- Autodesk Maya 2012: A Comprehensive Guide

ZBrush Textbook
- Pixologic ZBrush 4R6: A Comprehensive Guide

CINEMA 4D Textbooks
- MAXON CINEMA 4D Studio R16: A Tutorial Approach, 3rd Edition
- MAXON CINEMA 4D Studio R15: A Tutorial Approach
- MAXON CINEMA 4D Studio R14: A Tutorial Approach

Fusion Textbook
- The eyeon Fusion 6.3: A Tutorial Approach

Flash Textbooks
- Adobe Flash Professional CC: A Tutorial Approach
- Adobe Flash Professional CS6: A Tutorial Approach

Premiere Textbooks
- Adobe Premiere Pro CC: A Tutorial Approach, 3rd Edition
- Adobe Premiere Pro CS6: A Tutorial Approach
- Adobe Premiere Pro CS5.5: A Tutorial Approach

3ds Max Design Textbooks
- Autodesk 3ds Max Design 2015: A Tutorial Approach, 15th Edition
- Autodesk 3ds Max Design 2014: A Tutorial Approach
- Autodesk 3ds Max Design 2013: A Tutorial Approach
- Autodesk 3ds Max Design 2012: A Tutorial Approach
- Autodesk 3ds Max Design 2011: A Tutorial Approach

Softimage Textbook
- Autodesk Softimage 2014: A Tutorial Approach
- Autodesk Softimage 2013: A Tutorial Approach

AutoCAD Textbooks
- AutoCAD 2016: A Problem-Solving Approach, Basic and Intermediate, 22nd Edition
- AutoCAD 2016: A Problem-Solving Approach, 3D and Advanced, 22nd Edition
- AutoCAD 2015: A Problem-Solving Approach, Basic and Intermediate, 21st Edition
- AutoCAD 2015: A Problem-Solving Approach, 3D and Advanced, 21st Edition
- AutoCAD 2014: A Problem-Solving Approach

Autodesk Inventor Textbooks
- Autodesk Inventor 2016 for Designers, 16th Edition
- Autodesk Inventor 2015 for Designers, 15th Edition
- Autodesk Inventor 2014 for Designers
- Autodesk Inventor 2013 for Designers
- Autodesk Inventor 2012 for Designers
- Autodesk Inventor 2011 for Designers

AutoCAD MEP Textbooks
- AutoCAD MEP 2016 for Designers, 3rd Edition
- AutoCAD MEP 2015 for Designers
- AutoCAD MEP 2014 for Designers

Solid Edge Textbooks
- Solid Edge ST7 for Designers, 12th Edition
- Solid Edge ST6 for Designers
- Solid Edge ST5 for Designers
- Solid Edge ST4 for Designers
- Solid Edge ST3 for Designers
- Solid Edge ST2 for Designers

NX Textbooks
- NX 9.0 for Designers, 8th Edition
- NX 8.5 for Designers
- NX 8 for Designers
- NX 7 for Designers

SolidWorks Textbooks
- SOLIDWORS 2015 for Designers, 13th Edition
- SolidWorks 2014 for Designers
- SolidWorks 2013 for Designers
- SolidWorks 2012 for Designers
- SolidWorks 2014: A Tutorial Approach
- SolidWorks 2012: A Tutorial Approach
- Learning SolidWorks 2011: A Project Based Approach
- SolidWorks 2011 for Designers

CATIA Textbooks
- CATIA V5-6R2014 for Designers, 12th Edition
- CATIA V5-6R2013 for Designers
- CATIA V5-6R2012 for Designers
- CATIA V5R21 for Designers
- CATIA V5R20 for Designers
- CATIA V5R19 for Designers

Creo Parametric and Pro/ENGINEER Textbooks
- PTC Creo Parametric 3.0 for Designers, 3rd Edition
- Creo Parametric 2.0 for Designers
- Creo Parametric 1.0 for Designers
- Pro/Engineer Wildfire 5.0 for Designers
- Pro/ENGINEER Wildfire 4.0 for Designers
- Pro/ENGINEER Wildfire 3.0 for Designers

ANSYS Textbooks
- ANSYS Workbench 14.0: A Tutorial Approach
- ANSYS 11.0 for Designers

Creo Direct Textbook
- Creo Direct 2.0 and Beyond for Designers

Autodesk Alias Textbooks
- Learning Autodesk Alias Design 2016, 5th Edition
- Learning Autodesk Alias Design 2015, 4th Edition
- Learning Autodesk Alias Design 2012
- Learning Autodesk Alias Design 2010
- AliasStudio 2009 for Designers

AutoCAD LT Textbooks
- AutoCAD LT 2015 for Designers, 10th Edition
- AutoCAD LT 2014 for Designers
- AutoCAD LT 2013 for Designers
- AutoCAD LT 2012 for Designers
- AutoCAD LT 2011 for Designers

EdgeCAM Textbooks
• EdgeCAM 11.0 for Manufacturers
• EdgeCAM 10.0 for Manufacturers

AutoCAD Electrical Textbooks
• AutoCAD Electrical 2015 for Electrical Control Designers, 6th Edition
• AutoCAD Electrical 2014 for Electrical Control Designers
• AutoCAD Electrical 2013 for Electrical Control Designers
• AutoCAD Electrical 2012 for Electrical Control Designers
• AutoCAD Electrical 2011 for Electrical Control Designers
• AutoCAD Electrical 2010 for Electrical Control Designers

Autodesk Revit Architecture Textbooks
• Autodesk Revit Architecture 2016 for Architects and Designers, 12th Edition
• Autodesk Revit Architecture 2015 for Architects and Designers, 11th Edition
• Autodesk Revit Architecture 2014 for Architects and Designers
• Autodesk Revit Architecture 2013 for Architects and Designers
• Autodesk Revit Architecture 2012 for Architects and Designers

Autodesk Revit Structure Textbooks
• Exploring Autodesk Revit Structure 2016, 6th Edition
• Exploring Autodesk Revit Structure 2015, 5th Edition
• Exploring Autodesk Revit Structure 2014
• Exploring Autodesk Revit Structure 2013
• Exploring Autodesk Revit Structure 2012

AutoCAD Civil 3D Textbooks
• Exploring AutoCAD Civil 3D 2016, 6th Edition
• Exploring AutoCAD Civil 3D 2015, 5th Edition
• Exploring AutoCAD Civil 3D 2014
• Exploring AutoCAD Civil 3D 2013

AutoCAD Map 3D Textbooks
• Exploring AutoCAD Map 3D 2016, 6th Edition
• Exploring AutoCAD Map 3D 2015, 5th Edition
• Exploring AutoCAD Map 3D 2014
• Exploring AutoCAD Map 3D 2013
• Exploring AutoCAD Map 3D 2012

Revit MEP Textbooks
• Exploring Autodesk Revit MEP 2016, 3rd Edition
• Exploring Autodesk Revit MEP 2015
• Exploring Autodesk Revit MEP 2014

STAAD Pro Textbook
•Exploring Bentley STAAD.Pro V8i

Navisworks Textbooks
• Exploring Autodesk Navisworks 2015
• Exploring Autodesk Navisworks 2014

Computer Programming Textbooks
• Learning Oracle 11g
• Learning ASP.NET AJAX
• Learning Java Programming
• Learning Visual Basic.NET 2008
• Learning C++ Programming Concepts
• Learning VB.NET Programming Concepts

AutoCAD Textbooks Authored by Prof. Sham Tickoo and Published by Autodesk Press
• AutoCAD: A Problem-Solving Approach: 2013 and Beyond
• AutoCAD 2012: A Problem-Solving Approach
• AutoCAD 2011: A Problem-Solving Approach
• AutoCAD 2010: A Problem-Solving Approach
• Customizing AutoCAD 2010
• AutoCAD 2009: A Problem-Solving Approach

Textbooks Authored by CADCIM Technologies and Published by Other Publishers

3D Studio MAX and VIZ Textbooks
• Learning 3DS Max: A Tutorial Approach, Release 4
  Goodheart-Wilcox Publishers (USA)
• Learning 3D Studio VIZ: A Tutorial Approach
  Goodheart-Wilcox Publishers (USA)

CADCIM Technologies Textbooks Translated in Other Languages

SolidWorks Textbooks
• SolidWorks 2008 for Designers (Serbian Edition)
  Mikro Knjiga Publishing Company, Serbia
• SolidWorks 2006 for Designers (Russian Edition)
  Piter Publishing Press, Russia
• SolidWorks 2006 for Designers (Serbian Edition)
  Mikro Knjiga Publishing Company, Serbia

NX Textbooks
• NX 6 for Designers (Korean Edition)
  Onsolutions, South Korea
• NX 5 for Designers (Korean Edition)
  Onsolutions, South Korea

Pro/ENGINEER Textbooks

- Pro/ENGINEER Wildfire 4.0 for Designers (Korean Edition)
  HongReung Science Publishing Company, South Korea
- Pro/ENGINEER Wildfire 3.0 for Designers (Korean Edition)
  HongReung Science Publishing Company, South Korea

Autodesk 3ds Max Textbook

- 3ds Max 2008: A Comprehensive Guide (Serbian Edition)
  Mikro Knjiga Publishing Company, Serbia

AutoCAD Textbooks

- AutoCAD 2006 (Russian Edition)
  Piter Publishing Press, Russia
- AutoCAD 2005 (Russian Edition)
  Piter Publishing Press, Russia
- AutoCAD 2000 Fondamenti (Italian Edition)

Coming Soon from CADCIM Technologies

- Solid Edge ST8 for Designers
- NX 10.0 for Designers
- NX Nastran 9.0 for Designers
- SOLIDWORKS Simulation 2015 for Designers
- Exploring Primavera P6 V8
- Exploring Risa 3D 12.0
- Exploring Autodesk Raster Design 2016 for Image Processing

Online Training Program Offered by CADCIM Technologies

CADCIM Technologies provides effective and affordable virtual online training on animation, architecture, and GIS softwares, computer programming languages, and Computer Aided Design and Manufacturing (CAD/CAM) software packages. The training will be delivered 'live' via Internet at any time, any place, and at any pace to individuals, students of colleges, universities, and CAD/CAM training centers. For more information, please visit the following link: *www.cadcim.com*